UNION
of CROWNS

UNION
of CROWNS
THE FORGING OF EUROPE'S MOST INDEPENDENT STATE

CRAWFORD LITTLE

First published by

Neil Wilson Publishing Ltd

303 The Pentagon Centre

36 Washington Street

GLASGOW

G3 8AZ

Tel: 0141-221-1117

Fax: 0141-221-5363

E-mail: info@nwp.co.uk

www.nwp.co.uk

A catalogue record for this book is available from the British Library.

ISBN

Hardback 1-903238-39-0

Paperback 1-903238-70-6

Typeset in Baskerville Cyrillic Upright

Designed by Belstane

Printed in Finland by WS Bookwell

❦ DEDICATION ❦

I trace my descent in the male line through eleven generations of Scottish Borderers to Thomas Little of the parish of Redkirk. Born in 1541 when Henry VIII of England's troops burned Roxburgh and Kelso, he was three years old when they returned to plunder Edinburgh before marching through the Borders, killing and burning as they went, destroying seven monasteries and 240 towns and villages. He was in his teens when Mary Queen of Scots returned from France, and matured in a world of reiving, raiding and tit-for-tat killings, but unlike many of his family and neighbours, he survived both steel and rope.

Thomas was a man of 62 when the crowns of Scotland and England were united. Already old by the standards of the time, he learnt to adapt to the ways of peace and lived the rest of his life in comparative comfort. His gravestone states that he was 111 years old when he died. What tales he might have told …

This book is dedicated to Thomas and his wife Maisie Dalgliesh, and their ten-times-great grandsons, my sons Jamie, David and Justin. And to my wife Carolyn who has put up with me and my funny ways for 25 years. If there is a better woman in this world, I have yet to meet her.

Crawford Little
Auldgirth
Dumfriesshire

℘ Contents ℘

A MARRIAGE MADE IN HEAVEN?

Queen Elizabeth of England breathed her last at Richmond Palace on 24 March 1603, and Sir Robert Carey leapt into the saddle with 400 miles and a relay of fast horses ahead of him. Splattered with mud and blood, he finally galloped up to the gates of Holyroodhouse in Edinburgh. King James VI of Scots, soon to be James I of England, stretched out his hand and Carey touched it with his lips. One king for two crowns, uniting Scotland with England after centuries of hatred and warfare...

Union of Crowns examines those power struggles that decided the fate of kingdoms. High politics and low cunning in an age when men feared for the fate of their souls at the hands of a wrathful God – fear and betrayal, arrogance and impetuosity, hatred and warfare, glory and defeat, loving and loathing, deadly feuds and broken friendships, old alliances and new treaties in a world of constant change. Religion decided politics and politics dictated religion. And through it all ran the threads of self-interest and greed.

At the opening of the English Parliament in 1604, James was 'as royally attended as if the gods had summoned a parliament and were all in their steps of triumph to Jove's high court.' He declared his wish 'was at his death to leave one worship to God: one kingdom, intirely governed: one uniformity of laws.' This was his grand vision. He would speak of a Great Britain – and of himself as its king. Thus the Union of Crowns prompted the unification of the Scottish and English parliaments in 1707, laying the foundation stones for an empire that spread across the face of the globe.

For better or worse, it still affects the lives and attitudes of its children, at home and abroad. Without the Union, who would have provided the blueprints for democratic government in so many countries? Who would be Head of State in Australia? Would there be an India and Pakistan? What of Africa? What language would be spoken in North America? Come to that, what language would be spoken in Sauchiehall Street and the Royal Mile? And yet, many southern-based historians still regard the Union of Crowns as some sort of an embarrassing hiccup in what should be an essentially English story. In doing so, they fail to recognise how warring nations were knowingly and deliberately forged into the most independent state in Europe. Perhaps it is just too hard for some to accept that Scottish kings took over the English throne, so their narratives leap from Queen Bess to Absolutist Charles and that *English* Civil War – ignoring the inconvenience of who and what came in between ...

History will always be full of mysteries corrupted by misinterpretation or 'spin' in order to suit a variety of purposes. We may believe what is written in the history books of our home nations, but others will regard our inherited 'facts' as mistakes, exaggerations, or whopping great lies.

One people's facts might be viewed by others as little more than jingoistic propaganda, just as one man's traitor is another's freedom fighter. Historians asking questions of the dead may have to decide for themselves who was lying and who telling the truth. Advocate and jury perhaps, but still there may be no answers or none that we can find. 'Not proven,' may be all that we can say. Only a fool would suggest that their nation's historians have a monopoly on truth.

Union of Crowns is a book in two parts. The first gallops from the arrival of the Romans who divided the British island into a rich south and comparatively poor north through the forging of nations to the long centuries of bitter warfare when 'union by consent' was never an option. The pace then slows into the second part – beyond the marriage of King James IV of Scots to Margaret Tudor (daughter of Henry VII of England) and the signing of the Treaty of Perpetual Peace in 1503.

Another hundred years would pass before the crowns were united, but that joining of the Thistle and the Rose signalled a new understanding and an acceptance of the advantages that could be found in peace – rejecting essentially futile wars and the whims of kings. In this we see the growth of effective democracy.

At the same time – and vital to any historian – there was a more thorough approach to the recording of the affairs of state and, just as significant, a blossoming of correspondence both personal and public, much of which has been recorded and preserved. For example and comparison, the printed

Letters and Papers for the reign of Henry VIII runs to 37 volumes and parts of volumes, while just two volumes cover the reigns of Richard III and Henry VII. On the other hand, while acknowledging that such information is the historian's food and drink, we must introduce a note of caution. The wealth of documentation should not blind us to the possibility that much is missing, or that some of what remains was 'planted' with the intention of creating confusion, or manufacturing guilt.

The Protestant Reformation and associated Catholic Counter-Reformation encouraged international espionage and the planting of disinformation on a grand scale. Therefore, it seems safe to assume that much of the darker side of dealings both in and between Scotland and England, and the detail of their clandestine dealings with foreign powers, will remain difficult or impossible to trace – simply because much of the correspondence would have been destroyed in case it might fall into the wrong hands. Many historical questions cannot be answered with any certainty – whatever contemporary correspondence or the lack of it might seem to suggest.

So where do we go from there? A L Rowse wrote: 'To be able to make the dry bones (of history) live is a gift, and a rare one; it means that one must have a sense of the poetry and pathos of the past, some living inner spring of inspiration and intuitive insight.' Faced with conflicting accounts, inspiration and intuition may indeed be more useful than a decade of painstaking research.

Call it inspiration, intuition or whatever, but I am convinced that the fate of our nations was not decided by chance. Scotland and England would not and could not be united as the result of a constitutional coincidence. Instead, we can see the causes of the union as including complex political, cultural and religious elements, witnessed in the shifting *ménage à trois* relationship between England, Scotland and France. In a changing world, auld alliances became liabilities, and old enemies set aside their differences when faced with a new and common threat. It was as simple and yet as complicated as that...

At the start of the 16th Century, rifts fostered by the intertwining of religion and politics were widening in Scotland. Throughout Northern Europe, the move from Catholicism to Protestantism – rejecting the pope's authority – had gathered pace, polarising states and becoming an expression of political identity and autonomy as well as religious conviction and allegiance.

The world was changing, but not without opposition. In 1525, the Scottish Parliament had banned all 'heretical' literature and discussion of Protestant ideas, but it couldn't stop the new breed of radicals and free thinkers. Some were burnt at the stake, including dissident Catholic clerics, and more were exiled or fled the country, creating a vacuum in the country's religious, political and social leadership, but still their numbers increased. This persecution of Protestants in Catholic Scotland made a case for them to seek the protection of England, which had already been converted to Protestantism.

Since the times of the Romans, it had been recognised that the cost of defeating and garrisoning the thrawn northern land could never be financially justified. Thus it was accountancy as much as bravery that maintained Scotland's independence. After the death of the belligerent Henry VIII, the rules of the game had changed. The future would be decided by diplomats and politicians, rather than warrior kings and reckless adventurers. Or so it was hoped.

Mary Queen of Scots married the French Dauphin Francis in 1558. The marriage treaty included a secret clause granting the crown matrimonial to Francis in the event of Mary's death. Here was the full price of France's support – colonisation through the back door, perhaps, but colonisation nevertheless. News of this leaked in Scotland, heightening the crisis facing Mary of Guise's regency. Mary Queen of Scots was effectively handing Scotland to France. There again, as the future queen of France, what she gave with one hand she would take back with the other.

After a reign of five years, 'Bloody' Mary of England died on 17 November 1558. She left two main claimants to the English throne. Her half-sister, the Protestant Princess Elizabeth, was the daughter of Henry VIII and Anne Boleyn. The other claimant, Catholic Mary Queen of Scots, was a great-granddaughter of Henry VII.

Elizabeth's supporters won the debate. If the English had accepted Mary, they would have taken her husband and France into the bargain. For many, the choice between Elizabeth and Mary wasn't simply a matter of legal nicety or religious allegiance, but rather about maintaining English sovereignty or suffering the French yoke.

With Elizabeth's accession, England reverted to Protestantism. Refusing to acknowledge Elizabeth, Dauphin Francis and Mary Queen of Scots, future king and queen of France, assumed the titles of King and Queen of England and Ireland.

Protestants remained a minority in Scotland, but dominated the parliament. In the first weeks of 1559, the queen regent Mary of Guise – Queen Mary's mother – was suffering a deadly illness. She had neither the power nor the will to continue to suppress the Protestants. Their armed forces, describing themselves as the Army of the Congregation, seized Stirling then marched to Edinburgh. Although many were affirmed nationalists, they appealed to England for aid in ridding Scotland of the Catholic-French influence.

When French reinforcements arrived at Leith, the Protestants were forced to retreat into Fife, but then an English Fleet appeared off the coast and the French abandoned the area. A month later, the Scottish Lords of the Congregation and Elizabeth of England signed the Treaty of Berwick in which Elizabeth agreed to supply military aid against the French – the same French who would have supported a Catholic invasion of England and had formerly been Scotland's allies. The treaty heralded the start of intense cooperation between the Protestant power brokers of Scotland and England. Elizabeth's signature on it says more about her need to reduce a threat than any desire to promote a cause.

Mary of Guise died in June 1559. One month later, the Treaty of Edinburgh was signed, ending the civil war in Scotland. England and France were to withdraw their troops and let the Scots settle their own future. The Lords of the Congregation set up a provisional government and opted for Calvinism as the foundation for the Presbyterian Kirk, abolishing the authority of the pope and forbidding the celebration of Mass. The formality of asking the young queen (still in France) to ratify these enactments was gone through, but it was agreed that this was 'a mere Inglorious vane ceremony' and therefore unnecessary. The fight against Mary of Guise was then portrayed as having been a war of national liberation against French occupation. It created an atmosphere in which Protestantism could be equated with patriotism, attracting a new wave of eager Scottish converts who looked to England for a continuing alliance against France and Catholicism.

Mary Queen of Scots had been 15 when she married the 14-year-old Dauphin Francis in 1558. His father Henry II of France was killed in a jousting accident in June 1559 and they succeeded to the French throne, but then Francis died just six months after his father and one month before his 17th birthday. After the requisite period of mourning, the 18-year-old Queen Mary returned to an increasingly Protestant Scotland. She might have stayed in France, living comfortably on her large pension, so it may have been a sense of duty to which she responded – to be a focus for the Catholic cause in Scotland and England.

The Venetian ambassador summarised her position. 'Soon the death of the late king will be forgotten by all except his little wife, who has been widowed, has lost France, and has little hope of Scotland ... her unhappiness and unceasing tears call out for compassion.' None was given – Scotland had become an alien and hostile land in which strengthening forces laid plans for a Protestant pact with England.

While Elizabeth remained unmarried and childless, Mary was first in line to the English throne, through her descent from Henry VII. Thus Mary would unite the crowns of England and Scotland – but into a united Catholic kingdom. This was not an option for Protestants in both nations. It could be avoided if Elizabeth married and produced a Protestant heir, but she was clearly intent on remaining a Virgin Queen, and Scotland would still be left with a Catholic monarch.

Meanwhile, Mary was anything but virginal. She married Lord Darnley and produced a son, Prince James, first in line in the Scottish succession and second in line, after his mother, to the English crown. She was urged to baptise and raise him in the Protestant faith. Naturally enough, she refused.

Within a year, Mary was implicated in the infamous murder of her husband, and had married the chief suspect, the Earl of Bothwell. This enraged the capital, if not the country. The Edinburgh mob chanted 'burn the whore', while Mary and Bothwell fled from the city. By all means at their disposal – fair and foul – the Protestant lords blackened Mary's name, imprisoned her, forced her to abdicate and seized control of the young prince who was crowned King of Scots at the age of just 13 months. John Knox preached a sermon while two lords took an oath, on the baby's behalf, that he would defend the Protestant faith.

The Lords of the Congregation appointed one of their leaders, the Earl of Moray, to rule Scotland during the king's minority. At the same time, the Earl of Mar – another hard man of the Protestant cause – was made the baby's guardian. Formal provisions were made for the infant king's household at Stirling with a wet-nurse and servants. A Master of the Household and three Gentlemen of the Bedchamber were appointed. All Protestants, of course.

England was well satisfied. In effect, Catholic Mary Queen of Scots had become the surrogate mother of Elizabeth's Protestant heir. Before King James's fourth birthday, two scholars were appointed to supervise his education. The senior of the two was George Buchanan. He proved a harsh and unsympathetic master. Poet, humanist, historian and above all else a Protestant, his task was to produce a Protestant king to forge Protestant kingdoms into Europe's most independent state. The rest, as they say, is history ...

INTRODUCTION

I am not a professional historian who writes, but rather a professional writer who is fascinated by history. I beg forgiveness for failing to acknowledge all those who have contributed, helped or encouraged me in my work. My fear is that in remembering some, I might forget others. So at the risk of offending all, I will mention none ...

Crawford Little
Auldgirth
Dumfriesshire

June 2003

CHAPTER ONE

THE FORGING
OF NATIONS

Roman troops commanded by Julius Caesar invaded the southern shores of Britain in 55 BC. They met stiff opposition from the Celtic tribesmen, but once the Roman bridgehead had been won, their control expanded through what we now know as southern England. After that, it was just a matter of time before the Romans sought to dominate the entire island. In 80 AD, legions commanded by the governor, Gnaeus Julius Agricola, advanced north and established a frontier with a chain of forts on the comparatively narrow belt of land between the Forth and Clyde rivers, which is now known as Scotland's 'central belt'. Agricola then turned west, into what is now Ayrshire, and is thought to have considered an invasion of Ireland, but instead he focused his attention to the north, beyond the frontier already established. Battle groups marched up the east coast to the Moray Firth, defeating the 'Caledonians' wherever they found them.

Agricola's northern campaigns were a military success but a financial disaster, infuriating the 'civil servants' who handled the Roman Empire's administration. Their priority was to balance the books, and they insisted that any expansion must be subject to financial rules and constraints. Conquests were expected to produce wealth and revenues to finance further conquests, thus securing yet more wealth and still further expansion. However, the cost of Agricola's campaigns, together with the ongoing expenses of garrisoning the comparatively poor land he had seized, could not be justified. In the civil servants' opinion, too many Roman soldiers were tied up in northern Britain, so the northernmost legion was withdrawn from Inchtuthil to Chester, the construction of a massive military base in the newly-defeated territory was abandoned, and the Empire's northern frontier returned from the Moray Firth to the Forth-Clyde line. But it didn't stop there. The apparent retreat had encouraged the northern Celts to rise against the invaders. They harried the Roman withdrawal, forcing it into a rout. Forts were attacked and burned as far south as the River Tyne in what is now England. Here, in the years following 122 and on the orders of the emperor Hadrian, the legions drew a line, or rather built a wall, from east coast to west, in order to halt the advancing Celts.

Hadrian was in Britain at that time, as part of his tour of a vast empire beset with problems. The Mauri (Moors) were launching raids, the Sarmatae (Sarmatians) were waging war, Aegyptus (Egypt) was bubbling with sedition, Libya and Palaestina (Libya and Palestine) were in rebellion, and the Brittani could not be controlled. Hadrian's solution for Britain was to reform the army and build the wall *qui barbaros Romanosque divideret*, dividing Romanised Britain from its barbarian neighbours. Thus did Hadrian partition Britain, and lay the foundations of a north/south divide that would develop into the separate kingdoms of Scotland and England.

Rome's creation of a divided Britain served to define it further into a prosperous south and comparatively poor north – beyond the simple economic constraints of highland compared with lowland agriculture, and an imbalance in mineral wealth. The expense of administering and protecting the southern portion of Britain was acceptable, due to the income it generated, but the defeat of the north and its subsequent garrisoning, while militarily possible, couldn't be justified. This would be a recurring theme long after the Romans had departed, up to the Union of the Crowns in 1603.

Increasing southern prosperity created its own set of problems. Aggressive northern tribes repeatedly attacked the wall, attempting to plunder the lands it protected. In return, the Romans introduced a new policy, seeking alliances with the more powerful tribes and offering subsidies and other inducements for their good behaviour, while encouraging some controlled trade across the frontier. This calmed things for a time, but it wasn't very long before the tribes reverted to their old ways. In the fourth century, raids by Celts from both Scotland and Ireland were increasing and, in 387, they swept over the wall, leaving a trail of plundered settlements, murder and mayhem.

By the end of the fourth century, a new threat had emerged in the form of sea-borne attacks by Saxons based in northern Germany. The Celts adopted the same tactics, realising that it was easier to sail down the coasts, thus bypassing the empire's northern defences, in order to strike at its softer under-belly. The cost of protecting the British province was steadily increasing and at a time when Rome was beset with unrest, mutinies and uprisings throughout the empire. Finally, at the start of the fifth century, when Rome itself was threatened by invaders, the legions abandoned Britain to its fate.

The withdrawal of the Romans left southern Britain in a perilous state. Many Celtic people had become thoroughly romanised, both in attitude and mixed blood. For four centuries, they had relied on the Roman forces of occupation for administration and policing. Many believed they had learned enough to take over these roles – and a new wave of ruling families seized power in various regions – but they had little experience of military matters. This left them particularly vulnerable in the north, where the 'barbarians' were making the most of the Roman withdrawal.

The rulers of post-Roman, southern Britain realised that they must defend themselves from the Celts of Scotland and Ireland, as well as the Saxons. Recognising the military weakness of his people after four centuries of comparatively easy living, a new ruler, Vortigern, decided to look abroad for help and introduced a mercenary army. Ironically, these 'swords for hire' were Saxons, led by the brothers Horsa and Hengest.

Once the mercenaries had fulfilled their side of the bargain, they appeared reluctant to return home. The Romano-British realised that in avoiding the frying pan, they had fallen into the fire. The Saxon mercenaries announced their intention to become permanent colonists. With their backs to the wall, the southern fat cats tried desperately to transform into tigers. Unfortunately, though they were able to contain the Saxons into a comparatively small coastal area, their attempts to drive out the new invaders failed. Horsa and Hengest held on grimly, and sent for reinforcements.

This was later described in *De Excidio Britanniae Liber Querelus,* which was written by Gildas, a British cleric, and concerned 'the ruin of Britain'. Writing some 50 years after the events, Gildas proved that it is easy to be wise after the event. 'The proud tyrant (Vortigern) and all the members of his council were struck blind ... To hold back the northern peoples, they introduced into the island the vile unspeakable Saxons ... Of their own free will, they invited in the enemy they should have feared worse than death ... So the brood of cubs burst from the lair of the barbarian lioness ... Their dam, learning of the success of the first contingent, sent over a larger draft of her dogs.'

In *The Anglo-Saxon Chronicle*, the scholar Bede identified these reinforcements as coming from three nations of Germany: 'from the Old Saxons, from the Angles, and from the Jutes.' It was their clear intention to seize and settle, encouraged by descriptions of a rich land and weak people, though it seems improbable, as some have suggested, that they invaded in huge numbers. Nor would these proud warriors have invaded with the intention of tilling fields or herding pigs. Rather, they sought power, operating in aggressive bands, pushing out the Romano-British 'lords of the manor' but keeping the native peasantry in place. Slowly but surely, the Anglo-Saxon influence spread.

Compared to the Romano-British, the Saxons were militarily astute and capable. They were a race of warriors, chiefs and kings whose priority was the ownership of land, and the honour and wealth it bestowed. However, like the Romans before them, they did not indulge in land grabbing without consideration to potential incomes and projected costs. And so, again like the Romans, they concentrated their efforts where the rewards would be highest. By the end of the ninth century, most of what is now England was contained in Anglo-Saxon kingdoms such as Wessex, Mercia and Northumbria, stretching up the east coast as far as the Firth of Forth. This perpetuated a 'Celtic fringe' in what is now Cornwall and Wales, Ireland and most of what is now Scotland, all of which were, at that time, still a collection of minor kingdoms.

Then came the harbingers of the most persistent invaders of all. The Arabs of Spain called them *aljamus* (heathen). The Greeks of Constantinople called them *Rus* or *varangoi* while, to the Germans, they were *ascomanni* (shipmen). The Anglo-Saxons described them as *wicingas* or *Denes*, irrespective of whether they hailed from Denmark, Norway or Sweden. They called themselves the *vikingar*.

It is said that their arrival on British shores in 793 was presaged by a number of omens. A rain of blood fell on York Minster. There was lightning and whirlwinds, and dragons lit the night skies with their fiery breath. When they arrived they came as raiders, employing hit-and-run tactics. In fact, they had been making small forays for at least four years. Their scouting missions had sought to probe coastal defences, and found them lacking. They stormed ashore from their long-ships at Lindisfarne, a place so revered by Christians that they called it Holy Island. That didn't deter the pagan Vikings who razed the monastery, slaughtered many monks, and carried off others into slavery.

Scotland fared no better. When the Vikings attacked Iona in 806, it was for the third time in 11 years. They burnt the abbey and butchered 68 monks and laymen. In the wake of this atrocity, Abbot Cellach decided to abandon the island and found a new monastic community at Kells in the Irish kingdom of Brega, although a small number of monks, led by the Irishman Blathmac, decided to remain.

The Vikings returned in 825, demanding to be taken to the shrine of St Columba, which they intended to plunder. Blathmac refused to speak and was torn apart by merciless warriors who, as pagans, despised everything that Christianity stood for.

Within a decade of the martyrdom of Blathmac, there was a shift in the Viking's tactics. Where before they had killed and plundered, leaving as quickly as they arrived, they began to settle. They arrived with their families in northern Scotland and the Hebrides, settling the lands that they had so recently devastated. Where they were not allowed to settle peacefully, they resorted to violent conquest.

Once settled, the Norse took an active part in local politics. For example, in the middle of the ninth century, when Kenneth mac Alpin, King of Dalriadic Scots, sought to unite his south-western kingdom with that of the Picts who dominated the north-east, the Hebridean Vikings joined forces with him. After seven years of bitter but indecisive warfare, in or about 845, Kenneth proclaimed that he wished to make a peace. He invited the Pictish leaders to a banquet, where they were greeted as heroes, then seated on benches at a feasting table. On a signal, the cleverly constructed benches were overturned, tumbling the Pictish leaders into concealed pits where they were hacked to pieces. Or so the story goes ... Having removed the opposition, Kenneth unified his kingdom.

Meanwhile, far to the south the Norse were again shifting their intentions from raiding to settlement. In 865, a great army led by Ivar and Halfdan, the sons of Ragnar Lothbrock, landed in East Anglia, and as time passed it became clear that they had come to stay. Two years later, Ivar took advantage of the 'civil war' between the kings of Northumbria to seize York. When the kings laid aside their differences and attempted to regain the city, they were defeated. Osbert was killed in battle. The unfortunate Aella was captured and gruesomely sacrificed to the Norse god Odin in the ritual torture known as the 'blood eagle'. Held face down, his ribs were hacked from his spine, allowing his torturers to pull out his lungs, still pumping, and arrange them on his back to resemble the spread wings of an eagle.

Two years later, Ivar turned his attention to East Anglia where the king, Edmund, was either desperate or naïve enough to visit the invader's camp. Edmund was seeking to negotiate a peace, but the Norse took this as a sign of weakness. He was immediately seized and savagely beaten, then tied to a tree and shot with arrows. The archers were careful to keep him alive, however, and he was still conscious when he was cut down and, like Aella, given the blood eagle treatment. Later, having hacked Edmund's screaming head from his shoulders, Ivar turned his great Norse army on Mercia. He left it under the command of his brother and went to Ireland where he died.

In the middle years of the ninth century, much of what is now England was under Danish overlordship – the Kingdom of York, Danish Mercia and East Anglia – and Norwegians had settled in parts of Wales, Ireland and Scotland – along the Solway Firth and up the west coast, north of the River Clyde. King Alfred of Wessex was one of the few who succeeded in holding back the invaders, coming to the aid of his neighbours in Mercia. His exploits would fill the pages of a long book. Suffice to say he recognised the need to unite the country. In 886, he entered London and was grandly acclaimed as the sovereign lord of all the English people – other than those still under subjection to 'the Danes'. Some coins of the time style him *rex Anglorum* meaning 'king of the English'. In truth, however, he remained a king among kings.

After a period of relative calm, Viking raids resumed in the 990s, and these Danish invaders came with colonial ambitions. After twenty years of bloody battles, slaughter, betrayal and astute marriages, the kings of Denmark and England were one and the same. Cnut proved an astute ruler, relying heavily on those Saxons that he could trust or control. Under Cnut's leadership, England enjoyed 20 years of relative peace and prosperity, but when he died in 1035, there were too many claimants to his throne – English, Danish and Norman, and the whole question of who ruled what wasn't resolved until 1066.

In the north, following Kenneth mac Alpin's reign the royal succession was not father-to-son. Under the tanistry system, the succession alternated between two branches of his descendants. Thus when King Donald of Scots died in 900, he was succeeded by his cousin King Constantine II.

More than three centuries had passed since Columba and his 12 companions established a monastery on Iona, but Constantine's enthroning was a secretive, pagan ritual that took the form of a symbolic marriage between the king and the land and the people. The ceremony may have included the sacrifice of a horse, a feast on its flesh, and ritual bathing. It was not a coronation as such, because there was no crown, but Constantine was invested with a sceptre and ceremonial robes and seated on the sacred 'stone of destiny' that would later play its part in fostering enmity between Scots and English.

In his time, Constantine became the most powerful man in Britain, maintaining indirect control over the whole of Scotland, despite ruling only a part of it, and forging an alliance with the Vikings against King Athelstan's Wessex. But he lost that power in the closing years of his reign. Recognising that Athelstan was in the ascendancy, Constantine faced him with an alliance of Scots, Irish and Vikings, but the combined army was decimated at Brunanburh in Northumbria in 937 and he lost the will to rule. After more than 40 years on the throne, Constantine put his pagan past behind him and abdicated in 943 to become a monk at the monastery of St Andrews.

After Constantine came Malcolm. He started well, annexing Moray then making peace with Wessex and gaining Cumbria in return for maintaining a cordial relationship between the two kingdoms, but his alliances with the Norse kings of Dublin and York weakened his position. He reneged on his pledge to maintain peace, invaded English territory, but was defeated. In 954, he was killed in a skirmish on the banks of the River Forth.

Few of Kenneth mac Alpin's descendants enjoyed long reigns, or died in their beds. His cousin Indulf, who was killed by Danes in 962, succeeded Malcolm. He was followed by Malcolm's son, Dub, who reigned for just four years before ending up face down in a ditch at Kinross. It is thought that he was murdered by supporters of Indulf's son, Culen, who became the next King of Scots, only to be assassinated in 971 by Riderch, the sub-king of Strathclyde, reputedly for crimes committed during a campaign to assert control over Strathclyde – including the rape of Riderch's daughter.

Premature death was still a fact of life for Scottish kings as the first millennium drew to a close. In 994, King Kenneth II led a raid south in an attempt to assert his kingdom's claim on Bernicia – now Lothian but then that part of northern Northumbria lying between the rivers Forth and Tweed. He was not successful, and just one year later he was murdered.

He had been trying to persuade the Scottish nobility to set aside the tanistry system of succession, paving the way for his son to inherit. Instead, a distant relative, Constantine III, who survived for just two years, followed him.

In 1005 King Malcolm II of Scots had killed his last rivals to the throne, Kenneth III and his son Giric, thus securing the succession. With that business out of the way, he turned his attention to more weighty matters. Malcolm wanted the wealth and power that might only be gained by the acquisition of further territory, and kings of Scotland had long believed they had a claim to the northern part of Northumbria known as Bernicia. Originally, Northumbria was literally all land 'north of the Humber', running up the east coast as far as the River Forth. By 900, its southern part had been lost to Danish Mercia, but the remainder was a vast tract of highly fertile and productive land. King Malcolm was particularly interested in that part between the rivers Forth and Tweed and, despite a generation of comparative peace between the Scots and Northumbrians, he marched his forces south.

When he heard of Malcolm's advance, Earl Uhtred gathered men from all over Northumbria. Uhtred was a member of the family that had ruled northern Northumbria for at least a century. The opposing forces met outside Durham where the Scots were heavily defeated, losing many thousands of men. Their heads were hacked from their bodies, and placed around the walls of Durham. Malcolm was lucky to escape. He fled north, licked his wounds, and planned a second assault on Northumbria.

Malcolm returned in 1016, defeating Earl Uhtred at Carham on the River Tweed and imposing his control on Bernicia, thus succeeding where Kenneth II had failed. After this defeat, Earl Uhtred was assassinated, probably on Cnut's orders. His replacement was one of Cnut's closest henchmen, Eirik of Hlathir. Meanwhile, following the death of King Owen of Strathclyde, Malcolm was able to impose complete control of this formerly semi-independent kingdom, extending down the west coast and including what is now Cumbria.

Immediately following Malcolm's seizure of Bernicia, Cnut was attending to other matters, but he invaded and regained this territory in 1031. Three years later, Malcolm was killed in Moray and was succeeded by his grandson, King Duncan. Following the annexation of Strathclyde, he inherited a kingdom bigger than any held by his predecessors. He might have wished that it included Bernicia, but where there was a will ... Duncan attacked in 1039, but was defeated at Durham. He escaped, only to be killed the following year, leading an attack against Macbeth, who took the throne.

Duncan's three sons fled to Northumbria where they had kinsmen. Earl Siward of Northumbria was their uncle and it was he who defeated Macbeth at Dunsinane in 1054. However, King Edward of England (Edward the Confessor) was not best pleased with Siward's involvement in Scottish affairs, and he was replaced in 1055 by a southerner, Tostig, a brother of Harold Godwinson.

Two years later, Siward's eldest nephew Malcolm, Duncan's son, killed Macbeth and then his son, Lulach, to regain his father's kingdom in 1058. He then proceeded to raid Northumbria in 1061. Tostig was never popular in Northumbria and his *thegns* (minor nobles) rebelled successfully against him in 1065, and he fled to the continent.

CHAPTER TWO

NEIGHBOURS
FROM HELL

E dward the Confessor, King of England, died on January 5 1066 with the succession still undecided. In a staggering coup, Harold Godwinson, brother of the late king's wife, claimed that on his deathbed, Edward had promised the throne to him. He was crowned almost before the old king was cold, having good reason to act so promptly. Two years earlier, Edward had promised the crown to Duke William of Normandy. Indeed, William claimed that it was Harold Godwinson who had conveyed this message, and that Harold had sworn an oath of homage to him.

William was not one to accept what he perceived as treachery. As spring passed into summer, he obtained a papal declaration that he was the rightful claimant to the throne, and a blessing for an invasion of England. Fighting men from all over Europe quickly gathered in Normandy to prepare and dream – some of glory and land grants, others of English loot and unprotected women. William drilled them into an effective war machine, gathered an invasion fleet, and waited for a change in the weather.

Duke William of Normandy wasn't the only 'foreigner' with designs on the English throne. Having fled from Northumberland, Tostig, bitter brother of King Harold, had fallen in with the king of Norway, Harald Hardrada, who also coveted the crown of England. Together with allies from Scotland, Ireland and Iceland, Tostig and Hardrada ravaged the Cleveland Coast in mid-September. They then sailed up the Humber and along the Ouse, disembarking nine miles from York where they routed two armies led by local earls, forcing York to submit. Five days later, however, King Harold arrived at the head of an exhausted army and slaughtered his enemies in a running battle. Harald Hardrada and Tostig were both slain. Just three days later, on September 28, Duke William's invasion fleet set sail from Normandy.

On October 13 1066 William's cavalry and archers slaughtered Harold Godwinson's Saxon army at what is now known as the Battle of Hastings. Following this victory, even the faintest signs of resistance were met with great brutality. Norman forces sacked the Channel ports and ravaged much of south-eastern England.

The only serious Saxon claimant to the throne was the young Edgar the Atheling (royal prince), a grandson of Edmund Ironside, and with a better claim to the succession than Duke William. However, realising that he had few if any options, and with his supporters swapping sides in droves, Edgar led a delegation of Londoners to meet with the invader. They didn't have far to go. The Normans were already encamped on the outskirts of the city. Edgar offered William the throne. He accepted and was crowned at Westminster on December 25.

Due to various pronouncements, including the Declaration of Arbroath, the impression has been given by some that Scotland was ever a weak neighbour, cowering in the shadow of aggressive England. Nothing could be further from the truth – at least not at the time of the Norman Conquest of England. The Scots were a proud and warlike race, obstinately repelling the same waves of invaders that had conquered England. Also, generations of Scots kings believed they had a legitimate claim to most of Northumbria.

In the west, Strathclyde extended well south of what is now the border, including what is now Cumbria – the old counties of Cumberland and Westmoreland – and the Scottish kings believed their frontier should be extended just as far south in the east. It was their ambition to drive the English out of what is now Lothian and the Borders, extending the eastern frontier at least to the Tweed, preferably to the Tyne and, if possible, to the Tees.

It would be hard to overstate the importance of the old Northumberland. It was a highly fertile stretch of land, long before the fens of East Anglia had been drained or the vast tracts of native forest had been cleared. Indeed, the old Northumberland, stretching from the Humber to the Forth, included such a high proportion of the island's grain producing arable land that it was later known as 'the nation's bread basket'. It would be a jewel in the crown of whichever country secured it. A hungry Scotland watched and waited.

Having seized the throne of England, William the Conqueror might have been eager to inspect what he had gained and taken a royal tour of his domain. Instead, he appointed two regents, William fitzOsbern and Bishop Odo of Bayeux, before returning to Normandy in a triumphant parade, like a Roman general returning from foreign campaigns. Thus did William announce his priorities. He might be King of England, but he remained Duke of Normandy first and foremost. This Franco-identity would be maintained by many generations of English kings.

On Easter Day 1067, William staged a great assembly, having invited nobles from all over France to gaze upon his loot and prisoners including Edgar the Atheling, the earls Edwin and Morcar and Archbishop Stigand. He donated gifts to a number of religious foundations, and he did not return to England until the end of the year. Meanwhile, he planned the siting of a chain of castles.

Castle building was used by the Normans as a means of holding down conquered territories. Norman nobles used them as a defensive base from which to suppress the native population, and as a clear statement of who held the power in the land. The siting of these earliest motte-and-bailey constructions was significant. They were concentrated in the south of England and along the border with Wales, in areas that had been given to William's nobles in a carve-up of the spoils of war. However, if the Normans thought the north could wait, they were soon proved wrong. Matters were in fact forced when, in 1067, William sold the earldom of Northumberland to Gospatric.

Throughout 1068, the north was simmering with discontent. The city of York had become a focal point for resistance, and bands of rebels were sleeping rough in the surrounding area. The earls Morcar of Northumberland and Edwin of Mercia were in open revolt, and their combined threat was massively increased when it was learned that the Welsh King Bleddyn was marching to join them, at the head of a great army. William reacted swiftly, racing with an army to build a castle and defences at Warwick, and thus cutting off Bleddyn's advance. Without this support, Morcar and Edwin decided on discretion and surrendered.

Meanwhile, Edgar the Atheling had fled north to Scotland with his mother and sisters and they were welcomed by the still watching and waiting King Malcolm III of Scots, known as Malcolm Canmore (the great chief). By now, Edgar was set on driving out the Norman invaders, and negotiated for Malcolm's assistance. He also pleaded for help from King Svein Estridsson of Denmark.

Some of William's invading army had started to drift back to France. At least one bishop condemned the 'lustfulness' of Norman wives who were sending messages to their husbands, complaining that they were fed up sleeping alone – threatening that they might find their comforts elsewhere. Even knowing that they might lose their new English estates, many felt bound to return to fulfil their conjugal duties ...

Others were no less lustful. When the new Norman governor, Robert de Commines, a Flemish noble, arrived in Durham at the start of 1069, he did little to control his 500 men who set off on a drunken spree of rape and looting. The furious locals slaughtered all but two of the Norman soldiery, sparking an uprising throughout the north of England.

Hearing of the revolt, Edgar the Atheling hurried south, gathering Northumbrians to his cause. He joined up with the rebels who had been gathering near York, and besieged the two Norman castles that had been hastily erected in the city. He was then joined by forces from a Danish fleet commanded by Osbern, the brother of King Svein Estridsson. When the castles fell, more than 3,000 Normans were slaughtered.

William responded quickly and mercilessly. He marched his army north and routed the Danes and Northumbrians before devastating the land. His men scoured the north of England, torching villages, slaughtering herds, destroying crops and killing men, women and children. With no food, many refugees fled north to Scotland, some selling themselves into slavery to avoid starvation.

Edgar had fled back to Scotland and it was there, at Dunfermline, that his sister Margaret married King Malcolm of Scots. Malcolm had previously refused to back Edgar's northern revolt, but now he seemed to change his mind. His forces struck south in a ferocious assault, ravaging towns as far south as Cleveland, as if they hadn't suffered enough already. Many were killed, and more taken prisoner. Even churches were plundered and destroyed, including St Peter's at Monkwearmouth. Despite this ruthless savagery, the Scottish king's 'raid in force' seemed to suit no particular purpose. If Malcolm had intended to occupy Northumberland, he must have changed his mind for he soon returned to Scotland. Perhaps the devastated north no longer looked like much of a prize. Whatever the circumstances, Malcolm had angered the Normans and could expect to reap a bitter harvest from the seeds he had sown. This latest raid was Malcolm's fifth invasion of English-held territory.

William had other matters on his hands at the time – attempting to subjugate the Welsh Marches or borderlands, among others, and defeating a combined force of Danes and English rebels in East Anglia, including Hereward the Wake. It wasn't until the late summer of 1072 that he found time to turn his attention to Scotland.

William's army was an awesome sight. Famed commanders rode at the head of vast columns of well-equipped and war-hardened veterans. Few would choose to stand against them, and Malcolm wasn't one of them. Realising that he had bitten off more than he could chew, the Scots king sought to negotiate. At a meeting at Abernethy in Tayside, he agreed to submit to William, withdraw his men wherever they lingered in England, hand over his son Duncan as a hostage and, most importantly, to expel his brother-in-law, Edgar the Atheling. Having thus humiliated the Scots, William withdrew.

A few months later, William was fighting in Normandy against Count Fulk IV of Anjou who had seized the opportunity of William's absence to grab Maine – a province on Normandy's southern border. William led his army in a lightning campaign. When he arrived at the province's capital, Le Mans, he ordered them to surrender or be put to the sword. This was no idle threat and the citizens, like King Malcolm a few months before, saw they had but one option. It wasn't the first time that such a threat had been made, nor would it be the last. William wasn't the only king in Britain's history who was ready, able and willing to put populations to the sword, soldiers and civilians alike, if they didn't do what they were told. Such terror tactics were a convenient means to an end for those with no patience with time-wasters, and who were intensely irritated by the high costs involved in laying siege to a castle or city.

As much as William could be merciless, he was not such a fool as to disregard the will of his northern people. The politics of Northumbria might have foxed the wisest man in Christendom, but William had heard enough to realise that Earl Gospatric was anything but popular. So, Gospatric was forced out and replaced by Waltheof. The sulking Gospatric, perhaps fearing for his life, fled north in the footsteps of Edgar the Atheling to seek the protection of King Malcolm who was busily strengthening the fortifications of Edinburgh and its castle. For another 500 years and more, the border between Scotland and England would prove a welcome escape route to many who fell out of favour.

Malcolm was anything but mean in his hospitality. Two years after he had expelled Edgar, on William's orders, he allowed him to return. A few months later, the King of France offered Edgar a castle at Montreuil-sur-Mer, from where he could raid Normandy or England. There was no love lost between the French king and the Duke of Normandy and this may have been the first time that the kings of Scotland and France realised that they had at least one thing in common. A common enemy...

Edgar accepted France's offer, but his fleet was hit by a terrible storm. Edgar and the other survivors limped back to Scotland, where Malcolm suggested that Edgar should recognise that enough was enough and submit to William. Surprisingly perhaps, William accepted this arrangement.

In 1075, William was back in Normandy. His regular absence from his new realm encouraged plotters to attempt a coup – this time involving some of William's own men. Earl Ralph of Norfolk and Suffolk and Earl Roger of Hereford led the uprising with the backing of Cnut, the son of the late King Svein Estridsson of Denmark, who promised the support of those Danes who had settled in England prior to the Norman invasion. The coup was far from popular, however. Roger was quickly arrested and when Ralph's forces were defeated near Cambridge, he fled to Brittany.

Once again, Northumberland was involved. Gospatric's replacement, Earl Waltheof, had taken the rebels' side. He was taken prisoner and executed at Winchester. Northumberland was a major thorn in William's side, but once again he had other priorities and remained in France.

The years 1076 to 1080 were not good for William. In late 1076, he besieged the castle of Dol in Brittany, occupied by the rebel Earl Ralph of Norfolk and Suffolk. Before William could bring the siege to a conclusion, the French king sent an army and William was forced to retreat with heavy losses. This was his first defeat in France in more than 20 years; it severely dented his prestige, and worse was to come.

Following the conquest of England, William's son Robert Curthose had argued that his father should concentrate on his new realm and pass on the reins of Normandy and Maine. This William refused to do. Once again, the French king stirred Norman troubles, and placed the castle of Gerberoi at Robert's disposal. When William's army arrived to lay siege, Robert's forces swarmed out of the castle and beat them off. To add to William's humiliation, he was knocked from his horse by Robert himself, and his younger son,

William, was badly wounded. Some honour was recovered when William was finally, although uneasily, reconciled with Robert who subsequently involved himself in English matters for, once again, trouble had flared in Northumberland.

Following the execution of Earl Waltheof, William had been reluctant to appoint a replacement. Instead, he handed control to Walcher, the Norman Bishop of Durham. In one way, this was a wise choice, for Walcher did a reasonably good job, although he was unable to control some of his more aggressive knights, including his relative Gilbert, who were hell-bent on picking arguments with any Saxons who retained a modicum of influence and power. Ligulf was just such a Saxon, retained as an adviser to the bishop. When he was murdered by Gilbert, the local people were convinced that the bishop had acted as an accessory. Fighting broke out and Bishop Walcher, Gilbert and other Normans sought sanctuary in a church. It was set on fire by an angry mob. When the occupants tried to break out, they were all killed.

Robert Curthose came north to establish control. In the Norman way of things, he began by building a new castle (Newcastle) on the River Tyne. This added fuel to the northern flames and it was suspected that some Northumbrian leaders, believing the Scots to be more sympathetic to their way of life, were considering an alliance with their northern neighbours. The combined forces of Scotland and Northumberland would provide a strong opposition to Norman rule in the north – and the annexation of Northumberland was King Malcolm's ambition, above all other things.

In 1086, England was divided into seven areas or circuits for the purposes of King William's stocktaking inquiry – his *Great Survey of England* – but the northernmost area covered was North Midlands, Lincolnshire and Yorkshire. North of the River Tees, William's rule was insecure, at best.

Matters had not improved when William died on September 9 1087 from injuries sustained while attacking the French garrison at Mantes, which had been making raids into Normandy. While he lay dying, William handed the crown of England to his younger son, William Rufus, but the land that William had inherited in Normandy passed to his eldest son, Robert Curthose, in accordance with Norman tradition – the eldest son inheriting what his father had inherited before him, while any land conquered by the father went to a younger son. This did not please the new king's uncle, Bishop Odo, the former regent, who organised a rebellion seeking the crown for his older nephew, Robert. The rebellion failed, practically unsupported by

Robert who seemed content with Normandy, and Odo fled to join him.

In 1090, William Rufus planned to take Normandy from his brother Robert. When various Norman clergymen appealed to William Rufus to intervene in a campaign of harassment against them by Robert, he used this as an excuse to send over 300 knights to support his allies, but did not succeed.

In May 1091 King Malcolm III of Scots invaded Northumberland. William Rufus was in Maine and somewhat slow to react, but in September an English fleet sailed north to take part in a campaign against the Scots and their Northumbrian allies. This fleet was wrecked in mysterious circumstances – calm seas and fine weather – in the Tynemouth area. Some said that it was God's judgement on the sailors, but whatever the reason, William Rufus hurried back to England, raised an army and headed north.

The Scots and English armies met in northern Northumberland, in what is now Lothian, but did not fight. Once again, when push was answered with shove, the Scots king proved eager to negotiate. Robert Curthose had settled his differences with his brother, and handled the arrangements. Malcolm was forced again to pay homage and swear fealty to a king of England.

In the aftermath of Malcolm's humiliation, William took over Cumbria and expelled the 'sitting tenant' Dolfin, a son of the disgraced Gospatric – formerly Earl of Northumberland – who had ruled as a vassal of King Malcolm. Dolfin fled to Scotland, where Malcolm gave him extensive lands, and William started to build a castle at Carlisle.

William may not have been overly impressed with Malcolm's promises, remembering that this same king of Scots had broken an earlier oath. He certainly wasn't impressed when Malcolm rode to Gloucester the following April, demanding that William keep his side of the bargain struck by Robert Curthose. He may have miscalculated when he refused even to speak with the Scots king. Malcolm was furious at this snub to his royal pride. He galloped back to Scotland, raised his forces, and made his fifth invasion of English territory late in 1093. By now, however, his Northumbrian allies had lost faith in his ability or willingness to see this matter through to a conclusion. The new Earl of Northumbria, Robert of Mowbray, ambushed the Scots on the banks of the River Aln. Malcolm was killed, as was his eldest son Edward.

King Malcolm III of Scots had hoped for much, but gained nothing. Indeed, rather than seizing Northumberland, he had lost the southern part of Strathclyde now known as Cumbria. He was succeeded by his brother Donald Bane who ruled for little more than six months before he was deposed by supporters of his own nephew Duncan. Duncan had sworn homage and fealty to William Rufus of England, and was supported by an army of Normans and English in toppling his uncle. He was the late King Malcolm's eldest surviving son – but he didn't survive for long. Within a few months, Donald's supporters had murdered Duncan, and Donald returned to the throne.

King Donald III of Scots inherited his brother's ambition for Northumberland, and formed an alliance with the new earl, Robert of Mowbray. William of England responded quickly. Citing the homage made by the late King Malcolm, he claimed overlordship and 'gave' Scotland to Edgar, Malcolm's third son, as his vassal. In that summer of 1095, William and his younger brother Henry were fighting their eldest brother, Robert Curthose, in Normandy, and dealing with insurrection in North Wales, but the English king found time to conduct a lightning campaign to crush the Northumbrian revolt – threatening at one point to gouge out Robert of Mowbray's eyes.

One who sided with the earl was William the Count of Eu, a kinsman of the king. He was taken prisoner and submitted to trial by combat. Having been defeated by the king's champion, Geoffrey Baynard, the count was judged guilty. The sentence was that he was to be blinded and castrated – a fairly common punishment in those days and described as 'merciful' compared to hanging, in that the condemned survived. Despite the intention, the count later died from these mutilations.

As well as 'gifting' Scotland to Edgar, William had granted him that part of the old Northumberland that is now Lothian. There was a problem with this – Donald was still sitting on the Scottish throne.

Edgar's maternal uncle and namesake Edgar the Atheling, who had been reconciled with the English king, offered to intervene and raised funds from William to pay for an army. They marched north and defeated Donald's forces in a pitched battle at Rescobie. It is believed that Donald was blinded on Edgar's orders, but survived to 1107.

Others principal supporters of Edgar's cause included his brother Alexander, who was subsequently invested in the earldom of Gowrie; another brother, David; and Edgar the Atheling, who was rewarded with the earldom of Fife. The new king of Scots was faithful to his supporters, and he included

William of England among those to whom he owed a debt of gratitude. Throughout his reign in Scotland, Edgar remained staunch in his loyalty to England. He seemed to have been an admirer of most things Norman, and shortly after his coronation in 1097, he invited Robert fitzGodwin to settle in Scotland – the first Anglo-Norman to do so.

King William II of England (William Rufus) was shot dead by Walter Tirel while hunting in the New Forest in August 1100. Some said it was a terrible accident – that the arrow had been aimed at a stag that ran between Tirel and the king – but others suspected it might be murder. The illegitimate son of the king's older brother, Robert Curthose, had been killed in just such a New Forest 'hunting accident' only months previously. The moralists believed that William was a homosexual who 'provided a living for no one but mercenaries and whores'. They were convinced that Tirel's arrow had been steered to William's heart by the hand of God, as punishment for his wicked ways.

Whatever the true circumstances of William's death, his younger brother wasted no time in being crowned Henry I. His eldest brother Robert of Curthose was already returning from a crusade that had followed the standard form – visiting sacred sites, listening to sermons on the Mount of Olives, looting gold, silver and relics, and massacring men, women and children in the Holy City of Jerusalem – and might decide to seize England for himself.

At home, just two months after his coronation, Henry married Edith, sister of the king of Scots, though it was part of the marriage settlement that she would change her name to Matilda (or Maude) which was easier for the French-speaking English court to pronounce. This marriage served to strengthen the ties between Scotland and England, and such alliances would be regularly repeated in succeeding generations. Indeed, in 1102, Henry arranged the marriage of Mary, another sister of King Edgar of Scots, to the Count of Boulogne – highlighting the *ménage à trois* relationship between England, Scotland and France.

Robert Curthose did indeed want England, and crossed the Channel at the head of an army in 1101, declaring 'I demand the right due to me as eldest son'. When the opposing forces met in Hampshire in August, the brothers were able to make an agreement and avoid any bloodshed. In return for Robert dropping his claim to the English throne, Henry promised to pay Robert £2,000 per annum, in compensation, and gave up his claim to a part of Normandy. It was an uneasy agreement, and wasn't settled until Henry, viewing his older brother as a loose cannon, invaded Normandy in 1105. After a bloody battle, Robert was captured along with 400 of his knights and 10,000 men, and thrown into a dungeon.

King Edgar of Scots died at the age of 33 in 1107, having followed pro-English policies throughout his reign. It was said that he was a calm and godly man, certainly in comparison to his more warlike brother Alexander who succeeded him.

Despite his aggressive character, Alexander adopted a policy of appeasement towards England, inviting some Norman knights to settle in Lowland Scotland and encouraging them to introduce their feudal system and build castles. Following their example, he ordered the building of a castle on a high crag overlooking Stirling.

The ties between the royal houses of England and Scotland were pulled ever tighter when Alexander married Sybilla, an illegitimate daughter of Henry of England. Alexander's brother (and heir to the throne) David received the earldoms of Huntingdon and Northampton on marrying the widowed Maud de Senlis.

When Alexander died in 1124, David succeeded to the Scottish throne. It was expected that he would continue the close bonding with England. Already in his mid-40s, the sixth and youngest son of Malcolm Canmore had lived in England for a time, trained as a knight and probably fought in King Henry's successful campaigns in Normandy. Through his marriage, as well as being King of Scots he was an English earl. One of his first acts as king was to grant great tracts of land in Annandale to his old comrade Robert de Brus (Bruce), a Norman previously living in Yorkshire.

In November 1135, aged 67 Henry I, King of England and Duke of Normandy, died of food poisoning at his hunting lodge near Rouen. His only legitimate son had drowned 15 years earlier; therefore his only legitimate descendant (there were any number of illegitimate ones) was his formidable daughter, Empress Matilda. A widow of the Holy Roman Emperor Henry V, she had subsequently married Geoffrey Plantagenet, Count of Anjou and a bitter enemy of the Normans who, therefore, was far from popular with the English court. Indeed, at the time of his father-in-law's death, he was at war with Normandy.

Rather than let their enemy take the throne of England, the Anglo-Norman nobles supported Stephen of Blois, the late king's nephew, who grabbed the crown within a few weeks of his uncle's demise. He would soon realise that having the crown was one thing, but holding it was another matter.

One of Stephen's priorities was to settle matters with David, King of Scots, in order to secure an alliance. In February 1136, they signed a treaty, which settled their dispute over land in England. It was agreed that David's son would retain the earldom of Huntingdon, but Stephen retained Northumberland. Apparently satisfied with this deal, David then returned to religious matters, attending the consecration of a cathedral in Glasgow and announcing the foundation of the first Cistercian abbey to be established in Scotland, at Melrose.

In March 1137, Stephen made peace with Count Theobald IV of Blois. In May 1137, he was recognised as the true king of England by King Louis VI of France. But in April 1138, and despite the treaty of 1136, King David of Scots invaded England in support of Empress Matilda, in her claim to the throne.

David's campaign started with a succession of violent raids into Northumberland, and escalated when he rejected Stephen's terms for peace and marched south at the head of a huge army. The barons of Yorkshire were waiting for the Scots at Cawton Moor near Northallerton. The Archbishop of York had a ship's mast erected as a rallying point for the English. To it he tied a silver casket containing consecrated bread for Holy Communion, and an assortment of church banners. In memory of this, the encounter was named the Battle of the Standards. The English were outnumbered, but far better equipped than the Scots who, despite fighting bravely, were defeated. Another battle was lost that day. By involving the Scots, Matilda had united many English magnates against her.

Ironically, perhaps, David was able to snatch a victory from his defeat when a papal legate intervened to negotiate a treaty between the kings. Stephen had little option but to negotiate. Despite the defeat at the Battle of the Standards, the Scots army had been able to withdraw relatively intact, and was still in control of much of the north of England. It was agreed that in addition to retaining the earldom of Huntingdon, David's eldest son, Henry, would be given the earldom of Northumberland, excluding the castles of Newcastle and Bamburgh. For his part, David supplied some hostages as security for his promise to keep the peace.

Having neutralised the threat of Scottish support for Matilda, Stephen was able to concentrate on fighting the sporadic flames of rebellion within England. In October 1139, Matilda was at Arundel Castle in West Sussex as a guest of King Henry's widow, Queen Adeliza, who had recently married William d'Aubigny, the Earl of Arundel. Various nobles, some with separate grievances of their own, were rallying to Matilda's cause. One such aggrieved party was Ranulf, the Earl of Chester, who wanted Northumberland for himself, and deeply resented Stephen passing it into the hands of the son of the King of Scots. In protest, he captured Lincoln Castle. Stephen arrived with his army to lay siege, but was then attacked and captured by Earl Robert of Gloucester.

With the tables turned and Stephen a prisoner, Matilda started planning her coronation. Seeing which way the wind blew, King David of Scots broke his treaty with Stephen and marched into England in support of Matilda. Then the wind changed ...

Stephen's wife, also Matilda, raised forces still loyal to the king, now imprisoned in Bristol, and marched on London where Empress Matilda was holding a pre-coronation banquet. Encouraged by the arrival of Queen Matilda, the citizens rose in an angry mob and attacked the Empress Matilda and her dinner guests. The Londoners had been infuriated by her stubborn demands for huge sums of money, and the empress was lucky to escape with her life.

The empress rallied her supporters, including her uncle King David of Scots and half-brother Earl Robert of Gloucester, raised a strong army and besieged Winchester Castle, home of Stephen's brother, Henry of Blois, Bishop of Winchester. Once again the attackers became the attacked. Queen Matilda had given the command of her army to a professional soldier, William of Ypres, whose priority was to capture the empress. And he just about pulled it off. Finding themselves under heavy attack and almost surrounded, Empress Matilda's army adopted a policy of every man for himself, and devil take the hindmost. Matilda ran the gauntlet of enemy forces, accompanied by a handful of loyal knights. Robert of Gloucester was captured. The Earl of Hereford threw away his armour to avoid being identified, and walked home half-naked. David King of Scots was reputedly captured three times, and each time secured his release by paying a hefty ransom.

Later, King Stephen was released in a prisoner exchange and gratefully rejoined his queen, but Empress Matilda was still on the loose and her husband, Geoffrey of Anjou, was about to pull an ace from his sleeve. With his wife holding Stephen's attention in England, Geoffrey embarked on a campaign to seize Normandy, which he achieved after a decisive battle in 1145. Geoffrey's victory created a quandary for the Anglo-Norman barons who owned estates in both England and Normandy. If they supported Matilda against Stephen, they might lose their estates in England. However, if they allied to Stephen, they would lose their estates in Normandy. This went very hard with men such as the Earl of Worcester who was, at one and the same time, the Count of Meulan and the greatest landowner in Normandy. It wasn't simply a case of deciding which estate was most valuable, for while an English estate might be bigger and better, the barons were still Norman to the core and their lands across the Channel were the source of their prestige and family identity.

Despite her husband's stranglehold on the Anglo-Norman noble's allegiance, Matilda left England and joined him in Normandy in 1148, apparently content to relinquish her claim to the English crown. This was probably prompted by the death of her most loyal supporter, her half-brother Earl Robert of Gloucester, though some believed she was simply calling for a break rather than an end to the struggle as her son, Henry Plantagenet, seemed interested in pursuing the claim.

Over the previous ten years, King David of Scots had been revolutionising the system of government in Scotland. He had also adopted a policy of 'Normanising' his nobility, offering crown lands and titles to Norman 'settlers' and, like King Alexander before him, encouraging them to build motte-and-bailey castles throughout the lowlands while strengthening the feudal system where land was granted to 'inferiors' in return for services, often of a military nature.

Immigrants included Hugh de Morville, with estates in Huntingdon, and Walter fitzAlan, the younger son of a Breton noble living in Shropshire, who received land in Scotland and the title of 'steward of the household', from which arose the name Stewart (or Stuart) that would figure so prominently in Britain's later history.

The 16-year-old Henry Plantagenet met with King David, his mother's uncle, at Carlisle in May 1149, and was knighted by him. As a possible successor to the English throne, he clearly felt that it might prove sensible to have the Scots on his side. Indeed, he offered an enormous inducement,

☞ CHAPTER THREE ☜

THE EARLY MIDDLE AGES

At the start of the middle ages, England was ruled by a French-speaking, Norman elite. Many had 'dual nationality', holding lands in France as well as England. Some families even held land in Scotland. For the peasant in the field or the miller in the village, the nationality of the local landowners might have been irrelevant, as long as there was food on the table and a roof over their heads. However, the hands on the reins of power decided a nation's future.

Scotland had not been conquered, but the constant settling of Normans in the lowlands caused a crack that would eventually widen into a gulf between the Celtic north and increasingly Normanised south. On the still fluid frontier, the inhabitants of old Northumberland and Cumberland might have wondered whether their children would be born English or Scots. To most it probably wouldn't have mattered, if only they could be born in peace.

King David of Scots' only son Henry, Earl of Northumberland and Huntingdon, died in June 1152, leaving his 11-year-old son, Malcolm, heir to the throne. King David died one year later, in May 1153 and, with young Malcolm as king, doubts were expressed as to whether Henry Plantagenet would honour the promise he had made to David to recognise the King of Scots as ruler of Cumberland and Northumberland as far south as the Tees – though Henry had still to gain heir to the English throne from King Stephen.

In 1150, Geoffrey Plantagenet had declared Henry to be of age, and had given him the Duchy of Normandy. In May 1152, Henry gained Aquitaine through his marriage to the duchess, Eleanor, who was 11 years his senior and recently divorced from King Louis VII of France. At the beginning of 1153, he landed in Dorset with a small army to further his claim to the throne of England.

Once again, the country was torn apart by civil war. It was settled by negotiation, with King Stephen agreeing to accept Henry as his heir. Just one year later, Henry was in Normandy when he heard of Stephen's death. He quickly returned to England to claim his throne.

Henry Plantagenet was crowned Henry II in December 1154, becoming one of the most powerful men in Europe. His dominions included England, Normandy, Brittany, Maine and Anjou, Aquitaine and Gascony. They also included parts of Wales and Ireland and he claimed suzerainty over the rest, as well as Scotland. He was not a man to be trifled with and was described by many as an arrogant bully. He certainly reneged on the deal he had made with the late King David of Scots, forcing young King Malcolm to return both Northumberland and Cumberland.

Malcolm had been forced to withdraw his southern frontier and give homage for his lands in Huntingdon but refused to do homage for the kingdom of Scotland and tried to resist his bullying neighbour. It was perhaps fortunate for Malcolm that Henry concentrated on extending his power in Wales and the rich lands of France. At the same time Malcolm had made important alliances with Holland and Brittany through the marriages of his sisters. Malcolm died in 1165, aged just 24. His brother William succeeded him.

Henry II didn't spare his family from his bullying. It got too much for them and, in 1173, his three eldest sons rebelled, prompting a short but bloody war. The core of their complaint was that their father allowed them no authority, and denied them sufficient means to support themselves as royal princes.

King William of Scots, to be known as William the Lion, saw an opportunity – or at least thought he did. He offered to support Henry against his sons, on the condition that Henry returned Northumberland. When this offer was refused, the snubbed William proceeded to invade Northumberland, his forces raiding as far south as Yorkshire. However, the English king's chief deputy, Richard of Lucy, soon drove him back over the border.

Not one to give up easily, William was back in Northumberland the following year, 1174, laying siege to Alnwick Castle. He then set off with 60 knights for a ride through the surrounding countryside. They were resting in a meadow when they were surprised by 400 English knights under the command of Robert of Estouteville who had ridden out from Newcastle on a reconnaissance in force. The Scots put up a brave fight, while it lasted, but were hopelessly outnumbered. William's horse was killed under him, and he was taken to Richmond Castle in chains.

Just after William's capture, a fleet commanded by Count Hugh of Bar arrived at Cleveland in support of the Scots invasion. On hearing of William's capture they returned to Flanders and two weeks later William's brother David surrendered to Henry at Huntingdon.

William the Lion, King of Scots, was kept in chains from July to December when he signed the Treaty of Falaise in Normandy, just two months after Henry had made peace with his rebellious sons. William was allowed to return home, but only after giving Henry overlordship of Scotland and providing hostages, including his brother, to ensure his good behaviour in the future. At the same time, William had to hand over his major castles, forfeit his estates in England, and agree to the subjection of the Scottish church.

Henry's priority was to draw the lion's teeth, rather than destroy him. Apparently, beyond the retention of Northumberland and Cumberland, he had few if any territorial ambitions in the north. Instead, what he sought was security on his northern frontier, by neutralising the Scottish threat.

Henry's belligerent attitudes and bullying manner made him few friends and many enemies. He had placed his queen, Eleanor of Aquitaine, under house arrest for her part in their sons' rebellion – and for her objection to him taking Rosamund Clifford for a mistress. Though he apparently forgave his sons, at the outset, they continued to oppose him to the last – aided and abetted by the king of France. When he died at Chinon in July 1189, few mourned his passing. Certainly not Queen Eleanor who was finally free after 16 years of virtual imprisonment.

Henry is remembered most for his turbulent relationship with his queen and sons, not to mention Thomas à Becket, but like most men he had good points as well as bad. He was a passionate law reformer, and his reign saw a clear definition of the relationships between the monarch and the state, church and society in general. The civil war during King Stephen's reign had threatened the king's involvement in legal matters and the general administration, and Henry saw it as a priority to restore royal authority. His reign witnessed changes in land law (making it more efficient and allowing trial by jury), which was much more equitable than combat and the establishment of permanent professional courts. It was a vital period in the creation of English common law. Royal legislation, or assizes, brought a new measure of law and order to England. Royal justices travelled throughout the realm, seeking out criminals. 'Inquiry shall be made throughout every county and every hundred, through 12 of the more lawful men of the hundred and through four of the more lawful men of each village upon oath ... whether there be any man accused or notoriously suspect of being a robber or murderer or thief.'

'Twelve of the more lawful men' were referred to as juries of presentment. The introduction of these assizes was a major advance. Previously, the victim of a crime – or their relations in the case of a homicide – brought an accusation (action) against the suspect. But this left them open to pressure and threats. It wasn't easy for a defenceless widow to bring an action against local bullies.

The method of 'taking evidence' was decidedly medieval. All accused before the assizes were put to trial by water. The local priest blessed the water in some nearby pond, and then the accused was thrown in. If they sank, the water had accepted them, and their friends could pull them out – if the water wasn't too deep. However, if they were rejected by the water and floated, they were found guilty. Standard punishment was the 'amputation' of a foot or right hand. Even if they sank, they might not get off because if those 12 good men insisted that they were a character of 'ill-repute' they would be ordered to leave the realm, under oath never to return. Of course, the cheapest route was the road north, into the wild borderlands with Scotland.

A great deal of the 'law of the land' had been inherited from the dominant Roman Catholic Church, but Henry's reign witnessed a new era where dictates were questioned and, therefore, a new sense of national identity was born. One example of England's desire to go its own way in legal matters concerned the status of illegitimate children. Church law legitimised children born out of wedlock whose parents subsequently married, but English law did not, creating a major problem for illegitimate children as they could not be heir to the father's estate. Churchmen urged reform to bring English law into line with Church law, but the barons refused. This is likely to be more of a statement about legal precedent, rather than a moral stance. They were saying, in effect, that the Church would not rule them.

Although Henry's son Richard had been at war with his father at the time of the king's death, he was crowned King Richard I of England in 1189. He desired above all things to go on a crusade to the Holy Land. Such an expedition was a very expensive undertaking, but Richard had plans and, within a couple of months of his coronation, invited King William of Scots to meet with him at Canterbury.

Richard offered William a simple deal. In return for 10,000 marks, Richard would scrap the Treaty of Falaise forced on William by the late but unlamented King Henry 15 years earlier. William did not hesitate. Since signing the treaty, he had been humiliated in his own kingdom – unable to act without the permission of his English overlord.

Seven months later and suitably financed, Richard sailed on the Third Crusade, arriving in Palestine on June 8 1191. This crusade had been instigated by the Holy Roman Emperor Frederick and his son, Duke Frederick of Swabia, Richard of England and Philip of France. Their purpose was to recapture Jerusalem and restore the Christian kingdom that had existed there from the First Crusade in 1099 until its fall in 1187 to Muslim forces commanded by Saladin, the ruler of Palestine. Emperor Frederick died in 1190, and his son fell the following year, leaving Richard and Philip in command. Although they had been friends as young men – some suggesting they had enjoyed a homosexual relationship – they disagreed on many issues and, in the end, Richard effectively took control.

The crusade became a deadly game of cat-and-mouse. Richard was striving to bring the Muslim forces to a pitched battle. Saladin preferred to keep on the move, employing his mounted archers in lightning raids on the crusaders' extended column. They were two of the greatest generals of their time and both commanded exceptionally courageous troops. Certainly, the two commanders had great respect for each other, although Richard lived up to the Muslims' notion that all Christian soldiers were barbarians. On one occasion, angered that negotiations were not going his way, Richard ordered the massacre of about 2,000 defenceless Muslim women and children. Some of the crusaders then set about butchering the corpses, as it was rumoured that the women had swallowed their jewels to hide them from looters.

The campaign ended in a stalemate, with the crusaders unable to capture Jerusalem, and the Muslims unable to drive them out of Palestine. Finally, the two sides negotiated a peace treaty to run for three years, with Saladin allowing the Christians control of a narrow coastal strip of land from Tyre to Jaffa, and granting Christian pilgrims access to Jerusalem.

Richard returned to England in 1194. Later, after various adventures, he was hit in the shoulder by a bolt from a crossbow while besieging the castle of Chalus in France. Though not serious in itself, the wound became infected and, at the age of 41, the warrior-king breathed his last.

Richard I is remembered as a king, but acknowledging his lands in France he was, like Henry Plantagenet before him, effectively an emperor. He was succeeded by his brother, King John who, like many English kings before him, spent a great deal of his time fighting in France, having comparatively little to do with his Scottish neighbours in the early years of his reign. This was all about to change ...

King William of Scots had never given up his ambitions regarding Northumberland, but probably accepted, at least at the start of the 1200s, that he could not seize and hold the land by force of arms. Therefore, he was prepared to negotiate with King John of England. In February 1206 they met at York for four days of fruitless talks. The problem was, perhaps, that John didn't trust William's intentions. Certainly, over the subsequent years, John started to fortify his northern border as if in anticipation of a Scottish attack. This worsened the situation, with William seeing the building of a new English castle at Tweedmouth, near Berwick as an aggressive rather than defensive action. It was certainly a provocation to the Scots, who halted proceedings by killing the builders and demolishing their work. This in turn provoked King John, who marched north at the head of an army.

Faced with an English invasion of Lothian, William returned to the negotiating table. At the same time as securing his northern frontier, John demanded the then huge sum of £10,000 in compensation, and ordered that William must hand over his two daughters to be married to Englishmen – one to his eldest son Henry.

William the Lion, King of Scots, died in 1214 at the grand old age, for those times, of 71. During his reign of 49 years he had been a strong king within his realm, putting down a number of rebellions, although he had failed to regain Northumberland. When his 16-year-old son Alexander became king he was caught between the devil of England and the deep blue sea of Norway. In 1210 Hakon IV of Norway re-established Norwegian overlordship of Orkney and the Western Isles and had since been attempting to extend his power.

Some relief came to Scotland when the barons of England rose against King John in 1215, leading to the signing of the Magna Carta at Runnymede in June. Alexander decided to celebrate in Scotland's time-honoured fashion, by invading Northumberland, laying siege to Norham Castle, and receiving the homage of the northern barons.

King John must have been furious. Harried by his own barons and then invaded by the Scots, he marched north again in January 1216. Things were not going well for him. In England where the barons, seething that he now refused to implement the reforms to which he had placed his signature, albeit under duress, had invited the Dauphin Louis Capet, son of King Philip II of France, to claim the throne of England through his wife Blanche. John decided that the threat in the north could wait and retreated south to prepare for Dauphin Louis, whose fleet sailed into Dover in May.

Made bold by John's withdrawal, the Scots shifted their attention west and raided – Cumberland. After the surrender of Carlisle, Alexander apparently decided to hedge his bets. He travelled to Dover where he paid homage to the recently arrived Dauphin Louis for the northern counties of England. It was a curious situation – a Scottish king paying homage to a French prince for land in England.

King John's campaign against the invading dauphin and his supporters started well enough, but he contracted dysentery. He could hardly ride, let alone conduct a war, and quickly weakened. He died in October 1216.

Most of England's barons were quick to show that the French dauphin had meant little more to them than a means to an end. With the death of the king, the majority cast aside Louis Capet, denying his claim to the English throne, and handed the crown to King John's son. Henry III, the new king of England, was just nine years old.

William Marshal, the Earl of Pembroke, accepted the Regency at the baron's invitation, and dealt harshly with any who remained loyal to the dauphin and France. Alexander of Scots repeated his southern journey – this time paying homage to the child Henry for his northern counties.

A French fleet set off to support the dauphin, who was trapped in London, but it was intercepted and defeated by ships commanded by Hubert de Burgh, the justiciary of England. One month later, the dauphin made peace and returned to France where, on the death of his father in 1223, he was crowned King Louis VIII.

In June 1237, King Alexander of Scots recognised Robert Bruce of Annandale as heir to the Scottish throne. Three months later, he met with Henry III of England, now in his late 20s, to fix the border between the two kingdoms. It was agreed that it would run from just south of Gretna to just north of Berwick, with Alexander renouncing the Scottish claim to Northumberland. The two kings met again to renew their truce in 1244. It was not a cordial meeting, however, as England's king was deeply suspicious of Alexander's deepening relationship with England's old enemy, France.

England and Scotland had been drawn out of their isolationism. The fates of the two countries had become inextricably linked with France, and there was increasing contact with the continent as a whole, both in terms of commerce, diplomacy and alliances. This was witnessed in 1174 by the arrival of that Flemish fleet in support of William the Lion's abortive invasion of Northumberland.

Scotland's long struggle to integrate what is now Northumberland and Cumbria had failed, and this had serious consequences on the balance of power on the British mainland. If the north of England had become part of Scotland, then the two kingdoms would have been approaching some sort of parity. But as long as England retained its northern shires, it maintained a distinct advantage in terms of resources, revenues and therefore power. Added to which, England was not so much a kingdom as an empire, arising out of the English king's vast holdings in France. Indeed, looking at the 'French' lands bequeathed by King Richard I of England, from Normandy in the north and stretching continuously to Gascony in the south, it is tempting to suggest that the king of England held as much of France as the French king.

The English court remained 'Frenchified' in tongue, manners, and ambition. Throughout the Middle Ages, succeeding generations of English kings and nobles fought the French in a bid to increase their territorial holdings. Increased territories meant more resources, revenues and therefore the wealth and power to wage more wars in order to secure yet more territory. In 1214, the balance of power had shifted markedly in France's favour when it seemed that King John, disdainfully known as 'Softsword' due to his lack of martial ability, was about to crush King Philip II of France in a pincer movement involving William Longsword, Earl of Salisbury, on one flank and King John's allies, the counts of Boulogne and Flanders and his nephew Holy Roman Emperor Otto, on the other. However, the plan failed miserably. King Henry was forced to retreat to La Rochelle and accept that he had lost Normandy and other possessions in France – some of the finest jewels in his empire's crown.

France and England were two countries of roughly equal strength pushing against each other. Both knew that if they could get the upper hand they could gather momentum and crush the opposition. France wasn't fighting simply to drive the English out of their continental land holdings – they were defending themselves against an enemy bent on expansion. Equally, the English believed that if France were allowed to gain any measure of superiority, it would roll them back to the Channel, and perhaps beyond. After all, in 1216, the Anglo-Norman barons had come within a hair's breadth of accepting the son of King Philip II of France as king of England, and the situation was only saved by the death of the hugely unpopular King John. If Louis Capet had come to the throne, he would have eventually been king of both England and France and nobody could have stood against him. In time, the whole of the British Isles might have been little more than a French dominion, ruled from Paris.

Scotland was frustrated at its inability to gain Northumberland, and felt constantly threatened by the increasingly powerful England. Despite their pride, the Scots kings must have feared that they would be unable to resist a full-scale invasion, certainly without assistance from a foreign power.

The English might have felt, like the Romans before them, that the cost of invading Scotland could not be justified by the immediate financial rewards. They knew enough of the Scots to suspect that they would not be easily garrisoned. The Lowlands of Scotland might be worth the taking, and would suit the English army's style of warfare, but the mountainous region to the north was another matter. In the Highlands, a determined guerrilla army could cause all sorts of havoc and tie up English soldiers for decades – soldiers who might otherwise be fighting to gain far more valuable territory in France. Equally, they had to consider the possibility that a hard-pressed Scotland might settle its differences with the Norwegians, now settled in Orkney and the Western Isles. There was little to gain and too much to lose from invading Scotland – as long as Scotland minded its own business. However Scotland did feel threatened and therefore sought alliances – and France, already England's enemy, was the obvious choice.

There is a certain circularity to all this. When King John of England began to fortify his northern border as if in anticipation of a Scottish attack, William of Scots viewed this as an offensive, rather than a defensive manoeuvre, and attacked. This in turn provoked King John, who marched north at the head of an army, capable of invasion. However, the nature of the subsequent negotiations does seem to suggest that the Scots got things wrong. If John had indeed been planning an invasion of Scottish territory, then surely he wouldn't have been 'bought off' when he had the upper hand.

Because Scotland felt threatened by England they sought an association with France. However, any such an arrangement would have to suit both parties, so the Scots supported the French, making Scotland a threat to England. For the Scots, seeking a balance of power meant dancing on the blades of very sharp knives. Sometimes they ran with the hare while hunting with the hounds, seeking alliances with both sides. Marriages between the leading families of Scotland, France and England were increasingly common.

Another power struggle was taking place at home and abroad. The Roman Catholic Church, controlled by the Vatican in Rome, dominated Europe's kingdoms but there were numerous arguments regarding who took precedence in an assortment of issues. For example, in 1206, King John of England and Pope Innocent III were involved in an argument that quickly escalated into a feud over the choice of a new Archbishop of Canterbury – the highest ecclesiastical appointment in the country.

When the incumbent Hubert died in 1205, the monks of Canterbury had secretly elected one of their number, Reginald, to be his replacement. However, the king and bishops had chosen Bishop John of Norwich. Reginald visited the Vatican and brought this to the attention of the pope, who ordered an inquiry.

King John arrived at Canterbury, demanding an explanation. The nervous monks denied that they had elected Reginald, and declared their allegiance to Bishop John. Thoroughly confused, the pope ordered the king, the bishops and the monks to send representatives to Rome to explain what was going on. Finally, losing patience will all parties, the pope imposed his own candidate, Stephen Langton.

King John refused to accept Pope Innocent's decision. The pope gave the king a year to change his mind, but John was adamant and so the pope issued an interdict, forbidding the clergy in England to carry out any services, save the baptism of infants and the confession of the dying. The king then seized the property of any cleric who obeyed – a profitable exercise as the church was very wealthy. He then turned his anger on the monks of Canterbury, ordering that they be expelled and treated as public enemies. Finally, in response to the king's disobedience, and with his patience strained beyond breaking point, the pope excommunicated John in 1209.

King John held out for four years, but faced with increasing hostility from his barons (who would soon force him into signing the Magna Carta) and fearing that the pope might support the threatened French invasion (by Dauphin Louis Capet, at the barons' invitation) he finally admitted defeat, offering to make England a fief of the papacy, to do homage to the pope, and to pay him an annual tribute of 1,000 marks.

Returning to the difficult relations between Scotland and England, in 1249 King Alexander II of Scots died of a fever and was succeeded by his young son, Alexander III. King Henry III of England was by now middle-aged, and saw an opportunity to bring Scotland to heel, perhaps remembering his own naïvety when he too had been a boy king, following the death of his father King John in 1216.

It had been arranged that the new king of Scotland would marry Henry's daughter Margaret for a dowry of 5,000 marks. Alexander was just ten years old, and Margaret was 11. Well aware that this alliance would provoke a protest, the marriage was conducted in secret in York on December 26 1251, though a number of Scottish nobles accompanied their king. At the banquet after the wedding, Henry encouraged Alexander to do homage for the lands he held in England and, furthermore, to do homage for the kingdom of Scotland itself. The Scottish nobles rose as one to intervene, but there was no need. Alexander was young, but he was nobody's fool. He politely replied that he had come to York to marry and not to 'answer about so difficult a matter', which, he said wisely, would require deliberation with his nobles. Henry, for his part, was gracious enough not to press the matter. On the other hand, he demanded the resignation of some Scots in high office, stating that his suggested replacements would better serve the interests of his daughter, now Queen Margaret.

Henry had more marriage plans in hand for his other children. In 1252, he dismissed the violent Simon de Montfort, his brother-in-law, as vice-regent in Gascony. A year later, he visited the region, seeming to adopt a policy of appeasement. The situation was complicated by Gascony's geographical and political position between France and Spain, not to mention its rebellious nobles. Henry devised a cunning plan – a political pass-the-parcel – announcing that his eldest son, the 14-year-old Prince Edward, would marry his cousin, Princess Eleanor of Castille, sister of King Alfonso of Castille who would renounce his claim to Gascony. Edward was then granted Gascony together with great estates in England and Ireland, and Alfonso promised to aid his new brother-in-law in dealing with the troublesome Gascons, including Gaston de Bearn who virtually controlled the Pyrenees and had become a thorn in Henry's side.

Warming to this new theme of alliance and reconciliation, Henry then made peace with Louis IX of France. Peace between England and France? Cynics asked how long it would last ...

In 1255 it was Henry's turn to have dealings with the pope. This time it was Pope Alexander IV, who had granted the kingdom of Sicily, which included part of southern Italy, to Henry's second son, the ten-year-old Edmund. Sicily, however, was not free for the taking. Others had tried, and failed, for it was occupied by the Moors. Indeed, the pope accepted that conquering Sicily would be the equivalent of a crusade, thus freeing Henry from his vow to fight in the Holy Land. There may have been some hidden agenda, or unwillingness at the Vatican, as Henry was told, in no uncertain terms, that failure to take Sicily and meet all associated expenses would result in excommunication.

Whatever suited the pope and the king did not suit the English barons or clergy. The barons would have to raise a huge sum to pay for a venture that was of absolutely no interest to them. The clergy also refused to accept that the conquest of Sicily amounted to a crusade, arguing that it was nothing more than a land-grabbing exercise, and there was serious opposition to the Sicilian venture. The clergy produced some money, but the barons flatly refused to provide any financial support. Henry was extremely embarrassed.

He was hatching plans regarding matters closer to home. It was discovered that he had been planning a coup in Scotland and, in support of this had arrived in northern England with an army. In the wake of this discovery, the Scots were thrown into something of a panic and quickly formed a new council of regency, which was more acceptable to Henry, thus staving off the English threat for the time being but not pleasing everybody.

Two years later, two members of the powerful Comyn family – Walter Earl of Mentieth and William Earl of Buchan, seized the young King Alexander. They had been members of the original council of regency and weren't prepared to let 'Henry's lackeys' run Scotland. Patriotic stuff, no doubt, but not necessarily true. The Comyns were in fact power-hungry and had been throwing their weight about, to the point where Alexander had asked his father-in-law to help him get rid of them. Henry prepared again to march north to deal with the rebels. However in September 1258, Alexander presided over negotiations at Jedburgh at which, having reconciled the Comyns with their rivals including Henry, they were left as a dominant power in the land.

In that same year, Henry had his own problems concerning England's balance of power. His barons, while professing their loyalty, demanded that he hand over the government to a reforming council of 24 peers, and Henry had little option but to agree. Their main priorities were to put a brake on Henry's spending, arising out of the Sicilian venture, and to reduce the French influence at the court.

The council – 12 of whom had been appointed by Henry and the balance by the peers – reported some months later, in what is known as the Provisions of Oxford. Three parliaments were to be held each year, with powers over the chancellor, the treasury and certain forms of patronage. The council also recommended the creation of a council of 15 members and a legislative commission with 12 members, both to come under the joint direction of the king and the peers. They also revived the post of justiciar to act as the king's chief deputy. Significantly, the royal castles were to go to new holders swearing allegiance to the council rather than the king. Symbolically, this announced who would hold the reins of power in England.

This was a bad time for Henry. One year later, in 1259, he renounced England's claims to Normandy, Maine, Anjou and Poitou, which his father King John had lost 50 years earlier. At the same time, he paid homage to King Louis IX of France for the Duchy of Aquitaine. In return, however, Louis agreed to support the English claim on Sicily, and to cede lands north and east of Gascony.

Due to Henry's close links with France, this agreement might be viewed as a 'family affair'. Certainly, that is how many of the English nobles viewed it, and they were deeply suspicious of the French influence at the English court, suspecting that Henry might look to France to support him in curbing their reforming vigour. In 1263, Henry was still dragging his heels in upholding the Provisions of Oxford, agreed five years earlier. His brother-in-law Simon de Montfort, Earl of Leicester, ran out of patience, raised a rebel force and acted quickly to place himself between Henry's royal army and the prospect of French reinforcement through the channel ports. In 1264, Henry and his son, Prince Edward, were captured and imprisoned after their defeat at Lewes in East Sussex, and de Montfort set up a provisional government.

One year later, Prince Edward managed to escape from custody – probably with inside help. Within a couple of months, he had joined with the Earl of Gloucester and the Marcher lords. Together, they defeated, killed and mutilated Simon de Montfort. Henry was freed. He then gathered those councillors and nobles who had remained loyal and set about repealing the reformers' acts, and taking vengeance on de Montfort's supporters.

In Scotland, although the early kings had denied a complete Viking conquest, the Norsemen had made permanent colonies in the islands of Shetland, Orkney and the Hebrides, and had maintained toeholds on the western mainland. This continuing threat could not be tolerated, and in 1261 a Scottish envoy was sent to ask King Hakon IV of Norway to cede the Western Isles. This approach was not welcomed and Hakon reacted by plundering Islay and Kintyre, and capturing Rothesay Castle on Bute before mooring his large fleet off Arran, from where he could raid the Ayrshire coast at will – as long as the weather was in his favour …

At the end of September 1263, four of Hakon's longships were caught in a storm and stranded in Largs on the mainland. A quickly gathered gang of local men attacked the crews. Seeing what was happening, Hakon arrived with 1,000 of his Norse warriors, but a Scottish force led by Alexander Stewart of Dundonald joined the locals. After a terrible slaughter Hakon was forced to withdraw to his ships and flee. He died two months later at Kirkwall in Orkney.

HAMMER OF THE SCOTS

O ver the years, historians have chronicled the campaigns of medieval armies, using dates and places of their victories and defeats, to illustrate the who, where and when. But their behaviour towards civilians of both sexes and all ages as well as combatants – was disturbingly brutal, and few have sought to ask *why* they behaved in such a fashion. Brutalities and massacres were often part-and-parcel of the fighting between England and Scotland (and other countries, of course), and it seems worth asking how a Christian king could order the slaughter of a city's entire population, then eat a hearty meal while his troops murdered, raped and looted.

There are few if any records to explain the psychology of medieval warfare. One recent warrior race that left a record of its military philosophy may be considered as a guide.

The Prussian Army was a dominant force throughout most of the 19th century. One of its famed officers and thinkers was Karl von Clausewitz. Throughout his military career he wrote notes which were published after his death in 1832. These amounted to an instruction manual for young Prussian and German officers, and made the following comments regarding the nature of war and its conduct:

'War knows of only one method: force. There is no other, it is destruction, wounds, death, and this employment of brute force is an absolute rule. As to international law, which all lawyers are so full of, it imposes on the object and the law of war only insignificant restrictions; in effect, none whatever. Now, philanthropists may easily imagine that there is a skilful method of disarming and overcoming an enemy without causing great bloodshed, and that is the proper tendency in war. However plausible this may appear, still it is an error which must be extirpated, for in such dangerous things as war the errors which proceed from the spirit of benevolence are the worst ... To introduce into a philosophy of war a principle of moderation would be an absurdity. War is an act of violence which in its application knows no bounds ... We do not like to hear of generals who are victorious without the shedding of blood.'

Following on from Clausewitz, before the Great War of 1914 the German General Staff issued its officers with the *Kriegsbrauch im Landkriege*, the Handbook of War. It further defined the applications of violence, to include non-combatants. 'No citizen or inhabitant of a State occupied by a hostile army can altogether escape the burdens, restrictions, sacrifices and inconveniences which are the natural consequence of a State of War. A war conducted with energy cannot be directed merely against the combatants of the Enemy State and the positions they occupy, but it will and must seek to destroy the total intellectual and material resources of the latter ... By steeping himself in military history an officer will be able to guard himself against excessive humanitarian notions. It will teach him that certain severities are indispensable in war, and that the only true humanity very often lies in a ruthless application of them.'

Field-Marshal von Hindenburg made the following comments in 1915. 'The more pitilessly war is waged ... it will come to an end so much the quicker.' On the home front, Major-General Charles Ross wrote 'War is a relapse to barbarism ... Love and sentiment are out of place in the struggle for existence ... The exercise of barbaric qualities governs the day. Atrocities are the last recourse of strategy in its efforts to force an enemy to its knees.'

These military men described, but did not invent, the concept of total war. It had been in existence for many centuries. One of its greatest exponents was already making his first marks on the bloody pages of history in 1265 when he took a major role in defeating Simon de Montfort's rebels. He was King Henry of England's son and heir, Edward, later to be known as the Hammer of the Scots.

Edward I is remembered by some as the flower of chivalry and a man of great goodness. Tall and of athletic build, he was nicknamed Edward Longshanks. A king who did more for England than any other, so some say. What is the truth behind the legend?

Matthew Paris, a notable and independently-minded English chronicler of the day, wrote despairingly of King Henry's heir in the late 1250s, describing an incident in which Edward and some friends attacked a young man. On Edward's orders, the youth's ear was cut off, and an eye gouged out. Paris was moved to ask, 'If he does these things when the wood is green, what can be hoped for when it is seasoned?'

Writing in the 20th century, the famous historian R F Traherne described the young Edward thus: 'An irresponsible, arrogant and headstrong boy, treacherously selfish in the heedless pursuit of his own ends, indulging every whim at his own pleasure, and incapable of self-discipline or obedience to external authority in anything that conflicted with the passions and hatreds of the moment.'

The vicious boy matured into a vicious adult who took the concept of 'total war' beyond all bounds. Even by medieval standards, Edward redefined brutality and produced a new breed of English soldiery that would provoke an anonymous French chronicler to write: 'The war they have waged and still wage is false, treacherous and damnable, but then they are an accursed race, opposed to all good and reason, ravening wolves, proud, arrogant hypocrites, tricksters without any conscience, tyrants and persecutors of Christians, men who drink and gorge on human blood, with natures like birds of prey, people who live only by plunder.'

In the early years of his military career, following the destruction of de Montfort's rebels, Edward announced his desire to go on a crusade to the Holy Land. Such a crusade was felt to be sorely needed. Under the rule of Mamluk Sultan Baibars, Egyptian power had been extended. The kingdom of Jerusalem was in a sorry state and, one after another, castles and cities had fallen to Baibars's armies.

Crusades were initiated by the papacy, but it would be a mistake to view them simply as fights between Christians and Muslims. The crusades were as much, if not more, about politics as religion. It was the intent of Christian crusaders to wage total war on all Muslims in order to protect frontiers and territory. To that end, the crusaders were willing to make some surprising alliances – even with the Mongols, who had been defeated by Baibars in the late 1250s.

Pope Urban IV began to talk about a new crusade in 1263. The legate Ottobuono was ordered to preach its cause in 1266 and one year later, when King Louis of France announced his active support for the venture, it was clear that a crusade would indeed take place. There was little enthusiasm for it among the English, but Prince Edward announced his intention to join, along with his brother Edmund, Henry of Alamain, the Earl of Gloucester, Earl Warenne, William de Valence and others. We can only guess at their motives, though most of the rank and file were paid, and all received various privileges. Edward's total force probably amounted to less than 1,000 men. He undoubtedly wished for more, but there were tight financial constraints imposed on the expedition by parliament. They sailed from Portsmouth to France where they discovered that King Louis's fleet had already sailed for Sardinia. Edward's ships set off in pursuit.

The initial target for the crusade had been changed to Tunis. Disease and the intense heat of the African summer decimated the besieging crusaders. King Louis died in August. His successor Philip III all but died, and was too weak to take command. Charles of Anjou arrived, took stock of the situation, and decided to enter negotiations with the Tunisian emir. Edward arrived one week later and was furious that the enemy had been granted a treaty, effectively buying off the crusaders. He made his philosophy clear. However, he finally had to agree to sail with the rest of the crusaders to Sicily to over-winter, before going on to Acre in the spring.

Edward finally arrived in the Holy Land, but it was several weeks before he could mount a raid on the enemy. Very little was achieved, other than the destruction of some crops and houses. Elsewhere, the enemy simply melted away, or ignored Edward's presence, and there was little that he could do about it. His force was just too small to wreak sufficient havoc to force the enemy to come to him.

Things improved for Edward in the autumn, when his brother Edmund joined him with reinforcements from England, as well as Cypriot barons with their followers. The enlarged army marched on Qaqun where they engaged a force of Turcomans – a tribe of sheepherders. Accounts of the battle differed, with the crusaders claiming they had slain 1,500 of the enemy, and the Turcomans admitting to just a handful. Whatever the true number of the dead, Edward was unable to take the castle and withdrew.

The leaders of the crusade realised that they were getting nowhere fast, and negotiated a truce. Edward was the last to leave. During this dalliance he nearly lost his life when an Arab assassin wielding a poisoned dagger stabbed him. After an extended convalescence, Edward finally left Acre in September 1272.

The crusade taught Edward a great deal. His frustrations at not being able to effectively engage his enemy convinced him of the need for total war. Such a force would not hesitate to turn its violence on non-combatants, whenever deemed advantageous, in order to destroy what the German officers handbook would later describe as 'the total intellectual and material resources of the enemy nation'. As for 'humanitarian notions', they seldom if ever figured in the crusaders' creed.

Edward also learned that war was an incredibly costly business. He borrowed extensively, and many of his followers were forced to sell or lease their estates. The financial realities of campaigning prompted Edward to become an impatient warrior. Each day wasted on a siege or chasing an elusive enemy opened the tap on his war coffers. By following the total war concept of bringing matters to a swift conclusion – by the application of indiscriminate and brutish violence – he could achieve far more while reducing his costs.

Despite the setbacks, the crusade had huge benefits for England's prince. It made him a champion of the Church, and gave him the opportunity to gain the respect of his crusader contemporaries. By serving alongside the French royals as their comrade-in-arms, he had created a new friendship amounting to an alliance. He was criticised by some for being too subservient to the French, rather than maintaining his independence as a commander, but Edward wasn't troubled by such accusations. Instead, he looked to the future, making friendships with those who admired his zealous approach to warfare. Significantly, he met with Tedaldo Visconti who was later elected pope as Gregory X. Edward was making important connections in all the right places. Of course, this was very discomfiting to the Scots, as it seemed to threaten, among other things, their friendship with France.

Edward succeeded to the English throne when his father, Henry III, died in November 1272. At the time, Edward was resting at the court of Charles of Anjou in Sicily, on his return from the crusade. He did not rush to get home. His succession was secured, and it would be almost two years before he was finally crowned at Westminster, having spent time furthering his friendships and alliances in both Italy and France.

The coronation was a very grand affair, attended by Alexander III King of Scots (Edward's nephew) among a host of dignitaries and aristocracy, but one guest was notably missing. Edward was clearly irritated by the absence of

Llewellyn ap Gruffydd, Prince of Wales – a country that still maintained a large measure of independence from England despite the Anglo-Normans' best efforts over the past two centuries.

Seven years earlier, Henry III had formally acknowledged Llewellyn's authority and territorial claims in Wales, in return for homages and money. If Llewellyn imagined this gave him the right to snub Henry's son – if that was indeed his intention – he was mistaken. When it came to Edward's attention that Llewellyn was intriguing with the sons of the late Simon de Montfort, he sent orders to Llewellyn to come to England and pay homage to him. Repeatedly, Llewellyn refused. Edward ordered the mustering of his feudal army at Worcester, which then marched to Chester.

Llewellyn realised that he couldn't face the English host in open battle, and retreated into the stronghold of Snowdonia. Edward did not wish to indulge in a guerrilla war in the forests and mountains. So he surrounded Snowdonia, cutting off Llewellyn's lines of supply, and waited. The outcome was inevitable. Llewellyn capitulated, was heavily fined (partly to compensate Edward for the cost of his military action) and had most of his land 'confiscated'. This did not settle the Welsh. There followed an uprising led by those Welsh nobles who had supported Edward against Llewellyn, but felt they had not been properly thanked. Llewellyn had become embroiled in an argument with Edward as to whether Welsh matters would be administered under Welsh law. This argument led to the claim that Edward was threatening the national identity of the Welsh, which drew the various factions into a popular front against English interference. As tensions increased in 1282, what had started as sporadic killing and looting became outright war.

This time, Edward meant business, marshalling an army of 10,000 men. They quickly took control of the south and west of Wales. To the north, Llewellyn realised that Snowdonia was no longer an option, and marched into mid-Wales where English forces surprised him. Stephen de Frankton, an English squire, killed him in the heat of battle. Later, the Welsh prince's head was hacked off and taken to London, where it was set on a pike outside the Tower of London.

Llewellyn died fighting, but his brother wasn't so lucky. After Llewellyn's death, Dafydd retreated to the mountains to continue the fight. He was captured, hanged and quartered in 1283. Edward then set about 'anglicising' his new territory, building castles and fortified towns at Flint, Rhuddlan, Aberystwyth and Builth, and later at Caernarfon, Conwy, Criccieth and Harlech.

Edward was also involved in some far from friendly dealings with the king of Scots. In 1278, Alexander went to Westminster to pay homage to Edward for that land he held in England. It was then suggested that Alexander should acknowledge that he held Scotland only with the English king's consent. Alexander was anything but compliant, stating, 'To homage for my kingdom of Scotland, no one has right except God alone, nor do I hold it except of God alone.' The matter was left, but it was a clear signal of Edward's attitude and intentions.

Relations between Scotland and England remained frosty throughout the rest of Alexander's reign. When he was killed in a riding accident in 1286, his three children had already died and so the succession passed to his two-year-old granddaughter Margaret, daughter of King Eirik II of Norway. Her claim was recognised by the Scottish Parliament and six guardians were appointed to rule Scotland on her behalf – two bishops, two earls and two barons – but the situation was far from settled. Scotland's noble families were ever looking for opportunities to better themselves, and the Bruces of Annandale were perhaps the most ambitious of all.

Within days of Alexander's death, the 75-year-old Robert Bruce made it known to his supporters that he was preparing to make a claim to the Scottish throne, contesting Margaret's succession, as a female, and asserting his own as a descendant of King David. He was particularly annoyed that he hadn't been appointed as one of the guardians though his long-standing enemy, John Comyn, had been. Attacks on royal officials by Bruce's supporters, and outbreaks of fighting in the south-west, amounted to something of a rebellion, albeit on a localised basis. Besides letting off some steam and blood, it achieved very little and soon fizzled out.

Edward of England became involved in the problems of the Scottish succession three years later, in 1289, when negotiations were held in Wiltshire leading to a treaty signed by Edward, the Norwegians acting on behalf of Margaret (remembered as the Maid of Norway) and the Scots. It would later be claimed that Edward had made it a condition of his involvement that Scotland would be subject to England. In various ways, Edward showed his contempt for Scottish independence.

One year later, while undertaking the perilous journey across the North Sea to claim her throne, the Maid fell ill with acute sea-sickness and died in Orkney. The throne of Scotland was up for grabs. No less than 13 claimants stepped forward, ranging from the King of Norway to Nicholas de Soules, William de Ros and William de Vescy – the last three all claiming through illegitimate descent from Alexander II. The two outstanding claimants were Robert Bruce (Robert de Brus) and John Balliol.

No one contender had anything approaching universal support, and Scotland was teetering on the brink of civil war. It wouldn't matter who the Scottish powers chose – there would be opposition. The only alternative was to call in an outside authority to settle the matter, some authority who commanded respect abroad, including the papacy. Reluctantly, approaches were made to Edward of England to act as referee. In effect, the king of England was being offered the power to appoint the king of Scots. Edward agreed, but stated his price. He was bent on imposing some form of feudal overlordship in the northern kingdom – for himself and his successors.

The hearings began at Norham on Tweedside in May 1291, attended by Scottish and English powerbrokers. They didn't get off to a good start, with lengthy arguments over Edward's jurisdiction. From the English side, Roger Brabazon, the Chief Justice of the King's Bench, instructed the Scots to accept Edward's overlordship. The circumstances of Edward's role in choosing a Scots king seemed argument enough that he had this power. However, the Bishop of Glasgow, Robert Wishart, led the Scottish objection, stating that Scotland was not under feudal subjection to England.

The hearings were adjourned while both sides considered the matter. Finally, the Scots came back with the suggestion that they hadn't the power to make such a decision. Their argument was that only a king of Scotland could decide, and so it must be delayed until a new king had been appointed. This was good enough for Edward. After all, he would be interviewing the candidates, and it would be a simple matter to champion the cause of the most compliant. At interview, all the competitors for the Scottish throne accepted Edward's jurisdiction and the prospect of his feudal overlordship. To say otherwise would have put them out of the running.

A court of 104 auditors was set up. Twenty-four were appointed by Edward, 40 by John Balliol and 40 by Robert Bruce. Therefore, Edward's was only a minority interest, but Balliol's and Bruce's supporters cancelled each other out, leaving Edward's auditors with the final say. Their decision, after suitably lengthy deliberations, was that John Balliol had the best claim. A study of the case proves this was true. If Edward had noted that Balliol was a fairly weak and compliant character who might be content to rule as a puppet, it wasn't necessary to 'fiddle' the legal arguments. So, Edward could have his cake and eat it – choosing the best-qualified candidate, while getting the best deal for himself. In announcing the auditors' decision, Edward made it clear that he claimed sovereign lordship of Scotland, would exercise his rights, and expected to receive homage from Balliol. He also stated that if Balliol did not govern justly in Scotland, England would intervene.

John Balliol, King of Scots, was the fourth son of a wealthy Anglo-Scottish nobleman, and was probably intended for the Church. In many ways, he was more connected to England than Scotland, married to a daughter of Earl Warrene and with substantial estates in the north of England – factors which would perhaps have created an instinctive subservience to the English crown. He had no training in martial matters, being more intellectual. The problem was, of course, that the 'professor' was now matched against a heavyweight fighter.

The first rounds of the unbalanced contest took place in the law courts. Despite earlier assurances to the contrary, appeals against Scottish court decisions were heard in English courts, ignoring the Scots' claim that they had no jurisdiction. The most celebrated appeal case was that of Macduff, a younger son of Malcolm, Earl of Fife, who claimed that he had been unjustly deprived of his inheritance and imprisoned. John Balliol was summoned to appear in person before the English parliament. He may have prepared his arguments well enough, but Edward saw an opportunity to show who was boss, and instructed parliament accordingly. Balliol was humiliated. When threatened with the forfeiture of important castles and towns, he tucked his tail between his legs, acknowledged Edward's overlordship and agreed to an adjournment of the case. It was never concluded.

Scottish resentment at being forced into a subservient position came to a head in the summer of 1294. Feudal homage involved an undertaking to provide military service, and Edward summoned Balliol and other Scottish nobles to fight against the French – their old allies. This animosity between England and France suggested to some Scots that their old alliance might be renewed. Shoulder to shoulder with their old French comrades, they might stand against Edward's power and bullyboy tactics.

In 1295, Balliol was dithering – perhaps with a mind to follow Edward's demands. However, others were not so hesitant or compliant. A council of 12 seized power and affected a treaty of alliance with the French, effectively declaring war on England.

There had been earlier links between Scotland and France, but this was the first formalised agreement setting out the two countries' recognition of each other as kingdoms, and spelling out a policy of mutual support and defence. As such, it may be regarded as the first written evidence of the Auld Alliance, which the Scots valued so highly. Elements of the Scottish army then invaded Northumberland where, according to later English accounts, they committed many atrocities including murder, rape, sexual mutilation and infanticide – at Corbridge, it was reported, they rounded up two hundred children and forced them into a building which they then set on fire.

Edward's war with France continued until 1298. Somewhat ironically, in view of the Scottish situation, the problem was again one of overlordship. Under the terms of the Treaty of Paris, signed in 1259, the king of England held Gascony as a vassal of the king of France. Therefore, the French believed they could hear appeals against Edward's jurisdiction in Gascony, and receive military service from Edward, who had performed homage (for Gascony) to Philip IV in 1286. Edward refused on both counts, and Philip declared his intention to confiscate Gascony. Edward wasn't about to let that happen.

At the same time that he was fighting France, Edward was putting down a rebellion in Wales. As in Scotland, the Welsh rebellion had been prompted, in part, by Edward's demands for feudal military support against France. Despite already having these two fights on his hands, the English king prepared to invade Scotland in 1296. Fighting on three fronts would be vastly expensive, and was therefore very unpopular with those English who had to finance these campaigns. Faced with serious opposition at home, Edward would have to bring matters to a swift conclusion, and planned accordingly.

In early March, John Balliol renounced his homage, and a Scottish army was mustered near Selkirk. It included a small number of well-equipped and mounted knights and men-at-arms – mainly originating from those Norman families that had settled in Scotland – but the bulk of the force were armed with whatever came to hand, and had little if any military training or experience. One family was notably missing from the Scottish ranks. Robert Bruce had died one year earlier, and neither his son nor grandson, the new Earl of Carrick (also Robert Bruce) were about to fight for John Balliol. Rather the opposite, for they would have expected that if (when) Edward defeated Balliol, the Bruces would be next in line for the Scottish throne.

Therefore, it was in their best interests to ally themselves with Edward, and Robert Bruce rode off to join the English army, together with the Earls of March and Angus. Thus Edward was able to exploit Scotland's inherent factionalism. A nation divided by raw, personal ambitions would be far easier to conquer.

A Scottish force marched south from Annandale to attack Carlisle in the west. Edward's army was marching up the east coast. By the end of the month, the war machine, including 11,000 loyal Welshmen armed with the deadly longbow, had arrived at Berwick-upon-Tweed (then in Scotland) which closed its gates – the citizens placing too much faith in the town's flimsy defences and hurling insults at the English and Welsh host. Edward was in no mind to be held up by a siege, and ordered a full-scale assault. It is said that Robert Bruce was one of the first to cleave his way into the town.

Not content with a military victory, Edward ordered the massacre of Berwick's inhabitants – thousands of men, women and children – sending a clear message to any other Scottish city or town that might consider closing its gates to his army. According to one chronicler, the killing continued throughout the day until finally Edward, seeing a child clinging to the bloody skirts of its dead mother, signalled a belated end to the rape and butchery of Berwick's defenceless people. Some accounts recall the River Tweed running red with blood for many days after.

Edward's advance guard marched north, under the command of John de Warenne, Earl of Surrey. The ill-prepared Scottish army met with them at Dunbar on April 27. After the Welsh bowmen had thinned the Scottish ranks, Warenne's cavalry charged into what was left standing. They would later boast that 10,000 Scots had been killed on the field of battle. Countless more were slain as they fled in panic towards the distant sanctuary of the Ettrick Forest. The English advance was irresistible. As to Scotland's castles, their garrisons surrendered Dumbarton, Dunbar, Jedburgh and Roxburgh. Edinburgh held out for a week against heavy siege machines. And when Edward arrived at Stirling, the garrison had already fled, leaving the gatekeeper to hand over the keys.

Deserted by all but a handful, John Balliol had nowhere to turn. He was offered no option but to surrender the land and people of Scotland to Edward, while 'confessing' his wrongdoing and folly in allying himself to the enemy (France) of his overlord. Obliged to present himself in his royal splendour, he was ceremonially stripped off his crown, sceptre and sword, the ring from his finger and even the fur trimming on his surcoat.

After Balliol's humiliation, Edward set off on a short but devastating tour of Scotland, travelling as far north as Elgin. Wherever he went, Scottish nobles eager to make peace and pay homage, no doubt mindful of the lesson of Berwick, met him. Those who showed any signs of resistance were hanged and worse at their gates, alongside their kinsmen and servants. Their wives and daughters were raped and mutilated, their houses burnt, crops destroyed and livestock slaughtered or driven off. Nobody knows how many of both sexes and all ages were murdered while Scotland reeled under the full brutality of Edward's tour. Of course, these atrocities must be considered in context. The Scots could behave just as badly, and raiding parties operating in Northumberland had done just that – making a priority out of raping and looting, even while Edward's army was slaughtering their countrymen in Berwick.

Edward appointed sheriffs, and they too received submissions. By the time Edward returned in August to hold a parliament at Berwick, around 2,000 Scottish earls, barons, freeholders, burgesses and barons had sworn fealty to him and renounced the Franco-Scottish alliance.

There remained the matter of the empty Scottish throne, but Edward wasn't about to appoint a successor. The matter had been raised after the defeat of the Scots army, the 'loyal' Bruces taking the opportunity to ask to be installed in place of Balliol. Edward's bad-tempered reply was, 'Have we nothing to do but win realms for you?' Edward's intention was clear – there would be no replacement for Balliol. Nor would Edward assume the title of King of Scots for himself. He viewed Scotland as part of his English realm, rather than as a separate kingdom – and he would rule Scotland as King of England. He specifically referred to the land, rather than the kingdom, of Scotland. The Scottish regalia were sent to London, along with most of the nation's archives for Edward was ever the bibliophile. The enthronement stone – the Stone of Destiny – was taken from Scone to Westminster. Central government was in English hands. All this had been achieved in little more than 20 weeks.

CHAPTER FIVE

THE LION ROARS

Nigel Tranter's tale of *The Wallace* starts with a description of four young Scots arriving at a laird's home, Carleith Tower, which has been visited by English troops. Everybody is dead. Fourteen naked bodies including that of Cunninghame of Carleith, his sons, wife, three daughters and two serving women, are hanging by their ankles at the gateway, alongside grotesque bundles of children's limbs and body parts. When they enter the courtyard, the companions see the parapet of the deep well, buzzing with bloated flies and filled to overflowing with 30 or 40 bodies, the women naked and mutilated, men and children hacked to pieces ...

Such scenes were not uncommon in the time after John Balliol's defeat and humiliation, when Edward had returned to England leaving Scotland under the administration of the Earl of Surrey, Hugh Cressingham and other English officials who acted with bullying arrogance and brutal savagery. Throughout the land, whatever vestiges of Scottish pride remained were to be crushed under the heel of Edward's barons and soldiers in an effort to force the Scots to their knees, and keep them there.

The young Scots described by Tranter were William Wallace, a son of Sir Malcolm Wallace of Elderslie, Robert Boyd, John Blair and Wallace's nephew Edward Little – a son of his sister Margaret. Despite the English intention, they were not forced to their knees. Rather the opposite for, driven into a cold fury, they set off in pursuit, gathering like-minded young Scots along the way. One of these was Wallace's cousin, the 19-year-old Ranald Crawford, son of Sir Reginald Crawford. They circled ahead of the English column which they ambushed, and extracted their revenge. With English blood on their hands, there was no going back.

William Wallace and his companions didn't start the 'rebellion' against English occupation. There had already been trouble in Argyll, Ross, Moray and Aberdeenshire, fuelled by the actions of the army of occupation, Edward's imposition of taxes on the Scots and demands for troops to serve in France.

Wallace killed the English Sheriff of Lanark in May 1297 and, at or about the same time, James, the High Steward, William, Lord of Douglas and Bishop Wishart of Glasgow had assembled an armed force in the west. Significantly, Robert Bruce, Earl of Carrick, joined them. Probably, the 'loyal' Bruces, feeling snubbed by Edward's refusal to grant them the throne of Scotland, had decided to change tack. These western rebels lost their resolve when threatened by an English force in July. However, this did not settle matters. Cressingham wrote to Edward, warning him that Scotland was in turmoil and that Berwick and Roxburgh were the only shires remaining under effective control.

Wallace and his growing band of patriots suddenly appeared in Perth, where Edward's justiciar barely escaped from the surprise attack. A few weeks later, according to Cressingham, Wallace was to be found with a large, armed company in the Forest of Selkirk, and a few weeks after that, in August, he was apparently besieging the English-held castle in Dundee.

Further north, the castles of Aberdeen, Urquhart and Inverness fell to Scottish forces led by Andrew de Moray, son of Andrew de Moray of Petty. This daring young commander then took Montrose, Brechin and Forfar. Inevitably, he linked up with Wallace, and they declared themselves 'leaders of the army of Scotland', with most of the territory north of the Forth-Clyde line under their control. This corroborated what the Romans had discovered nearly one thousand years earlier – that while the north might be conquered, holding it was a very different matter.

The Earl of Surrey, Cressingham and the other Englishmen based in Scotland fully realised the seriousness of their position. However, Edward seems to have ignored or downplayed their concerns. He was still fighting his war with France and in late August he set sail for Flanders, having sent an impatient message to Surrey that if there was some problem with the newly-subjugated Scots, then he should deal with it.

English leaders in Scotland were thrown into a dilemma. There would be serious consequences for them if they lost their grip on Scotland, yet they would be in as much trouble if they ran up excessive expenses on a prolonged military campaign. Finally, they marched north with 300 heavy cavalry and 10,000 infantry – northern English levies and Welsh archers. No doubt they were feeling confident of a victory, as long as they could bring the Scottish army to battle. Their main concern was to bring matters to a swift conclusion, so it might have seemed that their prayers had been answered when it was reported that the Scottish army, under the command of Wallace and de Moray, was drawn up on the north side of the River Forth, near Stirling where the castle was still held by an English garrison.

Tacticians in the English army pointed out that the Scots held a strong position, and the English army would have to cross the narrow Stirling Bridge in order to get to them, but Cressingham shouted them down. 'Why should the king's treasure be wasted in prolonging the war?' he demanded.

On September 11, 1297, the Scots watched and waited while the English started to cross just two or three abreast, which was all the narrow bridge would allow. Finally, when about half the English troops were across, with Cressingham among them, the Scots attacked. They concentrated on the flanks, hacking their way through to the bridge, where they fought off the English attempts to reinforce their beleaguered comrades.

Unable to advance, the English on the southern side of the bridge could do little but watch while those who had crossed the bridge were surrounded and slaughtered, or driven into the river where they drowned. Cressingham died fighting. Wallace later ordered that his corpse should be skinned to make a sword belt.

What remained of the English army fled back to Berwick. The victorious Scots followed soon after – raiding through Northumberland and Cumberland in a vicious reprisal for atrocities committed by the English in Scotland and, perhaps, just for the hell of it. An eye for an eye, but where does it end when both sides seem blinded by hatred?

Andrew de Moray died from wounds received at Stirling Bridge. For ten months, while Edward remained in France, Wallace governed Scotland in Balliol's name. Wallace's continuing support of the disgraced king, still in captivity in England and later to be exiled to his French estates, was far from popular with the Scottish nobility, and the Bruces in particular. Nor were the Scots nobility happy to be ruled by the lowest rank of their class – a son of an insignificant laird. It would be a mistake to believe that Wallace had the full support of Scotland for, yet again, the nation was divided by personal ambitions and prickly pride.

Meanwhile, Edward was facing his own set of problems. During his absence in Flanders, a Parliament met at which the bishops and barons openly voiced their anger. They had two major grievances. Firstly, there were Edward's incessant demands for money to pay for his military campaigns in Wales, Scotland and France – a cost amounting to the enormous sum, in those days, of about £750,000. Secondly, they were angry that Edward was not observing the terms of the Magna Carta signed by King John in 1215. In Edward's absence, his council of regency agreed in October 1297 that the liberating charter should be renewed, the unpopular wool tax abolished, and any new taxes should not be imposed without 'the common consent of the whole kingdom'. In return, the barons and clergy would support alternative measures to boost Edward's coffers. The council reasoned that the king, in his current financial predicament, would have little option but to agree.

In the opening months of 1298, the expensive war between Edward and King Philip IV of France was concluded with a treaty. Most of Gascony was to remain under French control, but Edward hoped that what he had failed to hold by military means could be regained by diplomacy. For his part, Philip agreed to abandon his Scottish allies in their hour of need.

Edward returned to England in March, free to concentrate on the Scottish 'rebels'. He immediately ordered the raising of a strong army, and had the seat of government moved from London to York. At the start of July, he advanced into Scotland, apparently heading for Edinburgh.

As commander of the Scottish army, Wallace was faced with a dilemma. It was known that the tightly-financed English army was short of supplies, and that many of its already hungry infantry were on the verge of mutiny and desertion. Therefore, the best military option would perhaps have been to retreat before the English, leading them into the Highlands while destroying any stored food ahead of them – a 'scorched earth' policy – while harrying their lines of supply and employing hit-and-run guerrilla tactics. However, Wallace did not have the benefit of a professional army, and had to accept that his troops would soon be deserting in droves to return to their homes for the harvest. If the crops were left to rot in the fields, their families and ultimately the country would starve. The Scots were well aware of the English army's readiness to commit atrocities against undefended civilians. Wallace had little option but to prepare for the sort of pitched battle at which the English army's feudal cavalry and professional archers excelled. Edward heard that Wallace had gathered his troops at Falkirk, and pushed on to engage him.

Wallace arranged his army as best he could, organising them into schiltrons in which spearmen formed into compact squares, three ranks deep, presenting their spears to the enemy in what has been described as a 'bristling hedgehog' style. There were four of these schiltrons, linked by small groups of archers, and the few Scottish cavalry were kept in the rear. The schiltrons strength was, at one and the same time, its weakness. While it was effective at repulsing a charge of cavalry, there was little it could do against massed archers who kept their distance.

The schiltrons bravely withstood the first charge of Edward's cavalry, but the Scottish archers had little chance against them and were cut to pieces. The English cavalry then withdrew, making way for their own archers. The effectiveness of trained archers with longbows cannot be overstated – the medieval equivalent of machine guns, pouring tens of thousands of deadly missiles into the packed ranks of Scots in less than a minute. The only defence against archers was to sweep them aside with cavalry, but the mounted Scots had already fled the field. As the Scottish spearmen fell, huge gaps appeared in the schiltrons. Gaps big enough for the English heavy cavalry to pour in and carve up what remained.

Wallace was on the run. He crossed to France to plead for French support, but received little more than letters from King Philip, recommending him to the pope and King Hakon of Norway.

Meanwhile, despite his victory at Falkirk, Edward was unable to exert control in Scotland, which remained in revolt. The Scottish Lion had remembered how to roar, and would not be silenced. As 1298 drew to a close, and with Wallace's whereabouts uncertain, his place as guardian of Scotland was taken by two nobles – John Comyn, Lord of Badenoch and a nephew and supporter of John Balliol, and none other than Robert Bruce, Earl of Carrick.

It was hoped that by appointing leaders of the two main factions in Scotland – Balliol and Bruce – the country might be united against Edward's England. This was not to be. For whatever reason, Comyn and Bruce quarrelled. There was an almighty row at Peebles in August 1299, and it is said that accusations of treason were made, and that Comyn had Bruce by the throat. After this, it was deemed necessary to appoint William de Lamberton, Bishop of St Andrews, as a third and 'over' guardian – if only to act as a referee. But though the matter seemed settled, Bruce was far from content and, changing tack yet again, 'returned to Edward's peace'. His place as guardian was taken by Ingram de Umfraville, then by John de Soules.

Despite these quarrels, the Scottish resistance was proving effective. Territorially, the English controlled no more than the Borders and Lothian, and even there they were losing their grip. Edward came north in 1300 but achieved very little, other than the capture of Caerlaverock Castle near Dumfries. In October 1300, and perhaps at Wallace's instigation, the pope then 'pressured' Edward into granting Scotland a truce. It lasted one year before Edward returned to his Scottish campaigning, taking the castle at Bothwell. Increasing discontent in England outweighed these gains, for the expense was not justified by the rewards. Far from it. English barons, clergymen and merchants were loud in their complaints. In their opinion, campaigning in Scotland was a waste of money, time and effort.

In 1302, Edward's army defeated the French at Courtai, with the result that the Scots had to give up all hope of regaining France's support, other than at a diplomatic level in representing their interests to the already sympathetic pope. However, the Scottish morale was boosted at the start of 1303 when a force of English light cavalry, commanded by John Segrave, was routed at Roslin. Unfortunately, this seemed to prompt Edward into further action and, in May, he invaded again, making a savage progress to Kinloss, then turning back to winter in Dunfermline. The Scottish nobility appeared to crumple and, in the following March, Edward held a Scottish parliament at St Andrews, at which most of them declared their allegiance to him. Within a couple of months, William Wallace had been captured.

Wallace was taken south, and executed in London in August 1305. The Scots have their own view on the reasons for his death. They might be summarised by quoting William Croft Dickinson of Edinburgh University who wrote in the *A New History of Scotland* series that 'Wallace was "tried" in London and suffered an agonising death as a traitor to a king whom he had never acknowledged and to whom he had never sworn fealty and allegiance.'

A commission of gaol delivery tried Wallace, requiring no more than a description of the charges, followed by sentencing. The justices were an impressive group – Sir John de Segrave, Grand Marshal of England, Lord Chief Justice Sir Peter Mallory, Sir Ralph de Sandwich, Constable of the Tower of London, Sir John de Backwell, a judge of the High Court, and the

Mayor of London, Sir John le Blount.

Wallace was not allowed to make a defence to the charges laid against him – a composite charge including sedition, spoilation, arson, homicide, sacrilege, robbery and other felonies – most committed on English soil during the Scots' undoubtedly savage rampage through the northern counties of Northumberland, Cumberland and Westmoreland. He had been declared an outlaw and was literally outside the law, and so barred from taking part in the proceedings, other than as a spectator. Sir John de Segrave finally read out the sentence.

'That the said William, for the manifest sedition that he practised against the Lord King himself, by feloniously contriving and acting with a view to his death and to the abasement and subversion of his crown and royal dignity, by bearing a hostile banner against his liege lord in war to the death, shall be drawn from the Palace of Westminster to the Tower of London, and from the Tower to Aldgate, and so through the midst of the city to the Elms.

'And that for the robberies, homicides and felonies he committed in the realm of England and in the land of Scotland, he be there hanged, and afterwards taken down from the gallows. And that, inasmuch as he was an outlaw, and was not afterwards restored to the peace of the Lord King, he be decollated while he still lives, before being decapitated.

'And that thereafter, for the measureless turpitude of his deeds toward God and Holy Church in burning down churches, with the vessels and litters wherein and whereon the body of Christ and the bodies of saints and other relics of these were placed, that the heart, the liver and lungs as well as all the other intestines of the said William, from which such perverted thoughts proceeded, be cast into the fire and burnt. And further, that inasmuch as it was not only against the Lord King himself, but against the whole Community of England and of Scotland, that he committed the aforesaid acts of sedition, spoilation, arson, and homicide, the body of the said William be cut up and divided into four parts, and that the head, so cut off, be set up on London Bridge, in the sight of such as pass by, whether by land or water, and that one quarter be hung on a gibbet at Newcastle-upon-Tyne, another quarter at Berwick, a third quarter at Stirling, and the fourth at St Johnston, as a warning and deterrent to all that pass by and behold them. This for doom, by order of the High Court of England. God save the King.'

All this to be done in front of an excited, jeering mob ... English attitudes, as well as the manner of Wallace's death, are revealed in a description of the event contained in *Flores Historiarum* written by an eyewitness, Matthew of Westminster.

'About the feast of the assumption of the blessed Mary, a certain Scot, by name Wilhelmus Waleis, a man void of pity, a robber given to sacrilege, arson and homicide, more hardened in cruelty than Herod, more raging in madness than Nero, after committing aimless atrocities had assembled an army and opposed the King at Falkirk. This man of Belial, after numberless crimes, was seized by the King's agents, carried to London, condemned to a most cruel but justly deserved death, and suffered this, all in the manner prescribed by the sentence but with additional aggravations and indignities. He was drawn through the streets of London, at the tails of horses, until he reached a gallows of unusual height, specially prepared for him; there he was suspended by a halter, but afterwards let down half-living; next his genitals were cut off and his bowels torn out and burnt in a fire; then, and not till then, his head was cut off and his trunk cut into four pieces ... Behold the end of the merciless man, who himself perishes without mercy.'

A clever English lawyer might have argued that there was no question about Wallace's allegiance to Balliol, nor that Balliol, after the Scottish army's defeat at Dunbar, had surrendered the land and people of Scotland (including Wallace) to Edward, while confessing his wrongdoing and folly in allying himself to the enemy (France) of his overlord. What such intellectual or legalistic arguments fail to acknowledge is that the Scots' memory of Wallace, even to the present day, was and is emotional. The style of his execution, suffered by many 'traitors' throughout the centuries, made him a martyr in the cause of Scottish independence. Yet there is more to it even than that, for William Wallace is remembered as a symbol. In remembering him, Scots remembered and remember all those men, women and children who suffered and died at English hands, from Old Cunninghame of Carleith to the nameless body of a tortured child and the defenceless wives and daughters of Berwick. Slaughtered in tens, hundreds and thousands. Perhaps it is understandable that Scots give little acknowledgement to the English who suffered similar fates at Scottish hands ...

With the Scottish nobility having sworn their allegiance, and Wallace out of the way, Edward might have thought that he had solved his northern problem by effectively absorbing Scotland into England, under his rule.

There was still no question of him becoming both king of England and king of Scotland. One included the other, in Edward's opinion. This was to be the absorption of a kingdom rather than an act of union. In September 1305, he approved an Ordinance for the Government of Scotland, creating a framework of administration under which 'the northern land' was to be governed by a Lieutenant, with a Chancellor, a Chamberlain and a Comptroller.

These senior appointments were given to Englishmen, but the lower ranks of officialdom were to be divided between Englishmen and those Scots who proved most eager to submit to Edward. The king of England had many faults, but he certainly wasn't ignorant of how best to handle a Scottish noble. However, there is always an exception to any rule ...

On February 10 1303, Bruce and some companions murdered John Comyn in the Franciscan church at Dumfries. Nobody can be sure why these opponents met, though some have suggested that it was to discuss another uprising against the English – a meeting that, unfortunately and unexpectedly, dissolved into a violent argument. More cynical individuals might suggest that by slaying Balliol's main supporter in Scotland, Bruce was removing the opposition before declaring his hand. One thing is certain – almost immediately after Comyn's death, Bruce announced his intent to grab the throne of Scotland for himself.

One month after the murder, Bruce was crowned with a circlet of gold by Isabella, Countess of Buchan, the sister of Duncan, Earl of Fife, in the presence of his supporters including the bishops of St Andrews, Glasgow and Moray, and the earls of Atholl and Lennox. This 'coronation' did nothing to unite Scotland. The murder of Comyn had provoked a deadly feud with the powerful Comyns, and the fact that the murder had taken place on consecrated ground earned the wrath of many churchmen, other than Bruce's supporters. In May, Pope Clement V excommunicated Bruce for sacrilege.

In June, Edward's military commander in Scotland, the Earl of Pembroke, crushed Bruce's forces at Methven. Bruce and other survivors fled to Atholl before heading west where, in August, they were once again defeated – this time by the Lord of Lorne at Dalry near Tyndrum. Bruce found refuge in Dunaverty, then disappeared for four months. He may have fled to Ireland or Orkney, or even to Norway where his sister, Isobel, had married the Norwegian king.

Bruce's flight was insufficient to satisfy Edward, who had Bruce's wife, sister and daughter cruelly imprisoned, along with the bishops of St Andrews and Glasgow. Bruce's other captured supporters, including his brother Nigel and the Earl of Atholl, were executed.

Edward was sufficiently enraged to travel north to supervise Scotland in person, but by now he was quite old and frail. His health failed him and he was forced to convalesce for six months in Cumberland. This might have been an end to the matter, but Bruce was nothing if not determined. He appeared on the island of Arran in February 1307, then crossed to his earldom of Carrick. At the same time, his brothers Thomas and Alexander landed with a small Irish force some miles to the south, in Loch Ryan. This small army was quickly defeated and the brothers captured by Dougal MacDowell who sent them to Carlisle, where they were immediately executed.

Bruce had no option but to take to the Galloway hills with a small band of comrades. English troops were sent to hunt them down. They may have been over-confident, failing to recognise that Bruce was an experienced soldier and gifted tactician. They were given a beating in Glentrool and, in May 1307, Bruce displayed his military genius again at the battle of Loudon Hill where he defeated a force commanded by the Earl of Pembroke.

News of this defeat reached Edward, still convalescing near Carlisle. Now aged 68 and still in very weak health, he was nevertheless enraged. Deciding that he must direct proceedings against Bruce in person, he grimly mounted his horse and marched north at the head of his troops. In four days, they had covered just six miles, but even that effort was too much. Edward died of dysentery at Burgh-on-Sands on July 7, 1307.

Edward's successor was his son, Edward II. He had not inherited his father's zeal for military matters, but nevertheless determined on an advance into Scotland, at the head of the mighty army his father had assembled to crush the Scots, once and for all. It turned out to be, at best, a very half-hearted and futile affair – little more than a leisurely amble into Upper Nithsdale – before the young Edward turned back. The new English king had little stomach for a fight.

Bruce and his supporters were delighted. With the English wandering away, Bruce could tighten his grip on the kingdom he had claimed as his own. The lands of the Comyns were wasted 'with fire and sword', and John of Lorne was defeated in the battle of the Pass of Brander in Argyll. Throughout the land, men flocked to Bruce's cause. In 1309, Bruce was established to the point where he could hold a parliament in St Andrews.

That parliament wrote to the king of France, declaring that they recognised Bruce as their 'leader and prince', and those castles that were held by English garrisons – who found themselves virtually ignored by their king in England – had little option but to surrender to the jubilant Scots. In many cases, these castles were subsequently destroyed, in order to ensure that an invading English army could never again use them.

Edward's attention was on other matters, largely concerning his friend and lover Piers Gaveston, to whom he had granted the earldom of Cornwall. Nevertheless, Edward decided he must do something in the north, if only for the sake of appearances. In the autumn of 1310, he led a demoralised English army through southern Scotland. They achieved little, if anything, other than the increased enmity of the Scots, who quickly retaliated with a savage raid into Northumberland and Durham.

Edward's failure and the Scots' boldness proved too much for those English barons who effectively ran England, as a counter to Edward's inefficiencies. Determined to bring their king to heel, and angered by his attentions to his favourite, they seized Gaveston, who was executed without trial.

Meanwhile, the people of England's northern counties found that they were undefended against the marauding Scots. It was then that Bruce, now Robert I, King of Scots, introduced a form of blackmail or protection racket. The people of Northumberland, Durham, Cumberland and Westmoreland were told that if they paid the Scots, then the Scots would not raid in those counties. Instead, they would use them as 'corridors' down which they would travel in order to raid further south. It has been suggested that, in a fairly short period, Bruce raised £20,000 in this fashion. A king, no doubt, but also something of a racketeer.

By the early months of 1314, just one Scottish castle remained under English control. Stirling held out under the command of its constable, De Mowbray, but was closely besieged by King Robert's brother, Edward Bruce. Finally they negotiated, with De Mowbray agreeing that if he had not been relieved by Midsummer Day, June 24, he would surrender to the Scots. From the moment of that agreement, the clock was ticking ...

Edward and his barons had settled their differences. Thus united, England's pride was such that it could not stand back and watch while the last symbol of English rule in Scotland was handed over. England's mightiest warriors rallied to the cause, bringing their mounted knights, men-at-arms and archers. The English army that marched north to the relief of Stirling was about 20,000 strong and, most impressively, included some 3,000 heavy cavalry. Barring the way to Stirling were just 7,000 Scots. The opposing forces came within sight of each other outside Stirling on June 23 – just one day before the Midsummer deadline.

The English army camped that night on elevated but wet and uncomfortable ground, tightly restricted on a triangulated site between the River Forth and the Bannock burn, with marshy ground on both their flanks. It was their intention to advance in the morning, when they would spread on better ground in order to engage the enemy, but they awoke at dawn to find that the Scots were already advancing. The vast English army couldn't respond quickly enough. Hemmed in on three sides, only their advance troops could engage the Scots. Those of the English cavalry who were free to do so charged the advancing Scottish spearmen, but the schiltrons held firm and repulsed them. English archers moved to fan out on the flanks, but were cut down by the Scots' light cavalry. Slowly but surely, the Scots forced the English troops back onto their milling comrades.

At the rear of all this confusion, there was no option but to try to ford the River Forth. Edward managed to flee, guarded by a handful of his knights, but many others were swept away and drowned. Those who drowned in the Bannock burn were so numerous that, after a time, their bodies created a bridge for those who remained, but even they were not safe. Scottish irregulars and a mob of angry folk from Stirling and the surrounding countryside cut many throats that day. Those who were spared were noblemen, who would fetch high ransoms from their families. These ransoms, together with loot taken from the dead and abandoned baggage trains were such that one chronicler declared, 'Scotland became rich overnight'.

Victory at Bannockburn secured Scotland's independence and established Robert Bruce as the undisputed King of Scots. A Scottish Parliament, sitting almost immediately after the battle, passed sentence of forfeiture on all those Scots who had fought for England, and demanded that all should declare their loyalty and allegiance to King Robert.

CHAPTER SIX

RETALIATION
AND REVENGE

E dward Longshanks, Hammer of the Scots, had intended to bring Scotland to its knees, and to subjugate its people for all time. Instead, he made the prospect of union more distant than ever before. Atrocities committed by his representatives and troops in Scotland, their bloody-minded arrogance and punitive financial demands, had hardened Scottish hearts against a common enemy. In a climate of hostility to all things English, the Scottish king purged those Scots who had fought on the English side and maintained any semblance of lingering loyalty. The fact that Bruce had himself been driven by personal ambition to collaborate with the English, joining with their army while they slaughtered thousands of Scots including defenceless women and children, was conveniently ignored.

Poets and legend-makers have painted a picture of Robert Bruce as a heroic freedom fighter, perhaps confusing him with William Wallace. Within a year of the victory at Bannockburn, the Bruces were once again displaying their raw ambition, and contempt for the freedom of others.

In May 1316, Robert's brother, Edward Bruce invaded Ulster with an army of 6,000, which had been 'colonised' by English settlers under the pro-English Richard de Burgh, Earl of Ulster – ironically, Robert Bruce's father-in-law. Some of the native Irish nobility were sympathetic to Bruce's invasion and agreed that Edward might be crowned King of Ireland if only he would drive the English out. Clearly, this was the Bruces' ambition – to have two kings in the family. Indeed, Edward Bruce was crowned 'King of Ireland' at Dundalk in Co Louth. However, many Irish lords objected and there followed a complicated war in which the Bruces showed they could be every bit as ruthless as Edward Longshanks.

In December 1316, Robert Bruce, King of Scots, joined his brother Edward. Together with their Scottish troops and Irish allies, they advanced on Dublin. Finding the city was virtually impregnable, they then invaded middle Ireland and vented their frustration, slaughtering and burning as they went. After Robert returned to Scotland in May 1317, Edward continued the atrocities. In the end, it got too much even for the staunchest of the Bruce's Irish allies, and Edward had just 3,000 troops when the men of Meath and Drogheda formed themselves into an army to drive the merciless Scot from their shores. In Scotland, Robert made hasty plans to reinforce his bloody-handed brother, but was too late. Edward was defeated near Dundalk in October 1318 – not far from the scene of his coronation just two years earlier. Two years, but so much suffering for the Irish people ... The Anglo-Irish lords hacked off Edward Bruce's head, and sent it as a gift to Edward of England, restating his titular authority.

As they were devastating much of Ireland, Scots were regularly raiding northern England, often in considerable force. For example, at the end of July 1315, King Robert besieged Carlisle.

The fighting in the north cost England a great deal, but the capricious Edward II wasted vast amounts on luxuries, finery, feasting and lavish gifts for his favoured male companions. In 1315, his bill for wine alone amounted to some £4,000 – equivalent to the annual wages of more than 6,000 agricultural workers. A similar amount was spent on gifts. By comparison, alms (charitable donations) provided by the royal household amounted to less than £200. In total, the royal expenditure for 1315 amounted to £66,000 – the equivalent of 99,000 agricultural workers' annual wages.

The harvests of 1315 and 1316 were disastrous throughout England and Wales. The price of grain multiplied four-fold, so the poorer people couldn't afford bread and starved. There were riots in towns and cities, and rebellions in Lancashire and Wales.

Attempts were made to settle matters. In 1318, a treaty was signed between Edward and his openly hostile barons. Edward agreed to pardon the Earl of Lancaster, and to hand much control to a standing council of barons. This agreement allowed the English to return their attention to Scotland.

In April 1318, more than 20 years since Edward I had seized Berwick, it had returned to Scottish control. In 1319, Edward II marched north to get it back. He came at the head of a strong army, estimated at 8,000 men who besieged the town and its castle.

King Robert of Scots displayed his military guile. Rather than attacking the strong English army, he ordered a lightning raid as far south as York, led by Thomas Randolph, Earl of Moray, and Sir James Douglas. Archbishop Melton of York intercepted them with a militia, but they were swept aside at Myton-on-Swale to the tune of 3,000 dead.

One of the Scots' intentions was to seize a hostage for it was known that Edward's wife, Queen Isabella, was in York. She escaped, but the raid had the desired effect. The northern English earls abandoned the siege of Berwick and hurried south to defend their homes.

Learning of the Scots' success, France turned the screw on England. In the same month that he was forced to abandon the siege of Berwick, Edward received a demand from King Philip V that he should pay homage in person for the land he held in France.

With England repulsed – at least for a time – King Robert of Scots was more than keen to receive the pope's formal recognition for his kingship and thus, at the same time, a denial of England's continuing claim of overlordship in Scotland. Bruce had been excommunicated for the murder of John Comyn on consecrated ground, and papal legates restated this excommunication in 1320, at the instance of Edward of England.

In response, Robert urged his barons to send a letter to the pope – later to be known as the 'Declaration of Arbroath'. It was very probably drafted by the Scottish king's chancellor, Bernard de Linton, Abbott of Arbroath, and remains an impressive document (originally written in Latin) not least for its signatories: Duncan, Earl of Fife, Thomas Randolph, Earl of Moray, Lord of Man and of Annandale, Patrick Dunbar, Earl of March, Malise, Earl of Strathearn, Malcolm, Earl of Lennox, William, Earl of Ross, Magnus, Earl of Caithness and Orkney, and William Earl of Sutherland. The names go on and on, signifying Bruce's universal support within Scotland, ending with 'and other barons and freeholders and the whole community of the realm of Scotland'.

The document starts with a preamble about the origins of the Scottish people, independent of England:

'They took possession of that home with many victories and untold efforts;

and, as the historians of old time bear witness, they have held it free of bondage ever since. In their kingdom there have reigned one hundred and thirteen kings of their own royal stock, the line unbroken by a single foreigner.'

The document also reminds the pope that, 'Your predecessors gave careful heed to these things and bestowed many favours and numerous privileges on this same kingdom and people, as being the special charge of the Blessed Peter's brother.'

The Scots were keen to portray themselves as the innocent party in the dispute with England. Ignoring their long history of raids and invasions of English territory, they painted a picture of themselves as lambs among wolves – and offered a solution, urging the pope's acceptance of their new king and emphasising the Scottish people's resolve, irrespective of all things, with or without King Robert, to resist the English.

'Thus our nation under their [previous popes] protection did indeed live in freedom and peace up to the time when that mighty prince the King of the English, Edward, the father of the one who reigns today, when our kingdom had no head and our people harboured no malice or treachery and were then unused to wars or invasions, came in the guise of a friend or ally to harass them as an enemy. The deeds of cruelty, massacre, violence, pillage, arson, imprisoning prelates, burning down monasteries, robbing and killing monks and nuns, and yet other outrages without number which he committed against our people, sparing neither age nor sex, religion nor rank, no one could describe nor fully imagine unless he had seen them with his own eyes.

'But from these countless evils we have been set free, by the help of Him Who though He afflicts yet heals and restores, by our most tireless Prince, King and Lord, the Lord Robert. He, that his people and his heritage might be delivered out of the hands of our enemies, met toil and fatigue, hunger and peril, like another Macabaeus or Joshua and bore them cheerfully. Him, too, divine providence, his right of succession according to our laws and customs which we shall maintain to the death, and the due consent and assent of us all have made our Prince and King. To him, as to the man by whom salvation has been wrought unto our people, we are bound both by law and by his merits that our freedom may still be maintained, and by him, come what may, we mean to stand.

'Yet if he should give up what he has begun, and agree to make us or our kingdom subject to the King of England or the English, we should exert ourselves at one to drive him out as our enemy and a subverter of his own right and ours, and make some other man who was well able to defend us our King; for, as long as but a hundred of us remain alive, never will we on any conditions be brought under English rule. It is in truth not for glory, nor riches, nor honours that we are fighting, but for freedom – for that alone, which no honest man gives up but with life itself.'

The above paragraph, memorable for 'as long as but a hundred of us remain alive' has been interpreted as a declaration of the Scots' determination to resist the English. And so it is, but surely it is more? Is it not a clear warning to the Bruce that he must not revert to his old ways? A reminder that while the Bruces might fight for personal riches and honours, choosing their side accordingly, the Scottish people fight only for their freedom?

The document then builds steadily to its *raison d'etre*.

'May it please you to admonish and exhort the Kings of the English, who ought to be satisfied with what belongs to him since England used once to be enough for seven kings or more, to leave us Scots in peace, who live in this poor little Scotland, beyond which there is no dwelling place at all, and covet nothing but our own ... But if your holiness puts too much faith in the tales the English tell and will not give sincere belief to all this nor refrain from favouring them to our prejudice, then the slaughter of bodies, the perdition of souls, and all the other misfortunes that will follow, inflicted by them on us and by us on them, will, we believe, be surely laid by the Most High to your charge.

'To conclude, we are and shall ever be, as far as duty calls us, ready to do your will in all things, as obedient sons to you as His Vicar; and to Him as the Supreme King and Judge we commit the maintenance of our cause, casting our cares upon Him and firmly trusting that He will inspire us with courage and bring our enemies to nought.'

The pope was not impressed, still refusing to recognise Bruce's kingship. In correspondence, he addressed him simply as 'Robert Bruce' or 'Robert Bruce calling himself king' or anonymously as 'the noble man who at present governs Scotland.'

The pope's refusal to acknowledge Bruce as king was more significant than the modern world might acknowledge. That significance is bound up with the notion of 'the divine right of kings', which suggested that kings were chosen by God and, for that reason, must be obeyed without question. By refusing his recognition, the pope was suggesting that Bruce ruled against the will of God and, therefore, need not be obeyed. Equally, this would limit

Bruce's ability to deal with those kings who had God's seal of approval, and didn't want the pope to take it from them.

In return for this approval, kings were obliged to render many services to the papacy. The Scots had assured the pope that these services would be made, 'To conclude, we are and shall ever be, as far as duty calls us, ready to do your will in all things, as obedient sons to you as His Vicar...'

In another part of the Declaration of Arbroath, there is a specific reference to the crusades, with the suggestion that Edward should be fighting 'the savagery of the heathen raging against the Christians' and that the pope should 'rouse the Christian princes who for false reasons pretend that they cannot go to the help of the Holy Land because of wars they have on hand with their neighbours. The real reason that prevents them is that in making war on their smaller neighbours they find quicker profit and weaker resistance.' Predicting the pope's question, they go on to state, 'But how cheerfully our Lord the King (Robert Bruce) and we too would go there if the King of English would leave us in peace...'

Still the pope was unmoved, though four years later he was prepared to admit a concession. He would lift the ban of excommunication on Robert Bruce and recognise him as King of Scots, but only if Scotland formally recognised the English king's superiority. In other words, a return to the situation that had been forced on Scotland and John Balliol by Edward I. The Scots refused.

The stalemate between the papacy and Scotland might have continued, but this was the time of the Babylonish Captivity when seven successive popes were Frenchmen, resident at Avignon, and often subservient to French interests – just one more example of the intertwining of religion and politics.

Things were not going well for Edward II in England. He was anything but popular with his barons, and throughout his reign the country teetered on the brink of civil war. It all came to a head in September 1326 when Edward's wife, Queen Isabella, the sister of King Charles IV of France, returned home to Paris, living openly with her lover, Roger Mortimer of Wigmore, and announced her intention to declare war on Edward's 'favourite', Hugh Despenser. Her son, later to be Edward III, was with her in France and she had support in England. Her brother, King Charles of France, would also support her, because Edward still refused to give homage for lands held in France.

In October, Queen Isabella returned to England with an army of mercenaries and many influential supporters including the Earl Marshall, the Earl of Leicester, and several bishops. Sailors mutinied, and the citizens of London rebelled. They vented their anger on the Bishop of Exeter, Walter Stapledon, who had been placed in charge of London by the king. Having hacked off his head with a butcher's knife, the frenzied mob set off on a spree of murders and looting. Edward and Despenser were not to be found – they had fled to Caerphilly in Wales.

Hugh Despenser's father, the Earl of Winchester, was the first to be captured. In October 1326, he was tried at Bristol. The sentence was that he should be 'hanged for robbery, drawn for treason and beheaded for misdeeds against the church.'

Edward and Hugh Despenser were captured together at Neath Abbey on November 16. Queen Isabella wished a particularly gruesome death for her husband's lover, and was keen that it should take place in London. Despenser was refusing to eat and weakened rapidly, so the execution date was brought forward. Outside of Hereford, Despenser was stripped and crowned with nettles. Four horses dragged him to a high scaffold to allow the jeering crowd to witness his death. A contemporary illustration shows him tied with his back to a high ladder, propped against a wall. His genitals were cut off. He was then disembowelled – with sufficient expertise to keep him alive while his entrails were burnt. Finally, when sufficient time had passed to satisfy the watching Queen Isabella, he was lowered from the scaffold, beheaded and quartered.

Guided by Roger Mortimer, Isabella was keen to ensure that their coup should have a veneer of legality. The king's son, Prince Edward, was elected as guardian of the realm by a meeting of barons and knights in Bristol. Meanwhile, King Edward was powerless to oppose these proceedings, being a prisoner at Kenilworth Castle in Warwickshire. His abdication was announced in late January 1327.

In July, Edward was transferred to Berkeley Castle overlooking the Bristol Channel. In late September, he was systematically tortured over a period of days. Finally, a heated plumber's soldering iron was thrust up his anus and into his bowels. A fitting end, some thought, for a homosexual. Of course, it would later be claimed that it was all a misunderstanding, and no orders had been issued for his torture, let alone his execution.

Throughout this time, the King of France had been exerting pressure on the pope to recognise Scotland's independence, and the kingship of Robert

Bruce. For their part, the Scots had maintained pressure on England. Despite assurances that they only wished to be left in peace, they relentlessly raided over the border, laying waste to England's northern shires. The succession of Edward III to the English throne did nothing to dampen their enthusiasm.

Caught between Scottish raiders on the one hand, and the French king and pope on the other, the 14-year-old English king was forced to the negotiating table where he renounced forever England's claim to feudal superiority over Scotland. England would also respect the alliance between Scotland and France. Finally, Edward's sister, aged seven, married Robert's son, aged four. One year later, the 55-year-old King Robert I of Scots died after a prolonged illness and was succeeded by his now five-year-old son, who became David II. Despite everything, Robert Bruce had secured Scotland's independence. In his final days, he had received a letter from Pope John XXII addressing him as, 'Our dearest son, Robert, illustrious King of Scotland'.

Edward III announced his intentions three years after his father's agonising death. Queen Isabella's lover, Roger Mortimer, was closely involved in Irish affairs. His wife owned a large estate in Co Meath, and he had been appointed King's Lieutenant in 1316, to organise Anglo-Irish resistance to Edward Bruce, later becoming Justiciar (king's deputy) of Ireland, and made Earl of March in 1328. These advancements, together with his relationship with Edward's mother, may have convinced the young Edward that Mortimer had grown too powerful and ambitious. He was hung and drawn, but apparently not quartered, in October 1330. Just months later, the Westminster Parliament ordered that Ireland would be subject to English law.

Edward was not happy about the Scottish situation that had been forced on him. He was probably reluctant to break the agreement that he had signed, albeit under duress, when he came to the throne, but another possibility suggested itself. Like his grandfather before him, the young but cunning English king recognised that he could manipulate Scotland's inherent factionalism. Edward Balliol, son of the deposed King John, was keen to seize the throne of Scotland from the boy David Bruce. All he needed was financial support.

Accompanied by Scottish nobles who had been disinherited under the late King Robert's purge of pro-English families, Edward Balliol landed in Fife in August 1332. His force of 1,500 men was small but experienced and ably led. Most importantly, it was made up largely of war-hardened, mercenary archers – paid for by Edward of England.

The Scottish forces, commanded by the Earl of Mar, were either too cautious or over-confident. Despite having taken up a good defensive position on Dupplin Muir, they were rattled into making a shambolic attack – playing into the enemy's hands for the longbow was supreme as a defensive weapon. The Lanercost Chronicle states that the pile of Scottish dead was as deep as the length of a spear. Just one month later, Edward Balliol was crowned King of Scots, while paying homage to Edward of England and proclaiming his overlordship in Scotland. Edward could now openly involve himself in Scottish affairs.

When they had recovered from the shock of Balliol's invasion and coronation, many Scots declared their continuing support for David Bruce. Balliol was forced to flee in the face of this threat, under the command of Sir Archibald Douglas, but regathered his forces at Carlisle then crossed the country to besiege Berwick – still loyal to King David. Douglas prepared to attack, but Balliol had been reinforced by an English army. Edward was exercising his rights of overlordship in Scotland.

Ironically, the battle formation developed by Balliol and other Scottish commanders at Dupplin Muir had proved so effective that the English army immediately adopted it as their own. It consisted of a central group of dismounted men-at-arms, flanked by wedges of archers – like the head and horns of a charging buffalo – as the Zulu impis would later be described – but the English formation did not charge. Instead, they stood their ground and waited for the enemy. Then, as soon as they had come within range, the archers would start to shoot. A thousand archers might shoot ten thousand arrows in one minute, pouring their deadly shafts into the tightly packed enemy. And that is how it happened at Hallidon Hill – only there were thousands of archers in the English army. Few Scots survived the immediate slaughter. English cavalry hounded those that did as they fled, and any prisoners were immediately executed.

'And now it was the general opinion that the Scottish wars were over,' wrote one English chronicler. 'For no man remained of that nation who had either the influence to assemble or the skill to lead an army.'

At the start of 1334, Edward Balliol held a parliament at Edinburgh. Its purpose was to acknowledge the help he had received from Edward III, and to reward his supporters with vast tracts of land. At the same time, he surrendered the castle, town and county of Berwick to England 'for all time'.

One month later, the deposed boy king David Bruce fled to France where King Philip welcomed him and his English child-wife. And one month after that, Balliol granted to Edward III all the southern counties of Scotland. Edward immediately moved English garrisons into their castles, installed his own sheriffs, and appointed an English chamberlain and English justiciar to administer his new lands from Haddington in the east, to Dumfries in the west. Finally, Balliol did homage to his liege lord, Edward of England, for what remained of the kingdom of Scotland.

Dark days for Scotland, to be sure. However, the spirit of resistance was far from crushed and, yet again, the forces of occupation were to discover that it was one thing to conquer the northern land, but another to hold it.

Supporters of the exiled King David started a guerrilla war, avoiding pitched battles. A raid here, or an ambush there. Balliol found it necessary to winter in England. Edward decided to intervene and campaigned in southern Scotland in the autumn of 1334 and again in the summer of 1335. Even then, Balliol returned again to northern England in the winter for, 'he possessed no castle or town in Scotland in which he could live in safety'. Edward returned to Scotland in 1336 and 1337, but still a significant number of Scots continued to actively oppose Balliol, Edward's puppet king in Scotland.

Intentionally or otherwise, France came to Scotland's rescue. As well as being king of England, Edward was duke of Gascony and, in the spring of 1336, King Philip VI of France had accused Edward of harbouring his enemies and sent in an army to annexe Gascony for himself. In response, the infuriated Edward claimed the French throne as son of Queen Isabella, sister of Charles IV of France. Whatever the strength of his claim, the matter would finally be decided by strength of arms.

In August 1337, Philip confiscated Aquitaine, and Edward declared war on France. English troops sacked Cadzand in November. In response, a French fleet raided the Isle of Wight and Portsmouth. These were the opening rounds in the Hundred Years War between England and France. As Walter Bower recorded, 'Happily for Scotland, for if the King of England had continued his warfare in Scotland, he would have gained possession of the whole land, without difficulty, as far as it is humanly possible to judge.'

CHAPTER SEVEN

MÉNAGE À TROIS

The English are one of the great 'mongrel' races. Romans had interbred with the original Celts. Angles, Saxons and Jutes, then Vikings and Danes and finally the Normans of mixed Norse and Frankish descent had followed them. All had one thing in common – they were warriors by choice as well as necessity. Add a dash of this and a pinch of that, mix it all together, but don't expect to produce a dish of shrinking violets.

So, a race who, in the middle ages, were ready, willing and able to fight, whether at home or abroad. 'Do you know that I live by war and peace would be my undoing?' wrote Sir John Hawkswood. A greedy nation, some might say, who coveted the riches of neighbouring France. Was Edward III's claim to the French throne simply an excuse to follow the blood and thunder trail? It certainly seemed that way to the French.

At first, the French may not have been unduly concerned. After all, France was the wealthiest kingdom in Europe, with a huge feudal army having an abundant supply of chivalrous knights to provide heavy cavalry, and her ruler was, in the words of Matthew Paris, the famous chronicler, 'King of all earthly Kings' who had the pope in his pocket. Nor was he any stranger to combat. However, this failed to impress the king of England when he was instructed to pay homage for his lands in France, as reported by Sir Geoffrey Scrope in *The Raigne of King Edward III*.

Dare he commands a fealty in me?
Tell him the Crown that he usurps is mine,
And where he sets his foot he ought to kneel.
Tis not a petty Dukedom that I claim,

But all the whole dominion of the realm;
Which if with grudging he refuse to yield
I'll take away those borrowed plumes of his
And send him naked to the wilderness.

Edward proved as aggressive in his actions as his words. In 1339, together with French and German allies, he unleashed the rabid dogs of war in northern France. It is said that a French cardinal, Bertrand de Montfaucon, climbed a high tower to inspect the devastation, and collapsed from grief and shock. In every direction the air was thick with the pall of smoke. What they could not eat or plunder, they burned or killed – town and village, barn and shack, man and beast, woman and child.

In the following year, it came to Edward's attention that the French had gathered a huge fleet off Sluys in Flanders. He quickly gathered a fleet of his own, filled it with archers and men-at-arms and attacked with the wind, tide and sun at his back. The French fought desperately, but more than 20,000 were killed and 200 ships captured.

Philip of France no longer doubted that he had a real fight on his hands – or that he needed help to repel the English invaders. It was the time to remind Scotland that his alliance with them was one of mutual support. The English assault on France had taken the pressure off Scotland. David Bruce, the exiled king, now in his teens, joined the French campaign against the invading English in 1340.

A truce was signed in that same year between England and France, but not because of the Scots' involvement. Edward's war had already cost £300,000, and his own coffers were empty. The 12 month truce gave him time to sort out his finances and to appoint a council of regency to govern England in his absence, for he had every intention of returning to France. It was during this suspension of hostilities that David Bruce was able to return to Scotland and re-establish himself as King David II of Scots.

Edward returned to France in 1342, to involve himself in a dispute over the succession to the Duchy of Brittany – another excuse for fighting the king of France. However, as winter approached, he retired to England and despite vowing to return and continue the fight, he agreed to a three-year truce, instigated by the pope, but returned in 1345 before the treaty had run its course, after the French king had executed some of Edward's Breton allies and appeared to be threatening Flanders.

After initial skirmishing, the English and French armies faced each other at Crecy on August 7 1346. English longbows against French heavy horse and Genoese crossbowmen. The Genoese were quickly eliminated. Then it was the turn of the French cavalry to face the blizzard of English arrows. Fifteen times the flower of chivalry charged what was, in effect, a professional peasant army, and each time the archers drew and loosed, drew and loosed, then drew and loosed again – their arrows falling like murderous rain. At the end of the day, more than 10,000 French lay dead on the field of battle. Few of them had got within lance or sword striking distance of the English ranks, whose losses were less than a hundred. The jubilant English army looted the dead, and then marched to besiege the port of Calais.

Clearly, it was high time for the Scots to come to the aid of their French allies, by opening a second front against England. In keeping with tradition, they swept across the border into Northumberland, burning and killing as they went. In response, the Archbishop of York quickly raised a force including many archers. The two armies met at Neville's Cross, near Durham, on October 17 1346 – barely two months after the French defeat at Crecy.

The Scots army divided into three battalions, respectively under the command of the now 22-year-old King David, the Earl of Moray and Robert, the High Steward. The first two came under the heaviest pressure from the English troops and fought bravely, but Robert the Steward's courage dissolved. He virtually fled the field without engaging the enemy, taking his battalion with him. What remained of the now massively outnumbered Scottish army was faced with certain defeat. The Earl of Moray was among the many Scots who died that day.

King David fought bravely, despite being wounded by an arrow in the eye. He was among the last to accept that all hope was lost, and had to be dragged from the field. When overtaken by the pursuing English, he refused to yield. John Coupland was among those who overpowered him, but he lost two teeth for his efforts. Along with the king, four Scottish earls were taken prisoner.

King David remained a prisoner for 11 years. In his absence, Robert the Steward became regent of the realm, despite his conduct at Neville's Cross. Robert was the king's nephew although, in one of those quirks of extended families, he was in fact eight years older than his uncle.

Edward of England might have executed the Scottish king, but knew he was worth more alive, for he might fetch a ransom. Of course, Edward was desperately in need of cash to finance his campaigns in France. Negotiations for the king's release, and a treaty between England and Scotland, began in 1348. They dragged on until 1354 when it was agreed that David might be ransomed for a total of 90,000 merks to be paid in nine annual instalments of 10,000 merks each. It was also agreed that, while there were still monies outstanding, there would be peace between the two countries.

News of this agreement was anything but welcomed in France. The freedom of the King of Scots wasn't high on their list of priorities. By closing down the northern front, Edward could concentrate all his resources on fighting France. The French devised a plan ...

A group of French emissaries arrived in Scotland, accompanied by a small force of knights and men-at-arms – sufficient to guard the sum of money they had brought with them. Various members of the Scottish nobility were approached with the simplest of offers. If they would ignore the needs of their king, and maintain the fight with England, they would be rewarded. Thus a Scottish force was raised, now supported by the French knights and, together, they ravaged the eastern border and seized Berwick.

England's predictable retaliation is remembered as 'the Burnt Candlemas' of 1356. The French achieved their objective in that the infuriated Edward left France in order to deal in person with the Scots. Having regained Berwick, he marched with fire and sword from Roxburgh to Edinburgh. It is not known how many Scots perished to benefit those nobles who had accepted the French gold.

Edward upped the price of King David's release – 100,000 merks, to be paid 10,000 per annum over ten years – presumably to cover the cost of his northern excursion. This was agreed in October 1357, ending the Scottish king's 11 year imprisonment.

In order to put this ransom into perspective, it amounted to more than £6,500, thus exceeding the total annual income to the Scottish Exchequer – an income that was already outmatched by expenditure. Added to this, that same source was expected to fund the expenses of those 20 Scottish nobles who had been exchanged for the king – now hostages in England in order to ensure the Scottish king kept his side of the bargain – ten regular payments and ten years of peace.

King David's conduct after his return to Scotland was sadly remiss, but perhaps not without cause. He was kept in fairly open confinement during his time in England – but it was confinement, nevertheless. Just when he thought it might come to an end, a group of his nobles had muddied the waters, to say the least. He might have assumed that if so many Scots cared so little for him, he would return the compliment. He had little interest in Scotland's long-term prospects. Despite two marriages, he remained childless and in these circumstances, his successor would be his nephew Robert, the High Steward, who he hated for abandoning him at Neville's Cross, and accused of prolonging the ransom negotiations that left David a prisoner while Robert ruled as regent. Finally, David was an extravagant king with expensive tastes, which he didn't intend to curb, despite the fact that his exchequer was being driven into bankruptcy in meeting the ransom payments.

In 1362, five years after David's release, just two of the instalments had been paid. It wasn't that the ransom money hadn't been collected – through punitive taxation and other measures – but rather that the king was intercepting the payments and squandering them on extravagances.

Robert the High Steward had his faults as a soldier, but as an officer of the realm he was not prepared to let this continue. In 1363, together with the Earl of Douglas and the Earl of March, he led a revolt against King David. It failed, at one level, but succeeded in convincing the Scottish king that he must seek some practical solution to Scotland's financial burden.

King David travelled to London in November 1363, to meet with King Edward. At this meeting, the childless David offered that, upon his death, Edward or one of his sons would succeed to the kingship of Scotland. He made it a condition that the name and title of the realm of Scotland with all its laws and customs would be retained. In return for this, he asked that the rest of the ransom still outstanding would be written off, and that the noble Scottish hostages would be released.

Whatever his other intentions, the Scottish king was attempting to kill two birds with one stone – to cancel Scotland's debt while denying the succession to Robert, the High Steward. Edward, for his part, was sorely tempted, as long as David would undertake to maintain a peace between the two countries – thus allowing England to concentrate on fighting France. However, the English king was nobody's fool and realised that while the Scottish king might promise, his people could resist. Therefore, he ordered David to return to Scotland, to enquire of the Scottish people whether such an agreement would be acceptable to them.

David did as he was told, and held a parliament at Scone at the start of March 1364, at which he outlined the deal that was on the table. The Scots were having none of it. They would tighten their belts still further, rather than accept the rule of an English king. This was the legacy of Edward Longshank's brutality. The hardening of Scottish hearts. Better to starve, they said, than submit to English rule.

The Scots managed to keep their king's spending on a fairly tight rein, and imposed various measures in order to pay the annual ransom instalments to Edward. They were not to know it at the time, but relief was just over the horizon.

England's campaigns in France had been completed in 1360, after the fall of Calais to Edward, followed by the treaties of Calais and Bretigny. Fighting broke out again in 1369 and Scotland found that, once again, she could pose a threat to England. This time, Edward was without allies, and the last thing he wanted was the Scots opening a second front in the war, so he was prepared to listen when they declared their wish to renegotiate. They wanted a longer period for repayment, reducing the annual repayments to 4,000 merks. At that rate, it would take 14 years to pay off the outstanding balance. For their part, the Scots would sign a 14-year truce with England. Edward accepted this offer, and the payments were maintained until his death in 1377. The balance of 24,000 merks still outstanding at that time was never paid.

King David of Scots had died in 1371, aged 46 but still childless, after 40 years on the throne. Despite the king's feelings on the subject, the succession did indeed go to his 'older nephew' the now 54-year-old Robert, the High Steward or Stewart, thus founding the Stewart (Stuart) dynasty. In contrast to the childless King David, King Robert II of Scots had five surviving sons and seven daughters.

King Robert inherited a 'new style' Scotland. The Scots, as a whole, believed that King David's offer to 'sell' Scotland to England was a shameful denial of all that Wallace, Bruce and so many others had fought for, and this prompted a reaction. In brief, the Scots decided that their king must rule with their consent, and in line with their wishes. These were, in truth, the wishes of the nobility, rather than the people as a whole, but it meant the birth of a new level of 'democracy' in Scotland.

The first steps in controlling the errant King David were introduced immediately after the 1357 treaty, which secured his release from imprisonment in England. Recognising the terrible burden that his ransom would impose on Scotland, it was enacted that the King of Scots must not alienate the crown lands and rents. This was a back-handed way of stating that the king must live on the income provided by those lands in order that 'the community of the kingdom, already burdened with the payment of the king's ransom, may not be further burdened with his expenses.' The fact that the parliament wasn't able to bring this into effect did not reflect a lack of purpose, but simply highlighted the lack of a strong executive to enforce their acts against the king's will – but that might come.

Further attempts were made to shift the balance of Scottish power away from the king. In 1366 it was enacted that letters from the king could not cancel letters issued for the execution of justice – an attempt to block the king's veto on legal matters. Four years later, it was further laid down that the king's officers were not to execute any of his mandates that were contrary to common law or statutes.

Another change involved those towns that had been formed into burghs. As they had accepted part of the responsibility for raising the king's ransom – from income arising out of manufacture and trade – they were to be given their own representation in parliament which, up till then, had been exclusively the power base of the landed classes. It was in King David's time that the first written reference was made to 'the Three Estates'.

At the time of the succession of King Robert, Edward of England was still fighting in France, though the tide had gone against him and, indeed, England had lost more than she had gained. After his death, his ten-year-old grandson, Richard II, succeeded him though his uncle, John of Gaunt, Steward of England, effectively ruled the country. His attempts to finance the French Wars with a poll tax and other financial burdens were anything but popular, and led to what is remembered as the Peasant's Revolt in 1381.

One year later, in 1382, the French armies achieved a number of advances in Flanders, which was the main outlet for wool – a hugely important trade for both England and Scotland. These uneasy neighbours had experienced nearly 14 years of peace under the terms of the late King David's ransom treaty, but trouble was already simmering.

Despite the peace, the reiving families of the borders had maintained their raids across the border, in both directions, and in 1382 the Earl of Dunbar had defeated an English army led by Lord Greystoke at Benrig. This initiated serious military preparations in both countries. Just two days after the official expiry of the 14-year truce, the Scots announced their intention to regain their southern counties, expelling the English in the west from Annandale, and seizing Lochmaben Castle. Meanwhile, in the east, the Duke of Lancaster's army threatened Edinburgh, until the burgesses bought him off.

To show their appreciation for the Scots' efforts, the French sent over an expeditionary force of more than 1,000 knights and men-at-arms. Thus strengthened, the new Franco-Scottish army invaded Northumberland, only to withdraw when threatened by an English army led by Richard II and his uncle, John of Gaunt.

The French were far from happy. They would have preferred to charge into a pitched battle with the English. However, the Scots had learned their lessons and retreated while burning crops and driving away any livestock. This 'scorched earth' policy ensured that there was nothing to feed the advancing English. They got as far as Edinburgh, where they caused a certain amount of havoc before turning back and withdrawing south. Of course, this encouraged the Scots to resume the offensive, raiding ferociously in Cumbria and Durham. The French remained disillusioned, claiming that they were forced into an unchivalrous war for a country whose peasants did not show proper deference. As 1385 drew to a close, the border war ended in a stalemate.

While so many concentrated on making war, others had very different priorities. One such a man was John Wycliff who died in Leicester in 1384.

Wycliff was an intellectual theorist who spent much of his life in Oxford, pondering questions of theology. He came to oppose the practice of buying penances, paying taxes (tithes) to the Church, and going on pilgrimages. He also believed that the Bible should be translated into English so that the common man, independent of the priesthood, might study it. At the same time, he suggested that priests should be judged according to their deeds, rather than being given office on influence.

These views were far from popular with the establishment. Some suggested that Wycliff was a heretic, and should burn. He was allowed to retire to Leicester where he quietly spread his views, finding sufficient support to be regarded as the inspiration of the Lollard movement, thus laying the foundations on which later Protestant reformers throughout

Europe would build. Incidentally, the word Lollard comes from *lollen*, which means to mumble – a 'nick-name' derived from this pious group's habit of muttering prayers.

As if to confirm Wycliff's condemnation of many of the Catholic clergy, a sensational case was brought before the courts in 1385. Elizabeth Moring was found guilty of keeping a brothel and sentenced to three years' exile from London. That in itself was hardly noteworthy, but the accused was the wife of Henry Moring, a London alderman, and it emerged that many of the brothel's clients were supposedly celibate friars and chaplains.

One of the key witnesses was Johanna, a serving woman, who described how she had been forced to have sex with clergymen. Ostensibly, Mrs Moring had been running an embroidery business. However, it emerged that the girls who had been put in her care as apprentices had, like Johanna, been forced into prostitution to serve the pleasures of priests and other clerics

While the Scots had held England's attention by raiding her northern counties, the French were more than busy. In Antwerp, in 1386, they were building what they described as 'the greatest invasion fleet since God created the world'. While the shipbuilders raced to produce more than a 1,000 vessels, a great army was being assembled. The 60,000 foot soldiers and 40,000 knights and squires with 50,000 horses all knew that their destination was England. No doubt they were eager to visit on their enemies' homes the sort of destruction that France had been suffering for so many years.

The preparations dragged on into autumn and finally, in November, the ship's captains argued that the rough winter seas would make it very difficult, if not impossible, to mount the invasion. The French royal council announced that the invasion had simply been postponed, but they could not afford to hold together the vast army they had assembled, and it was doubted whether they would return a second time in sufficient numbers to ensure the outcome of such a venture.

The failure of the French invasion fleet to sail was great news for all of England, and particularly for King Richard II who was already beset with problems. Richard was king, but the great nobles held the military power of the land, and they weren't happy with the way the king conducted business. In brief, they suspected that the young king had inherited Edward II's sexual preferences. The Duke of Gloucester made a speech in which he hinted that

Richard might face the same fate – to be buggered with a red-hot poker.

The magnates were particularly critical of the king's closest male friend, Richard de Vere, recently promoted from marquis to duke of Ireland, and the Earl of Suffolk who parliament impeached. Finally, a new council (the lords appellant) with wide ranging powers was created, headed by Gloucester – the king's uncle and sternest critic.

It is known that in the spring of 1387 the king was plotting with de Vere to assassinate their principal opponents – the Duke of Gloucester and the earls of Arundel, Warwick, Nottingham and Derby. However, the young king seemed to lose his resolve in November, agreeing to a truce with the barons until the next parliament – these barons accused Robert de Vere, Michael de la Pole and Robert Tresilian, the chief justice, of treason.

De Vere hurried to the king's support with an armed force but was defeated at Radcot Bridge in Oxfordshire in 1387. Ambushed by the Duke of Gloucester, he immediately turned and fled, despite his own soldiers' urging him to stand and fight. His baggage was left behind. When it was searched, letters were discovered from the king, urging de Vere to hurry to London with an army. This hadn't been mentioned at the November truce, so Gloucester used it to point out the king's lack of honour. The king, he said openly, was not to be trusted.

At the start of 1388, King Richard was forced to hold a parliament at which five of his most loyal supporters were found guilty in their absence of treason, and condemned to death. In truth, their only crime had been to support the king against the nobles' parliament. Sir Robert Tresilian, the chief justice, was arrested and executed, as was Sir Nicholas Brembre. The earls of Suffolk and Oxford and the Archbishop of York fled abroad.

In later years, a maturing King Richard would assert his control and extract his revenge. His main opponents – the Duke of Gloucester, the Earl of Arundel and the Earl of Warwick – were all found guilty of treason and sentenced to be hanged, drawn and quartered. They were all executed, but not according to the sentence. Arundel was 'mercifully' beheaded, and Warwick was simply exiled to the Isle of Man. The Duke of Gloucester, on the other hand, was already dead before his trial, and the verdict's purpose was to justify the manner of his end. Arrested by the king, he was taken to Calais where he was murdered. It is said that the king's men smothered him with a mattress, but his death may have been a great deal more painful – remembering that he had made thinly-veiled threats to give his effeminate king the 'red hot poker' treatment. One thing is certain, however. The effeminate youngster transformed into a despotic king, guarded by a group of particularly tough archers from Cheshire. He also bullied parliament into granting control to a committee of his own men, and deprived it of many of its long-held responsibilities and rights, reversing the 'democratic development' of England to something like the situation that had existed prior to the Magna Carta.

It was a situation that many of his nobles were not prepared to tolerate. The king's main opponent was his cousin Henry Bolingbroke, the Duke of Lancaster, who gathered wide support in the northern counties. Henry Percy, the Earl of Northumberland, joined him. While the opposition grew, the king was campaigning in Ireland and by the time he returned, the quiet rebellion was complete. He was arrested and forced to abdicate in September 1399. Henry Bolingbroke was then crowned Henry IV. Richard was confined in Pontefract Castle where he was murdered within a few months of Henry's succession.

As well as involving themselves in matters of the royal succession, the Earl of Northumberland and Percys kept the pot boiling on the border with Scotland. Reiving families from both sides were constantly invading the other's territory. Sometimes it was a party of ten or 20, coming in the dark of an autumn night to lift a herd of cattle, but at other times they raided in force.

In 1388, Henry 'Hotspur' Percy, the son of the Earl of Northumberland, had raised what amounted to an English army, which was camped at Otterburn. Hearing of this, the Earl of Douglas decided that offence was the best form of defence, and attacked the camp in the fading light of dusk, catching the much stronger English force off-guard. The English put up a strong resistance, but many were slaughtered or captured. Ironically, while the defeated Hotspur was captured alive, the victorious Earl of Douglas was killed in the encounter.

But I hae dreamed a dreary dream,
Beyond the Isle of Skye;
I saw a dead man win a fight,
And I think that man was I.

My wound is deep; I fain would sleep;
Take thou the vanguard of the three,
And hide me by the bracken bush
That grows on yonder lily lee.

The outcome of Otterburn was reversed 14 years later, in 1402, at Homildon Hill near the small Northumbrian town of Wooler, two years after Robert III of Scots had refused to pay homage to Henry IV of England. After Henry's attempt to storm Edinburgh Castle had failed, peace negotiations came to nought when Robert questioned Henry's right to the English throne. After that, it was only a matter of time.

A force of some 10,000 Scots commanded by the latest Earl of Douglas, and supported by some 30 French knights, had gone raiding into Northumberland, plundering as far south as Newcastle. When they turned for home, they found their way blocked by 7,000 English archers, commanded by Henry Hotspur and his father, the Earl of Northumberland. Though outnumbered, such a force of English archers could be deadly efficient when properly commanded.

The Scots, with their French allies, adopted a defensive position on top of Homildon Hill, but this was of little use against the archers who manoeuvred into shooting range some hundred yards from the enemy, and proceeded to inflict a terrible toll on the defensive ranks. Realising the futility of their position, the Earl of Douglas ordered a charge, but the shower of arrows simply increased in its intensity and the Scots were driven back. Douglas was blinded in one eye by an arrow and captured. What was left of the Scottish force broke in panic and fled. It is said that 500 or more of them were drowned trying to cross the River Tweed.

It is worth stressing that an involvement in such encounters on the borders did not necessarily indicate unquestioning loyalty to the combatants' kings. Indeed, just one year after his victory against the Scots at Homildon Hill, 'Hotspur' was in open revolt against Henry IV, backing a rival claimant to the throne. In the end Hotspur was slain in battle near Shrewsbury.

King Robert III of Scots died in 1406, aged 69 – less than a fortnight after receiving news that English pirates had captured his sole surviving son, the 11-year-old James. The young prince had been travelling to France for his own safety. His elder brother had already died in suspicious circumstances, and the king had decided that James would be safer abroad.

Evidently, Robert simply lost the will to live. This sort of hysterical reaction to a reversal in circumstances emerged as a trait in various generations of the Stewart dynasty. Famously and melodramatically, Robert once announced that he should be buried in a midden (rubbish tip) and that his epitaph should read, 'Here lies the worst of kings and the most wretched of men in the whole realm'.

What is remembered as the Hundred Years War between England and France was conducted in fits and starts. There were various periods of peace and truces, sometimes involving Scotland. There was just such a treaty at the time of Prince James's capture, but when the pirates handed him to King Henry, he was not returned to Scotland. Instead, he was imprisoned in the Tower of London. Presumably, the English king had concluded that he could best achieve Scotland's non-interference in the wars with France by removing her new monarch. After Robert's death and with James imprisoned, Scotland was ruled by the prince's uncle, the Duke of Albany. He seemed to appreciate this role. James would later complain that his uncle had deliberately lengthened the negotiations for his release. This accusation was made in 1412, six years into James's confinement.

In that same year, another royal prince, Henry IV's second son Thomas, landed in France. In a complicated arrangement, the leaders of the Armagnacs, who supported the Duke of Orleans, would help England regain its control over Aquitaine, in return for England supporting them against the Duke of Burgundy. This situation had arisen out of the French king's incapacity, leading to a power struggle that developed into a war between Orleans and Burgundy.

After an illness, Henry IV died in 1413, having settled various differences with his eldest son, who was duly crowned Henry V. Within a year, the new king of England had offered to make peace with France, but he demanded a very high price – that he would marry the French princess and the crown and kingdom of France must be yielded to him. The talking began, but few were convinced, recognising that Henry's peace offer amounted to a declaration of war. He landed in France in August 1415, with an army of some 10,000 men, seized Harfleur and enjoyed a great victory at Agincourt in October. He returned with his army to London in November. A short campaign, but devastating to French morale, and they knew the English would return.

Henry V was and still is a hero to the English. They remember him as he was described by William Shakespeare – a courageous warrior, but having something of 'the common touch' and a measure of compassion. Why then did such a man evoke blind fury and hatred in the French? Because their version of history reveals a very different character ... Among other things, they remember Henry's conduct on his return to France in 1417.

Henry's intention was to conquer France, region by region, making the most of the opportunity created by the civil war still raging between Orleans and Burgundy. The French were literally too busy fighting among themselves to oppose him, and he was prepared to take his time, if necessary, starting in Normandy. It would suit his purpose if towns and cities surrendered to him without undue delay. And the best way to achieve that was to set an example, showing others what they might expect if they resisted.

In late August, Edward's soldiers were bombarding Caen. When their guns had breached the walls in several places, Henry called on the French to surrender, or expect no quarter. The French refused, and when the English finally stormed in, Henry proved as good as his word. More than 2,000 men, women and children were herded into the market place where they were literally butchered. The English troops then set off on a trail of rape and looting among the remains of the population.

Henry's terror tactics had their desired effect. A succession of Norman towns and cities opened their gates to his murderous army until, finally, they arrived at the Norman capital, Rouen, just seven miles from Paris on the banks of the River Seine. It was perhaps the most beautiful city in France, with five miles of city walls with six mighty barbicans and more than 60 towers protecting the town with its cathedral, three abbeys, more than 30 convents, and nearly 40 parish churches. And now the 'English devils' were howling at its gates.

In truth, the residents of Rouen were not unduly concerned. The Seine protected one side of their city. On the other three sides, they had dug an enormous ditch. All the food had been brought in from the surrounding countryside, together with a flood of refugees running in front of the English army. As well as a garrison of 4,000 men-at-arms commanded by Guy le Boutellier, many of the citizens showed themselves ready and able to defend the city with their crossbows.

The French in Rouen were hoping that the food supplies they had gathered in would last longer than the meagre pickings left for the English, and that a French army would relieve the city. However, the English were supplied by their own ships, which came up the River Seine, and the rest of France was too busy with its civil war to come to Rouen's assistance. Henry ordered the building of a gibbet within sight of the city walls, and proceeded to hang his prisoners.

In October, with food supplies running low, the people of Rouen were eating horseflesh. By Christmas, they were reduced to eating dogs and cats, then rats, mice and rotting vegetable peelings. Finally, they starved to death in such numbers that they could not be buried.

It was clear to the defenders of Rouen that drastic action was required. In the weeks before the siege, they had taken in many country folk and others, fleeing from the advancing English. If they stayed inside the city they would starve, so they were driven out, hundreds at a time from every city gate, to seek English mercy. On Henry's orders, however, they were driven back. Caught between the city and Henry's army, they cowered in the bottom of the defensive ditches that had been dug around the city walls. There were more than 12,000 of them – old men, nursing mothers and children. And there they stayed.

Despite their evil reputation, the English soldiery felt sorry for these starving civilians, huddled in the unceasing rain and chill winds of December. Some of the troops offered them a share of their bread, but it was far too little among so many. A witness, John Page, described the scene.

'There one might see wandering here and there children of two or three years old begging for bread as their parents were dead. These wretched people had only soil under them and they lay there crying for food – some starving to death, some unable to open their eyes and no longer breathing, others cowering on their knees as thin as twigs. A woman was there clutching her dead child to her breast to warm it, and a child was sucking the breast of its dead mother. There one could easily count ten or 12 dead to one alive, who had died so quietly without call or cry as though they had died in their sleep.'

Conditions were little better in the city. Finally, on New Year's Eve, there was a shouted message from the city walls. The French were ready to parley, but they were told they would have to wait. King Henry V of England was hearing Mass. This set the tone for the negotiations, which dragged on for ten days. King Henry had no reason to hurry, and denied any responsibility for the hundreds and thousands who starved to death with each passing day.

Finally, the terms were agreed. The city surrendered at noon on January 19, having agreed to pay an indemnity of 300,000 gold crowns. The garrison would be allowed to march away, but disarmed and on condition that they would not fight against the English for a year, and the citizens could keep their property in return for an oath of allegiance. It is said that Henry entered the city accompanied by one squire. They rode past the piles of dead and dying to the Cathedral, where the English king praised God for this victory.

Caen and Rouen were just two of the many atrocities committed by English armies campaigning in France. Thus in viewing the nature of the Auld Alliance between Scotland and France, one might ask whether the latter loved the former as much as they hated the English. They certainly had cause for their hatred, and without any doubt the alliance was born out of necessity rather than desire – but the deadly *ménage à trois* between Scotland, France and England was ever a strange affair.

CHAPTER EIGHT

RELIGIOUS AND SOCIAL CHANGE

History remembers warrior kings and their battles, but the history of the eventual unification of England and Scotland into a Protestant state depended more on social and religious change than military endeavour. In Scotland, the desire for reform of the Church, which mutated into violent, political revolt, is largely associated with John Knox and the latter half of the 16th century. English school children are still taught that the peculiarly English Reformation was instituted by Henry VIII alone, to obtain a quickie divorce from the first of his stable of queens. Both these pictures ignore the background to events – a background that encouraged freedom of thought and a hunger for the common man to have his say in moulding society, including how it might worship.

John Wycliff was an intellectual theorist who spent much of his life in Oxford and came to oppose many of the practices and theocracies of the Catholic Church. He believed that the Bible should be translated into English, so that all men might read it. He spread his views in middle England, finding sufficient support to be regarded as the inspiration of the Lollard movement, thus laying the foundations on which later reformers would build.

Wycliff was not alone in questioning the established order. He lived in a time of political and social change. The heavy expenses of a series of wars had prompted the English parliament to build on the achievements of the Magna Carta in order to further limit the king's powers. The country's barons introduced such reforms, but the common people also demanded to be heard.

In 1381, three years before Wycliff's death, a protest was made in the south against the imposition of a poll tax, and demanding that serfdom (the enslavement of common folk) should be abolished. Further demands were made regarding reforms to the church and court. When this protest was ignored, there was a rising among the common folk of Kent, Essex and London. They formed into a mob under a leader, Wat Tyler, and the rising became a bloody revolt in which more than 150 of 'the establishment' were murdered. This number included a judge, Roger Leggett, who was crudely beheaded, and the Archbishop of Canterbury, Simon of Sudbury, who suffered a similar fate.

Finally, the young King Richard II agreed to a meeting with the rebels and rode to Smithfield, where 60,000 of them had gathered. Recognising that he had few options, but knowing that what he agreed today might be denied tomorrow, he agreed to their demands. That might have been an end to the matter, but Wat Tyler wanted to make it clear that the king could not retract from what he had agreed. Evidently a belligerent character, he made some blunt remarks that overstepped the mark of what was deemed acceptable in addressing the monarch. In response the mayor of London, William of Walworth, drew his sword and cut down the rebel leader.

This might have instituted further violence, but the king was able to pacify the crowd, who then drifted away to consider the concessions they had won, and to wonder what else they might achieve. Later, many of them would swing at the end of rope, but they had enjoyed their small taste of freedom, when a peasant negotiated with a king, and would not forget how good it was.

Wycliff's teachings and criticisms of the Catholic Church were not forgotten – not while so many of 'celibate priests' lived openly with their mistresses, or consorted with prostitutes. Perhaps the greatest criticism was that they siphoned off so much of the wealth of the land, while others went hungry or homeless. Rather than accepting these criticisms at a 'political' level, many churchmen twisted them into a religious context. To question the Church was to question God, they insisted, and the questioner was therefore a heretic who should be burned.

Some of the clergy had recognised the threat posed to their comfortable lifestyle by Wycliff, and demanded that he should burn. Indeed, Pope Gregory XI condemned Wycliff in 1377 for his criticisms of the Church as an institution. This was largely ignored and it was only when Wycliff's thoughts were adopted and preached after his death that the Church became truly desperate for the king's support against dangerously radical notions.

In 1392, Bishop John Trefnant of Hereford got the royal nod of approval to arrest the leading Lollard preacher in the county, William Swinderby. His main crime seems to have been that he believed monks should live in poverty rather than luxury, and argued that the pope should stop selling indulgences to wealthy sinners. Before he could be arrested Swinderby fled into the wilds of the Welsh Marches. Described as an eloquent preacher, he was protected by his many followers.

While King Richard supported the Bishop of Hereford, he had his own axe to grind with the Catholic Church. In 1393, the third Statute of Praemunire limited papal power in England. In 1396, a lord appellant, Thomas Arundel, succeeded William Courtenay as Archbishop of Canterbury, thus increasing the secular influence over the Church.

Geoffrey Chaucer died in 1400, leaving the manuscript of the still-studied *Canterbury Tales*, which painted an illuminating and often bawdy picture of life in England at that time. His religious characters significantly include a merry friar, a hunting monk with his hounds, and a pardoner who sold indulgences, together with a dainty, French-speaking nun – this at a time when France was England's sworn enemy.

Seeing that their position was being usurped in so many ways, in or about 1396 the bishops had started campaigning for the death penalty to be used against 'heretics'. When they realised that they were getting nowhere with religious arguments, they changed tack, arguing that a criticism of the spiritual implied a condemnation of the secular establishment, and therefore the Lollards and their kin threatened the fabric of England's hierarchical society. This argument struck home. The Catholic Church was criticised from within as well as without. William Sawtre had been a Catholic priest, but turned to Lollardy. In February 1401, he was condemned to be burnt as a heretic.

Other members of the Catholic Church proved ready to support their flocks. In 1405, the Archbishop of York led what amounted to a citizens' army to press various grievances. At first, the authorities agreed to their demands, and the satisfied 'rebels' dispersed. However, the archbishop was later arrested, tried before Henry IV, condemned as a traitor and beheaded. In such ways did kings define what they considered was unacceptable.

Thomas Arundel, the still fairly new Archbishop of Canterbury, realised that there was a close intertwining in the increasingly puritanical desires for religious and social reform. This reflected the dependence between the secular and spiritual establishments, as did Arundel's appointment which illustrated, in part, why the king was content to see a wealthy Church. He was able to appoint his favourites to comfortable livings as a form of valuable patronage, at little or no cost to himself. Therefore, those who questioned the Church's selling of penances to those wealthy sinners who could afford them, and other money-making schemes including tithes, indirectly threatened the king – for what use would his patronage be without associated financial rewards?

In 1407 Arundel used theological arguments in the show trial of another eloquent Lollard preacher, William Thorpe, to stamp out the heretical notion that the Holy Sacrament remains nothing more than bread and wine after the consecration. However, the archbishop's motives in seeking to crush the Lollards were as much political as religious.

Arundel's intention was to humiliate the preacher by forcing him to recant when threatened with a hideous death, but the Lollards were about to discover a new weapon for their war of propaganda. They were not the first, nor would they be the last, to accept martyrdom – while not going out of their way to achieve it. The stuff of martyrs has a wide appeal in various, fundamentalist religious movements.

Unlike the priest Thorpe (who escaped with his life) John Badby was a layman (a blacksmith) but this didn't stop him becoming one of the most outspoken champions of Lollardy – described by the Church as heresy. It may have been that, as a layman, he seemed to be threatening social rather than religious reform. In 1410 he was arrested and the bishops, the king and his establishment were determined to make an example of him. This they did, but not in the way they intended.

He was sentenced to be burnt in a barrel. The mere threat of this might have caused him to repent, but he would not do so and, on March 5, he was taken to. Smithfield where a truly distinguished audience had gathered, including bishops and earls, the Archbishop of York and the king's eldest son, the Prince of Wales – later to be Henry V. The prince joined with the clergy in endeavouring to convince Badby to recant while there was still time, but he refused.

Finally, Badby was stuffed into the barrel, and the fire lit. As the flames seared his flesh, Badby cried out and the prince, thinking that the Lollard had broken, ordered that the fire should be extinguished. However, Badby had cried out from pain alone, and still refused to recant – even when the prince offered him a pension to do so. The fire was ignited for a second time, and the Lollards had their martyr.

Others were inspired to follow in Badby's footsteps, among them Sir John Oldcastle – an important member of the establishment and an old friend of the new king, Henry V. Despite this background, he was excommunicated in 1414 then arrested and put in the Tower of London to face charges of plotting to kill the king. There may have been some substance in these allegations because Oldcastle escaped and, with a small group of supporters, attempted to mount a coup. Oldcastle escaped a second time, but 60 of his followers were hanged on the king's orders. Oldcastle was finally caught and executed in 1417, but the spirit of Wycliff's teachings survived.

Kings came and went, together with saints and sinners, while the English wars in France continued through to the 1450s. The defeat of an English army at Castillon in 1453 led to the fall of Bordeaux, ending 300 years of English rule in Gascony. The then king of England, Henry VI, was so distraught that, within a year, he had been declared 'mad' by a delegation from the House of Lords.

The Scots celebrated the French victory. The Auld Alliance had been maintained throughout, with one or two breaks while various treaties were in force. Indeed, many Scots had taken an active role in the fighting. Henry V hanged those Scots he captured at the siege of Melun in 1420, and a large Scottish contingent, commanded by Sir John Stewart of Darnley, the Constable of Scotland, fought superbly alongside their French comrades against the Earl of Salisbury in 1423 at Cravant, but suffered heavy losses, as they did again in 1429 when they attacked a convoy commanded by Sir John Falstolf. The English particularly resented the Scottish involvement, regarding them as 'back-stabbers' by allying themselves to the French who noted that their Scottish comrades received harsh treatment but little mercy when captured. At home, the fighting continued all along the Scottish border – mainly raiding, but often in substantial style.

Now the campaigning was over. What would the English do without their French wars? How would those proud warriors pass the time? The Scots may have felt seriously threatened. However, within a few short years of the end of the Hundred Years' War, the madness of Henry VI sowed the seeds for an internal power struggle that led to a civil war which ripped England apart – remembered as the War of the Roses between the houses of York and

Lancaster. The warriors had their war.

Wycliff's urgings for reform were long before what is hailed as the Reformation in England. Some have suggested that education was not really popularised in Scotland until the reformation of the mid-16th century, prompted by men such as John Knox. And while this is true, up to a point, it ignores the emergence of Scottish universities long before that time. The first of these was St Andrews, in 1450, shortly to be followed by Glasgow.

Enthusiasm for universities and schools was widespread throughout Europe at that time, and prompted a more questioning approach to theology and other subjects, principally through the teaching of humanities – subjects designed to encourage the liberal application of rational thought. Indeed, it was the teaching of humanities in Italian universities – the foundation stones of the Renaissance – that led to the first questionings of the theocracies of the Catholic Church.

Within Scotland and England, another factor that prompted a move away from unquestioning acceptance was the steady drift of the population from the countryside into towns. As 'serfs' were no longer dominated by the lord in his castle, new freedoms of thought and expression emerged, as well as the artisan and mercantile classes demanding a say in the running of their country. Even in rural locations, the 'common workers' came to question their 'terms of employment'. Ironically, their position was improved by fairly regular bouts of plague and other maladies. By reducing the supply of labour, plagues and epidemics allowed those who survived to demand better pay and conditions. If refused, they might pack their meagre belongings and move to a more comfortable setting.

Scotland had lagged behind the rest of Europe in the creation of urbanised trading centres, but soon moved to catch up. Roxburgh and Edinburgh were among the first royal burghs – recorded in the 12th century – as was Berwick, which became a great centre for import-export, as reflected by the efforts of both Scotland and England to gain its control. Such burghs were the first sign of the move away from a self-sufficient economy, thus Scotland might trade its surplus wool and skins for minerals in which it was deficient – such as iron – or for spices and wine which, incidentally, was not altogether a luxury in those days of dubious water supplies.

The importance of a town becoming a royal burgh was significant. It set it apart from the surrounding countryside, making it the king's particular domain, under the supervision of the king's officers. Its citizens owed their allegiance to the king, rather than a family chief or earl, encouraging a national patriotism as much as fostering parochialism. Above all, perhaps, the burgh enjoyed special laws, apart from the rest of the land, often but not exclusively aimed at encouraging manufacture and trade. Added to this, the burgh was usually planned around one of the king's castles, thus ensuring a level of law enforcement which rural areas so often lacked. In return, the king received a revenue in hard cash – far more valuable, in times of peace, than the assurance that the tenant would turn up with a body of armed men, whenever required, which lay at the heart of the feudal system. By encouraging payment in cash rather than kind, a king would be able to hire professional soldiers, rather than relying on amateurs who otherwise spent their time working the land. The folklore of 'Merry Englande' is filled with tales of yeomen practising their archery on Sunday afternoons, but those who were paid to wage war in Scotland and France practised seven days a week, and had done so since childhood. A skilled archer could expect to be paid as much as a master craftsman – either by the king or some other patron.

The earliest burgesses remained farmers as much as craftsmen or merchants, and were granted 'common' lands, fisheries and so on for their support. However, those who could make more from their particular skills gradually concentrated their efforts away from tilling the soil or herding sheep.

The advantages to be gained from an increasingly urban population were realised to the point where country folk were offered inducements to move into burghs. A country peasant (practically a slave) who lived in a burgh for a year and a day became a free man, and new arrivals might hold their tenements rent-free for the first year. Other privileges included being able to marry, without having to seek permission from any lord. Burgesses were free to come and go as they pleased and, up to a point, could choose how they lived.

Trade inducements, timeous payment, the enforcement of contracts and so on were administered by a burgh court which, as well as protecting local traders, might encourage foreign merchants to settle. Thus it was that when Edward Longshanks seized Berwick, a group of Flemish merchants gained fame by holding out to the last man, refusing to surrender to the English troops.

After a time, the Scottish royal burghs became self-governing. Instead of being administered by royal officials, the burgesses elected their own officers from among themselves. As well as inspiring a sense of community, this created a new sort of freedom which was treasured by the burgesses. They

❦ CHAPTER NINE ❦

THE THISTLE
AND THE ROSE

King James IV Stewart of Scots married the 13-year-old Princess Margaret Tudor, daughter of Henry VII of England in Edinburgh on August 8 1503. The two kingdoms had fought through centuries steeped in the blood of battles, raids and feuds, but it was hoped this marriage alliance would herald a new era of peace and stability. The Scottish poet William Dunbar in *The Thrissil and the Rois* described the union of Stewart thistle and Tudor rose. Of course, it wasn't the first attempt at an Anglo-Scots alliance through a royal marriage; Alexander II of Scots had married Henry III's sister, Joan, and their son, Alexander III, aged ten, married his cousin, King Henry's daughter, in 1251 – but it was hoped that the marriage of 1503 might succeed where others had ultimately failed. To mark the event, the two kings signed the Treaty of Perpetual Peace.

It is said that the English guests flaunted their wealth in front of their poorer neighbours, the men wearing satin, velvet and damask cut in the latest Italian styles; the women in crimson and velvet with fur or embroidered borders to their close-fitting bodices and trains. Only the Scots king could seek to match the English finery. At a cost that nearly crippled his treasury, James Stewart was weighed down with jewels and resplendent in velvet, satin, silk and cloth of gold bordered with ermine.

The Stewarts had reigned in Scotland since 1371 when Robert II Stewart, a grandson on the maternal side of Robert the Bruce, gained the throne on the death of David II. Since then, the Stewarts had supplied Scotland with a string of kings in unbroken line. James IV was Robert II's great-great-great-grandson. In contrast, Margaret Tudor traced her lineage to a commoner, Owain ap Maredudd ap Tudwr ap Goronwy (son of Meredith, son of Tudor, son of Goronwy). A Welshman, he had joined Henry V's army in France, then served in the queen's household and changed his name to Owen Tudor.

After the death of Henry V, Owen 'comforted' the widowed queen, Catherine de Valois, youngest daughter of King Charles VI of France, and secretly married her. It caused a scandal, of course, but their two sons went on to become Edmund, Earl of Richmond, and Jasper, Earl of Pembroke, recognised as half-brothers of Henry VI. After the death of Richard III on Bosworth Field in the War of the Roses, Edmund's son Henry Tudor, of Franco-Welsh descent, was crowned Henry VII of England in 1485.

Eighteen years on, after the death of King Henry's eldest son, Prince Arthur, Margaret Tudor was second in line to the English throne, after her younger brother Prince Henry. If anything had happened to him, Margaret and James King of Scots would have been crowned king and queen of England, uniting the kingdoms, but it was not to be. Henry VII died six years later and his surviving son, Henry VIII, took his place on the throne. Margaret remained in the line of succession, as would her descendants.

The newly-crowned Henry VIII planned to marry his brother's widow, Catherine of Aragon – a daughter of King Ferdinand of Aragon and Queen Isabella of Castille – in order to maintain a Spanish alliance. A papal dispensation was required as Catherine was related to Henry 'in the first degree of affinity', but the Tudors saw this Spanish alliance as a priority, allowing England to concentrate on her old enemy, France. In return, Spain avoided the possibility of an Anglo-French alliance controlling the English Channel and blocking the sea routes between Spain and her territory in the Netherlands. This deal didn't suit everybody. England's old enemy was Scotland's auld ally.

In 1512, James renewed the 1492 alliance between Scotland and France, refusing to join Henry and other members of the Holy League – the Papacy, Venice and Aragon – as they prepared for war against Louis XII of France. When the Holy Roman Emperor Maximilian – head of what was nominally the senior state of Western Christendom – joined the league, James was urged to stay neutral.

With the benefit of hindsight, some might suggest that neutrality was Scotland's best option. However, the Scottish king did not see himself as a weakling to cower in the shadow of his powerful neighbour. James was a popular, brave and energetic king, and his kingdom was experiencing a new era of optimism and a flowering of the arts and ideas, as was much of Europe at that time. Scotland's foreign trade had increased significantly – as had her navy, converted from armed merchantmen to true men-of-war –as she began to prosper her friendship was encouraged throughout the courts of Europe. All this might be risked if Scotland appeared to come to England's heel like a timid spaniel fawning for a kind word.

This wasn't the first time that James had been asked to abandon the Auld Alliance with France. In 1498, a Spanish ambassador, Pedro d'Ayala, had sought to persuade him to take a Spanish bride and alter his country's foreign policy. The Spaniard's account of the Scottish king paints a vivid portrait. A man of noble stature, he said, as handsome in complexion and figure as a man can be, speaking six languages in addition to English and Gaelic. However, d'Ayala added that James was rash in warfare, not taking care of himself, and he was not a good captain because he began to fight before he had given his orders. The Spaniard was not alone in speaking of James's unguarded desire for military glory.

As to the treaty of 'perpetual peace' with England, obtained through his marriage to Margaret Tudor, James had grounds for complaint. On the Borders, still troubled by reiving clans and families, a Scottish Warden of the Marches – appointed to maintain the peace between the two countries – had been killed by Englishmen on a truce day. James was furious, but Henry declined to take any action. Also, in the summer of 1511, two Scottish ships commanded by James's captain, Andrew Barton, had been attacked and seized by the English Howards. Barton was killed in the fighting, but when James wrote to Henry, demanding that the ships should be returned and the attackers tried in accordance with the treaty, the English King contemptuously brushed aside the complaint. James then wrote to the pope, accusing Henry of encouraging trouble between the two kingdoms, attacking the Scots 'by land and sea, capturing and slaying'. Accordingly, he went on, he presumed the Treaty of Peace, renewed upon Henry's accession in 1509, was no longer binding.

At the end of June Henry landed with 35,000 men at Calais. Maximilian's German and Flemish soldiers joined his expeditionary force, and three months later they marched together into the defeated city of Tournai. That evening, flushed with success, Henry learned of the defeat of a Scots army in England. His attempts to keep his brother-in-law out of the war had failed.

Two months after Henry had landed with his army in France, James crossed the Tweed, invading England in support of Louis of France. His forces captured castles at Norham, Wark, Etal and Ford then took up a defensive position on Flodden Hill, some 11 miles south of Berwick. Meanwhile, an English army commanded by Thomas Howard, the Earl of Surrey, was hurrying north from Pontefract.

The Scots were in a strong position, but allowed the English forces to manoeuvre freely and cut off their line of retreat. Harried by English artillery fire, James threw away his advantage, impetuously ordering his phalanxes of pikemen onto lower, uneven and slippery ground. When the Scots inevitably lost their formation, the English swarmed into the gaps. What followed was a slaughter, the English taking few, if any, prisoners. The Scottish dead numbered 10,000, out of a force of only twice that number. Among them were a bishop, two abbots, 12 earls and 14 lords. James fell alongside his countrymen, leaving Scotland in the hands of his son, a 17-month-old infant, crowned King James V at Stirling on September 21 1513.

After the crushing defeat at Flodden, England might have pressed home her advantage and made an all-out invasion of Scotland, but the weather was appalling, Surrey's men were exhausted, and the army was short of supplies. And they had done enough. Scotland was left an enfeebled country and would be no trouble to anybody for some time to come. She had lost her political stability along with her king.

Margaret, now a 24-year-old dowager queen, acted as *tutrix* to her son. She was nominally the regent, but in practice a council of regency, divided by factionalism, ran the country. It was the best that Scotland could muster after the death of 'the flowers of the forest' at Flodden.

The following year, in August 1514, Henry signed a peace treaty with Louis of France. Tournai was ceded to England, and in return for not enforcing his claim to the French throne, Henry was to receive one million francs to be paid over ten years. Emphasising the belief in royal marriages as tools of diplomacy in creating alliances – a belief that still existed despite James's actions – it was agreed that 52-year-old Louis would marry Henry's 18-year-old sister Mary. Ribald courtiers suggested that if the ailing Louis consummated the marriage, it would be the death of him. Whether this was a contributory factor or not, Louis was dead within a few months. His successor was crowned King Francis.

In the same month that Henry gave his younger sister to the French king, his elder sister, the dowager Queen Margaret, widow of James IV, married Archibald Douglas, the Earl of Angus. This marriage upset many jealous Scottish nobles, who felt the 'Red' Douglas family were already too powerful. There was also a belief that Margaret, as Henry's sister, was actively pro-English. Scottish nobles were quick to argue that Mary was to be regent only for as long as she remained unmarried. According to the customs of those times, when a wife was subservient to her husband, Margaret had effectively handed the regency to the Douglases by marrying the Earl of Angus, and this was intolerable for their rivals in the Scottish parliament.

A year later, John Stewart, Duke of Albany, a grandson of James III and a cousin of the infant king, was accepted as the regent in Margaret's stead. Albany might have seized the opportunity to press his own claim to the Scottish throne, being next in succession, but seemed content to rule in practice if not in title. Raised in France and French in all but name, he was also appointed guardian to the king who was taken from his mother and entrusted to a small group of nobles. Margaret fled to England.

Two years later, with Henry busy in England, Albany travelled to France and renewed the Auld Alliance. The new alliance, the Treaty of Rouen, stated that the now five-year-old King James V would marry a daughter of the French king, assuming one was available. Unfortunately for Albany, this came to Henry's attention and as a result of diplomatic pressure the French authorities, in accordance with their new treaty with England, agreed to detain the duke. He was finally allowed to return to Scotland in 1521, eager for revenge, but the Scottish nobles refused to attack England without support from France.

The following year, an Anglo-Scots truce was agreed. This didn't stop Albany who was back in France one month later, seeking the military support that the Scottish nobles had demanded. He returned to Scotland with 4,000 French infantry and 500 cavalry. Hearing of this, Henry cast aside the velvet glove from his iron fist. In June 1523, English troops crossed the border and burnt Kelso Abbey. In July, Cardinal Wolsey, Henry's chief minister, forced parliament into agreeing to fund a new war with France. And in September, English troops again crossed the border, burning Jedburgh Abbey then relieving the castle at Wark in Northumberland. It had been besieged by the Franco-Scots army, which was forced to retreat back into Scotland.

It is said that neither the French nor the Scots seemed particularly distressed that their joint expedition was over. Scots were critical of the 'haughty' French who burnt too much winter fuel to keep warm. However, they must have realised that, once again, they had waved a red rag in the face of the English bull.

In May 1524, Albany set sail again for France, this time to discuss marriage proposals for the young James V. This confirmed what many Scots had been thinking – that the duke's anti-English, pro-French obsession was becoming a serious liability. They had told him that the wars with England were solely in the interests of France, and they were tired of fighting for others. In his absence, a coup returned Queen Margaret and her pro-English allies to power, thus taking the fire out of Henry's anger.

For several years, Margaret had been estranged from her husband Archibald Douglas, Earl of Angus, who had seized control of Edinburgh in 1520 in a bloody street battle with the Hamiltons that became known as 'Cleanse the Causeway'. This separation and the commencement of divorce proceedings won back the support of those nobles who had opposed the marriage, thus ensuring the success of the coup against Albany. Indeed, Margaret was so keen to be rid of her husband that she didn't wait to be formally divorced from him before secretly marrying Henry Stewart, Lord Methven, the Treasurer and Lord Chancellor, in March 1526.

The Scottish Parliament had agreed that, due to mistrust among the nobility, the young king should remain 'in company' with various nobles on a rotation – swapping from one to the next every three months. The Earl of Angus – now divorced from the queen – should have released the king in June 1526 when his tenure as custodian ended, but he was still intent on increasing the power base of the mighty Douglas family. By refusing to release his royal hostage, he maintained his stranglehold on the government of Scotland. The Earl of Lennox tried to rescue James in September, but was defeated and killed.

James remained under his stepfather's control for two more years. He was not an altogether unwilling prisoner, it has to be said, enjoying a certain level of freedom and gaining a reputation as a womaniser. It was a reputation for debauchery that stayed with him throughout his life. After his death, the protestant activist John Knox wrote that James cared not whether the women he took were another man's wife or otherwise, and his marriage did nothing to confine his promiscuity.

James finally 'escaped' from his stepfather in May 1528. In July, he entered Edinburgh at the head of an army of supporters to assert his right to rule his kingdom. Angus fled to England.

Scotland and England were both Roman Catholic countries, their kings acknowledging the supreme authority of the pope. In 1525, the Scottish Parliament had banned all heretical literature and discussion of Protestant ideas, and in February 1528, Scotland's first Protestant martyr was burnt at the stake in St Andrews.

Patrick Hamilton was a young but talented theologian from a prominent landed family. He had studied at St Andrews and Wittenberg, and later taught at the Lutheran University of Marburg. It is said that he was warned of his impending arrest, but refused to flee. If so, he may have courted martyrdom. Whatever his intentions, the damp conditions on the day of his execution made his sufferings more ghastly. It took six hours for him to die in the slow-burning fire.

Some hoped that the brutality of Hamilton's execution would deter other would-be heretics. However, his martyrdom served to inspire. Twenty more Protestants were burnt at the stake in the next 30 years, among them ten dissident, former-Catholic clerics. For every one that was put to death, more were exiled or fled the country, including many of Scotland's leading intellectuals. Thus the persecution of emergent Protestantism inevitably led to a vacuum in the country's religious, political and social leadership.

Long before Patrick Hamilton's martyrdom in Scotland, the flames of Henry VIII's passion for his queen, Catherine of Aragon, had died. In 1527, he declared that he should not have been allowed to marry his elder brother's widow, and they had been 'living in sin' for 20 years. Catherine counter-claimed that her earlier marriage to Prince Arthur had not been consummated and therefore, as she had still been a virgin when she married Henry, there was no question of an incestuous marriage, as her husband was claiming.

Catherine was concerned about the succession rights of her one surviving child from eight pregnancies. The 11-year-old Princess Mary would be made illegitimate if her father had his way. This question over her status halted plans for Mary to marry a French prince.

Henry had an ulterior motive in seeking a divorce from Catherine. He was hopelessly in love with a 26-year-old courtier, Anne Boleyn, who was resisting Henry's advances, saying that she wouldn't yield to the hungry king until she was his wife and queen.

Henry applied for papal approval for a divorce from Catherine in 1527. At the start of 1531 he was still waiting. When he was ordered by Pope Clement VII not to remarry until his divorce problem was solved, his patience broke. He decided to reject the papal authority.

Henry was then approached by Protestant German princes and invited to join an alliance against Maximilian's successor, the Holy Roman Emperor Charles V, Catholic ruler of Spain, the Netherlands and parts of Germany and Italy. While he joined them in rejecting the papal authority, Henry mistrusted their Lutheran radicalism. Equally, he was anxious not to give further offence to Emperor Charles, who was Queen Catherine's nephew, and there was no advantage to be gained from destroying the alliance with Spain.

In 1532, after months of intrigue, Henry gave notice to the bishops that they must take orders from him and him alone, making a break with Rome practically inevitable. He had already given up all pretence of a marriage to Catherine, and moved to Woodstock with Anne Boleyn whom he had created Marchioness of Pembroke. The title had convinced Anne to set aside her maidenly virtue. When Henry defied Rome to marry her in 1533, she was already pregnant.

On June 1, Anne was crowned Queen of England in Westminster Abbey by the Archbishop of Canterbury, Thomas Cranmer. This infuriated Pope Clement, who insisted that the king's marriage to Catherine of Aragon was still valid, thus questioning, at least, the legitimacy of the child that Anne was carrying. He gave Henry until September to take back his former wife or suffer expulsion from the Roman church, but the king wasn't for turning back.

Henry VIII's marital problems were the catalyst for England's break with Rome, although moves towards religious reformation had been taking place for many years – beginning with John Wycliff and his Lollards. All over Europe, voices were raised against the worst excesses of the Roman church. There again, it was because England's reformation was prompted for the king's convenience, rather than out of religious conviction, that Henry's brand of Protestantism would prove to be of a particularly conservative kind. A sort of halfway house between Catholicism and more radical forms of Protestantism. Indeed, some might suggest that rather than being Lutheran or Calvinistic the form of religion introduced to England did little more than replace the pope with the king as the head of what was still essentially a Catholic church. It was certainly a very different style of Protestantism to that which the Scottish martyrs were dying for.

The following year, 1534, the Act of Supremacy was passed, making Henry VIII the Supreme Head of the Church of England. The break with Rome was irrevocable.

On September 7, the new queen, described by some as 'the goggle-eyed whore', gave birth to a daughter, Elizabeth. In the eyes of the Catholic Church, the baby was undoubtedly illegitimate. What was far worse for Henry was that Anne had frustrated his desperate wish for a male heir. He was furious, believing his new wife had betrayed him, as if she could have chosen the sex of their child.

Catherine of Aragon died in January 1536 after languishing for two years under house arrest in Cambridgeshire. In May of the same year, Anne Boleyn was executed at the Tower of London. She had been charged with adultery with a number of men, including her brother. Confessions were obtained by torture. Her real crime, in Henry's eyes, was her failure to provide him with a son.

In regard to a royal consort, adultery was treated as treason. Therefore, Henry had the right to choose whether his wife would be burnt at the stake, or beheaded. He chose the latter option. It is reported that just before she bowed her head to the swordsman's stroke, she said, 'I pray God, save the king and send him long to reign over you, for a gentler, nor a more merciful prince was there never, and to me he was ever a good, a gentle and sovereign lord.' If she did indeed say those words, perhaps out of blind panic or relief that she would not perish at the stake, then she might be credited as the inspiration for the National Anthem. Life and death are full of irony ...

Once again, Henry had an ulterior motive in securing his wife's removal. Just 11 days after Anne's execution, he married the attractive 27-year-old Jane Seymour. As if in atonement, in July the Second Act of Succession declared the Princesses Mary and Elizabeth legitimate, but they would fall back in the line of succession if Henry's new queen produced a son.

The following year, 1537, Jane Seymour did indeed give birth to a boy, Prince Edward. Henry expressed his delight by making Jane's brother, Edward Seymour, the Earl of Hertford. In the same month, Jane died.

Throughout Northern Europe, the move from Catholicism to Protestantism was gathering pace – polarising states and becoming an expression of political identity and autonomy as well as religious conviction and allegiance. Henry was about to learn the significance of turning his back on Rome.

In June 1538, despite the war of 1513, France signed the Treaty of Nice with the Holy Roman Empire, creating an immensely powerful Catholic alliance and causing fears of an invasion in England. To add to those concerns, Pope Paul III had finally excommunicated Henry, and Henry's exiled Catholic cousin, Cardinal Reginald Pole, was attempting to rally the Spanish and French kings against newly Protestant England. Meanwhile, Henry was looking for new alliances and swelling his war chest, confiscating treasure from the Catholic monasteries – even down to their leaden roofs. What remained was demolished or left to the elements and looters.

Henry delayed marrying a fourth wife, Anne of Cleves, while he sought an excuse to avoid coupling with a woman described as tall, thin and pock-marked, and unable to speak any English. In the end, however, he put political gain ahead of personal taste. The marriage secured an alliance with North Germany's Protestant princes against the Catholics – a similar alliance to the one dangled before Henry in 1531. Unfortunately, politics and passion proved uneasy bedfellows and Henry's marriage to 'the Flanders Mare' was soon declared null and void on the grounds of non-consummation. A fortnight later, Henry married Catherine Howard, who also failed to give Henry a son and was beheaded in 1542. Again, the charge was adultery – that treasonable offence for a king's consort.

As well as dealing with supposedly treasonous wives, Henry was spreading his influence over all parts of the British Isles. An act called by Sir Anthony St Leger, the Lord Deputy, was passed through the Irish Parliament in Dublin in June 1541, making Henry of England also King of Ireland. 'The king's highness, his heirs and successors, kings of England, (shall) be always kings of this land Ireland.'

Two years later, an act of parliament at Westminster completed the Act of Union of 1536 between England and Wales. English law was extended to all parts, with the old distinction between the principality and the Marches abolished.

Another act sought to impose religious conformity and control extreme Protestants as well as Catholics still loyal to the Pope. This act was as much a social as a religious imposition in that it banned the lower classes and women, other than nobles, from reading the English Bible. The explanation is significant in revealing a royal wariness of Christ's teachings – the very thing that radical Protestants were trying to promote. Reading the Bible needed to be controlled, said the act, because it might mislead 'the lower sort' and encourage 'naughty and erroneous opinions'. 'No women, nor artificers, prentices, journeymen, servingmen, yeomen, husbandmen or labourers,' might read the Bible. The act also set severe penalties for unauthorised translations, illegal books, ballads, plays, songs and fantasies.

In Scotland, after two years of bloody border raiding, an Anglo-Scots peace treaty had been signed in 1534 and the following year James V was invested with the Order of the Garter by an envoy from his uncle. He also accepted the Golden Fleece from the Holy Roman Emperor and later the French Order of St Michael from King Francis. James then invoked the Treaty of Rouen, which entitled him to a daughter of the King of France. In 1536 he married the French princess Madeleine. She was just 16 and 'of pleasand bewtie, guidlie favour, luffing countenance and cumly manners,' but had a long history of ill health and died just seven months after the wedding. It is said that her health was worsened severely by the Scottish climate. Her father had certainly been reluctant to allow his frail princess to marry the Scottish king.

James retained Madeleine's dowry of 100,000 livres, and one year later married Mary of Guise, the eldest daughter of the Duke of Guise, one of the most powerful nobles in France. Like James, she was widowed, having been married to Francis of Orleans, Duke of Longueville, who had died just one month before Madeleine. Unlike James, she had a son, the new Duke of Longueville. A second son had died. Letters written to her mother after her marriage to James reveal that she was desperately sad about leaving her surviving son in France. It was also rumoured that James kept a mistress. Family duty was considered far more important than a mother's love for her children or concern over her husband's excursions and the Duke of Guise would have been more than happy if his grandson sat on Scotland's throne.

The French duke's daughter had attracted other admirers. It is known that, following the death of Jane Seymour, Henry of England made approaches and some appreciative comments about her stature, to which she replied that although her figure was big, her neck was small. Clearly, Mary was both intelligent and courageous. Henry might have been amused at this retort, but would not appreciate being thwarted.

Mary of Guise was indeed a tall and well-built girl of healthy vitality and high humour, in stark contrast to the lamented Madeleine. Her record in producing potential heirs would have appealed to James – as it had to the English king. Monarchs throughout the ages have treated the production of healthy heirs as a priority. Mary gave James a son, yet another James, in May 1540.

❦ CHAPTER TEN ❦

WINDS OF CHANGE

Scotland was still officially Roman Catholic though prepared to look at the alternative – and little wonder. The Catholic Church was gobbling up almost one half of the revenue of the entire kingdom. In a poor country such as Scotland, this led to an increasing alienation between the wealth of the Church and the poverty of its suffering people. While monks grew fat and lazy, the overworked people regularly faced the prospect of starvation. Many priests made a mockery of their holy vows. Cardinal Beaton, the Archbishop of St Andrews was just one of those who flaunted the vow of celibacy, living openly with his mistress. The court was reputedly shocked and amused by a new play, *Ane Satire of the Thrie Estaits*, which sought to expose, 'the naughtiness in religion, the presumption in bishops'. It was written by the diplomat-poet David Lindsay, a boyhood companion of James who had risen to an influential position at court and been entrusted with crucial diplomatic missions. The protection provided by his close relationship with the king allowed him to deal with various contemporary issues including the oppression of the poor, sometimes offering outspoken advice on how things should be improved. James was present for the first performance of the play in Linlithgow. After the final curtain, he is reputed to have told his Catholic bishops that if they did not act on the play's lessons he would dispatch them to England, where his uncle would know how to deal with them.

Uncle and nephew seemed happy enough to leave each other in peace. However, in September 1541, Henry embarked on a stately royal progress through England's northern shires, accompanied by a thousand armed men and an artillery train. His purpose was to remind his northern nobles that he was boss, and to settle any outstanding quarrels with Scotland, recognising that France and Spain were sufficient threats in themselves, without him having to worry about who or what might appear at his back door. He probably intended to encourage James to consider, at least, the advantages to be gained from breaking with Rome, thus opening the way to new Protestant alliances.

Henry invited James to meet with him at York, but the Scottish king didn't turn up. His privy council had warned him not to trust Henry, but there was more to it than that. In April 1541, Mary had given birth to a second son, Robert, Duke of Albany, who had died just two days later. As if this wasn't tragedy enough, shortly after, his elder brother, the young Prince James, died just days before his second birthday. Later, some in Scotland would claim that God was punishing the king for his sinful life. Whatever the cause, James was devastated, and simply wasn't well enough to meet with Henry.

The English king, suffering from the advancing stages of syphilis, had become unpredictable. As a young man, he had been graced with many admirable qualities, but the onset of madness left him an egocentric, vindictive bully. He ordered his northern levies to raid into Scotland, and his orders made his intentions chillingly clear. The Duke of Norfolk burned Roxburgh, Kelso and many villages, massacring all in his path, but Sir Robert Bowes was less successful in raiding Teviotdale, his army being heavily mauled at Haddon Rig by a force commanded by the Earl of Home.

Mary was pregnant again when James reluctantly assembled the Scottish host for a defensive counter-attack, only to discover that the bulk of his nobles would not follow him to the border, let alone into England. Their reasons were many and varied, but included 'the Flodden factor' and a lack of will to fight Protestantism – indeed some had already converted. Cardinal Beaton had been attempting to turn Scotland's retaliation into a holy war on the grounds that England lay under the papal interdict. While preferring isolationism, many Scots had decided that they would settle for an English rather than a French alliance. If nothing else, an English alliance might achieve an end to English aggression and, as they had told Albany years previously, the Scottish nobles were weary of fighting what they believed were essentially France's battles, and were no longer prepared to fight for the papacy. In brief, the Scots seemed war-weary.

Despite this lack of support, James proceeded with a small force, funded by the wealthy Catholic clergy. Weak as this army was by comparison to what

Henry might muster, James made it weaker still by splitting it in two. One group was commanded by Oliver Sinclair, a royal favourite but no soldier, whose force was caught and defeated by an English Army at Solway Moss – marshy ground between the rivers Esk and Sark – then harried all the way back into Scotland. Some had lost all interest in fighting, and even surrendered themselves to English women bystanders. Oliver Sinclair was captured 'fleeing full manfully'.

James retreated, a broken man suffering from nervous exhaustion, finally arriving at Hallyards, the Fife home of his treasurer, Sir William Kirkaldy of Grange. When asked by a servant where he wanted to spend Christmas, he replied, 'I cannot tell; choose ye the place. But this I can tell you, on Yule day, you will be masterless and the realm without a king.'

According to contemporary accounts, the Stewarts (later Stuart) had what might be described as a hysterical streak in their nature. What for others might have been harsh but tolerable stress could lead to a total, physical breakdown in members of the royal family. It is only in recent times, with the advance in medical knowledge, that their condition could be diagnosed. Serious, and in some forms hereditary, porphyria has symptoms including urine coloured red or purple, stomach pains, constipation, nausea, vomiting and sensitivity to light. It is not one condition, but a grouping of several related diseases, sometimes involving marked anxiety or disturbed behaviour, depression, dementia, convulsions and coma. Extreme sufferers might be described as obsessive and paranoid – and porphyria would dog the Stewart royal family down through the generations. Half of an affected parent's children are likely to inherit the condition.

Unable to recover mentally from the anguish of losing two sons (though he had nine other children, all born out of wedlock), followed by the defeat of his forces at Solway Moss, James grew increasingly despondent. He visited his heavily pregnant wife at the palace of Linlithgow, but by then he was beyond reason or cheering, and moved on to Falkland Palace. It was as if he had given up the will to live, turned his face to the wall, and slipped away into a deepening coma. Even with the benefit of modern medicine, severe cases of porphyria can develop into weakness and paralysis. There is still no cure, and fatalities still occur. James died on December 14, aged 30, leaving the throne and his medical condition to his daughter Mary.

She was just six days old, born premature and described as weakly. On hearing of her birth, James had sighed: 'Adieu, fare well, it came with a lass, it will pass with a lass', recalling that the Stewart dynasty had started with the marriage of Marjorie Bruce and Walter Stewart, and expressing his belief that it had no future. Once again, Scotland was ruled by an infant, this time a girl, and another red rag had been waved in the face of the English bull ...

Henry was undoubtedly angry at another Scottish invasion of his kingdom, but decided against an outright military response. Nor did he take retribution on the Scottish prisoners. Instead, he freed the nobles captured at the battle – including Cassillis, Glencairn, Maxwell, Fleming and the Douglas brothers – after having made them swear to support a marriage between his son, Prince Edward, and the infant Mary Queen of Scots.

The pro-English Earl of Arran brokered the marriage alliance – somewhat reluctantly, at first, as he had hoped that his own son might be a suitable candidate. However, he became very supportive when Henry suggested the boy might be a good match for his own daughter, Princess Elizabeth. Mary's grandmother, Margaret Tudor, may have suggested some features of the alliance before her death. She may have said that it would be better for Mary to be educated in England – under Henry's influence rather than that of her French-born mother, Mary of Guise. But whoever was the architect of the agreements sealed at Greenwich – known appropriately as The Treaty of Greenwich – it stipulated that Mary Queen of Scots would marry Prince Edward when she was ten years old.

Henry didn't want any new alliances between Scotland and France. This alternative strengthened the link between Scotland and England while significantly avoiding the expense of a military conquest – a relief to Henry whose hard-pressed military budget had already been allocated. He was planning to attack France, and had been discussing his intentions with the Holy Roman Emperor Charles V for over a year. Presumably, the Emperor was taking his time in considering whether to ignore the terms of the Treaty of Nice, signed with France in 1538, but at the start of 1543 he made his decision. Emperor Charles was officially allied with Henry against Francis – Catholic with Protestant against Catholic. To celebrate, Henry married his sixth wife, Catherine Parr. Everything seemed to be going his way – for now.

In Scotland, the Dowager Queen Margaret died at Methven Castle on October 18 1541. Her departure seriously weakened the pro-English faction in the Scottish Parliament. Following the death of her son, James V, in the aftermath of the Scots defeat at Solway Moss, they were ousted in 1543, allowing the anti-English and pro-French factions headed by the infant queen's mother, Mary of Guise, supported by Cardinal David Beaton, to denounce the Treaty of Greenwich. The infant Queen Mary was moved from Linlithgow to Stirling Castle, where she would be safer from outside interference and the threat of abduction by Henry's forces or agents. Catholic interests strengthened their grip on Scotland. The parliament annulled liberal religious legislation, including a law permitting reading the Bible in the vernacular. In 1544, various Protestant heretics were burnt at the stake, including Helen Stirk who was put to death for refusing to call on the Virgin Mary during childbirth.

The political situation in Scotland was further complicated by the emergence of a new pro-English grouping. After the death of Margaret, the vacillating Earl of Arran reverted to Catholicism and was reconciled with Beaton and Mary of Guise's anti-English faction. The Earl of Lennox stepped in to head the pro-English faction. He was joined by Archibald Douglas, the Earl of Angus – the estranged husband of Margaret – who had reappeared after 14 years of exile in England. One day after his about-turn, Arran bore the crown of Scotland at Mary's coronation. She was just nine months old.

Henry still had his alliance with Emperor Charles and in September 1544 he besieged and took the French port of Boulogne, but then the emperor hesitated. Negotiations for a joint, all-out military attack on France were inconclusive. Finally, the alliance with Emperor Charles collapsed.

On Henry's northern front, the Scots with renewed anti-English fervour 'loosed the border' in a series of bloody raids. Henry was driven to rant and rave when the opportunistic Earl of Angus, having witnessed England's failure in France, promptly turned on his former hosts, leading the Scottish force that defeated an English army at Ancrum Moor in February 1545. After the Scottish victory, and the collapse of Henry's alliance with Charles, the French were confident enough to send 5,000 troops to support the Scots. The Scots also received a papal subsidy.

Henry was undoubtedly furious, but was still sufficiently in control of his faculties to react cautiously to the defeat at Ancrum Moor and the continuing Catholic threat in the north. Rather than committing to any sort of invasion plan, his troops reconnoitred in force. Skirmishes between the English and Franco-Scots continued inconclusively throughout the year, before Henry's 'rough wooing' of Scotland finally began to gather momentum. As well as raiding across the border, he saw an opportunity in the Western Isles. It must have seemed a delicious irony to encourage an attack on Scotland's back door, remembering times when England's attention had been on France only to discover that the Scots had invaded their northern frontier.

Scotland had been trying unsuccessfully to pacify the Isles since 1493, and now faced the most serious uprising in support of a Clanranald Lord of the Isles. With Donald Dubh at liberty, the chiefs of the Lordship flocked to his standard. Their representatives met on Islay in 1545 to negotiate with Henry VIII's commissioners. Scotland was faced with the prospect of an invasion of 4,000 Islesmen from the west. However, the threat faded when Donald Dubh died without a credible heir.

After the failure in the Isles, Henry concentrated on the eastern Borders and coastline where he had already been active. In May 1544, an English force of 10,000 men commanded by Edward Seymour, the Earl of Hertford, made an amphibious raid on Edinburgh, looting the Palace of Holyrood and the Abbey Church, killing several hundred townsmen and seizing two ships and £50,000 worth of grain in Leith. The army then marched south through the Borders. They killed, burnt and spoilt as they went, later boasting of the destruction of seven monasteries and more than 240 towns and villages. At the same time, the Earl of Lennox harried the Scottish West Marches and Annandale in Henry's name.

As part of his plan to dominate Scotland by force or stealth, Henry revived the centuries-old suzerainty claim of Edward I, Hammer of the Scots, seeking to establish a pro-English party, rather than simply a faction, at the Scottish court. Hundreds were encouraged or threatened into taking assurance of the King of England – an oath of allegiance acknowledging Henry as their liege lord. They were promised pensions, received regular wages and were insured against losses arising out of any Scottish retaliation. Henry concentrated his recruitment drive on those areas where he exerted the heaviest military pressure, from Berwickshire and the eastern Borders through East Lothian to Fife and Angus. His 'blackmail with inducements' created what has been described as the most organised fifth column in Scottish history.

Rifts fostered by the intertwining of religion and politics were widening in Scotland. Catholic persecution of an expanding body of Protestant 'heretics' continued, thus strengthening the case, for some, to seek England's protection. One of the most vigorous of the persecutors was Cardinal David Beaton, the Archbishop of St Andrews, who presided at the trial of a popular Protestant preacher, George Wishart. Wishart was found guilty of heresy, and burnt at the stake in March 1546. The Cardinal and his bishops watched from cushioned seats while Wishart's prayers turned to agonised screams.

Two months later, Protestant militants sought their revenge. Disguised as stonemasons, they gained access to St Andrews Castle, but the alarm was raised and Cardinal Beaton barricaded himself in his chamber, where he had spent the night with his concubine, Marion Ogilvy. Not to be thwarted, the gang of killers threatened to set the room ablaze. It may have been one of Beaton's servants who opened the door. What is certain is that Beaton was killed. As he lay dying from numerous sword wounds, his last words were: 'I am a priest ... I am a priest. Fye, fye. All is gone.' The killers then dragged the mutilated body outside and, in front of a large crowd, urinated on the cardinal's face. His naked and mutilated corpse was then hoisted on the fore tower of the castle.

John Knox would justify Beaton's murder in his *History*, writing that the cardinal was slain in vengeance for 'the shedding of the blood of that notable instrument of God, Master George Wishart', and because he was 'an obstinate enemy against Christ Jesus'.

Knox had been Wishart's bodyguard, but was told by the preacher to offer no resistance when he was arrested. It is tempting to suggest that as well as being a bodyguard, Knox was a bit of a thug, but if so, he surely wasn't alone. Hard times breed hard men. These tit-for-tat killings weren't simply about religious intolerance and bigotry. Protestant militants were supported by Anglophile Scots – part of the late Queen Margaret's faction promoting union with England. Cardinal Beaton, as a leading Catholic figure in the country's French faction, had supported Mary of Guise in overturning the Treaty of Greenwich. His killing avenged that, as well as the death of Wishart and other Protestant martyrs.

After the killing, the Protestant militants seized St Andrews Castle. Just a few supporters rallied to their cause, including Knox, who became chaplain to the garrison – the start of his career as a Protestant preacher. Otherwise, the 'Castilians' were left stranded in the Bishop's Castle, set on a rocky headland, for more than a year. Henry was still maintaining a war of attrition in Lothian and around Dundee, well within striking range of St Andrews, but did nothing to relieve the castle's defenders. They had served their purpose in destabilising Scotland's government and, beyond that, he wasn't interested. His brand of Protestantism was poles apart from that being championed by Knox and other radicals. Henry was perhaps the most conservative Protestant of his time. Indeed, it might be suggested that while Henry had rejected the papal authority, he still held to the Catholic faith and made few concessions – he certainly had no time for the teachings of Luther or Calvin.

After 14 months, during which time Francis I of France had died, allowing the accession of his son Henry II, a French fleet bombarded the castle and the garrison finally surrendered to the Earl of Arran, Governor of Scotland. The 'gentlemen' were incarcerated in a French prison, while the 'common' defenders, including Knox, were sent to the galleys – brutal labour intended to break a man's spirit and, in many cases, amounting to a death sentence. Henry couldn't have cared less. In his eyes, extreme Protestants were as much of a threat as those who swore unwavering allegiance to Rome.

A year later, Henry's health was becoming the subject of speculation, to the point where discussions of his impending death had been outlawed. Aged 55, he was grossly fat, tormented by leg ulcers and barely able to walk. Worse, he had long been suffering from syphilis – the explanation for his 'erratic' behaviour and temper, and his incompetence in providing healthy heirs, despite putting the blame on his many wives. This sexually transmitted disease arrived in Europe in 1493, brought back from the New World by sailors who had accompanied Christopher Columbus.

Henry knew that his days were numbered, but had yet to declare who would act as regent during the minority of his nine-year-old son Edward. He favoured Prince Edward's uncle, Edward Seymour, the Earl of Hertford, but the powerful Howard family would resist this appointment. Therefore, the power of the Howards had to be broken. After ten days of investigation into a complex and sometimes baffling range of charges – including one that the Howards had sought to win influence over the king by encouraging Mary Howard of Richmond to become his mistress – Henry Howard, the Earl of Surrey, faced execution and his father, the Duke of Norfolk, was under arrest.

Henry VIII died on January 28 1547, and Edward was crowned in February. Henry's will provided for the country to be governed by a 16-man regency council, named by Henry, during Edward's minority. Hertford immediately set about having himself made Lord Protector by promising titles and lands, confiscated from the Howards, to his supporters on the council.

Henry had made a deathbed wish that the Scots be forced to observe the marriage clause contained in the Treaty of Greenwich. Hertford marched north and engaged the Scots army at Pinkie Cleugh near Musselburgh. Once again, the Scots rescued defeat from the jaws of victory under Arran's inept command. When it looked as if they were assured of success, a lack of discipline in their ranks allowed the English to inflict huge casualties and take many prisoners, though their butchering pursuers killed most out of hand.

After the Scots' defeat, the English controlled much of Lowland Scotland. The savagery displayed by them was, if anything, worse than had been witnessed in Henry's reign. However, they failed to capture the five-year-old Mary Queen of Scots who had been kept in the safety of Stirling Castle then moved to Dumbarton before being sent to France to live with the family of her mother, Mary of Guise.

The Scots queen had been betrothed to England's Prince Edward under the Treaty of Greenwich, but was now promised to the Dauphin Francis, heir to the French king, in a treaty under which France guaranteed to uphold the liberties of Scotland. The price of the Earl of Arran's agreement to this new treaty, as Governor of Scotland, was the French duchy of Chatelherault. Henry's 'rough wooing' of Scotland had failed.

The Seymours had come into favour when Jane produced Henry VIII's one and only son, now King Edward. They had extended that power on Edward's accession. Edward Seymour, Earl of Hertford, became Lord Protector and Duke of Somerset. His younger brother, Thomas Seymour, became Lord Seymour of Sudeley and Lord Admiral.

Thomas was certainly an interesting character. Tall and handsome, intelligent and very ambitious, but jealous of his brother and with a habit of letting his heart rule his head, he set his sights on the late king's widow, Catherine Parr, and won his vain prize. But after the marriage, he turned his attention on his wife's stepdaughter, the young Princess Elizabeth, who was living with the newlyweds in Chelsea.

It may have started out as little more than a mild flirtation, but soon, Seymour took to visiting his stepdaughter in her bedchamber. One contemporary account describes him as arriving 'bare-legged' on at least one occasion – another way of saying without his trousers. There is nothing to substantiate any suggestion that he ever indulged in anything more than 'playful kisses and cuddles', snatched from the young girl. There again, there is nothing to say that he didn't ...

Knowing Catherine Parr's reputation as a pious Protestant, it would be thought that she would have sought to stop her husband's antics with their stepdaughter. In fact, she began to take part in the fun and games, if that is how it can be described. On at least two mornings, she joined her husband in Elizabeth's bedchamber, where they both tickled and fondled the girl. Later, in their garden, their 'games' were continued. Catherine held Elizabeth while Seymour used a knife to cut the girl's dress 'into a hundred pieces'.

Kate Ashley, who had served as Elizabeth's surrogate mother for many years, was outraged and sought to intervene. When she remonstrated with Elizabeth – suggesting that the youngster was not an unwilling participant – the sulking princess simply shrugged off her objections. Kate then challenged Seymour for risking Elizabeth's reputation. He was not amused, swearing angrily at his accuser, and then growling 'I will tell my Lord Protector how I am slandered; and I will not leave off, for I mean no evil.' Catherine Parr gave Kate a more sympathetic hearing and, perhaps fearing that her husband would go too far, she agreed that Elizabeth should be sent to live with Kate's sister Joan and her husband, Sir Anthony Denny.

That might have ended the affair, but Catherine Parr died at Sudeley Castle eight days after giving birth to a baby girl, and just four months after Elizabeth's departure. It was a reflection of the widower's ambition that he chose to maintain the household that had been set up to reflect her status as Queen Dowager. All that was missing was a lady to reap its benefits. Lady Jane Grey, a granddaughter of Henry VIII's sister Mary, Queen Dowager of France, had lived with Catherine Parr in the past. Now she was invited to return, and accepted. There seems to have been some vague understanding that she might marry her cousin, King Edward. Whether this was enough to control Seymour's trouser-dropping habits is not entirely clear.

As for the now 16-year-old Princess Elizabeth, it was noted that she still smiled with pleasure whenever Seymour's name was mentioned. He, in turn, whispered his intention to marry her. Whispered, because he knew that such a proposal might not only prove unpopular, but dangerous. When he made his secret intentions known to Kate Ashley, insisting that they were entirely honourable, she became his ardent supporter. She may have introduced Seymour to Elizabeth's accountant Thomas Parry who certainly described the princess's finances to the prospective husband. Those discussions were sufficiently detailed to suggest that Parry acted with the approval of his employer.

Seymour had kept his late wife's ladies and female servants together after her death. Knowing the character of the man, he may have had personal reasons for doing so, but he now talked of their attending Elizabeth after their marriage. Indeed, the bold Seymour, probably blown up with self-importance, was talking too much, and it finally and inevitably came to the attention of his colleagues on the Privy Council. When John Russell, Earl of Bedford, took Seymour to task on the matter, it degenerated into a terrible row.

As he was making his marriage plans, Seymour was making other moves in royal circles, seeking to steal his brother's influence. As Lord Protector, the Duke of Somerset held the strings of the royal purse, and he held them tight, much to the young King Edward's annoyance. Seymour knew this, and showered money and gifts on Edward, suggesting that a change of government, with him as its head, would be far more beneficent. When Somerset heard what was going on, he had his brother arrested on January 17 1549, and interrogated.

Kate Ashley and Thomas Parry soon followed Seymour to the Tower. Within a couple of days, they spilled the beans about Seymour's intentions. Under more severe questioning, Kate broke down and told all she knew, including the details of Seymour's earlier visits to Elizabeth's bedchamber, and the dress-cutting episode.

Somerset laid the evidence before Princess Elizabeth. She did not panic, being fully aware of the terms of her father's will, and answering as if advised by the leading advocates in the land. She admitted her affection for Seymour, and their 'innocent' romps, but insisted that she would never marry 'neither in England nor out of England, without the consent of the king's majesty, your grace's and the council's.' Previously, in conversations with Kate Ashley and Thomas Parry, she had never gone so far as to admit that she intended to marry Seymour. That apparent vagueness now served her well.

Seeing that Somerset's accusations had run out of steam, Elizabeth went onto the offensive, claiming that scandalmongers were dragging her good name in the dirt. She demanded that rumours that she was with child by Seymour, and being held in the Tower, should be officially repudiated by the council.

Thomas Seymour was beheaded on March 20. The execution was not popular, many recognising that it was simply Somerset's solution to a rival, brother or not, in the power game. Somerset wasted no time, therefore, in prompting Hugh Latimer, the famed Protestant preacher, to blacken Seymour's reputation. According to Latimer, Seymour had been a debaucher of women, an atheist and a traitor. 'He was, I heard say, a covetous man ... a seditious man, a contemner of common prayer. I would there were no more in England. Well he is gone. I would he had left none behind him.'

When told of Latimer's preaching, Elizabeth said little, but probably thought a lot. From that time on, she often displayed contempt for both preachers and puritan piety.

Nobody could have known it at the time, but this was probably as close to love and marriage as Elizabeth ever got. And if they had married, and if they had been blessed with children, then the history of England, Scotland and Britain might have been very different. But there again, history is full of ifs, buts and maybes.

CHAPTER ELEVEN

BLOODY MARY

At the start of 1549, at about the time when Kate Ashley and Thomas Parry were hauled to the Tower, the House of Lords was passing the Act of Uniformity, making the Book of Common Prayer the prescribed liturgy throughout England. Effectively this meant that God would be worshipped throughout the realm using the same form of words and in the native tongue. Its architect was Thomas Cranmer, Archbishop of Canterbury, and it was regarded as a great victory for Protestantism. It was also the first act of parliament in a real sense, arrived at by dignified debate, rather than simply accepting or rejecting the king's will in a shouting match. But however well it was debated, it was not universally accepted.

Trouble erupted in July at Exeter in Devon, where rebels took up arms in protest against the new prayer book. The rebellion then spread to Cornwall, where Cornish speakers objected to the decree that services must now be in English, which they didn't understand. At least they were familiar with church Latin.

Back at Exeter, the rebels surrounded the city, cut its food and water supplies and mounted guns on nearby hillsides from where they could shoot into the city with greater accuracy. Rebel sympathisers among Exeter's leaders and citizens hampered the city's defence, and some plotted to open the gates.

The reaction to the West Country rebellion was cautious, at the start, because the royal troops in the region were heavily outnumbered. Under the command of Lord Russell, they advanced to the Devon village of Clyst St Mary where they defeated and killed almost 2,000 rebels. With his confidence raised, and after another successful engagement at nearby Clyst Heath, Russell was able to raise the siege at Exeter.

Rebel numbers were still formidable, but Russell settled upon a decisive encounter where the rebels had gathered at Sampford Courtenay. The Cornish contingent, spurred along by priests who fought alongside their parishioners, were most courageous and might have had the beating of the royal troops, but many were slaughtered and the rest forced to flee.

Rebellion also flared in Norwich, but for different reasons. There resentment of field enclosures, high rents and the overstocking of common land by greedy gentry drove the rebels led by Robert Ket, a radical landowner. The rebellion quickly spread throughout East Anglia, even as far as Cambridge. Ket's following quickly swelled to an estimated 16,000 men.

Armed with cannons, the rebels bombarded Norwich. When this seemed to be having little effect, they asked for a truce, which was formally denied, but when they stormed the city, it fell very easily. It is probable that many of the defenders, like those in Exeter, were sympathetic to the rebels' cause and simply 'going through the motions' of resistance in order to avoid royal retribution at some later date.

Social problems concerning the divide between the haves and have-nots had long been simmering, so it should have come as no surprise when the pot finally boiled over. The poor had been bearing the burden of inflation, high rents, unemployment and landlessness for too long. William Forrest, a priest from a rural parish, had long seen his parishioners driven from the land by enclosures, or selling their breeding stock to pay punitive rents, and eventually being forced to beg. He saw the empty villages that had once provided the men for English armies that crushed all before them. Now peasant farmers were destitute, beggars lined the roads, and the army relied on foreign mercenaries. Forrest described it in verse.

> The world is changed from that it hath beene,
> Not for the bettre, but for the warsse farre:
> More for a penny we have before seene
> Then nowe for fowre pense, whoe list to compare.
> This suethe the game called makinge or marre,
> Unto the riche it makethe a great deale,
> But much it marrethe to ther Commune weale.

In 1547, a law had been passed providing for vagrants to be whipped and 'run out of town'. If they then failed to return to their parishes and find work, they were to be branded with a V. Persistent offenders were enslaved. If these measures sound draconian, it should be noted that they repealed a law of 1535 imposing the death penalty for long-term offenders. The new law made a clear distinction between those who had no work or could not work, and those who would not work – drawing a distinction between the deserving and undeserving poor. The numbers of the latter, described as 'sturdy beggars' had become so vast, it is said, that they threatened England's social fabric.

State censorship was reinstated in August 1549 – the same month as the rebels' defeat. It had originally been introduced under Henry VIII in 1538 when he ordered that no publication might appear without a royal licence, but had been allowed to lapse under the new regime. Its reinstatement, conducted by the Privy Council, was a reaction to the flood of radical Protestant literature that had appeared since Edward came to the throne. It was becoming clear that while the Reformation had been welcomed by many, there was a significant minority who felt it had not gone far enough in rejecting 'popish notions'.

Edward Seymour, the Duke of Somerset, former Lord Protector and victor over the Scots at Pinkie, had led the Protestant faction that used its influence at court to relax the censorship laws. But while supporting Protestantism was one thing, undermining the throne, as it was now seen, was another matter entirely. With religious and social differences deepening, the duke came under attack. In October, he was taken to the Tower of London, together with many members of his family.

Somerset had been associated throughout with Henry's campaigns in Scotland. At the end of long years of campaigning, most recently to secure Scotland's compliance with the Treaty of Greenwich, England sought to balance her books. Prolonged wars were a very expensive business and, in this case, with the infant Queen Mary of Scots enjoying the sanctuary of France and now promised to the Dauphin, there was little to show for England's investment. Little wonder, then, that Somerset was no longer popular. He faced 29 charges, ranging from ruling without the assent of other councillors to encouraging rebels, and was executed on January 22 1552.

John Dudley, the Earl of Warwick, had played the major role in bringing down the Duke of Somerset, and stepped into the vacuum left by his departure. After four months of intrigue and what amounted to a palace coup, Warwick secured his appointment as Lord President of the Council, and Master of the King's Household.

Warwick was as ruthless as the times demanded. He used the Catholics at court, led by the earls of Southampton and Arundel. After they had served their purpose and Somerset was in the Tower, he cast them aside, exiling them from court. This allowed Warwick to gain favour with the Protestants under Archbishop Cranmer, to the point where he 'ruled' unopposed. The young king was little more than Warwick's puppet.

As well as being ruthless, Warwick was subtle, as he showed in his dealings with William Cecil, brother-in-law of John Cheke, the young king's staunchly Protestant tutor. Cecil had been a follower of the Duke of Somerset, even spending two months in the Tower with him. However, Warwick recognised Cecil's outstanding administrative abilities and Cecil, seeing the wind had changed, confirmed that he would be happy to swap allegiance. And so it was that he was made Secretary of State and a member of the Privy Council, planning to open up trade and abolish monopolies.

Warwick was soon elevated to become the Duke of Northumberland, and adopted hard-line Protestant attitudes. He became closely involved in a dispute between King Edward and his Catholic sister Princess Mary. Edward sent a series of stern letters to Mary, demanding that she conform to the Protestant religion. At the time, her defiance to Edward's demands caused annoyance, but little more. Only time would reveal its full implications. If the new duke had been able to foresee the future, he might have adopted a more conciliatory approach.

Since 1548 the French had been supporting the Scots who, following the Battle of Pinkie, were striving to rid themselves of English occupation. In the years 1548-50 France had made an even greater investment in Scotland than England, including the cost of a chain of sophisticated forts quickly established at Dunbar, Inchkeith, Eyemouth and elsewhere, balancing England's firepower and resources and thus forcing the war into attrition. In the year of 1549 alone, when she had 6,000 troops in Scotland, France's costs were in the region of 2m *livres* or £1m Scots.

The fighting was extended to two fronts when the French attacked and captured English-held Boulogne, leading to the Treaty of Boulogne in which the English agreed to abandon that city, and withdraw from Scotland. England's paymasters were not overly disappointed. The hostilities between England and Scotland had dragged on for some eight years and, while

England enjoyed greater wealth than her northern neighbour, this was balanced by the French investment. The prolonged war had brought England to the verge of bankruptcy.

After 1550, when England decided to cut her losses and concentrate on quelling internal strife, the French could reduce their forces in Scotland. However, they still maintained five garrisons with about 400 men. Like Henry before them, they were keen to establish a 'fifth column' in Scotland. They paid pensions to a number of Scots nobles and clergy. Some, including the Earl of Huntly, were granted full French citizenship.

At the end of the war, King Henry of France had decided to lay on a spectacular celebration at Rouen in Normandy. His guest of honour was Mary of Guise. Recognising this opportunity to display the French court's power and success, she insisted that she was accompanied by a large number of Scottish notables on what has since been called 'the brainwashing expedition'.

The celebrations at Rouen allowed Mary of Guise to be reunited with her now seven-year-old daughter, Mary Queen of Scots, who lived a cosseted life of splendour, her time divided between the Guises's magnificent palaces and the even greater luxuries of the French royal family's almost fairy-tale existence. To seal the Franco-Scottish alliance, it was reaffirmed that the infant queen would marry the Dauphin Francis, the French king's eldest son and heir, who was six. From that moment on, if not before, Mary Queen of Scots, who had been adopted into the French king's household as 'ma fille propre', saw her future in pleasure-loving France rather than the comparatively austere Scotland. She spoke nothing but French, and would have struggled to understand her mother's Scottish companions.

Mother and daughter enjoyed a long and happy year together. This time allowed Mary of Guise to consult with her brothers and others on how best to control rebellious Scotland. She also sought to improve her finances. It is hard to imagine that she relished the prospect of her eventual return to Scotland but duty, as ever, came before personal feelings. She must rule Scotland as best she could, as a caretaker for her daughter and to protect France's expansionist goals.

France's ultimate ambition was revealed when the French king asserted the infant Mary's right to the English throne. By marrying her to their Dauphin, the French hoped to annexe Scotland *and* England. This explains their willingness to buy off the Earl of Arran and the rest. The potential returns on France's investment were too good an opportunity to miss.

In late November, Archbishop Cranmer created the *Second Book of Common Prayer*, committing England to Protestantism. Mass was abolished and replaced with a Communion service, altars were replaced with Communion tables, and the new service was to be celebrated by clergy dressed in simple surplices, rather than rich vestments.

The following month, a royal commission set up by the Duke of Northumberland recommended drastic reform of the royal finances and revenue courts. He was striving to strengthen the royal finances, streamline the exchequer and create a centralised civil service, moving England towards becoming a modern state. Again, he revealed his ability to put the right man in the job, rather than favouring a circle of toadies. Sir Walter Mildmay was one of the best legal minds in the country and it was his mastery of the subject in general, and fiscal policy in particular, that ensured the commission's efficacy. But even Sir Walter couldn't have predicted what would happen next.

Edward VI died of tuberculosis on July 6 1553, aged 15. In his final days, he had been persuaded by the Duke of Northumberland to accept a declaration that the Princesses Mary and Elizabeth were illegitimate – directly contradicting the Second Act of Succession of 1537 which had declared them to be legitimate daughters of Henry VIII. This created an interesting situation, to say the least. Henry's marriage to Catherine of Aragon was legal, in which case Mary was legitimate, or it was not, thus enhancing Elizabeth's status. Equally important, for the purposes of royal succession, it was not necessary that the English monarch's children should be legitimate, but rather that they should be acknowledged, and this Henry had done. In later years, it was Charles II's refusal to formally acknowledge his illegitimate son's status, while giving him a dukedom that was the root cause of Monmouth's Rebellion.

Bearing in mind Henry's acknowledgement of his daughters, it might be asked how Mary and Elizabeth could later be declared illegitimate and unacknowledged. The simple answer was that it was so because King Edward had said it was.

As usual in those days of plots and intrigues, there was a hidden agenda. The Duke of Northumberland had been a witness to Princess Mary's defiance of her brother when he demanded she should renounce Catholicism. Therefore, like all hard-line Protestants, the duke was keen to deny Mary. Nor was he keen to support Elizabeth, albeit that she was a Protestant, because the duke had his own candidate for the throne, significantly his daughter-in-law, Lady Jane Grey, aged 15. Lady Jane was also a Protestant, descended from Henry VIII's sister – the one who exhausted Louis of France – and the duke proclaimed her as queen on July 10, just four days after Edward's death.

The 37-year-old Princess Mary was slower off the mark, but when she arrived in August she was at the head of 10,000 supporters prepared to fight for the throne. When she established herself in Framlingham Castle in Suffolk, the duke set out with an army to engage her forces, and it became clear that he had made a misjudgement. He wasn't popular in the country and had caused further resentment by keeping Edward's death a secret while he endeavoured to rally support for Lady Jane. His soldiers deserted almost as quickly as support for Mary was mounting. The duke was arrested and sent to the Tower where he was to be executed for treason.

In his last moments, the duke decided to employ his silvery tongue in an attempt to gain a last minute pardon. He begged for mercy, pledging allegiance to Queen Mary, renouncing Protestantism and confessing his sins. It didn't save him. His beheading was watched by the terrified Lady Jane, herself a prisoner.

Queen Mary's treatment of the unpopular duke caused little dismay, but many were deeply concerned about the new monarch's religious inclinations and intentions. Following weeks of rumour that she was planning to marry her Catholic cousin, Philip of Spain, a delegation from the House of Commons petitioned her to marry someone in her own realm. They found that she was determined to reject their advice, claiming that she was already half in love with Philip after seeing his portrait. She was desperate for an heir to sustain her Catholic principles – desperately worrying news for all Protestants in England. The queen was talking of giving herself to Philip 'following divine commandment', speaking of her intention to 'love and obey' this foreign king. Having accepted Mary as their queen, her council had little option but to accept this proposed Catholic marriage.

In truth, Mary was hardly likely to produce an heir. This may explain why this ageing queen was still unmarried. In her teens, she had been inspected by French ambassadors when it was proposed that she might marry the dauphin – heir to the French king. They reported back that Mary was too small for her age and physically immature for a betrothal. Furthermore, they expressed doubts as to her ever becoming fertile, which put her out of the running because noble and royal marriages were undertaken with the production of heirs as a priority. Mary suffered menstrual problems throughout her life.

Mary announced her desire to eradicate Protestantism. She dissolved her first parliament after repealing most of Edward's religious legislation. She also took the opportunity to pass an act declaring the marriage of her parents, Henry VIII and Catherine of Aragon, to have been legal, thus emphasising her own legitimacy and denying her half-sister Elizabeth.

England seethed with religious turmoil. Mary had grudgingly agreed in August that Edward's burial could be performed in accordance with Protestant rites, but then stated her resolve that Protestant services would not be legal in future. Her agents were soon busy rounding up leading Protestant churchmen and confining them in the Tower of London, charged with treason or sedition. Among them were the Archbishop of Canterbury, Thomas Cranmer, and three other bishops – Nicholas Ridley, John Hooper and Hugh Latimer.

The almost inevitable Protestant rebellion started at the end of January, led by Sir Thomas Wyatt of Allington in Kent. He was very nearly successful in toppling the Catholic queen from her throne. For a time, London appeared defenceless, but Mary roused the City's government with a moving speech at the Guildhall, reminding them that at her coronation she had been wedded to the realm and its laws. 'On the word of a prince, I cannot tell how naturally the mother loveth the child, for I was never mother of any. But certainly, if a prince and governor may as naturally and earnestly love her subjects, as the mother doth the child, then assure yourselves that I, being your lady and mistress, do as earnestly and tenderly love and favour you.'

Mary went on to make various assurances – most of them lies as it turned out, but they served their purpose. When the rebels arrived at London Bridge, the drawbridge was up. Eventually, they managed to enter the city via the bridge at Kingston, leading to street-to-street fighting in which the queen was finally saved by the heroics of her gentlemen pensioners. Wyatt was led off to the Tower.

Queen Mary's response was to order the execution of the 17-year-old Lady Jane Grey, the guileless focus for the Protestant rebels' cause. She was beheaded on February 12 1554, just hours after being forced to see the still bleeding corpse of her husband, Lord Guildford Dudley, son of the Duke of Somerset. Lady Jane met her death with an unexpected measure of courage and dignity for one so young and obviously terrified. As 'a true Christian woman' she forgave her executioner but begged him to dispatch her quickly. 'Lord, into thy hands I commend my spirit,' were her last words.

Mary heard of a second conspiracy when her agents discovered the secret dealings of various Protestants including Edward Courtenay, the Earl of Devon, who had been named as a prospective husband for Princess Elizabeth. On the same day that Lady Jane was executed, Mary had Elizabeth arrested, giving orders that she should be held in the Tower as a suspected traitor.

Elizabeth was charged with being involved with both Wyatt and Courtenay. It was a close run thing for a time, but nothing was proved or fabricated, despite Sir Thomas being offered a pardon if only he would implicate the princess. He was executed on Tower Green in April, his final speech exonerating the royal prisoner. 'And whereas it is said and whistled abroad that I should accuse my lady Elizabeth's grace and my lord Courtenay, it is not so, good people. For I assure you neither they nor any other now in yonder hold or durance was privy of my rising or commotion before I began. As I have declared no less to the queen's council.'

With his speech finished, Wyatt was handed to the team of executioners. Hanging, drawing and quartering was open to interpretation, and Sir Thomas was lucky that he was beheaded at the start. Then he was gutted, his bowels and organs being burnt on a fire while his body was quartered and prepared for display at Newgate. Ninety of his followers were also executed in Mary's savage reprisals and left on public display in various parts of London – some whole, but others in pieces.

Elizabeth was moved from the Tower, but remained a prisoner at Woodstock for nearly a year. Her popularity and influence in the country probably saved her. Mary had no desire to risk a more serious uprising and Elizabeth was as much a hostage as a prisoner. The execution of Lady Jane Grey had proved what Queen Mary could do, if forced into a corner.

Philip of Spain disembarked amid magnificent celebrations at Winchester in late July. The son of the Holy Roman Emperor Charles V made little effort to speak English, other than to dismiss Mary's courtiers as he led his new wife to the bedchamber, announcing his intention to satisfy Mary's desire for a Catholic son and heir.

Philip had been in England for just over a year when it was discovered that after months of confinement and preparations for a royal birth, the queen was suffering an entirely phantom pregnancy – either that or she had miscarried and could not accept it. One contemporary account, from the Venetian ambassador, suggests, among other things, a strangulation of the womb. Whatever the true diagnosis might have been, Philip decided that he had done as much as could be expected and departed for the Netherlands (which had been granted to him by his father) leaving the grieving queen in his wake. He told her that he would be back in a few weeks, but that extended to months then years.

Mary vented her anguish on the Protestant bishops languishing in the Tower. Nicholas Ridley, the Bishop of London, had been chaplain to Henry VIII and supported Lady Jane Grey on the death of Edward VI. Hugh Latimer, the former Bishop of Worcester, had been a chaplain to Henry's second wife, Anne Boleyn, and had devoted his last 20 years to furthering the Protestant cause. Found guilty of heresy, the bishops burned together outside Balliol College in Oxford. 'We shall this day light such a candle by God's grace in England as, I trust, shall never be put out,' Latimer told Ridley.

Thomas Cranmer, Archbishop of Canterbury, was burnt on the same site five months later, on March 21 1556. His faith had faltered in his final months. Since the burning of his fellow bishops, he had signed seven recantations in an understandable attempt to save himself, but hearing that he would still burn, he retracted them. It is said that when he was taken to the stake, he thrust his right hand into the flames – the one that had signed the recantations – and cried out, 'This hath offended! Oh this unworthy hand!'

The Catholic queen insisted on witnessing the horrible fate of the man who had been the main promoter of Protestantism in her father and brother's reigns. Mary was no shrinking violet when it came to executing those she described as heretics. She never made a secret of her intention to rid England of heresy, and was ready to use all and any means at her disposal.

This is something that modern Christians might find impossible to understand, but it is a fact. Of course, Protestants could be every bit as merciless in their dealings with Catholics. Once again, we see the complex intertwining of politics and religion at a time when religious faith was such that many would willingly kill or die for their beliefs. Three days before Cranmer burned, Mary had ordered the arrest of various nobles after discovering another plot, this one led by the exiled Sir Henry Dudley, to put Elizabeth on the throne.

Cranmer's replacement as Archbishop of Canterbury was a Catholic. The same Cardinal Reginald Pole who had been exiled by Henry VIII more than 20 years earlier, after the king's break with Rome, who had then attempted to rally the Spanish and French kings against Protestant England. He had been made a cardinal in 1536 by Pope Paul III and returned to England in 1554 as papal legate after Mary's coronation, reconciling the Church of England to Rome while, at one and the same time, backing the queen in her persecution of Protestants. Now that England had joined Spain in its war against France, and as the pope was now allied with France, the pope regarded Cardinal Pole's position as untenable and he was recalled to Rome to face heresy charges. Mary intervened, refusing to allow Pole to leave England, or to recognise his replacement, Friar William Peto. A strange situation – the devout Catholic queen resisting papal authority.

To speak of 'Queen Mary' without qualification might have caused confusion in the 1550s. There was Queen Mary of England. Then there was the infant Mary Queen of Scots – still in France and betrothed to the dauphin. And finally there was the Scottish queen's mother, the dowager queen, Mary of Guise, widow of James V.

Mary of Guise replaced the unpredictable Earl of Arran as the regent of Scotland in 1554, but her appointment was not universally popular. She was a Catholic, and from a leading French family. Indeed, one of her brothers commanded the French army and another was a cardinal. So with Catholic Mary on the English throne, many Protestants – both in Scotland and England – were doubly afraid of the growing French influence. They were resentful also of the presence of those French troops who had remained in Scotland after 1550, ostensibly to protect the Scots from the English, but ultimately to protect France's investment regarding the infant Mary Queen of Scots – the vehicle for French designs on both Scotland and England

Talk of pro-English and pro-French factions in Scotland does not deny that most Scots were simply pro-Scottish. This group resented any intrusion in their affairs, be it English, French or whatever, and recognised that Scotland was becoming little more than a French satellite under Mary of Guise's influence. Their resentments were aggravated by a ruling that made it illegal to 'speak evil against the queen's grace and of Frenchmen'. Nationalists united with Protestants and the pro-English faction to ensure the failure of Mary's government to secure a permanent tax to pay for the French army in Scotland, and other defensive measures.

Resistance to taxation had other causes. Quite simply, the people couldn't pay what they didn't have. Throughout the British Isles, the harvest had failed for three consecutive years and prices had risen sharply. In 1556, grain cost twice what it had in 1553, and that at a time when the majority of the population lived at subsistence levels and wage earners reckoned to spend 80 to 90 per cent of their meagre income on food. Many were literally starving to death, or dying of diseases and sicknesses, 'the like whereof has never been known before'.

Matters might have reached a head in December 1557 when a 'Covenant with God' championing Protestantism was heralded in Edinburgh. This attracted only a few signatures, including just five nobles headed by the Earl of Argyll, who pledged themselves to 'forsake and renounce the Congregation of Satan with all the superstition, abomination and idolatry thereof'.

The apparent lack of support wasn't enough to reassure the dowager Mary of Guise, however, who employed the French troops to persecute Protestants – just what the 'soft-liners' who abstained from signing the covenant had been hoping to avoid. In 1558, the authorities executed 80-year-old Walter Myln, a parish priest and teacher from Lunan near Montrose, burning him at the stake in St Andrews. With another martyr to the Protestant cause, serious rioting broke out on the streets of Edinburgh.

Mary Queen of Scots married the French Dauphin Francis, heir to the French throne, in Notre Dame Cathedral on April 24 1558. The 15-year-old Mary was resplendent in lily-white, sumptuous silk robes. The rubies, pearls and sapphires in her gold crown surrounded an enormous diamond, said to be worth 500,000 crowns. The beautiful Mary grabbed the guests' attention. The 14-year-old Dauphin, who was widely described as ugly, dull and stunted in height, was virtually ignored.

Even by the standards of the time, the royal couple were very young. But there were compelling reasons to hurry matters along, as explained in a report from Giacomo Sorenzo, the Venetian ambassador. The French were keen to ensure the involvement of Scotland's army against England in an imminent military campaign. In return, the powerful Guises needed assurance that the marriage would not be called off if, as was the common custom, any subsequent peace treaty with the English included a marriage alliance for the dauphin with an English bride. Now that he was married to Mary, this was no longer a possibility.

As well as satisfying these considerations, the marriage treaty included an infamous clause granting the crown matrimonial to Francis in the event of Mary's death. In other words, whether Mary lived or not, Francis would remain Scotland's king, ruling in his own right if Mary predeceased him. Therefore, in the subsequent generation, the successor to the Scottish throne would be one and the same as the successor to France. Here was the full price of France's support. It was just 26 years since Brittany had been annexed to the French crown as a dukedom, using similar means. This clause should have remained secret, but news of its content leaked in Scotland, heightening the crisis facing Mary of Guise's regency.

There were, in fact, two marriage treaties – one open and one secret. Mary Queen of Scots put her signature to both. The second, secret treaty not only confirmed the crown matrimonial in regard to Scotland, but also in regard to Mary's rights to the throne of England as a descendant of Henry VII. While France agreed to defend Scotland, all that country's revenues would be made over to the king of France and his successors until the cost of such defence was fully reimbursed. Finally, there was a curious clause renouncing in anticipation any agreement that Mary might enter which could interfere with these arrangements. There was no going back.

By signing this document, Mary was effectively handing Scotland to France. In her defence, it has been said that Mary, at 15, failed to recognise the significance of the secret document. There again, as the queen of Scotland and future queen of France, what she gave with one hand, she took back with the other. By now, Mary was more French than Scottish. She knew from her mother that it would be virtually impossible to rule Scotland without France's support. At a personal level, Mary must have felt that she had much to gain and little to lose by signing the document – and Mary tended to see everything at a personal level.

England's people had suffered the same natural disasters as the Scots in the mid-1550s – famine and disease taking a heavy toll. What they described as hot, burning fevers or 'the shivering sickness' was influenza. Then as now, it was particularly lethal to the elderly and thousands died, including many politicians and churchmen. To add to the country's woes, Mary's Spanish husband had returned, and he wasn't bearing gifts.

Holy Roman Emperor Charles V had abdicated at the start of 1556. His son Ferdinand succeeded as Emperor, but Ferdinand's brother Philip, Mary of England's husband, ruled Spain and the Netherlands. These territories brought great wealth, but Philip had been provoked into a war against Pope Paul IV and France that proved an expensive business. He was virtually bankrupt when he returned to England in March 1557, seeking financial support.

Queen Mary might have kept England out of Philip's war, but in June 1557 she was provoked when a disaffected aristocrat, Thomas Stafford, raided Scarborough Castle supported by French troops. Declaring war on France – and therefore the pope – was another sad irony for this devout Catholic queen, and it did not go well for her. The English garrison at Calais fell to French forces led by the Duke of Guise at the start of 1558.

Following the defeat at Calais and fearing invasion, an act was passed at Westminster to improve England's defence forces. The reforms obliged all sections of society to provide men, horses and equipment. This act was forged out of military necessity but it would have political consequences, accelerating a shift in leadership away from the aristocracy to the gentry – from the House of Lords to the Commons.

The loss of Calais was a bitter blow to Mary and, after suffering another phantom pregnancy, her health failed. She died on November 17 1558 – just hours before Cardinal Reginald Pole. It is reported that in her last hours she said, 'When I am dead and opened they shall find Calais engraved in my heart.'

Queen Mary's persecution of Protestants in England, with Pole's support, had brought about the deaths of hundreds of men and women. Little wonder that she is remembered as 'Bloody Mary'. She died unloved and alone, knowing that despite her desire to produce a Catholic heir, her Protestant half-sister, Elizabeth, would probably succeed her.

❧ CHAPTER TWELVE ❧

SEEDS OF REVOLT

Following the death of 'Bloody Mary' in 1558, there were two main claimants to the English throne. They were Princess Elizabeth of England and Mary Queen of Scots. Choosing between these two would divide the country.

Princess Elizabeth was the daughter of Henry VIII and Anne Boleyn and half-sister to the two previous monarchs, Mary and Edward. However, she was a Protestant and those who wished to further the Catholic reclamation of England resurrected the rumour that Henry wasn't Elizabeth's father – adding that even if he was, his marriage to Catherine of Aragon was still valid when he married Anne. Mary Queen of Scots, on the other hand was a legitimate granddaughter of Henry VIII's sister Margaret Tudor (who had married James IV of Scotland in 1503). It could also have been argued that it had been Henry VIII's stated will that Mary should rule in England, though it would have been as the wife of Prince Edward under the terms of the Treaty of Greenwich.

Princess Elizabeth's supporters weren't simply seeking to ensure that their monarch would be of the Protestant faith. Nationalistic Englishmen didn't want a Scot on their throne, whatever her connections. Others were aware that Scots had long been voicing their fear that under the influence of Mary's mother, Mary of Guise, Scotland was fast becoming little more than a French province. Then there was the matter of the 'crown matrimonial' clause in Francis and Mary's marriage treaty – in accepting Mary, England would take her husband into the bargain who, as Dauphin, was heir to the French throne. For many, the choice between Elizabeth and Mary wasn't simply a matter of legal nicety or religious allegiance, but rather about maintaining English sovereignty or suffering the French yoke. At that level, there wasn't a contest.

Within two months of Elizabeth's accession, the French laid their cards on the table. Francis and Mary, King and Queen of Scotland and the future King and Queen of France, assumed the title of King and Queen of England and Ireland. An attempt at colonisation through the back door, perhaps, but colonisation nevertheless.

The fine balances between religion, politics, nationalism and self-interest were displayed in a marriage proposal to Elizabeth from King Philip of Spain, the Catholic widower of the late Queen Mary, who sought to maintain England's support in his war with France – the common enemy as he saw it. It has been suggested that Philip formed affection for Elizabeth at an earlier date, preferring his lithe sister-in-law to his demanding but dowdy wife. What is certain is that Philip knew that by marrying Elizabeth, and producing an heir, he would effectively deny the English succession to Mary Queen of Scots who, already betrothed to the Dauphin, would have sided with France against the Habsburgs. Also, by avoiding an Anglo-Scots-French alliance that would have dominated the English Channel, Philip would have ensured the shipping lanes stayed open for craft sailing between Spain and the Netherlands.

Elizabeth declined Philip's offer, and was crowned at Westminster Abbey on January 15 1559. There was the traditional splendour, but the Gospel and Epistle were said in English as well as Latin. The lack of Catholic ritual emphasised the new queen's Protestantism.

The following month, parliament passed the Acts of Supremacy and Uniformity, renouncing papal jurisdiction over England, but these acts barely scraped through the House of Lords, and would have been defeated if it had not been for the absence of three leading Catholic churchmen (two were in prison). The acts in their original form sought to restore the religious situation that existed immediately prior to the death of Edward VI, but a growing body of conservative opinion, and those wearied by the swings of the religious pendulum, demanded concessions. Most significant, perhaps, was a concession concerning the Protestant Communion service, allowing religious conservatives to regard the bread and wine as containing the actual presence of Christ's body and blood. Elizabeth's title was to be Supreme Governor rather than Supreme Head of the Church.

Meanwhile, back in Scotland, although Protestants remained a minority in the country they now dominated the Scots parliament. They ordered friars to vacate their premises, to be used in future by the sick and poor. In response, Mary of Guise announced her determination to stamp out Protestantism. And in response to that response, the burgh of Ayr outlawed the Catholic mass. Finally, the regent lost her patience and issued a summons for various Protestant preachers to appear before her.

Numerous references have been made to the Reformation with its champions and hard-line opponents. It was a long drawn-out affair affecting all aspects of life, human endeavour and devotion – not only in Scotland and England but also throughout Western Christendom.

Any study of its events and influences must be approached with infinite caution. Its history is riddled with suspect interpretations, misinformation and downright lies. What is launched as propaganda may be accepted as fact through repetition. A glorious renaissance for some was an unmitigated disaster to others. One person's meat is another person's poison.

The Reformation resulted in the establishment of the Protestant Churches, thus ending the totalitarian, ecclesiastical supremacy of the pope in Western Christendom. It started in the early 16th century, but its causes had existed for centuries. Those causes were not founded in religious differences alone, but included complex political, economic and cultural elements, all nurturing grievances that had been smouldering since the end of the first millennium.

In 962 Otto I revived the Holy Roman Empire, thus initiating a continuous struggle between the spiritual and temporal – generations of popes and emperors who sought to attain supremacy. The popes argued that they had an all-embracing role to play, and this was God's will. At the start, in promoting the establishment of the empire, they had sought to create a powerful secular deputy to command Christendom in their name, and according to their instructions. Instead, they found they had created a rival. A succession of elected emperors argued that the papacy should limit itself to strictly religious matters.

By the end of the 13th century, and despite its democratic beginnings, the empire had become virtually hereditary among the Habsburgs. Centuries of antagonism were fuelled by the rise of German nationalist sentiments in the 14th and 15th centuries. In other regions of Western Christendom, there was just as much resentment against papal taxation and the assumption of supremacy by officials of a distant authority.

In England, the first moves toward independence from papal jurisdiction were witnessed long before Henry VIII sought to rid himself of an unwanted wife. Statutes enacted in the 13th and 14th centuries limited the powers of the church to seize land, make ecclesiastical appointments without reference to the civil powers and to retain absolute judicial authority. The reformer John Wycliff attacked the papacy itself, highlighting the corruptions inherent in the sale of indulgences and the appointment of priests who were often of limited intellect and low morals – feasting while their parishioners starved and openly flaunting their mistresses despite their vows of chastity. The Lollards sought to neuter what they saw as a corrupt priesthood that employed itself as a barrier between the people and their creator. They translated the Bible into English and delivered sermons in the vernacular, rather than Latin.

Wycliff's teachings were taken up in Continental Europe, notably by the Bohemian reformer Jan Hus. His execution as a heretic in 1415, allied to a popular Bohemian nationalist movement, prompted the Hussite Wars. This combination of religious dissatisfaction and nationalist fervour threatened both the Roman Catholic Church and the Holy Roman Empire, prompting the pope and emperor to set aside their differences. Though the suppression of Bohemia by their combined forces affected a temporary cure of the symptoms of a national ill, it did nothing to treat its causes.

Whatever the intentions of the papacy may have been, it was judged at local and national levels by the behaviour of its clerics and officials. It has been estimated that the church held between one-fifth to one-third of the lands of Europe, and these vast tax-free possessions incited as much envy and resentment among land-hungry peasants as they did among kings and nobles. A greedy, ignorant and immoral hierarchy demanded much of the produce of these vast estates in rents, with little concern for its producers.

The assumed superiority of the Catholic Church – achieved through a monopoly on learning and the championing of mysteries – was further questioned at the start of the 15th century by those who revived classical learning in Italy. That time is remembered as the early Renaissance. It fostered Humanism, based on sceptical enquiry and thus encouraging an intellectual opposition to the apparently narrow-minded teachings of the church. Scholars such as Lorenzo Valla appraised the accepted translations of the Bible, and found them wanting. 'Not only has no one spoken Latin correctly for many centuries,' Valla stated 'but no one has even understood it properly when reading it ...'

That was one possibility. The other was that they understood it well enough, but sought to ignore some parts of it, and massage others, to serve their own ends. Valla and others of the Renaissance intellectuals seemed to be suggesting that many of the church's traditions were little more than self-serving dogma, foisted on an uneducated population.

The intellectual sceptics were not confined to Italy. England had the likes of John Colet and Sir Thomas More; Desiderius Erasmus operated in the Netherlands, Johann Reuchlin in Germany, and so on. Together, they put the scriptures and church practices under the microscope. Their studies paved the way for better-remembered reformers – principally Luther and Calvin – to claim the Bible rather than the Church as the source of all religious authority.

The Catholic Church reacted to the intellectual movement like a strict father faced with a wilful child. It is so, because we say it is, and who are you to question it? They saw no room for compromise, and their public stance was one of entrenchment.

Martin Luther, a German Augustinian friar, published his theses in 1517 challenging the theory and practice of indulgences – selling pardons for sin – as had John Wycliff. The papal authorities were intensely irritated with Luther's criticism. At that time they were actively promoting such sales in order to pay off the debts of Pope Leo X. They ordered Luther to retract and submit to church authority, or face excommunication.

Luther's teachings were seen to be promoting social as well as religious revolution at a time when German peasants were already discontent due to an agricultural recession, so the Holy Roman Empire became involved. Charles V, the German princes and ecclesiastics assembled in 1521 at the Diet of Worms, and Luther was again ordered to recant. He refused, was declared an outlaw, and went into hiding for a year during which he concentrated on writing pamphlets expounding his theories. The printing press proved mightier than the sword – or imperial edicts, which sought but failed to prohibit the sale of Luther's work. Mass-produced, they were openly sold, widely popular and quickly converted the great German cities to Luther's way of thinking.

Despite assertions to the contrary, Luther's message was spiritual. He proclaimed a doctrine of 'justification by faith alone' and 'the priesthood of all believers'. Religious observance in itself would not bring salvation, he said. A man was justified by his belief in the redemptive power of Jesus Christ alone. And every man had direct access to God and the truth of the Gospels – suggesting that the hierarchy of the Catholic Church was an irrelevance to spiritual health.

Luther saw himself as a reformer, but was regarded by many as a revolutionary in an increasingly divided Germany. The explanation is that his message was hijacked. Some who witnessed Luther's popularity saw an opportunity to harness his message to their agenda for social and political reform, and ultimately a class revolution.

The emperor felt ever more threatened by the prospect of social and political change, and so maintained his alliance with the Catholic Church in order to preserve the traditional order. However, the North German princes actively supported Lutheranism's spiritual message with its implied independence from Catholic control, as did the commercial classes and peasantry, though perhaps for different reasons. Many members of the lower Catholic clergy supported Luther and matters came to a head in 1524 with the outbreak of the Peasants' War.

Luther was against this violence, believing that its instigators were simply seeking to better their economic lot – a reduction in rents and services – while hiding behind a smokescreen of religious conviction. Though he urged the landlords to satisfy their claims, he made his feelings known in a pamphlet entitled *Against the Murdering, Thieving Hordes of Peasants*. The peasants were defeated in 1525, but the matter was not settled.

The word Protestant arose out of the failure of an agreement reached at the Diet of Speyer in 1526. The agreement was that those German princes wishing to practice Lutheranism should be free to do so, while others could stick with the traditional faith – some measure of religious tolerance, even if it was left to the princes rather than the people to decide the fashion of their worship. The failure came three years later at a second Diet of Speyer. One version has it that the Roman Catholic majority abrogated the agreement, seeking to impose Catholicism on all states irrespective of the wishes of their princes and people, causing the Lutheran minority to protest, and thus be known as 'Protestants'. Another version has it that the agreement was that individuals would be free to worship as they chose, and that it was the Lutherans who objected to this, protesting that they would not tolerate Catholics. The arguments and accusations flew back and forth, then as now.

In the next decade, Emperor Charles V was involved in wars with the Turks and France, giving the Protestant states an opportunity to flourish. By 1546, however, the emperor was free to turn his attention to his own backyard. Maintaining his alliance with the pope, and aided by Duke Maurice of Saxony, he waged war on the Schmalkaldic League of Protestant princes. Despite a promising start to the campaign, Duke Maurice decided to swap sides and Charles had little option but to make peace.

The terms of the Peace of Augsburg of 1555 stated that the rulers of the 300 or so German states could choose between Lutheranism or Roman Catholicism, and enforce that faith upon their subjects – again, religious tolerance for the princes, but not for their people. Whatever the rights and wrongs, one thing was certain. The unity of a single Christian authority and community in Western Europe had been effectively destroyed.

In the Scandinavian countries, reformation was achieved with little opposition. Not so in Switzerland, however, where the country was split. The commercial classes and town councils turned to Lutheranism as an expression of their independence as well as an expression of religious belief. In Zurich, the town council supported and made legal, at a civil level, the burning of religious relics. Priests and monks were released from their vows of celibacy and the Mass was replaced by a simpler communion service. These moves were far from popular with the conservative peasantry whose allegiance remained with the Catholic Church. Fighting broke out on at least two occasions, but peace was finally agreed with each canton allowed to choose its own religion.

Religious reform in Switzerland would have an important bearing on events throughout the British Isles, and it was in Switzerland that the brand of Protestantism known as Calvinism – which was finally accepted in Scotland – was developed. Calvin was a French Protestant theologian who fled intolerance in his own country to live in the newly-independent Protestant republic of Geneva. It was he, above all others, who introduced the notion of 'the God-fearing Christian' by developing a strict moral code to be enforced by democratically elected pastors and members of the church. The dress and personal behaviour of citizens was prescribed to the minutest detail. Recreations such as dancing and card playing were forbidden. Under this strict regime – effectively a Puritan theocracy – nonconformists were persecuted or put to death.

As the new faith centred on personal study of the Bible – reflecting Luther's message that every man was his own priest, requiring direct access to the Gospels – all Geneva's citizens were provided with a rudimentary education. In 1559, Calvin founded a university in Geneva for educating and training Protestant pastors and teachers who subsequently imposed a Calvinistic stamp on the theology and organisation of the Protestant faith throughout Western Europe.

In France, reformers had translated the New Testament from Latin into French in 1523. At first, their work was tolerated or even encouraged by the church and state, but as the more radical doctrines of Calvin's disciples began to filter through, there was a reaction to the perceived threat and the reformers were persecuted. Many fled to Geneva where they came directly under Calvin's influence. He trained more than 120 of them as pastors before they returned to France to champion the Protestant cause and establish an active Protestant church. Its members were known as Huguenots. Efforts were made to suppress them, but their numbers rapidly expanded until they were perhaps a tenth of the population. By 1561 there were more than 2,000 Calvinistic churches in France, and confrontation between the old and new seemed practically inevitable.

The situation in the Netherlands was as complicated as anywhere else. The territory was part of the Holy Roman Empire and ruled by Spanish overlords. Therefore, when the people embraced Lutheranism, it was as much an expression of nationalist fervour against the occupying forces of Catholic Spain as an objection to the Catholic Church. Emperor Charles V sought to suppress the political and religious upheaval by public burnings of Luther's books, and the establishment of the Inquisition in 1522. However, the people of the northern provinces, known as Holland, proved very determined. Their struggle to establish an independent Protestant nation would continue into the middle of the 17th century.

Holland was not alone in producing determined Protestants. One of the most determined was the Scotsman John Knox, and for this he is remembered by some as something of a national hero. But not by all ... Knox is explained by some as a passionate reformer who had no alternative but to resort to extreme measures. Others say that he was a vindictive psychopath who employed all and any means, necessary or otherwise, to achieve his goals. There can be no argument that he was an ardent Calvinist, but can a man who openly incites religious intolerance and persecution, and apparently gloats over the violent deaths of his opponents, be described as a good Christian?

It has been said that in order to understand Scotland, one must understand John Knox. And at the risk of repetition, he demands a close inspection. His influence on events in the decades leading up to the union of the crowns cannot be overstated. It could be said that it was Knox, acting as the Protestants' enforcer, who ensured a Protestant king on a Protestant throne.

In Scotland, as in other countries, the causes of the Reformation were not founded in religious differences alone, but included complex political, economic and cultural elements. The commercial classes and many of the nobility were already active in furthering the Reformation for political and religious ends, long before Knox barnstormed onto the scene. Early religious reforms in Scotland had followed the Lutheran model, but the revolution brought about under Knox's leadership was firmly Calvinistic. It was Knox who persuaded the Scottish Parliament to adopt a confession of faith and book of discipline modelled on those used in Geneva, thus introducing a stern, Puritanical theocracy. Out of this, the Parliament subsequently created the Scottish Presbyterian church, governed by a general assembly and local kirk sessions.

Knox's origins are not entirely clear. He was born in Haddington, but nobody is sure when. Suggestions range from 1505 to 1515. Nor is anybody certain as to his father's occupation, though it is known that his mother was a Sinclair. Glasgow and St Andrews universities both claim him among their *alma mater*, but there is little evidence that he received any formal education after his days at Haddington burgh school. In terms of theology, law and other matters, he may have been self-taught.

According to his own account of his life, he was raised a Catholic and became a priest. 'One of Baal's shaven sort,' as he described it. But nothing is known of any ecclesiastical career, and it is widely assumed that it was over almost before it began. We know that in 1540 he was engaged as a private tutor to various children, and that he continued in this employment for some years.

At that time, the famed exponent of Protestant doctrines in Scotland was

George Wishart who, recently returned from Germany, used Haddington as his main base while preaching throughout the Lowlands. He found a devoted disciple in Knox, and a man who knew how to handle himself. In those troubled times, Wishart needed a bodyguard, and Knox fulfilled that role.

Wishart's most dangerous opponent was Cardinal Beaton, the great champion of the Catholic cause. Wishart, in turn, was involved in the intrigues of Scottish Protestants and Henry VIII of England to kidnap or murder the cardinal. Knox was with Wishart, and carried a double-handed sword, when Wishart was arrested in January 1546. However, Wishart had ordered Knox not to offer any resistance.

Wishart was tried, sentenced and burned at St Andrews in March. Just two months later, Beaton was murdered at the same place. It is hard to believe that Wishart's frustrated bodyguard took no part in planning this revenge for his mentor's death. Certainly, he applauded the assassination and later described the deed with a gleeful and mocking levity.

Following his capture by French forces at St Andrews, along with Beaton's assassins and their supporters, his time on the galleys must have been hard, but Knox had an indomitable spirit. His captivity was not so rigorous as to prevent him from writing a theological treatise and preaching to his fellow prisoners. Surprisingly, perhaps, he was released from captivity in 1549. The short duration of his sentence seems to suggest that the Catholic authorities in Scotland and France didn't see him as much of a threat. If so, they were very much mistaken ...

After his release, Knox decided to spend time in newly-reformed Protestant England, rather than risk fresh arrest in still Catholic Scotland. He was a licensed preacher at Berwick for two years, and was then appointed a royal chaplain and transferred to Newcastle where, after the death of Henry VIII, he preached before the young King Edward on at least two occasions. In 1552, he was nominated to the Bishopric of Rochester, which he refused, declining also a benefice in the city of London. In later years, he stated that he had refused these preferments because he thought the Anglican Church too favourable to Roman doctrine, and that he could not bring himself to kneel at the communion service.

When Protestant King Edward died in July 1553, and Catholic Queen Mary came to the English throne, Knox continued his preaching for a time, but was careful not to cause offence to the new sovereign, for whom he even published a devout prayer. It was at about this time that Knox married Marjorie Bowes. She was younger than him – young enough to have been his daughter, some said.

When the queen stepped up her persecution of Protestants in 1554, Knox settled on discretion rather than valour or marital ties. He left his young wife and sought refuge in Dieppe. From there he travelled to Geneva, partly to consult Calvin and other divines as to the lawfulness and expediency of resisting the rule of Mary Tudor in England and Mary of Guise in Scotland. It is said that he got little satisfaction from his advisers and, in September 1554, he accepted the post of chaplain to the English Protestants at Frankfurt. There his strengthening Puritanism revolted against the use of King Edward's prayer book and the Anglican ceremonial, and he was in dispute with a number of his congregation. Finally, he was accused of comparing the Emperor Charles to Nero in a published tract, and was ordered by the authorities to leave Frankfurt. He returned to Geneva where he ministered for a time to the English congregation.

In August 1555, Knox received an urgent summons from his mother-in-law, causing him to return to Berwick, but 'most contrarious to mine own judgement'. However, slipping over the border into Scotland, Knox was to be pleasantly surprised at what he found. The new Protestant doctrines had made headway during his absence, and he found himself able to preach both in public and in the country houses of many nobles and gentry. At a historic supper, given by his friend Erskine of Dun, it was formally decided that no Protestant could attend Mass; and the external separation of the party from Catholic practice, as well as doctrine, thus became complete.

Knox boldly proclaimed that adherents to the old faith were as truly idolaters as the Jews who sacrificed their children to Moloch, and that the extermination of idolaters was the clear duty of Christian princes and magistrates, and, failing them, of all individual believers – by which he meant Protestants. On the dubious advice of two of his noble supporters, he wrote to the queen regent. His tone swung from conciliatory to confrontational. He was supplicatory when petitioning for toleration for his coreligionists, but then abusive of Catholics and their beliefs, even going so far as to threaten the regent with 'torment and pain everlasting', if she did not act on his advice.

The queen regent may have sought advice about how best to respond to Knox's letter. It is said that he resented her lack of reply, at least at first, then once again he put discretion before valour and returned to Geneva with his wife and mother. In fact, he was none too soon in making his departure. On the day that he sailed, he was cited to appear in Edinburgh, where he was condemned and outlawed in his absence as contumacious (stubbornly disobedient) and publicly burnt in effigy.

Back in Geneva, Knox embraced Calvin's autocratic ideas of church discipline – a repressive regime that he was subsequently to introduce into Scotland. And with Knox able to spend more time with his young wife, they produced two sons, Nathaniel and Eleazar.

Glencairn and others tried to persuade Knox to return to Scotland in 1557, arguing that persecution was diminishing, and the Protestant cause needed a champion. However, his confidence seemed to evaporate at Dieppe where he halted his journey, ministering for a time to the Dieppe Protestants before turning tail and heading back to the comparative safety of Geneva.

Some have chosen to question Knox's readiness to disappear at this and other times. Others might argue that any fool can get himself killed, and that while martyrdom had been a tradition of the Christian faith since the Cross, it is best avoided whenever possible. Indeed, to actively seek martyrdom, or to do little or nothing to avoid it, might be considered tantamount to suicide. Knox believed that there was much of God's work to be done, and he was the man to do it. Unlike his mentor Wishart, Knox wasn't the sort of man to place his head in the lion's mouth.

During 1558 his pen was constantly busy: he published his earlier letter to the queen regent with supporting comments, and his famous *First Blast of the Trumpet against the Monstrous Regiment of Women*, aimed at Mary Tudor, Mary of Guise, Catherine de Medici, and the youthful Queen Mary of Scots, who had just married the French Dauphin. In other writings he reiterated his inflammatory view that every Protestant had a right to slaughter every Catholic, if he got an opportunity. In a *Brief Exhortation to England* he insisted on the expulsion of all the 'dregs of Popery' and the introduction of the full church discipline of Calvin and Geneva.

❦ CHAPTER THIRTEEN ❦

PAPIST AND PURITAN

In the first weeks of 1559, following the death of Catholic Queen Mary of England who was to be succeeded by her Protestant sister Elizabeth, Knox deemed it opportune to return home. Having been refused a safe-conduct through England, he sailed from Dieppe to Leith, arriving on May 2. He had heard by letter that the Scottish Protestants were no longer in any serious danger. The queen regent was suffering a deadly illness, and had neither the power nor the will to suppress the Protestant party in Scotland, which was growing daily in power and influence. St Giles's Cathedral in Edinburgh had been the scene of a riot, followed by the flight of the Catholic clergy. The Lords of the Congregation – those nobles who had converted to Protestantism and were taking a leading role – were practically in arms against the regent. Knox, who had so carefully avoided martyrdom while others perished, was suddenly full of fight and courage.

Soon after his return to Scotland, Knox was in the fortified town of Perth where he preached an inflammatory sermon in support of the Protestant preachers who had defied the regent's summons. A riot ensued, in which the monasteries of the Black Friars, Grey Friars and Carthusians were razed. Control of the town was seized, and the rioting transformed into a rebellion with the arrival of the Earl of Glencairn and armed forces from the west.

Knox moved on to St Andrews, accompanied by a retinue of friends and bodyguards. Once again he preached, and once again a mob was incited to sack and pillage. The wrecking of other great abbeys, including Scone and Lindores, followed. Knox and his band of followers, now describing themselves as the Congregation, seized Stirling and then marched to Edinburgh where the devastation of churches and monasteries was repeated.

The regent had retreated to Dunbar but in July, and with the promise of French troops to support their efforts, the regent, her advisers and troops marched upon Edinburgh in an attempt to drive out the Congregation before it could gather any more forces. The opposing sides came to terms and decided that the capital was to be free to choose its own religion. The regent, who believed that the majority of citizens were not in favour of the new doctrines, accepted this. The Congregation, who left preachers in possession of the churches and retired to Stirling, openly broke this and many other points of the agreement.

By abandoning Edinburgh, the Protestants bought some time for themselves. The Lords of the Congregation were calling the shots, though they remained shadowy figures, and they used the time to seek aid from Protestant England. Although so many of their number were affirmed nationalists, they determined to appeal to Queen Elizabeth, and Knox was ordered to seek an interview with her most powerful minister, Robert Cecil. Knox's first action was to write to Elizabeth, more or less apologising for his *Monstrous Blast*.

Knox sailed from Fife, and later returned to Stirling with letters from Cecil, who seemed more or less favourable to the requests of the Congregation for help. The master of intrigue was cleverly indefinite in his terms, offering little more than a definite maybe. It was enough. The Protestants returned to Edinburgh and, on July 7, Knox was appointed Minister of St Giles's. Mary of Guise agreed to an armistice and retreated into Leith, Edinburgh's seaport, which was now the only part of Scotland where her rule prevailed. The Lords of the Congregation then suspended her from the regency – a measure of their power. With the Protestants in Edinburgh, but the regent and her forces in neighbouring Leith, there was a stalemate between the antagonists.

Considering the strength of feeling expressed in his sermons, and his ability (and willingness) to whip a mob into a violent frenzy, Knox made what might seem like an excuse for himself and his followers. 'We meane no tumult, no alteratioun of authorities, but onlie the reformation of religioun, and suppressing of idolatrie,' he wrote to one of his female followers in Geneva. And yet, at the time he wrote those words, Knox was inciting violent revolt against the 'authoritie' of the regent of the realm, with the professed desire of preventing the lawful queen, Mary Stuart, from enjoying her hereditary throne.

Elizabeth was wary of being seen to support the Protestants in Scotland, but provided some money and munitions. Beyond that, she would not go. In April, she had signed the Treaty of Cateau-Cambresis, bringing a peace between England and France too valuable to risk on the throw of a Scottish dice – at least, not at that moment.

Mary of Guise was not abandoned. French reinforcements arrived in August to help with the fortification and defence of Leith and when the rebels finally attacked in November, the port's defenders were ready for them. The 'Army of the Congregation' was beaten off and forced to retreat in disarray to Stirling, hotly followed by French troops who occupied the town, drove out the rebels, and chased them into Fife.

With the Army of the Congregation on the verge of annihilation, Elizabeth finally set aside discretion. An English Fleet commanded by Admiral Winter arrived off Fife in January 1560, and the French abandoned the area. A month later, Scottish Protestants led by the Lords of the Congregation and Queen Elizabeth of England signed the Treaty of Berwick, in which Elizabeth agreed to supply military aid against the French – the same French who would have supported an invasion of England in support of Catholic Mary Queen of Scots – now queen of France, against Protestant Elizabeth.

England's queen was still young, but she already knew not to place too much faith in treaties and alliances. She would have known that the French would break the Treaty of Cateau-Cambresis whenever it was convenient to do so, just as she might ignore the Treaty of Berwick. Elizabeth's signature on the Berwick document says more about her need to reduce a threat than about any desire to promote a cause.

Mary of Guise died in June. One month later, the Treaty of Edinburgh was signed, ending the war in Scotland. England and France were to withdraw their troops and let the Scots settle their own future – including religion – as long as Dauphin Francis and his wife, Mary Queen of Scots, approved it. In the meantime, the victorious Lords of the Congregation would set up a provisional government. The Congregation held a thanksgiving service at St Giles's. Knox took centre stage.

Elizabeth's reward for her involvement was that the treaty stated Mary Queen of Scots would effectively recognise Elizabeth as Queen of England, and renounce her own claim to that throne. However, Mary was in France and did not ratify the treaty. Nor did she ratify the enactments of the Reformation Parliament.

Scotland's provisional government banned the Latin Mass, opting for Calvinism in the Geneva form. As the sovereign was not represented, it was in fact not a parliament at all, but an assembly. This did not stop them adopting the new Confession of Faith, drawn up by Knox, abolishing the authority of the pope and forbidding the celebration of Mass – the penalty for the third offence being death. The formality of asking the young queen to ratify these enactments was gone through; but Knox said that such ratification was 'a mere Inglorious vane ceremony,' and therefore unnecessary.

The Catholic Church of Scotland was extinct, as far as human power could extinguish it, and the Protestant religion officially established. This despite the fact that the majority of the Scottish people still adhered to the Catholic faith.

The new Protestant church approved *The First Book of Discipline*, essentially a plan for the future of the church, drafted by John Knox. One of its major achievements was its influence on education, linking it to religion and establishing Scotland as a front-runner in this field.

'Seeing that God hath determined that his Church here in earth shall be taught not by angels but by men ... of necessity it is that your Honours be most careful for the virtuous education and godly upbringing of the youth of this realm ... Of necessity therefore we judge it that every several church have a schoolroom appointed, such a one as able, as least, to teach Grammar, and the Latin tongue, if the town be of any reputation.'

The move to a reformed faith for Scotland was uncompromising, though the Protestants remained a minority, concentrated in relatively few localities, and were faced with strong opposition. It was, perhaps, more popular in the burghs than the countryside. The creation of the royal burghs gathered together both craftsmen and merchants, subject to their own laws and with a direct involvement in parliament, thus fostering an independence of mind and spirit. There again, it should not be imagined that the towns and cities were exclusively Protestant while the countryside remained Catholic. There were many who accepted the Protestant faith for political as well religious arguments.

The Lords of the Congregation's success was due, in part, to what we would describe today as a propaganda machine, linking religion with politics. The fight against Mary of Guise was portrayed as having been a war of national liberation against French occupation. It created an atmosphere in which Protestantism could be equated with patriotism.

Mary Queen of Scots was not asked for her opinion. She had been 15 when she married the 14-year-old Dauphin Francis in 1558. Her father-in-law, Henry II of France, was killed in a jousting accident when a splinter from a shattered lance pierced his eye, entering the brain. Francis and Mary then succeeded to the French throne, but they did not reign for long. Francis's health had always been a cause for concern. His breath was foetid and his blotched skin alarming, suggesting to some that he might be suffering from leprosy although it was probably eczema. In his childhood, he had a respiratory infection that developed into a chronic inflammation of the middle ear, evidenced by a purulent discharge. He must have been in near constant pain. Finally, the infection spread to the surrounding tissues. The doctors could do nothing for him. Mary nursed him through his final days of acute pain, fever and delirium. He died on December 5, just six months after his father and one month before his 17th birthday.

Calvin set aside the spirit of Christian compassion to pen the following to a Protestant colleague. 'Did you ever read or hear of anything more timely than the death of the little king? There was no remedy for the worst evils when God suddenly revealed himself from Heaven, and He who had pierced the father's eye, struck off the ear of the son.'

Nor was there much sympathy from the French royal family for the widowed Mary. Her hostile and devious mother-in-law, Catherine de Medici, was now regent of France. On the day immediately after Francis's death, she wrote to Mary demanding the return of the French crown jewels. Within a year, Catherine would have pushed Mary aside into a position of obscurity, albeit a financially well provided for obscurity.

After the requisite period of mourning and visits to her Guise relations, the young Catholic queen finally made a sad farewell to France and returned to an increasingly Protestant Scotland. It is said that she did not return from necessity but by choice. She could have stayed in France, avoiding her mother-in-law, living on her comfortable estates and with a large annual income – a fine prize for amorous suitors. So it may have been a sense of duty to which she responded – perhaps to honour the memory of her beloved mother, Mary of Guise, who had sacrificed so much to ensure her daughter's position in Scotland. Whichever way you look at it, it cannot be said that she returned happily. As future events would reveal, she was very probably pressurised by her uncle, the Duke of Guise, who was among the most ardent of Catholics. If Mary had stayed in France, there would have been no focus for the Catholic cause in Scotland or England. Of course, that was why Mary of Guise had been pressurised into staying in Scotland. The two Marys, mother and daughter, were expected to put the needs of France and the Catholic Church before personal happiness.

Once again, the words of the Venetian ambassador summarise Mary Queen of Scots' position. 'Soon the death of the late king will be forgotten by all except his little wife, who has been widowed, has lost France, and has little hope of Scotland ... her unhappiness and unceasing tears call out for compassion.'

Mary had been just five when she fled Scotland from the English invasion that sought to enforce the terms of the Treaty of Greenwich. She was 18 when she returned, accompanied by a small retinue of household servants and, despite Catherine de Medici's earlier demands, a considerable quantity of the French crown jewels.

After the splendour of the French court, the land of her birth, now in the grip of Knox and his disciples, must have seemed an alien land. After speaking French for most of her remembered life, she could barely understand the Scottish tongue. Neither could she write it, or so it seemed, for she signed her name Marie Stuart, rather than Mary Stewart. It was a custom that she maintained throughout the rest of her life, and one that would be adopted by her son and other royal descendants.

Mary's illegitimate half-brother James Stewart, the Earl of Moray – a natural son of James V by Margaret Erskine, daughter of Lord Erskine, and a leading member of the Protestant party – in fact, one of the Lords of the Congregation – warned her what to expect, and to tread gently. 'Abuiff all things, Madame, for the luif of God presse na matters of religion, not for any mans advice on the earth.' After consultation with her late mother's family, the Guises, she wisely decided to follow this advice, rather than accepting the Catholic Earl of Huntly's offer to raise his northern clansmen and reduce the kingdom to obedience.

Mary concentrated her thoughts on financial matters, and quickly realised that her status, if not her surroundings, was very comfortable. She had her own income as a dowager queen of France, amounting to about £30,000 Scots a year. This met the cost of the royal household. In addition, and somewhat ironically, she was the main financial beneficiary of the break with Rome, because those revenues that had formerly been directed to the Vatican now came to the royal purse. Of those revenues that the remaining Catholic Church retained, it was negotiated that one third would be divided between the crown and the Protestant Church. This was a masterstroke of fiscal diplomacy, with something for everybody – even the Catholic Church who accepted that two-thirds of something was better than nothing. The arrangement acknowledged Protestant interests, while suggesting the Catholics had a secure place in Scotland's future.

Mary's half-brother Lord James had advised her that she would be free to attend Mass. However, when she attempted to do so in the comparative privacy of Holyrood Palace, she found that religious tolerance had become a one-way street in Scotland's capital. Protestant onlookers were enraged, one shouting that the priest should be put to death, inciting others to storm the chapel, where their progress was barred only by the presence of Lord James who came to the rescue. The service was concluded, but the atmosphere inside the chapel was understandably tense and fearful.

Mary's response was well measured. The next day, she issued a proclamation that sought to please Catholic and Protestant alike. She said that she would not allow, under pain of death, any man to interfere with the Protestants' worship. In return, she demanded that no man would interfere with her personal worship, or that of her French servants and companions, again under pain of death.

This must be seen as a laudable attempt to introduce some note of tolerance in Scotland's religious differences, but it simply infuriated the more stubborn Protestants. The following Sunday, John Knox thundered from his pulpit that one Mass was more fearful to him than ten thousand armed enemies being landed in the realm.

Mary had many faults, but she was quick to recognise Knox for what he was, commenting to a companion that she regarded him as the most dangerous man in her kingdom. Even so, she made the mistake of thinking that she might influence him, and demanded an interview.

When she had heard him out, the exasperated Mary was moved to say,

'Well then, I perceive that my subjects shall obey you and not me; and shall do what they list and not what I command; and so must I be subject to them and not they to me.'

The intransigent Knox refused to acknowledge the sarcasm in those words. Instead, he treated them as an admission of Mary's acceptance of the Protestant position, suggesting that this subjection to God, as represented by his Protestant Church, would carry her to everlasting glory.

Mary had heard enough. 'Yea, but ye are not the Kirk that I will nurse,' she exploded. 'I will defend the Kirk of Rome, for, I think, it is the true Kirk of God.'

Lesser men might have quailed at this statement of royal intent. Knox simply shrugged it off. 'Conscience requireth knowledge,' he said. 'And I fear right knowledge ye have none.'

The interview was over. The queen and the preacher may have been sparring to discover the other's strengths and weaknesses. 'If there be not in her a proud mind, a crafty wit and an indurate heart against God and his truth, my judgement faileth me,' Knox told his friends. Some have suggested that these words show a grudging respect for his opponent. Others conclude that he was simply stating that she would not easily be beaten into submission to the Protestant faith, but beaten she must be.

The prospect of an unmarried Catholic queen, newly arrived from France, deeply alarmed the champions of Scotland's Protestant and Nationalist causes. According to John Knox, 'the very face of heaven, the time of her arrival, did manifestly speak what comfort was brought unto this country with her, to wit, sorrow, dolour, darkness and all impiety ... The sun was not seen to shine two days before, nor two days after. That forewarning gave God unto us.'

Because Mary had failed or refused to ratify the Treaty of Edinburgh, Elizabeth in London feared that the queen of Scotland who had been queen of France intended to press her claim to become queen of England. In that claim, the papacy and France, not to mention the many English Catholics who would dearly love to see a Catholic monarch on England's throne, would support her.

Elizabeth had refused to grant safe passage through England, requiring Mary to sail direct from France to Scotland. It was rumoured that a squadron of English ships had been lying in wait to intercept the returning queen, but missed her in a thick fog. In fact, Elizabeth had relented but did not issue the safe conduct until after Mary had set sail, and the English ships did indeed intercept the returning queen, but merely saluted her as she went on her way. Presumably, they had received new orders.

Mary was keen to settle differences with Queen Elizabeth, and she found the perfect envoy in William Maitland. He was an experienced and skilled diplomat, and already known in England having served as Mary of Guise's envoy to London in 1558, and to Paris the following year, despite having converted to Protestantism in 1555. He had also served as envoy to London for the Scottish Protestants in 1560, having joined them in 1559. He belonged to a new class of laird, excellently educated and politically astute – a cynic perhaps, certainly a pragmatist – who believed in the merit of public service. To say that he had converted from Catholicism to Protestantism might say more about his politics than anything else, and faced with a queen who seemed genuinely dedicated to toleration, he was prepared to employ his skills on her behalf.

Queen Mary's half-bother, Lord James Stewart, Earl of Moray, had already written to Queen Elizabeth, setting out what he believed was the Scottish position, and suggesting that Mary would do as she was told. Clearly, he was confident in his own abilities, not least to control his half-sister. It was a confidence born out of the support he could command within Scotland, as a leading Lord of the Congregation.

He offered a straightforward deal. Mary would ratify the Treaty of Edinburgh in return for Elizabeth acknowledging that Mary was next in line to the English throne. At the meeting with Elizabeth, also attended by Cecil and Lord Robert Dudley, Maitland had to admit that this suggestion was not possible, as one would cancel out the other. That is, if Mary ratified the treaty, she would be giving up all claims to the English throne both before and after Elizabeth's eventual death.

The meeting continued with Elizabeth acknowledging that she knew of no better right to the throne than Mary's, and that Mary was her personal favourite among the claimants, but she would go no further. Pressed for an explanation, Elizabeth told Maitland that to declare Mary as her successor, should she die without issue, would put an impossible strain on their relationship. For one thing, nobody wanted to face up to his or her own death. 'The desire is without example to require me in my own life, to set my winding sheet before my eyes. Think you that I could love my own winding sheet? Princes cannot like their own children, those that should succeed unto them ... How then shall I, think you, like my cousin, being declared my Heir Apparent?'

Elizabeth then went on to voice more immediate fears. She acknowledged that in her time she had become the focus of opposition against her sister's reign. Protestants and others had plotted to oust her sister, Queen Mary, in order to return the throne to the Protestant faith. In turn, if she now acknowledged her cousin Mary as her heir, then Catholics would surely plot to hasten her end. Even ignoring religious differences, she suggested that the English people had a penchant for revolt. 'I know the inconsistency of the people of England, how they ever mislike the present government and have their eyes fixed upon that person that is next to succeed. They are keener to worship the rising than the setting sun.'

Maitland had little option but to sympathise with Elizabeth's opinion. However, he was able to gain a concession to the Treaty of Greenwich. Mary would not have to deny her claim to the English throne for all time – only during Elizabeth's lifetime, and that of any lawful offspring.

Elizabeth stated that she wasn't seeking to close a door on the subject, and that Maitland and Cecil should continue to correspond, thus maintaining a point of contact between the two countries. Of course, this contact would be maintained in the utmost secrecy. Elizabeth did not need to explain to Maitland that his mistress was widely despised in Protestant England, and in particular by the increasingly Puritan parliament. Not only was she a Catholic and practically French – she was also a relation of the Guises, who had emerged as the most ruthless persecutors of Protestants in France. What could English Protestants expect from a queen with such credentials? As for Mary's attempts to champion religious tolerance in Scotland, with Protestantism on the ascendancy these efforts were cynically viewed as nothing more or less than the first moves in a long term strategy to return the country to Catholicism.

Maitland returned to Scotland, and duly started his secret correspondence with Cecil. It was clear that Mary was not prepared to ratify the treaty but, instead, wished an entirely new agreement to be negotiated. Of course, this would have brought the matter into the public domain, so Elizabeth refused. By now, the two queens were corresponding directly, and they eventually agreed that they should meet. York was suggested as the most convenient venue, then Nottingham. Maitland returned to London in order to finalise the arrangements.

At the last moment, it was learned in early March 1562, that the Duke of Guise had ordered an attack on a Protestant prayer meeting at Vassy. This sparked a war between the French Catholics and Huguenots. Clearly, this was not the time for a Protestant queen of England to be seen consorting with the half-French, Catholic queen of Scotland. Mary was devastated, but somewhat consoled when Elizabeth suggested the meeting might be held in a year's time. In fact, that meeting never took place and no treaty was ever ratified, or agreement made. The two queens were at a stalemate in which neither could make a concession.

As a Catholic queen in a Protestant country, Mary would seek to run with the hare and hunt with the hounds. She was not the first to do so, nor would she be the last. At the start of her 'active' reign, she confused Scottish Catholics by fiercely defending her personal devotion to Rome while seeming to favour Protestants. It all got too much for George Gordon, the Earl of Huntly.

Known as 'the Cock of the North' and one of Scotland's most powerful Catholic nobles, the leaders of the Protestants were confident that, given time and the rope to hang himself, the insolent Huntly would provide the cause for his own downfall. He had got too big for his boots, was a notorious double-dealer and plotter, and his family had been involved in a number of scandals, both moral and legal. Others coveted his estates and all this made Huntly an obvious target for the new regime, seeking an opportunity to display its muscle.

They didn't have long to wait. Huntly rebelled, but was defeated in battle at Crouch in Aberdeenshire by troops loyal to the queen (and the Congregation, of course) commanded by her half-brother James Stewart, the Earl of Moray. Immediately after the battle, Huntly was taken prisoner but died of a heart attack. His vast corpse was then sent to Aberdeen where it was disembowelled and embalmed because an ancient law demanded the presence of the offender, dead or alive, for trial before the Parliament in cases of treason. Seven months later, the embalmed corpse, brought before the queen and Parliament, was declared guilty. The sentence was forfeiture of it and its erstwhile belongings, and the title of the earldom of Huntly was attainted. Only when the corpse had been removed could anybody breathe a deep sigh of relief that the matter was closed.

Mary had earned the respect of her countrymen in this northern campaign, riding all day at the head of her troops. Huntly's son, Sir John Gordon, had been taken prisoner at the battle and Mary showed that she didn't have the Tudor stomach for retribution and bloodletting, collapsing in tears at Sir John's botched execution. He had been just one of the queen's many suitors, or rather, he had been a maker of wild schemes as to how he might take her for his own. Sir John was rather keen on wild schemes. At one time, he had earned his father's wrath by bedding his stepmother. Not that she was unwilling, for she then became his mistress.

Other advances on the royal personage came from equally unexpected quarters. The handsome French courtier and poet Pierre de Chattelard was so encouraged by Mary's appreciation of his verse that he hid under her bed to await his reward. Contrary to his expectations, when he was discovered, Mary banned him from her court. Undaunted, he then followed her to St Andrew's, broke into the royal rooms and attempted to take her by force. Her half-brother, Lord James, answered Mary's desperate cries for help. The besotted Frenchman was still reciting verse as he mounted the scaffold.

Mary was not alone in suffering from the attentions of unwelcome suitors and uninvited comment. In the first year of her reign, Queen Elizabeth had turned down Philip II of Spain, Prince Eric of Sweden and Charles, the Archduke of Austria. After this string of refusals, the House of Commons was desperate to know her marriage plans, repeatedly urging her to marry for the sake of the succession. They wished her to choose an Englishman, to avoid the country being swallowed up by some foreign dynasty, as had happened in the case of Burgundy, Spain, Bohemia and Hungary with the Habsburgs, and as had very nearly happened under her sister, Queen 'Bloody' Mary. Parliament knew that Mary Queen of Scots would press her claim to the English throne in the event of Elizabeth's death – which would prompt a return to Catholicism. Unmoved by their fears, Elizabeth replied that she would be happy to live and die a virgin, but reassured them that if she changed her mind, she would choose a husband as committed as herself to the prosperity and security of the realm.

Hardly reassured, in 1560 the royal court was buzzing with rumours associating Elizabeth with the death of the wife of Lord Robert Dudley. He had attended the secret meetings with William Maitland, the Scottish envoy, emphasising the regard in which he was held. A son of the late Duke of Northumberland and, more importantly, one of Elizabeth's favourite courtiers, Dudley was married to Amy Robsart, who, after having lived apart from him for two years, had mysteriously tumbled to her death down a flight of stairs.

❦ CHAPTER FOURTEEN ❦

THE MATING GAME

Scandalmongers and the Queen of Scots weren't the only threats, real or imagined, to Elizabeth's throne. In 1561, Elizabeth learned that Lady Catherine Grey – a younger sister of the Lady Jane Grey who was queen for nine days then beheaded by Bloody Mary – had given birth to a son. It emerged that she had married Edward, the Earl of Hertford, son of the former Lord Protector, the Duke of Somerset.

Being in the line of succession to the throne – Lady Catherine was a great-niece of Henry VIII – she should have sought Elizabeth's permission to marry, but had kept the wedding a secret. Elizabeth didn't like secrets, suspected a plot, and had Lady Catherine arrested and placed in the Tower.

Whatever else they might have been, it seems the Grey girls were slow learners. In 1565, Lady Mary Grey, younger sister of Jane and Catherine, repeated the same mistake, secretly marrying Thomas Keys, described as one of the queen's men, and later joined her sister in the Tower. If Elizabeth viewed them as legitimate threats to her throne, the Greys could hardly have been more obliging in providing an excuse to remove them from the scene.

In 1562, Elizabeth's life was undoubtedly threatened, but not by the rivals and shadowy assassins she so feared. She had been feeling unwell for some time and this developed into tiredness and a high temperature. Her doctor was called, but Elizabeth dismissed him when he diagnosed smallpox – she distrusted his opinion because she had no red marks on her skin. Four days later, however, her condition had rapidly declined and her servants, fearing the end was near, sent for her councillors. When they arrived, she insisted that Lord Robert Dudley be appointed Protector of the Realm. She was still making other arrangements for her imminent departure when Dr Burcot returned and, following a 14th-century cure, wrapped the queen in a scarlet cloth and laid her in front of a fire. The queen quickly recovered, her skin unblemished, but her true feelings for Lord Dudley no longer a secret – or so it seemed.

Once again, parliament urged Elizabeth to marry in order to provide a Protestant heir. Once again, she refused. In 1564, she gave Dudley the title of Earl of Leicester, with lavish grants of land including Kenilworth Castle, but then confounded both matchmakers and gossips by suggesting that he should marry Mary Queen of Scots, again confirming her intention to rule as 'the virgin queen'. It may be that she was prepared to 'sacrifice' Dudley in order to neutralise the Catholic threat.

The scandalmongers came up with other possibilities, stated or hinted suggesting the object of her affections might have changed. A contemporary painting called *A Handsome Catch* portrays three people seated at a table loaded with baskets of fish. A plainly-dressed woman on the left is busy. A more expensively-attired woman on the right seems to be little more than her spectator, while a man is reaching over her shoulder, one hand enveloping her breast. His other hand is grasping her hip. It has to be said that she bears a likeness to portraits of Queen Elizabeth. If that were intended, then presumably the 'fondler' would be William Cecil, gathering a reward for boosting the economy.

Cecil was the architect of the Statute of Artificers passed in 1563, introducing measures concerning the fishing industry (hence the baskets of fish?) as well as generally regulating wages and conditions of employment. Its stated intention was to make all males aged between 12 and 60 work for a living and so 'banish idleness, advance husbandry and yield unto the hired person a convenient proportion of wages.'

Workers feared it meant more work for less pay. It fixed the hours of work in agriculture from dawn to sunset in winter, and from 5am to 8pm in summer – a 15-hour working day. Justices of the peace, all drawn from the employer class, were given the power to set wages, a few pennies a day being the going rate, and those missing work could be fined.

In the same year, England became actively involved in the supply of an alternative labour force. Captain John Hawkins had been trading with the Canary Islands for nine years before discovering the profits that could be made out of human cargoes, exporting blacks from West Africa for sale to Spanish settlers on the Caribbean island of Hispaniola. The funds raised were then used to buy pearls, ginger, sugar and hides. The Spanish in Seville, who had been keeping the slave trade to themselves, declared Hawkins a pirate and confiscated half his returning ships and their loads. He still made a huge profit.

Behind the scenes, Hawkin's voyage was just one part of an emerging, long-term English strategy to establish new trading outlets. For example, the Muscovy Company started trading with Russia in 1553, before the East India Company was formed.

The need for a policy to expand outlets for English exports was highlighted by Spanish hostility to the English wool trade – vital to England's economy. For years, practically all wool exports had been channelled through Spanish-controlled Antwerp. In 1563 the Spanish banned English imports, stating this was a precaution against the spread of a plague raging in Southern England. The English dismissed this as an excuse and switched part of their trade to the Dutch port of Emden. Spanish hostility to English foreign trade was prompted, in no small part, by English privateers' attacks on Spanish shipping,

In 1563 the 'Wars of Religion' had begun in Western Europe, and Scotland became increasingly concerned with Queen Mary's marital plans. Buchanan later set out the Protestant view: 'The case was different for an heiress to a kingdom, who by the same act (marriage) took a husband to herself and a King to the people. Many were of the opinion that it was more equitable that the people should choose a husband for a girl, than that a girl should choose a King for a whole people.'

The Protestant faith would be threatened if she chose a Catholic, so when Don Carlos of Spain was mentioned, John Knox was moved to preach another of his thunderous sermons. 'This, my lords, will I say ... whensoever the Nobility of Scotland professing the Lord Jesus, consents that an infidel; and all Papists are infidels; shall be head to your Sovereign, ye do so far as in ye lieth to banish Christ Jesus from this Realm; ye bring God's vengeance upon the country, a plague upon yourself, and perchance ye shall do small comfort to your Sovereign.'

In terms of bolstering her power and prestige, a Spanish alliance had much to commend itself to Mary. In fact, she had been in negotiations for a Spanish husband. Not necessarily Don Carlos – others had been suggested. Certainly, the Spaniards didn't want her to marry a Frenchman. So when she heard of Knox's interference, she was not best pleased and demanded he should come before her. She got straight to the point. 'What have ye to do with my marriage? Or what are ye within this Commonwealth?'

'A subject born within the same, Madam,' Knox replied. 'And albeit I neither be Earl, Lord, nor Baron within it, yet has God made me (how abject that I ever be in your eyes) a profitable member within the same.'

Mary was absolutely furious. 'I have sought your favours by all possible means. I offered unto you presence and audience whensoever it pleased you to admonishe me; and yet I cannot be quit of you.'

Knox was clearly delighted to cause the young queen so much distress. Later, he would gloat that she shed so many tears that the chamber boy could scarcely find enough napkins to mop them up.

This wasn't the first time that Knox had been summoned to appear before Queen Mary. The first occasion was in September 1561, soon after the queen's return from France, after he had thundered from his pulpit against the Mass. He had been summoned again in December 1562, after he had preached against the vanity of princes and the danger that they were more exercised in their delights than in hearing and reading God's word. Once again, he wouldn't back down, and after the agitated Mary had dismissed him, somebody commented that he was not afraid. 'Why should the pleasing face of a gentlewoman effray me?' he responded. 'I have looked in the faces of many angry men, and yet have not been afraid above measure.'

At a third interview, Mary had sought Knox's support, asking him to use his influence to prevent the Roman Catholics in the West from being punished for observing their own rites. She may have been counting on her 'pleasing face' to soften Knox's resolve, but he arrogantly reminded her that princes and subjects alike were bound to observe the laws, that 'the Sword of Justice is God's' and that if a ruler failed to do justice, then the servants of God could do so. Of course, when Knox spoke of the 'servants of God', he meant Protestants alone.

Taken together, these exchanges illustrate the shift in power away from the Scottish throne. It is difficult to imagine the likes of James V tolerating such hectoring insolence; it can only be surmised that it was fear of a Protestant backlash that stayed Mary's hand.

Threatened on all sides in a strange land, and surrounded by courtiers she did not trust, the widowed Mary yearned for the support that only a husband could give. Still in her early 20s, she was not the sort of woman who would easily accept the lonely life of the celibate. So it came as no surprise when she announced her intention to marry. Her choice of husband, on the other hand, raised more than a few eyebrows and just as many hackles for he was Mary's cousin, the 19-year-old Henry Stewart, Lord Darnley, a son of the Earl of Lennox.

Darnley's mother Margaret, and Mary's father James V, were half-siblings being children of Margaret Tudor, Henry VIII's sister, from her first two marriages. It was not uncommon for royal families to fail to draw a line on incest, and Mary was totally and hopelessly in love with the lad. He had many attractions. A tall and slender youth with fair hair over a boyish face, and courtly manners, it is said. Darnley had been raised in England – indeed, he had only just returned to Scotland – and attended the reformed Anglican Church, though his background and inclination was Roman Catholic.

Mary was still obsessed with her right of succession to the English throne. By marrying Darnley, also a direct descendant of Henry VII, she was strengthening that claim. His religious vagueness also served a purpose. His background would please Catholics, while his involvement with the Anglican Church might encourage Protestants in both Scotland and England to hope that he would declare in their favour. Equally his vagueness ran the risk of antagonising both faiths. Time would tell.

Some Scots acknowledged certain advantages to be gained from the marriage. Above all, it avoided any alliance with England, while maintaining a claim on its throne. To say that Elizabeth disapproved of the Scottish marriage would be an understatement. Mary and Darnley were not only cousins and Catholics, but as great-grandchildren of Henry VII of England, both had claims to the English throne. Elizabeth was hot in her condemnation of what she described as nothing more than another move against her rule in England. She had previously given permission for Darnley to travel to Scotland from England. Now she demanded his return, but Mary would have none of it. Her heart ruled her head, moving Randolph to write of the 'poor queen whome ever before I esteemed so worthy, so wise, so honourable in all her doings', but now distracted 'to the utter contempt of her best subjects'.

Others tried to find some advantage in the marriage. Those who wanted Scotland to escape from the French influence said it would be up to Darnley to make his mark. As Mary's husband, they said, it would be within his power to make her a 'patriot queen'. In this regard, a Scottish husband had the tentative approval of the anti-French, anti-English and pro-Scottish factions. They would soon realise their mistake.

Mary's love for Darnley served to inflate his already abundant ego. The more she gave, the more he demanded. His character was emerging as that of a spoilt child and bully. When Mary made him Earl of Ross, he demanded to know why he could not also be made Duke of Albany. Mary simply pandered to his wishes. He was given the coveted title on July 22. Soon after, the heralds proclaimed that he would be named and styled 'King of this our Kingdom' after the marriage, which took place on July 29.

On the day after their marriage, this proclamation was repeated by the heralds, with the added proclamation that the couple would sign all future documents and proclamations jointly, in the names Marie and Henry. The news was heard in silence. Of all those who were present, not one so much as said 'Amen'.

The marriage had disappointed many and threatened the interests of others, added to which Darnley was very unpopular because of his arrogant behaviour, which the Scots detested. The fact that Henry had spent his early years in England, returning just shortly before his marriage, ensured that he had anglicised speech and manners. This did nothing to endear him to the Scottish nobility. Seeing all this, an English diplomat was moved to remark, 'He can have no long life among these people.'

Scotland was still divided by faction and feud, and the young queen needed the support of a wise head as well as the soft shoulder of a strong and trustworthy consort to stand by her side. Mary was deeply and totally in love with her new husband. Unfortunately, it seems to have been an unquestioning love that blinded Mary to Darnley's faults, for the man who appeared so handsome, elegant and accomplished was truly weak-willed, vain and jealous.

Mary was wise enough to recognise that those who were prepared to give this new king the benefit of the doubt could be encouraged, and some who did not could be bought over. In Scotland, it was ever thus. Mary's various incomes allowed her to support a glittering renaissance Court and she became a noted patron of poetry, ensuring that the royal couple's praises would be sung in the 'popular press' of that time. Added to that, the queen announced a huge honours list, creating five new earldoms and 20 knighthoods. The English ambassador, Thomas Randolph, commented that he could hardly turn round in the Scottish court without bumping into a new peer. He added, with more than a hint of arrogance, that 'the Scots begin to think themselves as great as we.'

The Scottish nobility was easily bought. Not noted for taking the long-term view, or for learning from history, the majority of them were driven by nothing more than financial gain and family ambition. Mary had sent an ambassador to investigate her kingdom, prior to her return from France in 1561. He had scathingly reported that it would be a waste of time to try to remind the nobles of their duty to the monarch, or to attempt to teach them of the honour to be found in just and virtuous actions. This left them open to corruption and they might change their allegiances in the blink of an eye. Mary knew that if she failed to buy their allegiance, they would look elsewhere.

The pleasures of the expanded court began to cast their spell. John Knox fumed at what he described as 'the holy water of the court by which all men are bewitched.' At first, he had little support. He was even criticised in the General Assembly of the reformed church for his implacable hostility to the queen (who he described as a dangerous Jezebel).

By elevating some, the royal couple inevitably alienated others. Mary's half-brother James, the Earl of Moray, had quarrelled with the arrogant Darnley and his presence was no longer welcomed at court. He resented his loss of influence following the marriage and he led a rebellion in the Borders. He soon discovered that many of those who might have supported his revolt had been charmed away by Mary's money and gifts of titles. The Earl of Arran, now Chatelherault, was among the few who joined him. Other supporters were a mixed bunch, some being Anglophiles, others Protestants, and some who had simply had enough of Darnley's insufferable behaviour, or felt snubbed at being missed off the royal honours list. Scots nobility regularly fought and died for far less serious affronts to their grandiose notions of self-importance.

Lacking confidence, commitment or a common sense of purpose, the rebels avoided a conclusive engagement with the royal troops that followed in their wake. Instead, they were ignobly chased from one town to the next in what is remembered as the Chaseabout Raid.

The rebels may have expected help from England, but Elizabeth's hands were tied. The French had warned her off, making it plain that any interference would prompt another Franco-Scottish pact. Phillip of Spain had also shown his disapproval of the Scottish rebels by sending a small subsidy to Mary. His involvement, however small, roused Elizabeth's fear of turning the Catholic League against England. The only thing that England could provide was a sanctuary for the fleeing miscreants.

Despite the royal couple's successes at court and the failure of the Chaseabout Raid, Lowland Protestants grew increasingly confident in pressing their case. Tens of thousands of Catholic Highlanders had perished in the terrible winter of 1564. In some areas, forests were denuded of timber for fuel, despite the best efforts of some landowners to prevent this. Presumably, the landowners had concluded that forests would be harder to replace than people. Massive numbers of livestock had also frozen to death, ensuring the severe winter was followed by a time of food shortages and high prices. Men, women and children died in their hovels, too weak to search for food. Entire glens were depopulated in some areas, and the loss of so many Catholic fighting men did nothing to hinder the Protestant cause.

It is impossible to say when Mary realised that Henry wasn't fit to be a queen's consort, let alone a king. It may have been during or immediately after the Chaseabout Raid in the closing months of 1565, that she started to see his true colours. A drunken and boorish womaniser, he behaved with insolent brutality to his wife who was already pregnant, causing constant rows and arguments whenever he returned home from his frequent hunting and hawking expeditions. He was away so often that a stamp was made to replace his signature on official documents.

Mary showed her disappointment by refusing to give Henry any real authority, or to grant his frequent and sometimes violent demands for a grant of the 'crown matrimonial' – the same grant that had been made in favour of Dauphin Francis, her first husband. It would have meant that if Mary predeceased Henry and left no issue, Henry would continue to reign as king in his own right. He demanded this for the status it would bring, ignoring the increased responsibilities which, as he regularly displayed, he was unfit to undertake.

Lord Herries outlined the royal couple's conflicting positions in his memoirs. Mary's position was that all the majesty and honour Darnley had came from her, and as so many of her nobles had been opposed to the marriage, she did not want to upset them any further. Darnley didn't agree. He believed that their marriage had received the full backing of the nobility, who thought him worthy to be king in his own right and would follow him into battle, if necessary, but would think it 'a shame a woman would command'.

Some were keen to fuel the fires of Darnley's indignation. Those who sought to enhance the Protestant cause saw Catholic Mary as a continuing threat, with her soft and insinuating talk of religious tolerance. They encouraged Darnley, in order to foster trouble for the queen. Wise heads on old shoulders saw that the infantile king could be putty in their hands, as long as they pandered to his egomania.

Mary's dwindling passion for Darnley may have been exacerbated by her pregnancy. She was four years older than her husband – who was anything but mature anyway – and there had been an element of maternalism in their early relationship, with Mary insisting on nursing him when he was ill and indulging his boyish demands for honours and favours. The impending birth may have convinced her that it was time for Darnley to grow up. Instead, she found that he was going from bad to worse. The pregnant queen may also have lost interest in the physical side of their relationship, which the petulant Darnley would have viewed as a rejection. If so, his jealous temperament might have sought more sinister explanations than the obvious.

Mary must have felt threatened by her husband's demands and overtly bullying manner, but was determined to keep the reins of power to herself. As time passed, she increasingly relied on the advice of a small circle of members of her household, to the point where she excluded not only her husband, but also her nobles. Clearly, they did not inspire her trust.

King Henry, or Lord Darnley as he is better remembered, has been variously described as unstable and weak, but he was also proud and aggressive – a potentially explosive combination. On Christmas day, 1565, he chose to return to the Mass while the General Assembly was sitting in Edinburgh, apparently signalling a Catholic revival at court and infuriating the Protestants. One month later, at the start of February, he was invested with the Order of St Michael, the greatest order in French chivalry. After the ceremony, he strode up Edinburgh's High Street with a group of his cronies, boasting loudly that he had returned Scotland to the true faith. His eventual fate may have been sealed at that time.

Just a few weeks later, Mary was enjoying a quiet supper at Holyrood

Palace with members of her close household, including her Italian secretary David Riccio, when Henry and an 'angry gang' broke into the room. It is said that Riccio clung to Mary's skirts, but was dragged from the room crying, 'Save me lady, save me,' in French.

The queen, who was six months pregnant, was roughly handled and could do nothing. According to one account, one of the gang pushed the queen in Henry's direction, telling him to hold her while the deed was done, and another of the gang pressed a pistol to her breast, though another account suggests it was pointed at her pregnant belly. Riccio died in a whirlwind of stabbing daggers. It was later discovered that there were more than 60 wounds in his lifeless body.

Suggestions have been made that the queen and her secretary enjoyed a certain intimacy, and the murder was the actions of an outraged husband, supported by his closest friends. But despite his appearance in paintings portraying his death, it is said that in reality Riccio was a hunchback, little taller than a dwarf and notoriously ugly. Mary's taste in men was more toward the tall and handsome ... Then there is the identity of the gaunt figure in full armour who followed Darnley into Mary's chamber. Lord Ruthven was a hard-line Protestant – as were the bulk of the murderous mob – while King Henry was now openly Catholic – fellow conspirators, for sure, but they were not his friends.

Henry's wild jealousy was undoubtedly a major factor in the murder, but that is not to say Riccio was killed solely as the result of some amorous indiscretion with the queen. By terrorising Mary, Darnley might force her to make him king in his own right, and a king in more than name and style. In this regard, Catholic Henry and his Protestant allies might ignore their differences to deal with a common cause – ridding Scotland of French interference. And Darnley's religious convictions were never so strong that he wouldn't have converted to Protestantism if it suited his ends. It would be far too simplistic to suggest that all Protestants were pro-English and all Catholics were pro-French. Even one awarded the Order of St Michael might put self-interest before foreign alliance.

Riccio's personal relationship with the queen has been highlighted as the motive for his murder, but his link with the queen's maternal French family – the Guises – was most significant, and Riccio did not die alone. Murdered on that same night was John Black, a Dominican friar recently selected by the queen to join her household. He wasn't an innocent bystander who simply got in the way. He was deliberately sought out and attacked by more than 20 prominent members of the Protestant party.

It would later emerge that Henry had entered a plot with those Protestant lords who had been exiled for their part in the Chaseabout Raid, including Mary's illegitimate half-brother, Lord James Stewart, the Earl of Moray. The plan had been that they would be pardoned for their part in the revolt, and allowed to return to Scotland, their properties intact, in return for supporting Henry's demand for the crown matrimonial and other royal authority. They knew that Mary must be bullied into accepting this arrangement, and Riccio and Black's murders were just the first step in their terror tactics. After the murders, Henry kept his side of the bargain, discharging the Parliament which was due to meet to forfeit in life, lands and goods the exiled Protestant lords.

Mary was kept captive in her own palace, a prisoner of Riccio's murderers. At first she was angry and hysterical, fearing a miscarriage, but she calmed down enough to gather her thoughts and change tactics. The beautiful queen fooled the conspirators with her charming manner and promises of a pardon – the same pardon offered by Henry – before setting to work on her husband, persuading him to desert his co-conspirators.

Within 48 hours, Mary and Henry had escaped from the palace through underground passages. The queen was mounted behind Sir Arthur Erskine, her master stabler, and the captain of the guard took one of the queen's maids behind him. The king, Sir William Stanley and Sebastian Broune accompanied them. Despite the queen being six months pregnant and again fearing a miscarriage, they rode the 20 miles to Dunbar, arriving at a castle belonging to James Hepburn, the Earl of Bothwell, in less than five hours. From there, Mary sent out a call to arms. The confused plotters, realising they had been deserted by Henry, fled to England and Queen Mary returned triumphantly to Edinburgh.

CHAPTER FIFTEEN

DARNLEY'S MURDER

Mary had promised forgiveness to David Riccio's murderers, but only to secure her liberty. Returned to power, she could seek a cautious revenge. Cautious because if she made one wrong move, Scotland would burst into flames, particularly if her vengeance was interpreted as another persecution of Protestants and anti-French nationalists.

Mary needed to know the whole truth. Henry was trying to deny all knowledge of the plot that had led to Riccio's murder, but those he had deserted saw their opportunity to regain some favour with the queen. In secret meetings, they revealed Henry's complicity. Mary might have wondered if Henry had hoped that her terrifying ordeal would prompt the miscarriage of their child, or her own death, clearing the way for him to reign. She was learning to hate the man she had so recently loved, but still she did not act.

On Wednesday, June 19, 1556, between the hours of nine and ten in the morning in a small retiring room in Edinburgh Castle, Mary gave birth to a boy. To the world, he would be known as James VI of Scots and James I of England or, as he would style it, of Great Britain. But to his weary mother, reverting to the French of her younger years, he was Jacques. Even in old age he would use this name when signing documents.

Guns at the castle boomed out news of the birth, and nobles and common folk gathered at the Great Kirk to give thanks to God. That night, a chain of bonfires carried the news across the length and breadth of the land. Couriers were dispatched to England, France and Savoy. As a great-great-grandson of Henry VII, the heir to the throne of Scotland was also heir to the throne of

England, as long as Queen Elizabeth remained childless. When she heard news of the birth, Elizabeth reeled back as if struck, crying out 'Alack, the queen of the Scots is lighter of a bonny son and I am but of barren stock.' Later, she would learn to be more philosophical about this turn in events.

At about two in the afternoon, Mary's husband, King Henry, arrived to see the child. 'My Lord, God has given you and me a son, begotten by none but you,' Mary said, taking the child in her arms. 'My Lord, here I protest to God, as I shall answer to Him at the great day of judgement, this is your son and no other man's son.'

Sir William Stanley, an Englishman who had accompanied Mary on that desperate ride after Riccio's murder, was in the room. Mary may have emphasised her statement about the baby's legitimacy as much to impress him as her husband, knowing that Stanley would report back to Queen Elizabeth, who was all too familiar with the problems caused by the possibility of illegitimacy in regard to a royal succession.

'This is the son whom I hope shall first unite the two kingdoms of Scotland and England,' the queen said.

'Why, Madam, shall he succeed before your Majesty and his father?' Sir William enquired.

'Because he has broken to me,' was Mary's somewhat confusing reply. Perhaps she was hinting that Henry's days as her consort were numbered. 'Because he has broken to me.' Few words, but packed with meaning.

Sir Henry Killigrew, another Englishman in Scotland, was summoned to see the baby. He reported back to Queen Elizabeth that he 'was brought to the young Prince, sucking of his nurse, and afterwards saw him as good as naked. I mean his head, feet, and hands, all to my judgement well proportioned and like to prove a goodly prince.'

Mary and her baby were also visited by John Spottiswoode who brought congratulations from the General Assembly, and a request that the boy be baptised in the Protestant faith. Mary had the prince brought from his nursery. The elderly Spottiswoode fell upon his knees, said a short prayer, and then playfully invited the baby to say 'Amen'. A suitable gurgle was interpreted as consent, much to everybody's delight and amusement.

Mary ignored the General Assembly's request for a Protestant baptism. She had other plans. Six months after his birth, James was baptised in a Catholic ceremony at Stirling Castle. It was an occasion for pomp and festivity. The Earl of Bedford represented England and brought a gold font from Queen Elizabeth, who had agreed to be the baby's godmother though she did not attend the ceremony. There was an ambassador from Savoy, and France was represented by the Count de Brienne who carried the prince from his chamber to the chapel, flanked by two rows of barons and gentlemen and followed by a number of Scottish nobles, all Catholics, bearing the great cierge, the salt, the rood, and the basin and laver. The Archbishop of St Andrews, attended by other Catholic prelates, met them at the door of the chapel.

The Archbishop baptised the prince with 'all the ceremonies accustomed in the Roman Church'. Lyon King of Arms then proclaimed the baby's name and titles. 'Charles James, Prince and Stewart of Scotland, Duke of Rothesay, Earl of Carrick, Lord of the Isles, and Baron of Renfrew,' but to his mother he was still Jacques, the son who might unite the kingdoms of Scotland and England.

The baptism was followed by an elaborate banquet for the guests. Attending were those Protestant lords who had boycotted the baptism itself on religious grounds. The banquet was seen as an opportunity for making conciliatory gestures. Protestants sat side-by-side with Catholics. The Earl of Argyll, the Protestant champion of the west, and Lord Seton, described as the most resolute of the Catholic lords from the south-east, carried white staffs – the traditional emblem to mark the end of a feud.

A young Protestant minister, Patrick Adamson, wrote a celebratory poem to mark the event, and predict the future.

'Our leader has transposed Mars ablaze with civil war into peace in our time ... A powerful young woman, whose race was from the lofty blood of kings, controls by her rule the warlike Scots ... The importance of kingship is eternal; it will be in the power of the Stewart family; the crown of Mary awaits her grandsons ... The fates will grant you to extend the territory of your realm, until the Britons, having finished the war, will learn at last to unite in one kingdom.'

The boy's father, King Henry, was in Stirling but did not attend the baptism. Some say that he refused, but it may not have been his choice to make. 'Neither was he required nor permitted to come openly'.

In the period between his son's birth and baptism, Henry had time to reflect upon his life. He wrote a poem for his wife at about this time, acknowledging that she, and not he, would reign in the future. He titled his verse, *To the Queen*.

Be governour baith guid and gratious,
Be leill and luifand to thy liegis all;
Be large of fredome and no thing desyrous;
Be just to pure for ony thing may fall;
Be ferme of faith and constant as ane wall;
Be ready evir to stanche evil and discord;
Be cheretabill, and sickerlye thou sall,
Be bowsum ay to knaw thy God and Lord.

Be traist and conquese they awin heretage,
Be ennemyes of auld now occupyit;
Be strength and force thou sobir thai man swage,
Be law of God – thair may no man deny it;
Be nocht as lantern in mirknes unspyit;
Be thou in rycht thi landis suld be restored,
Be wirschop so thy name beis magnefeit;
Be bowsum ay to knaw they God and Lord.

Be to rebellis strong as lyoun eik;
Be ferce to follow tham quhairevir thai found;
Be to thy liegemen bayth soft and meik;
Be thair succour and help them haill and sound;
Be knaw thy cure and caus quhy thow was cround;
Be besye evir that justice be nocht smord;
Be blyth in hart; thir wordis oft expound;
Be bowsum ay to knaw thy God and Lord.

A sympathetic person might look at those words, and ask if the queen's husband was really as bad as he was painted. Is it possible, they might ask, that Henry's downfall was prompted by some deep-seated belief that Mary wasn't fit to rule?

The historian D H Willson certainly had a low opinion of Mary. 'Had she been the consort of a strong and wealthy monarch who could have controlled and protected her, she might have charmed the world. But as a ruler in her own right she was beneath contempt. Frivolous, extravagant, careless, emotional, utterly self-centred, lacking in judgement and temper, unmindful of the interests of her country, she looked upon the world largely as it advanced or retarded her personal aspirations. Her diplomacy and plotting, though daring and clever, were brittle and unrealistic, for her preoccupation with personal interests blinded her to the gulf between hope and hard reality.'

Could it be that Henry was a patriot, trying to wrestle the throne from a contemptuous ruler who put personal gain and her allegiance to France before the needs of the Scottish nation? The balance of evidence suggests otherwise. Henry might have done better to write, 'Be not as I am,' and left it at that.

Returning for a moment to Willson's appraisal of Queen Mary, he ended by saying that her preoccupation with personal interests blinded her to the gulf between hope and hard reality. By insisting on a Catholic baptism, she was expressing her hope that her son would be raised in the Catholic faith, to become a Catholic king – presumably of both Scotland and England if Queen Elizabeth remained childless. The hard reality was, however, that the General Assembly had requested a Protestant service. They might have decided that this was neither the time nor the place to insist, but if the queen imagined that the Protestant lords of the Congregation would simply sit back and allow the heir to the throne to be raised as a Catholic, she was fooling nobody but herself.

Once Henry had broken with the Protestant lords after Riccio's murder, only to realise that his wife would never accept his claims of innocence, he returned to plotting. This time, he would present himself as the true champion of the Catholic cause in Scotland. He secretly sought to convince the papacy that he would be merciless in dealing with the Protestant heretics and in return, he hoped, they would give him support in overthrowing the queen who advocated tolerance. After that, perhaps he would take his place alongside the great Catholic kings of Europe as the saviour who had rescued Scotland from the Protestants. But the papacy was not impressed, and whispered to Mary of her husband's intentions.

Mary's loathing of her husband must have intensified when she discovered that as well as plotting against her, he was suffering from syphilis. She whispered that she wanted a divorce, but said she feared it might affect the legitimacy of her son, the prince. Of course, a short conversation with a lawyer or priest would have set matters straight. However, she chose to insist that she could see 'no outgait'.

In a world of feud and faction, where men were ready to use whatever means secured the desired end, 'the outgait' was obvious, and Mary would have known this. To some, it must have seemed that she was not so much stating her position as dropping hints. Married or divorced, as long as Henry was alive he would remain a loose cannon, capable of causing all sorts of mischief.

Mary knew that many Scots hated the king. There were the co-conspirators he had abandoned, and nobles who resented his position and loathed him for his arrogance – men who would be delighted to see Henry dead. Intentionally or not, Mary was giving them the royal nod of approval.

Events that occurred at the end of 1566 and into the start of the following year are still the subject of speculation. What is known is that on 24 December 1566, the queen pardoned most of those who had been involved in the murder of Riccio, and allowed them to return to Scotland. These men hated Henry for his duplicity, and had proved that they were ready to resort to violence when it suited their purpose.

Six weeks later, Henry was staying on the outskirts of Edinburgh. He wanted to be at Holyrood, but Mary had insisted that he should stay at Kirk o' Fields, where she had brought him from Glasgow, while he convalesced from a serious fever. Mary was lavishing attentive care on her husband, just as she had in the early days of their marriage, while refusing him access to Holyrood and thus avoiding any risk, she said, of infecting their son.

On the evening of February 9, Henry was left in the care of a manservant, but without guards. Mary was attending a masked ball being held in honour of the marriage of her favourite architect, and was to return to Kirk o' Fields the following day. At two o'clock in the morning, there was an almighty explosion – so loud that it was heard throughout the city. It was, they said, as loud as 30 cannons firing simultaneously. Kirk o' Fields was reduced to rubble.

When people rushed to the scene, they found the king's body in the garden. He had been strangled. His servant lay at his side, also strangled, and there was a chair, some rope, a dagger, and a furred cloak. It was surmised that the king had heard some disturbance – something that put him in immediate fear of his life – and had himself lowered in the chair, on the rope, from a window. It was clear that he had got out before the explosion because there wasn't so much as a scorch on his body. His assassins who were, presumably, waiting to see the explosion had intercepted him.

Women living in nearby houses would later testify that they had heard him pleading for mercy. 'Pity me, kinsmen, for the sake of Jesus Christ, who pitied all the world,' but he had fallen into pitiless hands.

One man was arrested, attempting to flee from the scene though he claimed that he had simply been drinking with friends in a neighbouring house. He was Captain William Blackadder, a notorious henchman of James Hepburn, the Earl of Bothwell who, from that moment on, became the prime suspect in Henry's murder. Some said openly that as Mary's love for her husband faded, her affection for the bold Bothwell had grown, implying that she might have been an accomplice in her husband's murder. Certainly, few doubted Bothwell's involvement, though it was clear that he did not act alone. Indeed, he may have been little more than a pawn, though the authorities would later insist otherwise.

The Privy Council announced a reward of £2,000 for information leading to the capture of Henry's murderers, but very little effort was made to investigate the matter and the queen was badly supported by her advisers. When the old women who claimed to have heard the king's dying words – and may have seen his killers – were questioned, their interrogators decided that they were too free and easy with noble names, and so dismissed them with a warning – this amounted to the deliberate suppression of vital evidence from the only eye witnesses. Suppressed because the interrogators didn't like the names they were hearing.

If Mary was an accomplice to her husband's murder, she played her part badly. At first, when she might have given a performance of the sort of histrionics expected of a widow in despair, she seemed outwardly calm. Indeed, it is said that just two days after his death, she took part in an archery competition. It was later that she went to pieces.

After the initial shock, if shock there was, she may have considered whether the assassins had intended to murder her, as well as her husband. Alone in what must have still seemed like a foreign land, her previous advisors alienated by Darnley, their replacements murdered or in fear for their lives, and surrounded by hostile faces, Mary experienced a mental and physical breakdown. She retched uncontrollably for long periods, bringing up black and bloody mucus. The porphyria inherited from her father was manifesting itself, her moods swinging uncontrollably between exhaustion and hysterics. Clearly, she was deeply troubled and terrified of those around her, and was incapable of fulfilling her duties for many weeks.

Darnley's distraught father, the Earl of Lennox, ran out of patience with the establishment's indolence, indifference or inability to find his son's killers. In a letter of March 24, 41 days after her husband's murder, Mary finally agreed to allow Lennox to bring a private action, to be heard by the Scottish Parliament, accusing Bothwell of the murder.

The trial was a farce. Bothwell flooded Edinburgh with 4,000 of his armed supporters who intimidated witnesses, including the victim's father who was 'persuaded' not to attend. Bothwell walked arrogantly from the court, free to celebrate with his cronies.

One week later, Mary attended Parliament. Significantly, Bothwell carried the sceptre. The proceedings of Bothwell's trial were ratified, and land grants were confirmed. Bothwell received the land that went with Dunbar Castle, and Huntly and four other Gordons received back their estates, which had been forfeited in 1562 after George, 5th Earl of Huntly, had rebelled against the queen.

Bothwell, Maitland and Bellenden then approached Mary. Their purpose was to convince the queen that she must quickly take a husband if she were to hold together her kingdom, and to assure her that Bothwell was the man for the job, being 'a man of resolution well adapted to rule, the very character needed to give weight to the decisions and actions of the council.' According to her later accounts of this meeting, she pointed out that there were too many scandals surrounding her husband's death, and she firmly refused Bothwell's proposal.

On April 24, Mary had been to Stirling to see her baby son, James, and was returning to Edinburgh with an escort of 30 riders when Bothwell intercepted her with a force of about 800 armed men. To resist would have been futile, and Mary had no option but to accompany Bothwell to his castle at Dunbar. What came next is not certain; some say Mary was raped while others argue that she was not unwilling. Certainly, we have the account of one who was in the castle at the time. Melville had been taken to Dunbar, along with the queen, though he was released after the first night. According to his account of events, 'The Queen could not but marry him, seeing he had ravished her and laid with her against her will.'

Bothwell did not return Mary to Edinburgh until May 6, by when she had agreed to marry him – willingly or otherwise. Even if taken by force, Mary would have been obliged to consider the possibility that she might be pregnant by Bothwell. If so, there would be another heir to the Scottish throne. It was unthinkable that a queen should produce an illegitimate child, however common such offspring might be in the case of royal princes and kings, as witnessed by Mary's illegitimate siblings – the fruit of her father's philandering habits. The code of that time favoured the rapist, so long as he married his victim. This was why the daughters of nobility were so closely guarded, lest their parents be foisted with an unwanted son-in-law, demanding a substantial dowry to save the family's honour. Bothwell was clearly intending to marry Mary, and had freed himself to do so by both granting and obtaining a quick divorce from his wife.

Three days earlier, in the Commissary Court of Edinburgh, the Lady Jean Gordon had secured a divorce from Bothwell, her husband of just one year, on the grounds of his adultery with one Bessie Crawford. And four days after that, and at the instance of Bothwell, the newly re-established consistorial court of the Archbishop of St Andrews nullified his marriage to Lady Jean on the grounds that they were within 'the forbidden degree'. This despite the fact that a dispensation to marry had been sought and granted – a fact that was conveniently suppressed ... Later, the judge-delegate would complain that he had given the sentence of nullity under threats of violence and other pressures.

Significantly, the consistorial court had been re-established by Mary in order to help her secure a divorce from Darnley. This seems to suggest that it was divorce, rather than murder, that had been uppermost in the queen's mind – though some might see it as a smokescreen hiding her true intentions.

Clearly, things were happening in a rush. The day before he had been granted his St Andrew's divorce, Bothwell had demanded that John Craig, a colleague of John Knox, should proclaim the banns of marriage between himself and Mary. Craig refused to do so without written warrant from the queen. When this was produced, charging him to make the proclamation, Craig did so, while simultaneously denouncing the marriage. His objections were told to the Privy Council in May, and appear in the record of the General Assembly, *Booke of the Universall Kirk*, for December 30 1567. He denounced Bothwell, citing the laws referring to adultery and ravishing, the suspicion of collusion between Bothwell and his wife, Lady Jean Gordon, in their sudden divorce, the hasty proclamation of marriage to the queen, and lastly the suspicions that had been raised in connection with Darnley's death.

Bothwell's response to Craig's outburst had been to threaten to hang him.

Yet the bold clergyman had simply said what most were thinking. They recognised that Bothwell was forcing the pace, and criticised Mary for allowing it to happen.

On May 15, Mary and Bothwell were married at Holyrood. The Bishop of Orkney conducted the service according to the rites of the Protestant church. This hasty marriage, just three months after Darnley's death, shocked public opinion. The facts seemed obvious enough. The queen must have been Bothwell's lover, and together they had planned her husband's murder. The abduction had been a charade. Later, after Bothwell's 'quickie divorce', the evil couple had married.

The pope decided to have no further communication with the Queen of Scots 'unless, indeed, in times to come he shall see some better sign of her life and religion'. After due consideration the pope might have concluded that the devoutly Catholic queen would not have been a willing participant in a Protestant marriage – not with Bothwell nor anybody else. Instead, he abandoned her when, perhaps, she had most need of his intervention.

This long after the event, it is impossible to discover the truth of what really happened in the time from before Darnley's murder until Mary's marriage to Bothwell. Certainly, it is well nigh impossible to sort the truth from the propaganda. Attempts to blacken the names of Mary and Bothwell served to hide the truth about others who might have been implicated in Darnley's and earlier murders.

Before the killing of David Riccio and John Black, the queen had already 'turned in on herself', relying on her immediate household for advice, trusting neither her husband nor her nobles. Immediately after the murder, with two of her closest advisors taken from her, she was very vulnerable. When she arrived at Dunbar with her husband, who she neither loved nor trusted, Mary's marriage was over in all but name. It may be that she looked at the strong, confident and handsome Bothwell and decided that he was a man who could protect her against her enemies. In the coming months, a friendship developed.

Mary must have known that a divorce would have left Henry free to cause trouble and rally support against her. He had tried to grab the reins of power in the past, and might try again. He had been involved in the murder of her advisor and close friend. Above all, perhaps, he had betrayed her love. So it is easy to imagine that she would have wanted him removed from the scene. For a moment, let's imagine that she had plotted with Bothwell to murder her unwanted spouse ...

Mary moved her husband from Glasgow to Kirk o' Fields, despite his suffering from a grave fever. She tucked him up in bed and set off for the masked ball where she would be surrounded by witnesses. There was no question of her returning to Kirk o' Fields that night. It would have been a simple matter for Bothwell to slip away. On the other hand, there really was no need for his presence at Kirk o' Fields. Others could murder the convalescing king – Bothwell's henchmen, perhaps, or the rebels of the Chaseabout Raid, recently returned from exile. Mary had pardoned them – Bothwell may have acted as an intermediary, promising that he would secure them that pardon in return for 'a favour'. Then the explosion rocked the city.

This begs an obvious question. Why would Mary have agreed to a plan that announced to the world that Henry had been murdered? Surely, a more sensible option would have been to quietly smother the king, and say he had died from his fever. So, the question persists. Why the explosion?

To make a stab at answering that question, we should look more closely at the man described as 'this reckless Earl, a man high in his own conceit, proud, vicious and vainglorious above measure, one who would attempt anything out of ambition'. The sort of man who might murder a king, then abduct and rape his queen in order to force her to marry him?

Queen Mary of Scots had arrived from France at a time when the long-running feud between James Hepburn, Earl of Bothwell, and the Hamiltons, principally the Earl of Arran, took a new twist. It was an open secret that Alison Craik was, or had been, Arran's mistress. She lived with her stepfather, an Edinburgh merchant, and one night three masked men visited their household. Bothwell was in the lead. He was accompanied by two of the queen's kinsmen – her half-brother Lord John Stewart (one of the nine children that James V sired out of wedlock) and her Guise uncle, Rene of Elbouef. They gained entry to the house and gang-raped Alison – her ordeal being Arran's insult.

Not content with this, next night the three returned. This time, however, the household was ready for them. The uproar was enough to convince Lord John that discretion was the better part of ardour, but Bothwell and Elbouef forced their way in and raped Alison a second time.

The following day, the outraged Church Assembly presented a petition to the queen, and she administered a 'stern rebuke' to the delinquent pair. It wasn't enough to deter them. They boldly announced that they intended to repeat the offence that night, and challenged anybody to try and stop them. Clearly, they were spoiling for a fight with the Hamiltons, and the repeated rapes of Alison Craik were simply their means to that end.

The Hamiltons assembled with spears and jacks to defend the Craik household. In turn, Bothwell mustered his supporters. Murder and mayhem was about to start when Lord James Stewart, the Earl of Moray, Argyll and Huntly rushed down from court, supported by troops, and broke up the bristling antagonists.

Bothwell was ordered to leave Edinburgh while the matter cooled, and a few months later he and Arran seemed to be on better terms. But this didn't last long. Arran went to John Knox, claiming that Bothwell had recently invited him to join a conspiracy. The queen's trusted supporters, her half-brother Lord James and her envoy William Maitland were to be killed and the queen abducted by force to Dumbarton Castle. Bothwell and Arran would then rule Scotland.

As well as reporting this to Knox, Arran wrote to the queen and Lord James, making the same claims. While it was an open secret that Arran was mentally disturbed, and unreliable in distinguishing between fact and fantasy, Lord James decided not to take any risks. Arran and Bothwell were arrested while the reported conspiracy was investigated.

Arran was detained in his father's house but escaped, half-naked, by climbing down a rope made from his bed sheets. He made his way to the home of Kirkaldy of Grange. By now, it is said, the poor man was howling of devils and witches, and claiming that everybody wanted to kill him. He was moved to St Andrews, where he seemed to calm down, but continued to accuse Bothwell of high treason.

Bothwell demanded the satisfaction of trial by combat, but Arran's mental condition would not allow it. He was taken to Edinburgh Castle and confined in the grimmest conditions. Twelve years later, desiring only solitude and fearing all around him, he was released on a caution of £12,000 and allowed to live with his mother.

Despite Arran's mental health problems, the authorities were not prepared to ignore his testimony. However, they were faced with a dilemma.

If they brought Bothwell to trial, Arran would have to be produced as the main witness, and if Arran were shown to be a liar then, according to the law, he would have to be executed, irrespective of his condition. And his closeness to the royal family would provoke a scandal. Lord James brought it to Mary's attention that Bothwell had also been intriguing with the English. Taking all this under consideration, it was decided that Bothwell should be left to cool his heels in Edinburgh Castle, without trial.

The details of the relationship between Arran and Bothwell tell us a lot about Bothwell's character. Firstly, he was prepared to take a woman by force, and to repeat that crime even when it had been publicly disclosed. Secondly, he didn't care what others thought of him. Thirdly, he resorted to violence at the slightest provocation. And fourthly, and perhaps most significantly, he had apparently planned to abduct and ravish the queen (before she was married to Darnley), hoping to get her pregnant and thus forcing her to marry him, for her honour and that of the child. Indeed, he might have succeeded in his ambition, had he made a better choice of co-conspirator.

Things changed after Mary's marriage. It was Darnley, rather than Moray and Maitland, who was the obstacle between Bothwell and the throne. Such an obstacle might be removed, and a man such as Bothwell had no reason to fear conviction. Backed by hundreds of armed supporters prepared to intimidate witnesses and judges, he literally held the courts in contempt, believing (rightly, as it turned out) that he could obtain a 'not guilty verdict' whatever the charge. However, by announcing to the world that a murder had indeed been committed, he would have placed the queen in a terrible predicament.

One word from Bothwell – a hint would have been enough – would have brought Mary down, and what would happen to her son James? It wouldn't have mattered whether she had been a party to the murder or not. The Protestant party wouldn't allow such a chance to go begging. Shortly after the explosion at Kirk o' Fields, a poster appeared in the streets of Edinburgh depicting a mermaid, and a hare surrounded by daggers. The hare was Bothwell's family crest. A mermaid was a colloquial Scots name for a prostitute. The Edinburgh mob would believe what it wanted to believe, and they were already chanting 'Burn the whore!'.

These are only suggestions, but if Mary were indeed expecting her drunken, bullying and syphilitic husband to be disposed of and to be disposed of quietly, in a way that suggested he had died of natural causes, she would have been thrown into a panic, realising that she had been double-crossed. She would have found it hard to resist any of Bothwell's demands, though she may indeed have resisted him at his castle at Dunbar.

Simply because they might have been lovers in the past does not imply that Mary wished to marry Bothwell, nor would it alter the fact that rape is rape, and it may have been repeated many times. Bothwell kept Mary in his castle for nearly a fortnight before returning her to Edinburgh, 'leading her like a captive' according to at least one witness. Such a prolonged, brutal assault – if it occurred – would have emphasised Bothwell's dominance of the threatened queen.

Perhaps we should leave the queen with the last word on her abduction. Not long after her hasty marriage, she described her 'courtship' to the Bishop of Dunblane. 'Albeit we found his doings rude, yet were his words and answers gentle.'

CHAPTER SIXTEEN

QUEEN MARY'S DOWNFALL

The Scottish envoy Robert Melville, in reporting to Queen Elizabeth of England on the marriage of Mary and Bothwell, highlighted the quarrelsome nature of the Scots as an explanation. He argued that Mary had been exhausted by their plotting against her, and needed the support of a strong husband. However, Elizabeth was not impressed. After all, she ruled 'unruly England' alone, and was constantly beset with intrigue and plotting. Her main objection was that Mary had married a man suspected of her former husband's murder. The argument that Bothwell had been acquitted of that charge would not have impressed Elizabeth, who knew the circumstances of those farcical court proceedings.

Realising the difficulty of his position, Bothwell wrote to Elizabeth. 'I will thus boldly affirm that, albeit men of greater birth and estimation might well have been preferred to this room, yet none more careful to see your two Majesties' amity and intelligence continued by all good offices.' Even his attempts at insinuation verge on self-aggrandisement. His letter may have done nothing more than steel Elizabeth's resolve against him.

The English queen had another concern. Bothwell had made himself stepfather to her godson – heir to the English throne as well as the Scottish, as long as Elizabeth remained childless. Before doing that, he should have sought her approval. In forging ahead, Bothwell had made himself England's affair and risked incurring her wrath, and Elizabeth was not of a forgiving nature in such matters. To those who knew the full circumstances of the case – and Elizabeth's agents within Scotland were certainly efficient – it might have been feared that Bothwell could persuade or force Mary into granting the 'crown matrimonial' to her new husband, as she had done previously for

Dauphin Francis. After that, who could say? Mary and her son, the infant prince, could meet with 'accidents', leaving Bothwell to rule in his own right. Bothwell may have been maintaining a sexual relationship with his former wife after his marriage to the queen. There had been accusations of collusion between Bothwell and Lady Jean. With Mary out of the way, there would have been nothing to hinder them from remarrying. They were certainly a formidable pair.

Since the marriage, Bothwell had become obsessively suspicious of the queen. She wasn't allowed to close doors, and was shadowed by an armed guard. He insisted on being present at any meetings. Those nobles who managed to gain an audience reported back that the queen was certainly distressed, and almost deranged. It is known that Bothwell was involved with sorcery, and some suggested that he was 'managing' Mary with some sort of drug. All this would have been reported to Elizabeth. Certainly, Bothwell would later admit that he had used 'magic' to seduce the queen into marriage.

Scottish nobles opposed to the hasty royal marriage and fearful of what it might lead to raised an armed force, declaring their intent 'to deliver Mary from Bothwell and her enemies, to secure the person of the young prince, and to prosecute the murderers of the king.'

The queen had another explanation for their opposition, as she mused in later years. 'It may have originated in some secret feuds among the lords of recent date, or possibly from grievances of remoter origin which, though long hidden, at last came to scatter their poison on the surface.'

This may have been a reference to William Maitland, Mary's trusted envoy to the English court. His loyalty was, in fact, to the Protestant party. Within days of the marriage, he was given cause to hate Bothwell to the point where he was prepared to set his face against the queen. In a letter to Cecil, he reported that Bothwell, in a fit of rage, had tried to kill him. This had occurred in the queen's presence and it was the last straw for Maitland. While he regretted any disloyalty to the queen, enough was enough. Indeed many Scots, not least those who took part in the Chaseabout Raid and were then exiled, had grievances of various origins – not necessarily as remote as the queen suggested.

Maitland's correspondence with Cecil reveals something that is kept hidden in the lords' proclamation that they intended to deliver Mary from Bothwell, for it contains the hint that the queen, as much as her new husband, was held responsible both for Darnley's death, and the subsequent marriage. There can be little doubt that Cecil and Elizabeth were kept fully informed of the developing situation, at the same time as suggesting that the situation must not be allowed to continue.

Mary's illegitimate half-brother Lord James Stewart, Earl of Moray, was another who had been disappointed, to say the least, by Mary's marital decisions. He had been her closest advisor on her return from France. As a leader of the Protestant cause, he had guarded and guided her well and wisely. In fact, she had become almost completely dependent on his wise council to the point where he had become a real power in the land. Then she married Darnley, who he could not abide, leading him to rebel, becoming one of the leaders of the Chaseabout Raid. After a time in exile, he returned just in time for Riccio's murder. And then, just when he might have expected to regain his half-sister's favour and his role as her closest council, she married Bothwell. It was no coincidence that many of those now opposing Bothwell were members of Moray's original Protestant party.

On June 6, barely three weeks after their marriage on May 15 and faced with hostility from all quarters, Bothwell decided to leave Edinburgh. He took Mary from Holyrood Palace to the Castle of Borthwick, a stark fortress just two miles from his own castle at Crichton. Quite why he decided against his own battlements is not known. Perhaps he thought that it was the first place that any rebels would come looking for the royal couple. If so, he underestimated their intelligence network. The rebels were soon there in force, and prepared for a siege.

Bothwell made his escape – galloping through the startled besiegers. A companion was captured, but Bothwell got clean away, leaving Mary to fend for herself. Some have criticised this action, but Bothwell was no coward and must have believed that the only way to save the situation was by raising an armed force from his own estates, and then counter-attacking. There was nothing to be gained from having Mary at his side in the desperate bid to break out of the castle that had suddenly become their prison.

In the wake of Bothwell's escape, the besiegers called upon the queen to open the gates of the castle and return with them to Edinburgh where she might renounce her husband. When she refused, she was effectively sealing her fate. She may have feared for her own life at the hands of the mob of irregular soldiery. But whatever her reason – and it might have been blind panic – now that she had publicly refused to abandon Bothwell, it was presumed that the wildest rumours must be true. Those who had so recently declared their intent to 'rescue' the queen were now screaming abuse at her as she looked down from the castle battlements. Abuse that was, according to one witness, 'too evil and unseemly to be told'.

Faced with this vulgar hostility, Mary retreated out of view, but the abuse didn't stop and the siege continued. Perhaps disillusioned, or tiring of the venture, some of the besiegers drifted back to Edinburgh. Those who remained were not best organised and, seizing the opportunity, Mary disguised herself as a man and managed to escape on horseback. She met Bothwell at the nearby Black Castle at Cakemuir, from where they made their way to Bothwell's castle at Dunbar where forces still loyal to the queen and Bothwell's brigands were already gathering.

Mary and Bothwell might have waited longer at Dunbar, and raised a far greater force, but for an invitation to return to Edinburgh. Sir James Balfour promised them the protection of the castle and its guns. Thus encouraged, they left Dunbar with just 250 men, though this number had swelled to 600 by the time they reached Haddington. They then marched onto Seton Palace at Prestonpans, where they spent the night. Next morning, they resumed their march to Edinburgh, but eight miles east of the city, at Carberry Hill, an army was waiting for them. The invitation from Edinburgh Castle had been a ruse to draw them out of Dunbar.

The opposing forces lined up in battle array, but there was no fighting. Instead, the leaders rode out to parley. Again, Mary refused to abandon her new husband. After much talk and argument, Bothwell fled north and Mary was placed in what might be described as 'protective custody' – arrested and imprisoned in a remote island fortress in Lochleven, near Kinross, while her captors weighed up the evidence against her.

Bothwell lingered for a time at Spynie Castle where he was sheltered by his kinsman, the Bishop of Moray, then made his way to Orkney, then Shetland, and finally to Norway where his ship was seized, and he was accused of being a pirate. He was then confronted by the Lady Anne Throndsom who he had married then deserted in Denmark in 1560 – so he hadn't in fact been free to marry Lady Jean, let alone Mary.

He was transferred to a Danish castle and chained to the wall of a tiny dungeon, without light or sound, becoming totally deranged and dying some 18 long years later. A prolonged and brutal end to an evil man, some might say.

The stories of Mary Queen of Scots, Lord Darnley aka King Henry and Bothwell have intrigued historians, romanticists, conspiracy theorists, and religious propagandists for four centuries. Today, we are faced with mountains of faction, innuendo and downright lies. Who killed Lord Darnley? In truth, nobody can say. Was his wife an accomplice? Again, who can say? Did Bothwell rape Mary, or was she a willing participant? Yet again, who can say for sure?

Perhaps we are asking the wrong questions. It might be better to concentrate on asking who had the strongest motive – the most to gain, or, taking a slightly different slant, who did gain the most from the decline and fall of these three figures?

In the murder of Darnley, Bothwell certainly had his motives and opportunity, but this doesn't deny the possibility that he may have been little more than a puppet. Vain seekers of aggrandisement are often prone to manipulation, if they think that whatever is proposed will help to serve their own ends. Whose hands on the strings, then? Again, we come back to that question about who had most to gain, or lose.

Talk of 'the Protestants' in Scotland in that time suggests that they were a cohesive force, all working for the same end, a Protestant monarch for their Protestant land. But they were split over what means would best achieve that end. Faced with a Catholic queen, they divided roughly into two camps – the doves and the hawks. Or, to put it another way, those who favoured the carrot and those who would employ a stick.

Queen Mary's half-brother Lord James Stewart, Earl of Moray, was a leader of the doves, offering himself as the queen's advisor. Whenever she got into trouble, he was there to rescue her. He became her strong protector and it was hoped that, under his influence and given time, she might have converted to Protestantism. Her stated belief in religious toleration seemed to signal that she might be open to persuasion. After all, every Scottish Protestant had either been a Catholic in the past, or was descended from Catholics.

One of the few flies in the dove's seductive ointment was the rampant John Knox whose sustained insolence pushed Mary into defending her Catholic faith. He might be described as the leader of the hawks. By all accounts, Mary was a passionate woman. Above all, she was a queen. But the rabid preacher refused to see that while she could not be ordered, she might be persuaded and finally converted. Heaven knows, she wouldn't have been the first. Her mother, Mary of Guise, had been an ardent Catholic and a willing persecutor of Protestants. In these circumstances, the Protestants needed to take a tough line in defending themselves. A man like Knox, who could incite a riot or inspire a revolt, was a useful man to have on your side. But the young queen was altogether different to her mother, even preaching religious toleration. This was probably as much as most Protestants had ever wanted – toleration rather than confrontation and persecution – but it didn't suit Knox. He continued his tirades against the queen both privately and from the pulpit, sometimes reducing her to tears by his violent statements.

Knox was going too far, and the doves tried to rein him in. He found himself in trouble for having written a letter summoning the 'brethren' from all parts of Scotland to Edinburgh to defend – apparently by violence, if necessary – one Cranstoun, who was to be tried for brawling in the chapel royal. Knox's letter was interpreted by the council as treasonable, but when brought to trial he was judged to have done nothing more than his duty in summoning the brethren in time of danger.

In the summer of 1564, the Lords of the Congregation publicly censured Knox for his violence in speech and demeanour against the queen, but Knox retorted with his usual references to Ahab and Jezebel, maintaining that idolaters must 'die the death'. In vain, the lords cited the opinions of Luther, Calvin, Melanchthon, and other Continental Protestants as being entirely opposed to Knox's views, and requested him to write and ascertain their judgment on the questions at issue. Knox flatly refused and, as he always produced Scriptural texts to back up his opinions, the Lords were silenced if not convinced.

Mary was clearly not intended for a celibate life. As far as the doves were concerned, this would not be a problem if she followed her half-brother's good advice. Indeed, it might have been employed to the Protestant's advantage. Moray could suggest a Protestant, and if he was tall, handsome and fair, he might woo the queen away from the Roman faith. And queen or no, a wife was expected to accept her husband's dictates – a vehicle for kings.

Then Mary chose the Catholic Darnley – though not, on first impressions, so Catholic or incorruptible that he might not be encouraged to think again. He seemed to hover on the fence, so might be persuaded to fall on the Protestant side. Therefore, the Lords of the Congregation would have seen little advantage in forcing a confrontation. Better to appear to welcome

Darnley, then set to work on winning him over. The carrot rather than the stick.

Knox had other ideas, and made a vehement attack from the pulpit on Mary and Darnley, in their presence, about a month after their marriage. He was formally suspended from preaching, but he seems to have disregarded the prohibition, remarking that if the Church (not the council) commanded him to abstain, he would obey 'so far as the Word of God would permit' – in other words, he would obey only so far as he himself thought fit. Ironically, Knox's opposition to Mary may have influenced her decision to marry Darnley – if only for a husband's support.

Unfortunately, the marriage was a disaster and Darnley turned out to be as arrogant as he was foolish. When her husband fell out with her former advisors, Mary found it increasingly difficult to take sides. She had never coped well with stress – part of her Stewart inheritance. Not knowing whom to trust, Mary fell back on her French connections, taking advice from David Riccio. He was known to be an agent of Mary's uncle, the Duke of Guise, a hard-line opponent of Protestantism. The doves among the Lords of the Congregation realised to their despair that instead of creating the ways and means to convert the queen to Protestantism, the marriage to Darnley had pushed her deep into the Catholic fold. They might have seen little alternative but to unleash the hawks in their camp. Riccio was the first to go. Whether Knox was actually privy to his murder before the queen's eyes on March 9 1566 is a matter of doubt; but his own statement that 'the act was most just and worthy of all praise' shows his approval. Darnley followed Riccio within a relatively short space of time.

Something else must be considered. Once Mary had produced an heir, the baby Prince James – heir to the throne of England as well as Scotland – she became expendable. Easier to control a baby than a wilful queen. Even if Mary had perished in the explosion at Kirk o' Fields, the future of both countries wouldn't have been altered one jot. Removing Mary from the scene would, indeed, have removed the only major obstacle to having her son raised in the Protestant faith. At some point, it must have crossed somebody's mind that Mary had become more a liability than an asset.

Then the vain Bothwell thrust himself to the fore. Scottish nobles who opposed the latest royal marriage raised an armed force, declaring it was their intent 'to deliver Mary from Bothwell and her enemies,' and yet, when Mary made it clear that she neither sought nor welcomed their deliverance, they arrested her – an arrest that would lead to years of imprisonment and

❧ CHAPTER SEVENTEEN ❧

PROTESTANT PERSPECTIVES

W hat was to be done with Mary Queen of Scots? Despite her Protestant marriage to Bothwell, she remained a devout Catholic and would raise her son in that faith if left free to do so – the son who was heir to the thrones of Scotland, England and Ireland. Those eager to ensure a Protestant succession would have been determined to stop her, and the best way to do that, short of killing her, was to implicate her in her husband Darnley's murder, thus proving she was not fit to rule.

Mary was brought captive to Edinburgh in June 1567, abused by her captors and the mob, (who chanted 'burn the whore') then confined to Lochleven Castle. A month later, and under duress, she signed an abdication conveying the Crown to her baby son, still referred to affectionately as Jacques, and appointed her Protestant illegitimate half-brother, Lord James Stewart, Earl of Moray, as Regent.

On July 29, the one-year-old Jacques was crowned King James VI of Scots. Mary would never see him again. Under the direction of Moray, the young king was to be raised in the Protestant faith and guarded from unwanted influences – unwanted, that is, by the Protestants who had seized control of the Scottish kingdom. These Protestants maintained a close working relationship with the English court, acknowledging that the Scottish king was heir to the throne of England. Meanwhile, the Protestants were free to develop a case against Mary, in order to justify her continuing detention.

At the time of Mary's capture, John Knox had retired to Ayrshire, to write his *History*. She was already a prisoner at Lochleven when he returned to Edinburgh to resume his sermons against her although, ironically, after her fall he never regained his former prominence in the country. 'I live as a man already dead from all civil affairs', he wrote a little later to the Earl of Moray's agent in England. He had served his purpose as a rabble rouser, and Scotland's new breed of Protestant politicians set him aside. In his later years, Knox's declining energies were devoted to his ministerial work, which he seems to have carried on with many intervals of weariness and depression. In the autumn of 1569, he was struck by apoplexy and never entirely recovered. He died in 1572, still making denunciations of Mary and 'that cruel murderer and false traitor, the King of France'.

'Knox cannot be said to have possessed the impetuous and heroic boldness of a Luther,' wrote his biographer and editor, Dr Laing. 'On more than one occasion he displayed a timidity or shrinking from danger scarcely to have been expected from one who boasted of his willingness to suffer death in his Master's cause.'

A less sympathetic biographer had this to say. 'He was most valiant when he had armed men at his back, and the popular idea of his personal courage, said to have been expressed by the Regent Morton, is entirely erroneous'.

As to Knox's religion, it may be sufficient to suggest (without questioning the sincerity of his convictions) that his reaction to the Catholicism of his youth and the persecution of his early, Protestant colleagues, seems to have landed him outside the pale of Christianity altogether. The ferocity and unrestrained violence of his public utterances stand out, even in the rude and lawless age in which he lived, as surpassing almost everything recorded of his contemporaries.

How did this thing that started out as a desire to reform the Catholic Church transform into a religious, social and political revolution – even to the point where 'the people' would decide how the young king was to be raised or, as was sometimes threatened, be 'removed'? Perhaps the first question that needs to be asked is whether or not the Catholic Church was truly in need of reform.

In the 15th century, James I of Scots had been increasingly angered by slack standards within some Scottish monasteries, and introduced the strict Carthusian order to act as a balance. However, they made little impact on those monasteries and friaries where easy living was the order of the day. Seeing this, lay people tended to stop making endowments to these 'institutions of sloth', preferring to put their money into town churches and collegiate establishments.

The sex lives of some Catholic churchmen, who had taken the oath of celibacy, are said by some to be a cause of the Reformation. However, there was a fairly straightforward attitude towards sex in pre-Reformation Scotland, and an acceptance that men with 'natural' desires would break some rules. For example, the 'conditions of employment' of a Linlithgow chaplain stated that he would not maintain 'a continual concubine'. So a priest wasn't to live with a woman as if husband and wife, but this needn't stop him having casual sex whenever the opportunity arose. With predictable results ... In Scotland there was a legal process by which illegitimate children could be legitimised. Nearly one-third of these were the offspring of priests, at a time when priests were a tiny fraction of the population – less than one in six hundred. This moral laxness was found throughout the hierarchy of the Catholic clergy – one of the outstanding examples being Cardinal Beaton, Archbishop of St Andrews, whose lust for women seemed to be matched only by his desire to burn heretics. Some nuns were described as being as immoral as they were illiterate.

While some turned a blind eye to fornicating priests, the hypocrisy inherent in this did not go unnoticed. It wasn't so much the act itself as the breaking of an oath. What respect would be afforded to a priest who was 'living in sin' – a priest who openly flouted his solemn vows, while claiming to be an intermediary between men and God without whose involvement there could be no salvation?

The sex lives of some priests were as nothing compared to the avarice to be seen at individual and institutional levels in the Catholic Church in Scotland. It was this greed of a rich church in a poor land that sowed the most fertile seeds of discontent. At a local level, people saw that for all the money gathered in, only a tiny proportion was returned to the parish, while the bulk was siphoned off by the prelates, abbots and commendators (lay protectors of monastic establishments). Often this left the local priest in dire straits. Paid less than a pittance, some took the livings of five, six or more parishes – spreading themselves thinly between the needs of a hugely inflated number of parishioners – while some took to begging in the streets. Others traded in goods to the point where their priestly duties had to take second place. They charged fees to carry out particular rites of the Church, often demanding payment in advance. In some cases, they refused to bury the poor, whose families couldn't afford the requisite cow and cloth. In brief, a significant number became little more than predatory parasites – or so it appeared to their parishioners – either from need or by choice.

Such an unhappy situation clearly affected the quality of people the Church could attract to the priesthood. At the local level, low pay and impossible conditions were not the stuff to attract the right sort of candidates. Many priests were barely literate – some could hardly sign their own names let alone read a service, either in Latin or Scots. It was not unknown for a priest to be staggering drunk while conducting a Mass. In 1562, a Jesuit described the Scottish Catholic clergy as 'extremely licentious and scandalous'.

In some cases, churches were literally falling about their parishioners' ears. Wars with England had long been used as an excuse. Why repair when the English might return in a few years time and knock it all down? It was a good question, certainly in the Borders. Nevertheless, many believed that the Catholic Church in Scotland, and the monasteries in particular, had converted into some sort of conglomerate property company with the ethics and priorities of what we would now describe as 'slum landlords'. By failing to repair, they reduced costs, thus boosting profits.

Such corruption, involving huge urban and rural wealth, and vast incomes, could not have been achieved without the complicity of the establishment. Generations of Scottish monarchs took a share of the loot. If it had been denied, the monarch might have acted to purge the money grabbers. But as long as the money kept rolling in, the monarchy complied. James V of Scots was probably without equal in his ability to use the Church to benefit himself and his extended family. When Henry VIII of England declared for Protestantism, James recognised that if he kept the Church guessing he could bend it to his will. The pope was determined not to see any more countries slipping from the Catholic grasp. In 1532, when James was 20 years old, he already had a number of illegitimate children. He told the pope what he wanted for three of his sons, all of whom were still babies, and it was done. One became Abbot of Kelso and Melrose, another Prior of St Andrews and Pittenweem, while the third became Abbot of Holyrood. All appointments effective forthwith. Later, a fourth illegitimate son was made Prior of Coldingham and a fifth was Abbot of the Charterhouse. All these appointments brought huge incomes. No wonder the king was so popular with the ladies. Lord James Stewart, Earl of Moray and Regent of Scotland, came from this illegitimate royal brood, but this didn't stop his criticism of its means of support. Rather the opposite, particularly when he had secured alternative incomes for himself.

It would be wrong to suggest that all the Catholic clergy in Scotland were steeped in immorality, indolence and avarice. Far from it. As in any institution, for every rotten apple there may be at least one that is good. Archbishop John Hamilton of St Andrews, who replaced the murdered Cardinal Beaton, was one good priest. Witnessing the growth of Protestantism abroad, and the tide of unrest at home, he was keener than ever to set the Church in order. He echoed the judgement made by another contemporary critic within the Church, John Major, who wrote that 'piety the mother was smothered by luxury the wanton daughter'.

Men like Hamilton and Major were prepared to rattle a few gilded cages in order to save the Church. It is, ironically, these Catholic churchmen who should be remembered whenever reform is discussed, for it was they who sought reform, as such, rather than the revolutionary alternative of the Protestants.

Under Hamilton's leadership, programmes of reform were outlined at the General Councils of the Scottish (Catholic) Church in 1549, 1552 and 1559. Various abuses were considered, such as absentee priests and uneducated preachers. Recognising that Protestantism was attracting many of the country's intellectuals, the larger abbeys were ordered to send students to universities, though they may have been trying to make silk purses out of sows' ears.

In hindsight, it might be said that these reforms were too little, too late. While they acknowledged abuses at local levels, they could do little to correct them. By the time these reforms were considered, the whole of the British mainland – both Catholic Scotland and Protestant England – was experiencing social unrest and revolt. South of the border, it was in 1549 that the Prayer Book rebels besieged Exeter, and agrarian protesters captured Norwich.

In 1550, leading Scots were entertained by the French king at Rouen, to convince them of the benefits of remaining Catholic and allied to France, but only a few were convinced. Among them, of course, were members of the Scottish royal family, headed by Mary of Guise. This extended family of Scottish royals, and various aristocrats, did nothing to support Archbishop Hamilton's proposed reforms because the Church, in its corrupt form, was their gold-plated meal ticket.

It might be said that Hamilton's reforms were aimed at the wrong level of the hierarchy within the church. For the common people of Scotland, it did not matter whether the monasteries became seats of learning. What concerned them, above all things, was the misappropriation of local funds. The Church, as an institution, must have seemed like a hostile tax collector, robbing from the poor to feed its self and rich friends. This was the problem that Archbishop Hamilton and his reformers could not solve, and it was this failure that led to a surge in Protestant numbers. If the Catholic Church could not reform itself – and many had concluded that it could not – then it must be swept aside.

A significant number of the early Protestant preachers were disillusioned Catholic clergy – John Knox among them. The lower ranks of the Catholic priesthood suffered as much as any from the Church's financial priorities. These reformed rakes were among the main instigators for seeking 'a different way', convinced that the Catholic hierarchy was simply paying lip service to reform.

Where did the Protestants find their converts? The rise of the burghs and increasing power of the burgesses provided an ideal environment to encourage freethinking and Protestantism. Knox affirmed the important role played by mariners in coastal burghs, for here were a class of men 'who, frequenting other countries, hear the true doctrine affirmed and the vanity of the papistical religion openly rebuked.' On returning from their voyages, they described what they had seen in the ports of the North Sea and Baltic.

The merchants and craftsmen of the burghs liked what they heard. Their increasing involvement in government at local and national levels had encouraged a growing sense of independence, and a will for self-determination. For them, perhaps, the choice between Catholicism and Protestantism was, rightly or wrongly, about dictate or democracy. It has also been said that the merchants and craftsmen, with their secretive guilds, were well placed to spread the doctrine of Protestantism without drawing the attention of the Catholic Church and Crown.

As well as merchants and craftsmen, the towns, burghs and cities had attracted an 'under class' of poor folk, including those who had fled from a succession of famines in the countryside, or been evicted for failing to pay inflating rents. These poor, living from hand-to-mouth, felt a deep resentment against the established order. In that frame of mind they could be incited, as a group, to riot or rebel. John Knox exploited this social unrest to the full – in Perth, Edinburgh and elsewhere. When the mob attacked and looted major Catholic establishments, it was not so much an expression of dissatisfaction with theological doctrines as the disenfranchised poor attacking the ostentatiously rich.

More affluent people were prone to disenchantment with the Church. After all, wealth is relative and most people can convince themselves that they don't have enough. In the countryside, standing between the poor and the great aristocrats, were the minor lairds or landowners – particularly common in the south-west of Scotland. With fairly heavy expenses and comparatively small rentals from their let farms, they were caught financially between a rock and a hard place. Therefore, they were deeply resentful at having to pay tithes to the wealthy Church. Few like paying taxes and the minor lairds swore at the wealthy clergy riding on their backs, and hoped that Protestantism might relieve this burden. Hope became belief, and the emergent 'Protestant Party', as it was developing politically, did nothing to disillusion them.

What about the Scottish nobility? What would they have found attractive in the broad sweep of Protestantism, leaving aside the theological niceties? Not a lot, might be the obvious answer. At least, not in those families who had been able to obtain a share of the Church's wealth – perhaps by talking the monarch or regent into arranging for a younger son to be given a church office requiring a modicum of work in return for a comfortable living. However, you can't please all the nobles all the time and James V, Mary of Guise and their daughter Mary Queen of Scots had the unhappy knack of offending most while honouring many. Certainly, in the time of Mary of Guise's regency, many Scottish nobles felt they were ignored in matters of state. They grew to resent the regent's French advisors who filled the highest offices, and saw the French and Catholic Church as being mutually supportive, and thus exclusive of themselves. For disillusioned nobles including Argyll, Morton and Arran, replacing the Catholic Church would remove this unwanted French control, and clear the way to power for themselves. For them, perhaps, the rallying cry of Protestantism was 'Scotland for the Scots', admittedly with a selfish slant.

In 1559, while the General Council of the Scottish (Catholic) Church debated fairly minor reforms, the stated intention of The Lords of the Faithful Congregation was to defend the Protestant faith, and to free Scotland 'from the bondage and tyranny of strangers'. The truth, however, was that they sought to rid the country of the Catholic French in order to open the way to a full alliance with Protestant England – an alliance that did not depend on 'bondage and tyranny' along the lines imposed by Mary of Guise's French troops. What they were hoping for was a working partnership with England, based on mutual respect and support.

The leaders of the Protestant Party in Scotland – for by now it was as much a political as a religious movement – were not so independently minded as to imagine that Scotland could rid itself of French interference without English help, or that a future Scotland would be strong enough to 'go it alone' in a changing world. The burgesses, craft guilds, merchants, traders and mariners recognised that the country's future prosperity would depend on the development of international trade. The lairds and aristocrats also saw that this trade might be the source of huge fortunes for investors.

As a group, the upper echelons of the Protestants recognised that centuries of war with England had held the country back, wasting its already meagre resources. The continuance of such wars as they had witnessed in their own lifetimes would destroy any future prosperity. Alliance with France meant war with England. Alliance with England therefore seemed a happier prospect. In a united Britain, all might prosper. Many Scots were sick and tired of the alternative. It is one thing to dislike or distrust your neighbours, but something else again to waste your sons on fighting them.

The Reformation in Scotland has been described as a great and popular revolution, but this is a half-truth. In fact, the revolution was far from popular in some areas, including the Highlands and the Borders. Without wishing to indulge in sweeping generalisations, it might be said that the Reformation received far more support in the burghs of the central belt, south-west and south-east than it did in essentially rural areas.

The worker in the fields was probably quite indifferent to the niceties of theological doctrines. He would have had more pressing matters to consider, like the passing of the season's wind and rain, and whether there would be a roof and food for his family in six months' time. These basic needs helped to ensure agricultural workers and minor tenants would worship according to the dictates of the local landowner, aristocratic or otherwise. If the laird had converted to Protestantism, then it was expected that his tenants would do likewise – or find somewhere else to live.

Consider the case of Lord James, the Earl of Moray, and his kindly Catholic tenants. 'Kindly' referred to their legal status, rather than a helpful attitude. They had no legal right to the ground they occupied and upon which they depended for their survival – though they enjoyed informal rights of heritable tenure, in return for a fairly nominal rent. In the late 1500s, Moray decided to ride roughshod over those rights and evicted his 'kindly' tenants to make way for others who would pay more, and whose religion was more to his liking. The original tenants were of Clan Chattan and their chief led an uprising against the oppression and evictions, but it was not successful. Little wonder, when you consider the power wielded by Moray once the Protestants began to seize control.

With Protestantism meaning different things to different people – from the desperately poor to the ambitious rich – it was inevitable that there would be conflicts of interest. Widening cracks appeared in the façade of the Protestant movement. To the reforming priests, theology and closely connected issues were the primary objective. However, the intellectuals, merchants, craftsmen and 'small lairds' sought to link religious with social change, including greater democracy. Of course, this did not necessarily suit the ambitions of the upper tiers of the nobility. Without questioning the sincerity of their religious allegiances, it seems that some were intent on personal and family gain – seeing a chance to feather their own nests at the expense of the Catholic Church, by taking its lands while seizing control of the government of the kingdom. They would certainly have cocked an eyebrow at the notion that they were taking a leading role in a glorious revolution! For some, the Reformation was 'just another power struggle' and they looked long and hard before placing their bets. The notion that such men would dance to the rabble-rousing tunes of John Knox is, quite frankly, bizarre.

In his role as Regent, the Earl of Moray sought to strengthen an alliance of Protestant nobles into a ruling elite, with himself at its head, but this proved too much for old rivals – including the Hamiltons – who were jealous of Moray's power. These Hamiltons had not 'reformed' and remained supporters of the still imprisoned Queen Mary. They could see that Moray would not consider her restoration. There was, of course, an alternative. In 1570, three years after becoming Regent, Lord James Stewart, Earl of Moray, illegitimate half-brother to Queen Mary and uncle of King James, was shot dead while riding down the main street in Linlithgow.

This assassination brought Scotland to the brink of civil war. Queen Mary's supporters raised her standard and rallied to the cause, if only to regain the status they had enjoyed before the Protestants came to power. They were joined by Catholic rebels from the north of England, prompting a short but violent border raid, but Queen Elizabeth ordered them to withdraw while she intervened in Scottish affairs in a more conciliatory fashion. Finally, it was agreed that Matthew Stewart, Earl of Lennox, father of the late Lord Darnley and grandfather of King James, would be Moray's replacement. He didn't last long – killed by the Marian Lords (Queen Mary's supporters) in 1571.

Lennox's replacement, the Earl of Morton, selected as Regent in 1572 when James was six, had long been the strong man of the Protestant party. Moray had been strong, for sure, but Morton was stronger. His aim was absolutism in Church and State, and he pointed the way that the country was to follow. He was described as a stern and extortionate ruler, yet possessed a wonderful courage and fortitude and a statesman's grasp of the problems confronting Scotland. His major role in dethroning Mary left him no other course but reliance upon Elizabeth of England, with whom he skilfully maintained good relations without becoming the tool of her policy – no easy task. True, even his most ardent admirers admit he was a tyrant, but 'it was only by tyranny that Scotland could be governed'.

Morton was nobody's fool – that much is certain. He took up the established contacts with Queen Elizabeth and the English court, recognising that William Cecil was the secretive power behind the English throne. By now, William Cecil was perfecting the English Secret Service, though it was never known as such. His nameless web of informants and agents were to play a major role in gathering civil and military intelligence both at home and abroad. They made mistakes, for sure, but in their time they were very good indeed. Certainly, they had plenty of practice.

Morton and Cecil both knew that Scotland and England must expect a Catholic reaction to the Protestant Reformation. In the broad scheme of things, from now on they could accept that what threatened Scotland threatened England, and vice-versa. Plotters were already whispering in clandestine meetings, both at home and abroad. It was only a matter of time.

Many of the plots centred on restoring Queen Mary to the Scottish throne and – eventually or at one and the same time – to the throne of England, thus achieving a universal restoration of the Catholic Church. This common threat created a unity of purpose between Protestants in both countries.

Even before Morton came to the Regency, Mary had escaped from imprisonment. In May 1568, a number of nobles and bishops had come to her support with 5,000 armed men. Archibald Campbell, Earl of Argyll, commanded these forces, which were largely supplied by the Hamiltons. An incompetent general, Campbell was defeated by a smaller force, commanded by the Earl of Moray, and Mary was forced to flee.

Rather than taking a ship to France, Mary had headed south to throw herself on Elizabeth of England's mercy. This seems a strange choice to have made. In France, Mary could have lived in comfortable retirement on the very substantial income she received as widow of the French king. Why take the risk of fleeing to England? The French may have let her know that she would not be welcomed. They still had their colonial ambitions in regard to Scotland and England – ambitions that might be best served with Mary in either one of those countries, rather than languishing on a French estate. Clearly, she remained a threat, and Elizabeth had little option but to renew her imprisonment.

England's premier nobleman and Catholic, Thomas Howard, the fourth duke of Norfolk, entered the scene. He had been devastated by the death of three wives in childbirth, and it was rumoured that he might be about to marry Mary and seek a Catholic restoration. In the spring of 1568, while loyal forces were rushing to support the recently escaped Mary in Scotland, Norfolk attempted to undermine Cecil at court. As attempts go, it was a rather clumsy affair. Elizabeth and Cecil recognised the threat posed by Norfolk if he married Mary, but came to the conclusion that the man had been overcome with grief and wasn't thinking straight. When he declared that he was still loyal to the crown, he was given a stern telling-off and imprisoned, but kept his head.

Norfolk's former Catholic allies, Thomas Percy, Earl of Northumberland, and Charles Neville, Earl of Westmoreland, rebelled at the end of 1569, seizing Durham before marching south towards Tutbury where Queen Mary was being held. Clearly, they intended to secure her release. However, when they heard that a royal army commanded by the Earl of Sussex was moving to intercept them, they had a change of heart and turned for home. With the royal troops still hot on their heels, they continued north and crossed the border into Scotland. They entered Liddesdale – a 'no-go area' for any official troops, either Scottish or English – where they were harboured by the reiving clans who had little allegiance to any side other than their own. Some weren't lucky enough to find such a sanctuary. In January 1570, it was reported that 450 of the northern Catholic rebels had been executed.

In August, perhaps assuming that the executions had settled the Catholic threat, Cecil persuaded Queen Elizabeth to free the Duke of Norfolk into house arrest. One month later, negotiations were resumed for the marriage of Elizabeth to the Habsburg Archduke Charles. Another name that was mentioned was Henry the Duke of Anjou, the Catholic heir to the French throne. Clearly, the queen or her advisors were prepared to consider all possibilities. It is quite impossible to follow the major and minor thrusts of Elizabethan diplomacy with all its subtleties and hidden nuances.

In July 1570 the Protestant Queen Elizabeth was excommunicated by Pope Pius V, partly in response to the execution of the Catholic rebels. The purpose of the excommunication was to release those of her subjects who remained Catholic from any allegiance to her. In effect, it said that Elizabeth was no longer queen, and need not be obeyed. Thus the English Catholics were being urged to rebel. However, this made little if any impression on the majority of them who, despite their religious differences, remained staunchly loyal to the crown. One of the exceptions was John Felton who nailed a copy of the papal bull to the gates of the Bishop of London's palace. He was arrested and tortured, but still refused to acknowledge Elizabeth as queen. Finally, he was executed.

A far more serious threat to Elizabeth was about to emerge. It would later be discovered that since his release from the Tower of London in August 1570, and despite his earlier protestations of loyalty, the Duke of Norfolk had become involved in a plot to overthrow the queen. Robert Ridolfi, described as a Florentine banker with close connections to the papacy, had hatched this plot. Indeed, the pope was one of the plotters, along with Philip II of Spain and the Duke of Alva, the Spanish military commander.

By devious means, the still imprisoned Queen Mary was kept abreast of the plan, which was that 6,000 Catholic soldiers would be landed at Harwich, to march on London. The Duke of Norfolk would seize Elizabeth and hold her hostage to ensure Mary's safety. Then, with Elizabeth and London under the rebels' control, Mary and Norfolk would marry and rule as queen and king in both England and Scotland – returning both countries to the Catholic faith.

It might have worked – except for Ridolfi's loose tongue and the efficiency of the Secret Service created by Cecil, who had recently been raised to the peerage by an already grateful queen. It was as Lord Burghley that he reported the threat to Elizabeth. His agents had trailed Ridolfi's messengers, and seized some coded correspondence. When these codes were deciphered, all was revealed. Norfolk was immediately arrested, and returned to the Tower. He was found guilty of treason in June 1572. This time, he failed to keep his head.

CHAPTER EIGHTEEN

THE VIRGIN QUEEN

Queen Elizabeth I of England is remembered as the 'Virgin Queen', and was famed as such during her lifetime. This was reflected in the naming of the then new territory of Virginia – an early example of English colonialism in the New World and among the first steps towards galloping imperialism across the face of the globe.

Elizabeth's unmarried and childless status was a rarity in royal circles. One cannot help but suspect, therefore, that it was something she chose. Heaven knows, there was no shortage of suitors, and there is plenty of evidence that she relished the company of men, but she politely refused them all, despite being under constant pressure from Parliament to find a suitable mate and start breeding. Eventually her proclaimed virginity (real or otherwise) created an image of noble sacrifice that prompted an unrivalled loyalty from her people. Godfrey Goodman remembered this loyalty when he was Bishop of Gloucester. He recalled how, as a boy of five, he had been in the crowd that hailed the queen at Whitehall Palace one evening in 1588.

'Then we cried "God Save Your Majesty". Then the Queen turned to us and said, "God bless you all my good people." Then we cried again "God Save Your Majesty". Then the Queen said, "You may well have a greater prince, but you shall never have a more loving prince" ... This wrought such an impression on us ... what an admirable queen she was and how we'd adventure our lives to do her service.'

This brief exchange encapsulates Elizabeth's deepening love affair with her people. By resisting the desire to love one person, she was able to give her all to all her people – and she gave her love with a modesty that suggested vulnerability. A mother's love, she seemed to suggest, offered in a decidedly masculine society. She knew how to pull the right strings. Ironically, perhaps, it was this portrayal of a celibate and virginal mother that secured the loyalty of Protestants as well as Catholics.

Elizabeth was brave, wise and charismatic. It must also be said that she was arrogant, spiteful and incredibly manipulative. It was this blend that made her the queen she was – inspiring devotion, while trusting nobody – charming, but cunning. Above all, perhaps, she was a gritty survivor in a hostile world. Certainly, it would not be too surprising to discover that she had achieved her iconic status by design.

Elizabeth's father, Henry VIII, had inspired awe in his early life, and terror in his later years. From him, the young Elizabeth had learnt 'that vanity of princes', believing in absolutism, and developing a jealous pride in personal power. Pride in a power that paid little more than lip service to democracy. As far as Henry and Elizabeth were concerned, it was not necessary to be a Roman Catholic in order to practice absolutism. A king, married or not, could yield that power to its utmost, as might an unmarried queen. However, a married queen – inevitably subservient to her husband at that time – could not. Knowing this, Elizabeth had cause enough to avoid giving herself to any man. Elizabeth's mother, Anne Boleyn, had paid the ultimate price for failing to please her husband, and who would choose to follow that route? She might, in that age of high natal mortality, have been terrified of childbirth. Whatever the reasons, she firmly decided against marriage.

Following her father's death, Elizabeth was given a salutary lesson in the ways of men – a lesson that ended in shame and scandal when she was sent to live with her father's widow, Catherine Parr, who married the Lord Admiral, Edward Seymour. He couldn't keep his hands off the young princess. There is little to suggest that Elizabeth was an unwilling participant in what was presumably her formative sexual experience. Rather the opposite, and Elizabeth learnt a lesson that she would remember and use throughout her life. Seymour was like putty in her hands. His desire to possess her, both as an attractive woman and heir to the throne, came between him and reason, and played a major role in his downfall. Elizabeth may have concluded that a person in love or driven by lust could act like a complete fool, so these emotions were better avoided by herself, and might be exploited in others. In the course of time, she might achieve her ambitions by using her sexuality along with her status. Flirtation could be used as a weapon. Men could be manipulated.

Elizabeth was as clever as she was cunning. When she was later questioned about her relationship with Seymour, she could not deny what had happened. Witnesses had already been interrogated, and provided the juiciest details. However, that didn't stop Elizabeth from turning the tables by accusing her accusers – playing the outraged innocent in a communication to her lover's brother, the Lord Protector Somerset.

'My Lord. Master Tyrwhit and others have told me that there goeth rumours abroad which be greatly against my honour and honesty (which above all I esteem) which be these: that I am in the Tower; and with child by my lord admiral. My lord these are shameful slanders for the which besides the great desire I have to see the King's Majesty I most heartily desire your lordship that I may come to the court after your first determination that I may show myself there as I am.'

The style of Elizabeth's letter reveals much more about her than the content, for it is written in a particularly mature way for one who was so young. She had been well schooled by John Cheke and Roger Ascham – the tutors appointed by Henry VIII to supervise his children's education.

In some circles, Ascham is remembered as the author of *Toxophilus*, the first and most famous book on the practice of archery. This was one of the first books written and published in English, when archery was still regarded as part and parcel of England's power – the means by which she had enjoyed great victories in France and Scotland. It is likely, therefore, that it was written at the command of the then king, Henry VIII, to serve as an example of the benefit of fostering universal study, thus championing the principles of Protestantism amounting to self-salvation. A roundabout route, no doubt, but if a man might achieve competence in archery by study of the written English word, then it pointed the way to what might be gained from enabling a wider, personal study of the scriptures, rather than simply relying on priests.

Ascham was no soldier, and his experience of archery was as a recreation – providing a marked contrast to his scholarship. Before he moved into royal circles, he was known as a gifted tutor among the country's brightest stars, specialising in what we might now describe as 'communication skills'. As well as being a master calligrapher, he was appointed Public Orator at Cambridge University.

When he sought to pass on something of his skills to the king's children, he discovered that Elizabeth was a particularly gifted, able and willing student. He wrote that 'her mind has no womanly weakness and her perseverance is equal to that of a man and her memory long keeps what it quickly picks up. She talks French and Italian as well as she does English and has often talked to me readily and well in Latin, moderately in Greek. When she writes in Greek and Latin nothing is more beautiful than her handwriting. She delights as much in music as she is skilful in it. In adornment she is elegant rather than showy.'

Ascham was writing to an academic colleague, so had no reason to make false praise, and knowing Ascham's background at Cambridge, we can assume that what he describes as good was very good indeed. Ascham's role was to polish an already bright mind. Elizabeth's very survival would soon depend on this.

When Protestant King Edward died and Catholic Queen 'Bloody' Mary came to the throne, their half-sister Princess Elizabeth became the focus for Protestant opposition, whether she liked it or not. Therefore, she was kept under Mary's control, and when she was not physically imprisoned and humiliated, was shadowed by the queen's watchful Catholic agents. If Elizabeth had put one foot wrong, Mary would not have hesitated to have her head.

Elizabeth knew she must convince her half-sister that she was no threat, and knowing Mary's obsession with finding a husband and bearing children, Elizabeth proclaimed her intention to do the opposite. This was prompted by a suggestion made by Queen Mary's new husband, King Philip of Spain – to marry off Elizabeth to a Catholic prince who would bring her to heel and, no doubt, to Catholicism. This was well within Mary's power to order. Faced with this threat, Elizabeth was shrewd enough to realise that rather than refusing this suggestion in particular, she must object to it in more general terms. She wrote to Mary of her intention to embrace spinsterhood, while keeping her options open.

'I so well like this (unmarried) estate as I persuade myself there is not any kind of life comparable unto it ... What I shall do hereafter I know not but I assure you upon my truth and fidelity and as God be merciful unto me I am not at this present time otherwise minded than I have declared unto you, no though I was offered to the greatest prince of all Europe.'

It was enough. Queen Mary may have enjoyed certain advantages, but a high intelligence wasn't one of them. Rather, she passed her short and unhappy reign displaying the mentality of a brood mare – albeit one with a vicious temper. She took Elizabeth at her word, and left it at that. Of course, she may have been right to do so. After all, Elizabeth never did marry.

In the early days of Elizabeth's reign, the country felt uncomfortable at having a 'mere woman' on the throne. Threatened by continental Catholic powers, they wanted the country to be led – in practice if not in theory – by a 'strong man' of the Protestant cause. Parliament left the queen in no doubt as to their concern.

To Protestant eyes, an unmarried queen was at odds with the divinely sanctioned, and therefore universally accepted, relation between the sexes. They believed that women were the 'weaker vessel' as described in Tyndale's 1526 English Bible. Printed in Germany, in the English vernacular, thousands of copies had been smuggled into pre-Reformation England, to spread the Protestant faith, and it was regarded as a foundation stone of their faith. To Protestants, the subservience of women to men was ordered.

John Knox had his say on this subject as author of *The First Blast of the Trumpet against the Monstrous Regiment of Women*, published in 1558. In it, he described women as 'weak, frail, impatient, feeble and foolish and experience hath declared them to be inconstant, variable and cruel ... in the nature of all women lurketh such vices as in good governors are not tolerable.'

Ironically, this may have prompted Elizabeth to strengthen her resolve to go in the opposite direction. Her vanity and arrogance would have rebelled at such suggestions. Why should she, the strongest and brightest of women, share her power with a man, simply because his arm was stronger than hers? The more she was pushed, the more she resisted – though she was prepared to go along with parliament, entering 'negotiations' with a long list of suitors, till they were driven to distraction by her apparent indecisiveness.

The Virgin Queen might choose to avoid marriage, but this still left her and England with a problem. Short of an immaculate conception, or the unthinkable scandal of an illegitimate child, England would remain without an obvious heir. Or rather, without an obvious Protestant heir, for the Catholic Mary Queen of Scots was next in line.

That was the threat. As long as Elizabeth was unmarried and childless, England faced the prospect of Frenchified Mary who, like Bloody Mary in the recent past, may seek to return the country to the Roman faith. This simply wasn't acceptable to English Protestants.

The news of 1566, that Mary Queen of Scots had produced a son by her husband Lord Darnley (proclaimed but hardly acknowledged as King Henry), served to underline the threat, for Darnley was a cousin to Mary and therefore, like her, in the line of succession to the English throne as a descendant of Margaret Tudor, daughter of Henry VII and sister of Henry VIII. Therefore, their baby would have a legally indisputable right to England. No wonder Elizabeth reeled in shock at the news, knowing how the English parliament would react. There was every likelihood that they would force her into a marriage with the next available Protestant suitor.

The news from Scotland would have done little to settle Elizabeth's mind on the unavoidable prospect of marriage. William Cecil (later Lord Burghley) had still to hone the cutting edge of the Elizabethan Secret Service, but it was already good enough to keep the English monarch informed of her royal cousins' marital problems. Might she be stuck with such a disloyal spouse, simply to provide England with an alternative heir?

Elizabeth couldn't have known it, but Mary was about to score an own goal. Implicated in the murder of her unwanted husband Darnley, marrying the chief suspect, Bothwell, then publicly giving him her unqualified support, the Queen of Scots would give the Scottish Protestants all the excuse they needed. By all the means at their disposal – fair and foul – they blackened her name, imprisoned her, forced her to abdicate, and seized control of the young prince, who was crowned in his first year.

It is hard to believe that such a coup was gained without design. Whatever was done behind closed doors and in the whispering corridors of power, the outcome is certain. The King of Scots who might one day become King of England would be henceforth closely guarded and raised in the Protestant faith. In this way, Mary Queen of Scots had unwittingly provided Elizabeth and England with a suitable son and heir.

English Protestants might prefer an English king, but Elizabeth was not about to sacrifice herself for preference alone. In her eyes, it was enough that the country would be saved from Catholicism. And if it was enough for her, then it should be enough for others.

From that moment on, Elizabeth played her part in every aspect of her godson's upbringing – through the offices of a succession of pro-English and Protestant Scottish regents. As if by divine intervention, the virgin queen had found a surrogate mother to produce an heir.

CHAPTER NINETEEN

THE BOY KING

Mary Queen of Scots saw very little of her son James in his first year, and never saw him again after her imprisonment and abdication. He was crowned at the age of 13 months in the parish kirk at Stirling. It must have been a strange affair. John Knox preached a sermon and two lords took an oath, on the baby's behalf, that he would defend the Protestant faith.

The Lords of the Congregation, headed by the regent Earl of Moray, instructed that the Earl of Mar would be the baby's guardian, and that his wife would care for the physical needs of the infant king. Formal provisions were made for his household at Stirling with a wet-nurse and her servants – four young ladies described as 'rockers', presumably because it was part of their duties to rock the king to sleep – and two more to keep his clothes. Three Gentlemen of the Bedchamber were appointed and Cunningham of Drumwhassel, Moray's cousin, was appointed Master of the Household, which included two musicians, Thomas and Robert Hudson.

The only boyish company the infant king enjoyed was with Mar's son, eight years his senior. He slept under black bed linen in a singularly gloomy room, with no decoration other than a small portrait of his grandfather, James V. His diet was hardly what one would expect. Among the food and drink for the servants and household, a daily allowance had been made 'for the King's own mouth' of two and a half loaves of bread, two capons and three pints of ale. The ale would have been a weak brew, given because it wasn't safe to drink water that might be infected or contaminated.

Before James's fourth birthday, two scholars were appointed to supervise his education. The senior of the King's tutors was George Buchanan – poet, humanist, historian and, above all else, a democratic Protestant who took a dim view of the monarchy. In his 60s, suffering constant ill health and often morose and irascible, he proved a harsh and unsympathetic master. He was a bitter enemy of the young king's absent mother, and never missed an opportunity to denigrate her in James's presence.

On one occasion, when a pet bird had been killed in a boyish tussle, Buchanan flew into a rage, struck the young king, and told him he was 'a true bird of the bloody nest from which he sprang'. Buchanan thrashed James for fairly trivial mistakes and once James and the Mar's son were playing somewhat noisily, close to where Buchanan was intent on his own books. When the tutor threatened to punish the boys, James made some clever but impudent reply. Again Buchanan flew into a rage, thrashing the young king. When Lady Mar sought to intervene, she was met with a torrent of obscenities and abuse. Such beatings and verbal abuse were part and parcel of Buchanan's involvement in deforming James's character.

As a break from Buchanan, the boy king probably looked forward to his lessons with Peter Young, a young man who had recently completed his studies in Calvinist Geneva, and made every effort to build a library for the King's use. Most of these books were in Latin, many in French, some in Greek, Spanish and Italian – surprisingly few in English. In short time, James could read them all. Even the curmudgeonly Buchanan declared the boy king was highly intelligent, that he learned with admirable ease and possessed an excellent memory.

James led a cloistered life at Stirling, distanced from events that shook the foundations of his kingdom. Many Scots remained Catholic and loyal to Mary. The Marian Lords led them in opposition to the Lords of the Congregation. They weren't prepared to stand idly by while their queen was kept imprisoned by Protestants who had already received financial and military support from the English queen.

For many Scots, England remained the 'auld enemy' and while they might not welcome French interference in their nation's affairs, they saw this as a necessity to avoid the English yoke. They didn't accept that England would treat Scotland as an equal partner in any relationship between the two countries. Therefore, they believed that men like Moray and Morton were traitors to Scotland, and should be dealt with accordingly. The ensuing civil war, assassinations and killings dragged on for years.

After the killing of the Earl of Moray, the replacement regent, King James's grandfather, the Earl of Lennox, summoned his Protestant supporters to a convention at Stirling. He decided that it would boost their morale if the young king were present. James was just five years old, but he made a short speech with apparent confidence. Later, while they were eating, he noticed a hole in the cloth that covered the banqueting table before announcing, 'This parliament has a hole in it'. They laughed at the time, but this statement was remembered as prophetic when, within a short time, the Marians killed Lennox. The Earl of Morton then filled the hole, becoming the third regent in James's reign. Meanwhile, the five-year-old had returned to his sheltered life of intellectual endeavour.

Peter Young described a typical day in the life of the boy king. 'First in the morning he sought guidance in prayer, since God Almighty bestows favour and success upon all studies. Being cleansed through prayer and having propitiated the Deity, he devoted himself to Greek, reading either from the New Testament, or Isocrates, or from the apophthegms of Plutarch, with practice in the rules of grammar. After breakfast he read Latin, either from Livy, Justin, Cicero, or from Scottish or foreign history. After dinner he gave some time to composition; and during the rest of the afternoon, if time permitted, he studied arithmetic or cosmography, which included geography and astronomy, or dialectic or rhetoric. But these subjects were taken up in turn, not followed all at the same time.'

The boy king's tutors pushed him very hard. On numerous occasions, James was called upon to 'perform his party pieces' before visiting dignitaries, who were suitably lavish in their praise.

In his autobiography, the Protestant minister James Melville tells how he and his uncle, Andrew Melville, visited James at Stirling in 1574. He speaks of the eight-year-old king as being, 'the sweetest sight in Europe that day for strange and extraordinary gifts of wit, judgement, memory and language.'

Visitors came from the English court – reporting back to Elizabeth on how the heir to her throne was developing. Sir Henry Killigrew, Queen Elizabeth's emissary, made encouraging noises. 'The King seemed to be very glad to hear from her Majesty, and could use pretty speeches, as how much he was bound to her Majesty, yea, more than to his own mother.'

Killigrew told what he had heard, but that is not to say that the young king was sincere in his stated devotion to Elizabeth. He already had a habit of recognising what people wanted to hear and telling them it was so, rather than blurting out his true feelings. He was cleverly cautious, and cunning into the bargain, even at such an early age.

It may seem odd that so much of James's education was given over to a study of Latin as one of the objectives of the Protestants was to have the Bible printed in the vernacular, and services conducted likewise. It was, however, the language of scholarship and the law, as well as the Catholic Church. James learnt it well, being able to read, write and speak it an early age, though there is a hint of juvenile revolt scribbled in one of his copybooks. 'They gar me speik Latin ar I could speik Scots'. For those whose tutors gar them speik English ar they could speik Scots, this means 'They made me speak Latin before I could speak Scots'.

James's scribbling was written as he spoke – in the Scots tongue of those among whom he was raised. In later life, this would be a factor in his dealings with English courtiers, some tittering that he was barely intelligible to their dandified ears.

As his reputation as an academic prodigy spread, the great at home and abroad decided that books would make suitable presentations to the young king, and his library expanded. He was surrounded with the classics, Bibles, Psalters and books of devotion, history and science (military and otherwise) and many more hefty tomes. Just occasionally, some visiting personage, perhaps remembering his own youth, presented a book on hunting. For these, James was particularly grateful.

In addition to his scholarly tutors, the young king had two instructors in horsemanship and 'manly sports'. David and Adam Erskine were the lay abbots of Cambuskenneth and Dryburgh. Presumably, as well as being Protestants, these lay abbots were cast in the 'muscular Christian' mould. Horses, hounds and hunting became the young king's greatest passions, and would remain so throughout his life.

These Erskines were connected to the Earl of Moray and related to the Earl of Mar, the young king's guardian. When Mar died in 1572, his replacement was his brother, Sir Alexander Erskine. The Earl's widow continued her domestic care of the king.

Despite his scholarly achievements and manly pursuits, James received little if any training in gentlemanly manners or courtly graces. Lady Mar might have tried, but the curmudgeonly Buchanan would have intervened. He regarded such things as unimportant and even reprobate, and told the infant king that flattery was a loathsome vice. This lack of training was a fault, for while a 'rough approach' suited Buchanan, it did not prepare James in the social niceties that he would need in later life, when he took his place at court.

For all his intellectual strengths, James had many faults and weaknesses. He was an awkward lad with spindly legs and staring eyes. His narrow jaws made it difficult for him to eat and drink with becoming dignity. He was slovenly and careless about his appearance and manners, and had fits of temper, despite being described by some as a good-natured boy.

He saw much of dogs, hawks and horses, but little of young ladies and as he grew into a youth, he held them in contempt. Indeed, through all his life, he believed in the superiority of the male – views first inculcated by the boorish bachelor Buchanan, who thought that women did nothing but cause trouble and make cuckolds of their husbands – James's own mother being paraded as an example.

Buchanan had his own views on kingship. In his opinion (and he paid scant regard to any other) a king should be a lover of piety, his life a pattern for every citizen, his countenance the terror of evildoers and the delight of all good men. A king should exist for his subjects, the old tutor growled, and not for himself for he was the father of his people. Buchanan thundered that kings had been chosen originally by the people and ruled only by their will. Kings could not override the law and those who did could be called to account, and in the last resort put to death. James knew better than to argue with his tutor at the time, but his later life shows he refused to take this lesson on board.

Peter Young was more interested in theology than politics and kingship, and ensured that James received a thorough grounding in Calvinism, as taught in Geneva. Reflecting the Renaissance origins of the Reformation in which men were encouraged to think for themselves, Young believed in the application of logic and was keen to foster argumentative solutions to complicated theological questions. Thus encouraged, the young king branched out into logical discourse on all manner of problems, often displaying huge confidence in the value of his own conclusions. After all, those who came to visit him were lavish in their praise of his intelligence and wit. It was enough to turn any boy's head. Timid, yet immensely confident – it was a strange mix.

To quote one historian 'Thus the young King was an interesting and intelligent boy, precocious and learned beyond his years, very much of a prig though sincerely attached to his books, thoroughly convinced of his own piety, delighting in puns, fond of weighty pronouncements, amiable for the most part though capable of tempers, with bad manners and a high opinion of himself.'

Some of these characteristics were to be seen when a rare playfellow told a long tale in French. Growing impatient, James interrupted explosively, 'I have not understood a single word that you have said, and what the Lord Regent has said of you seems to be true – that your French is nothing and your Scots little better.' Young intervened to tell James that he should control his anger, but the boy king retorted, 'Then I should not wear the lion in my arms, but rather a sheep'.

The regent, the Earl of Morton, the strong man of the Protestant party, aimed for absolutism in Church and State. He had played a major role in the removal of Queen Mary, and worked hand-in-glove with Protestant England, without becoming its puppet. Described as a stern tyrant by grown men, showing neither pity nor remorse, he must have been truly awesome to a young boy. It is no surprise that the young James regarded Morton with great fear.

The nervous James developed a sly cunning, believing that he must win the approval of those in power over him. He appeared to go along with virtually anything that was suggested to him. The Frenchman Fontenay wrote: 'Owing to the terrorism under which he has been brought up, he is timid with the great lords, seldom venturing to contradict them.' Already, James sought to run with the stag and hunt with the hounds. It was a habit that he retained throughout his life. Nobody could be sure of his true feelings or intentions.

As the king's junior tutor, Peter Young's influence was limited, but he did what he could, inspecting what was left of the queen's comparatively light-hearted library at Holyrood. Much of it had been lifted, but he unearthed some medieval romances and a collection of French poetry that he presented to James.

This poetry came as a shaft of sunlight into the young king's otherwise austere life. It prompted a desire to become a rhymester, if not a poet, and perhaps planted seeds of wonder in the young king's mind. Whatever the likes of Buchanan and Morton might say about his imprisoned mother, he realised that she had a love of life and laughter. Equally, such poetry may have stimulated an admiration of the French, for was he not related to the dukes of Guise, and hadn't his mother been Queen of France as well as Scotland?

Unwittingly, Peter Young had introduced James to the notion that there was a better life, beyond the confines imposed by the Lords of the

Congregation. His fear of Buchanan and Morton was mixed with anger and hatred. As soon as he could, he would strive to break their grip.

The Earl of Morton was successful in achieving a conclusion to the civil war in Scotland, but the resentment lingered on. As long as Mary Queen of Scots was imprisoned in England, and the stern Morton tightened his inflexible grip on Scottish affairs, there would be unrest.

Where warfare had failed, subtle means might secure the desired end. For some, the priority was to remove Morton. Assassination was a possibility, as ever, but there was an alternative. In 1578, the Earls of Argyll and Atholl formed a secretive coalition to oust the regent.

At first, they adopted a cautious approach. They made discreet enquiries and learned that Morton kept a very tight rein on the royal household's spending. This penny-pinching had led to dissatisfaction among those who surrounded the king. In such a condition, men are apt to look kindly on those who suggest their lot might be improved, and that is what Argyll and Atholl promised, in return for seemingly harmless information.

Deals were made. James's guardian, Sir Alexander Erskine, was weary of Morton's tyranny and miserliness. Argyll and Atholl were told of James's character – that strange mix of timidity and self-confidence, which might be exploited. They also learned that James both feared and hated Morton. Again, this could be exploited.

In the spring of 1578, Argyll and Atholl arrived in Stirling and were ushered into the 11-year-old king's presence by their new friends in the royal household. They told the king a simple tale, with which he could sympathise. Playing the innocents, they explained that they had fallen out with Morton, who was now hounding them. They begged the boy king to intervene. Growing bold in the company of fellow sufferers, James allowed his self-confidence to take over. He told Argyll and Atholl to remain in Stirling while he put his bright, kingly mind to their problem, and contacted Morton.

In Edinburgh, Morton flew into a fury at this news. Argyll and Atholl had acted outside the law, and Morton sent a stern rebuke to the king, including evidence of the 'evil intent' of the rebel lords. Finally, he declared that Argyll and Atholl must be punished, or he would have no option but to resign from the regency. That last part was a mistake, which he would soon regret.

Argyll and Atholl were delighted. With the guidance of Sir Alexander

Erskine, they knew exactly which buttons to push. Was James not king? Who was Morton to order him thus? All of Scotland was proud of their king's great intelligence and wisdom. None was better qualified to rule. And of course, if he ruled as king, then nobody would argue when he wanted to buy a new horse or a couple of hounds.

James was convinced. Never the victim of modesty, he decided that he could do a better job of running the country than Morton. He announced that he would accept the regent's resignation, and planned to publish his acceptance of the government.

For a time, Morton didn't know where to turn. His offer of resignation had been made as a threat. He had never dreamed that James would accept it with such alacrity. Without his influence, there could be no guarantees about James's behaviour. The solution, however, was close at hand, though it came from an unexpected quarter.

The wife of James's first guardian the Earl of Mar had looked after the infant king's domestic arrangements and their son, despite being eight years older than James, was his boyish companion. That boy had now grown into a man, succeeded to his father's title and had a sensible head on his shoulders. He could see that Argyll, Atholl and his uncle, Sir Alexander Erskine, were manipulating James and the young earl was not prepared to let this continue. With armed supporters at his back, he charged Erskine with fraud and demanded the keys of the castle. It turned into a running fight in which several men were slain, but finally the castle was taken and with it the king. Morton arrived to restore the peace, and James shuffled back to his studies.

Queen Elizabeth was hardly amused when she heard what had been happening in Scotland. In fact, she was furious, knowing that Argyll and Atholl were sympathetic to Mary. Cecil's spies reported that she had made contact, and discovered the contents of various letters while doing nothing to alert the correspondents. Mary had asked the men she trusted to spirit her son away to France and into the care of the Guises, who would return him to Catholicism. After which, in her vivid imagination, he would become her champion and restore her to the throne. It didn't enter her mind that he might be happy to continue filling the monarch's role. Whenever James heard of her intrigues, he would see her as a competitor and therefore a threat.

In the meantime, the Protestant powers were not so severe as to be indifferent to the demoralising nature of the restrictions borne by the young king. In brief, all work and no play – other than his hunting – had made Jacques a rebellious boy, and they had seen the trouble this might bring. His 13th birthday, in June 1579, seemed a good time to allow him some freedom – albeit under close supervision. Various short excursions were arranged, and when these went well enough it was announced that James would visit Holyrood in September.

Morton was not so reassured as to allow James to travel without an impressive escort of 2,000 mounted troops, led by loyal Protestant members of the nobility who were there to guard the king, in both senses of the word. They skirted Edinburgh where cannons fired a salute from the castle as the young king's cavalcade entered Holyrood.

James remained in the confines of Holyrood for a month before making a formal entry to Edinburgh. The provost, baillies, councillors and citizens turned out in force, decked in their finery, to welcome him. In a glittering pageant, he was presented with silver keys to the city. There was a service in St Giles's, bringing a note of seriousness to the events, and then the carnival continued. In the same month, James opened Parliament and was entertained by Morton, who showed a softer side to his character, though he may have been smiling through gritted teeth.

James lingered at Holyrood until February before returning to Stirling. That summer, he made a royal progress through Fife and Angus. On this trip, he was clearly delighted with a horse that had been presented to him – a gift from the Earl of Leicester in England – and which he ran in a race. Another gift that had clearly taken his fancy was a latch or crossbow. The nervous youth carried it wherever he went.

It was clear that James was revelling in his newfound freedom, after years of work and not much play. This would have been reported back to Elizabeth through William Cecil. She may have sighed with relief, although Cecil's agents would have been reporting that foreign powers were watching the young king's progress, and making plans that could destabilise Scotland and therefore threaten England. It was only to be expected.

Elizabeth was still unmarried and childless. In these circumstances, it was practically certain that the young King James VI of Scots would become King James I of England upon her death – if he lived that long. So whoever controlled James would gain control of both kingdoms – something that the French had long been trying to achieve. Only now the stakes were higher, for under French instruction the two Protestant countries would be returned to Catholicism.

※ CHAPTER TWENTY ☙

RIPE FOR CORRUPTION

In September 1579 Esmé Stewart, Seigneur d'Aubigny and a first cousin to James's father, the murdered Lord Darnley, arrived in Scotland from France. At a time when King James was being allowed more freedom to mix with his countrymen, Esmé Stewart's rank gave him a 'right of passage' to the Scottish court. This man of great charm, easy conversation, affection and courtly manners, immediately fascinated the young king. Into dour surroundings, d'Aubigny brought colour, amusement and, for some, a degree of panic. The seigneur was an agent of the Duke of Guise, sent to win James's friendship and promote the cause of Catholicism, France and Mary Stuart.

The Duke of Guise is seen by many as little more than 'the French connection', but he was a great deal more than that. The Wars of Religion were raging in Europe, and France came within an inch of converting to Protestantism under Henry of Navarre. The Catholic who opposed this most devoutly and violently was the Duke of Guise and he was implicated in many massacres and atrocities in his persecution of Protestants.

The duke did not stand alone. He was a member of the Holy Roman League – a confederation of Catholic nobles throughout Europe who were prepared to use all and any means to protect the Roman Catholic Church. Again, the reasons were as much political as religious. They viewed the Reformation as a social revolution that threatened their positions. The King of Spain was the league's nominal head, and he worked in partnership with the Vatican. Ergo, an agent of the duke was an agent of the Holy Roman League, established to protect the Vatican's interest. And it was not in the Vatican's interest to sit back and do nothing while a king, baptised a Catholic, was converted to Protestantism.

If James was aware of his new friend's true background, he ignored it. 'Deeply affectionate by nature, the King delighted all his life in the love of intimate companions. Of this he had been starved, reported D H Willson. 'Now he found a person whom he could truly love, and he loved him with a passion and abandon scarcely normal in a boy. He was too young to know that d'Aubigny's charms were tawdry and superficial, that the depraved court of France had made him no fit companion, that love for such a man had many pitfalls.'

The astute d'Aubigny quickly realised that he had as much to gain from the favour of King James as he had by serving France and Spain. He was soon playing an astonishing and successful game of double intrigue. James gave him the rich Abbey of Arbroath, created him Earl then Duke of Lennox, admitted him to the Council, and placed with him the custody of Dumbarton Castle.

Morton remained Regent, but his old enemies, led by Argyll, were flocking to Lennox. There would be a day of reckoning between the factions, but for now the star of Lennox continued to rise.

Elizabeth recognised the Catholic threat, and intervened in support of her old ally Morton, her emissary speaking to James with great severity, threatening the loss of England's friendship should he prefer 'any Earl of Lennox before a Queen of England.' Caught in a quandary, James promised to please Elizabeth in any way he could, but he would not part with Lennox.

On the last day of 1580, as King James sat in Council, an argument was forced on Morton by one Captain James Stewart. Morton was arrested. James was now completely in Lennox's control and turned against Morton, who was finally tried and executed in June 1581. Elizabeth's control of her successor was slipping from her grasp.

At 15 years of age, James was passing from childhood into youth, and more contradictions were appearing in his character – prematurely old and sophisticated in certain ways, simple and naïve in others. Esmé Stewart, now Duke of Lennox, recognised that James was ripe for further corruption.

Lennox had a group of hangers-on. Among them was a Monsieur Momberneau, described as 'a merry fellow, very able in body, most meet in all respects for bewitching the youth of a prince'. Lennox introduced him to James. When they became friends, James demanded less of Lennox's company, leaving the duke free to concentrate on strengthening his position.

With Morton and his tutors removed from the scene, James was encouraged to spend his time in riding and hunting, delighting in six pairs of fine horses, a gift from the Duke of Guise. Meanwhile, James was steeped in 'licentious and filthy tongued' company and developed a taste for oaths and bawdy jests that remained with him through life. 'The age was not over-nice in such matters, but James achieved a florescence of obscenity that contrasted painfully with his interest in holy things.' Among those whose company he kept was the grasping and immoral Captain James Stewart, who had taken a major role on Lennox's side in Morton's downfall. His reward was the title of Earl of Arran. His wife, a daughter of the Catholic Atholl, was now the chief lady at court, despite having been married to Arran's uncle, the Earl of March, whom she had divorced on the ground of impotency, though she was pregnant at the time – already Arran's mistress.

Concerns were openly expressed about his relationship with Lennox. 'His Majesty, having conceived an inward affection to the Lord d'Aubigny, entered in great familiarity and quiet purposes with him,' wrote the chronicler Moysie, delicately recognising the special connotation contained in that idiom. The Scottish clergy, on the other hand, were painfully blunt, declaring 'that the Duke of Lennox went about to draw the King to carnal lust.'

Lennox may have enjoyed seducing the young king, but carnal lust wasn't his principal motivation. He had been sent on a specific mission, dictated by the Holy Roman League. And so he encouraged James to question the teachings of his old tutors, particularly in regard to religion and politics. As a Protestant with Puritan inclinations, Buchanan had taught that kings had been chosen originally by the people and were continued in office through their will; that kings could not override the law, and that those who broke it could be justly called to account and in the last resort put to death. In direct opposition to this, Lennox encouraged James to believe in the notion of 'the divine right of kings'.

It is an indicator of the style of Lennox's double dealing that he converted to Protestantism – at James's urging – but then encouraged James to admire the absolutism of Catholic France, with its attitude that Protestant ministers were little more than seditious disturbers of the peace.

Despite the florescent obscenities, carnal lust and addiction to hunting, the king maintained his interest in theology and intellectual matters. The ministers complained that he indulged in pastimes on the Sabbath, was remiss in attending the Kirk, and no longer called for preachings after dinner and supper, but these complaints were largely unfair. In truth, a chapter of the Bible was read at every meal, he attended the Kirk with exemplary regularity, and his interest in theology never flagged. The ministers also complained that he disliked hearing his shortcomings reproved from the pulpit. If so, little wonder.

With the Kirk becoming ever more vociferous in its criticism of the young king, he became increasingly entrenched in his opposition. Like many a young man, the harder he was pushed, the harder he resisted. With Lennox and his cronies egging him on, James came to regard the Scottish Reformation as an anti-monarchical revolt. 'Some fiery spirited men in the ministry got such a guiding of the people as finding the gust of government sweet they began to fancy to themselves a democratic form of government,' James complained. 'They settled themselves so fast upon that imagined democracy as they fed themselves with the hope to become *tribuni plebis*; and so in a popular government by leading the people by the nose to bear the sway of all the rule.'

James was justified in his fears. John Knox had held that the laws of God, needing no confirmation from king or parliament, were to rule the State. Kings who opposed the Kirk fought against God, thundered Knox, and should be brushed aside.

The situation needed a peacemaker. Andrew Melville, who led the Kirk, sought to dilute Knox's theocracy into the famous doctrine of the two kingdoms – making a distinction between the civil power of the King and the spiritual power of the Kirk. But there was a sting in the tail of Melville's argument for in the Kirk, according to Melville, the King must obey the clergy in all matters of the spirit.

Clearly, this left scope for further argument. *The Second Book of Discipline*, set forth in 1581, held that while the independence of the Kirk was inviolable, the independence of the State was less secure. 'The ministers exercise not the civil jurisdiction, but they teach the magistrate how it should be exercised; and all godly princes and magistrates ought to hear and obey.' This opened the way for ministers of the Kirk to dictate to the State. James had no option but to resist such claims if he wished to preserve his authority.

In opposition to the Kirk's desire to control the State, James sought to impose his control on the Kirk. The argument centred on bishops. To the Presbyterians, bishops were symbols of Roman error and royal tyranny. To

James, they seemed the only safeguard against the authoritarianism of the clergy. 'No bishop, no king,' held as true in Scotland as in England.

When Henry VIII had converted his realm in England to Protestantism, it was of the Episcopalian kind – catholic, but not Roman, and with bishops to safeguard the royal prerogative – and it was as head of that church that Elizabeth ruled. She must have been relieved, therefore, to discover that the Scottish king seemed to favour this English system. From the exchanges between the Scottish king and the Kirk, it must have appeared that while he had many arguments with the Scottish Presbyterians, he was very close to the Anglican form of Protestantism – far closer than he was to Roman Catholicism, despite Lennox's best efforts.

At home and abroad, James faced a complex intertwining of religion and politics – the strands so closely intertwined as to be inseparable. Lennox may have publicly converted to Protestantism at James's suggestion, but he privately maintained his Catholic contacts. It was probably Lennox who encouraged James into subtle courses of double diplomacy – but not subtle enough to fool the arch-schemers of Elizabeth's court where espionage was being raised to an art form. James quickly acquired a reputation for deceit, offering protestations of friendship to Elizabeth, while secretly being in negotiation with Catholic states.

'The King's fair speeches and promises will fall out to be plain dissemination, wherein he is in his tender years better practised than others forty years older than he is,' wrote one English noble. 'He is holden among the Scots for the greatest dissembler that ever was heard of for his years.'

In connection with another matter, Bowes reported: 'And into whose hands soever he should fall, they should note in him such inconstancy, perjury and falsehood that they would shortly regret their action.'

Elizabeth would not have been surprised to receive such low opinions of her royal cousin. Speaking of his part in Regent Morton's ruin and execution, she is said to have exclaimed, 'That false Scottish urchin! What can be expected from the double dealing of such an urchin as this?'

However, James was not about to apologise for his part in Morton's downfall. As a boy, James had resented open criticism of his mother. And that resentment had grown. He described the late Earl of Moray as 'that bastard who unnaturally rebelled and procured the ruin of his own sovereign and sister.' He obtained from Parliament a condemnation of Buchanan's writings. And he savagely denounced the clergy for their part in Mary's disposition.

At Lennox's urging, the young king started a correspondence with his mother – loving letters reassuring her that he would act in all things as her obedient son. Mary decided to take him at his word. In 1581, she proposed a plan that came to be known as the Association. Her terms were high. She expressed the hope that her son would be reconciled with Rome. James would rule, but in their joint names and her authority would be such that no important decision could be made without her approval. James answered that he would joyfully accept, but never had any intention of playing his part in it. 'If he had a tender love for his mother, he had a love for himself more tender still.' And he wasn't about to share his power.

Unfortunately for Mary, encouraged by James's stated acceptance of the Association, she continued with her intrigues. She contacted Philip of Spain, placing herself, her son and 'her' kingdom in his hands. Philip was prepared to offer his support, but only if James converted to Catholicism. Jesuits were sent to discuss matters with James. He blew hot and cold. Other Jesuits came. Things got out of hand. There was even a plan to invade Protestant England, the enterprise to be led by Lennox.

The Kirk got wind of what was going on and their anger was fanned to a white heat by the arrival in Scotland of an emissary from the Duke of Guise. Factions were forming, and there was no shortage of enemies for Lennox and Arran. Morton's former allies, Protestant nobles, led those enemies.

Lennox was still hoping to strike the first blow when James was lured to Ruthven Castle and practically kidnapped. After some threatening speeches, James burst into tears. Unmoved, the Master of Glamis said: 'It is no matter of his tears, better that bairns should weep than bearded men.'

The 16-year-old King James was virtually a prisoner. Once again, he was under the Protestant's thumb. Lennox was ordered to leave the country. Indeed, the Ruthven Lords went so far as to threaten to kill James if Lennox did not go. Though he lingered for a short time before going into exile, Lennox never saw James again.

Back in Protestant hands, James realised he should make peace with Elizabeth. The Ruthven Lords urged him to do so without delay, recognising that they could not maintain control of Scotland without English support. Along with his fawning messages, Elizabeth received a request for financial support. James asked for £10,000 to satisfy his immediate needs, and £5,000 per annum thereafter – a high price for his loyalty, which Elizabeth considered exorbitant.

Elizabeth then entered a negotiation with James – probably to test him. She suggested that if they could make an alliance, she might see the way clear to releasing Mary, who had been languishing as a prisoner in England – provided that James and the King of France guaranteed her good behaviour. However, James was soon complaining that his mother was using the offer to advance her own interests, and that she was claiming precedence over him. He went on to insist that her involvement with Catholic powers rendered her unfit to rule either Scotland or England. He, on the other hand, would be a fit ruler for both.

The threat of his mother's release served to focus James's mind. He recognised that the English succession, which he coveted above all else, was to be gained by friendship with Elizabeth. Of course, this was what Elizabeth had intended, so she may have breathed a long sigh of relief. If so, it was premature. The Holy Roman League were already conspiring. Lennox might be out of the way, but his supporters were still in place. Principal among them was Captain James Stewart, now Earl of Arran.

The new Earl of Arran was a younger son of Lord Ochiltree – well educated, accomplished and able, but arrogant and 'capable of many things'. Above all, perhaps, he and his wife were inordinately greedy and ambitious. When the 17-year-old James escaped from the Ruthven Lords, Arran was waiting. James was lazy about the running of government, and Arran took this over on his behalf – leading to all manner of fraud and corruption. At the same time, Arran and James sought to deal with the Ruthven Lords, who fled to England where there was a growing colony of threatened or disenchanted Scots.

James and Arran determined to overthrow Presbyterianism, which discounted bishops. They forced through laws, and many clergy fled south, swelling the Scottish colony, which included exiled Protestant lords. The Presbyterian leader and reformer, Andrew Melville, attempted to make a stand against the Episcopacy – Protestant, but with bishops – championed by King James. However, this brought him into conflict with Parliament and, knowing Arran's reputation for violence, he fled to England to join the other Scottish clergymen. It may seem somewhat ironic that Scottish Presbyterians found sanctuary in Episcopalian England, but Elizabeth was still angry about Morton's downfall. Equally, the Scottish king's correspondence may have been brought to her attention.

Estranged from Elizabeth, menaced by the exiled lords and ministers, and aware of the widespread discontent in Scotland, James had returned to his secret correspondence with foreign Catholic powers. The Duke of Guise was among the first to offer him protection. James then wrote to the pope, hinting that military and financial aid might persuade him to convert to Catholicism. He also appealed to the kings of France and Spain, suggesting schemes to free his mother and seek revenge on Elizabeth. Clearly, James felt very threatened and might have accepted help from any quarter. Elizabeth acted quickly, when the opportunity arose.

Patrick, Master of Gray, had been one of Mary's agents in France, but had finally turned against her, advising James to make his peace with Elizabeth. James sent Gray to negotiate with Elizabeth. Mary thought Gray was negotiating for her release but, in fact, he was telling Elizabeth about Mary's plotting and conspiracies. He confirmed what England's agents had already reported. In these circumstances, Elizabeth was minded to offer an alliance with Scotland – one of mutual support against the possibility of invasion of either country.

Mary was furious when she found out what had happened. In short, her son had sold her out, in order to gain a league with England.

Negotiators came north to settle the details of the Anglo-Scottish treaty, and then everything went pear-shaped. Sir Francis Russell was killed in a border scuffle by an ally of Arran. Elizabeth demanded that Arran be held responsible – recognising that he was a 'loose cannon' in any negotiations with Scotland. Unfortunately, James had an undying loyalty to his 'close friends' and let Arran escape. Elizabeth was exasperated, to say the least, and let slip the exiled Presbyterian lords in the autumn of 1585. They arrived at Stirling at the head of 8,000 armed men. Arran fled, and spent the rest of his life in political obscurity. James was back under Elizabeth's thumb. Or so it seemed.

The Scottish nobles were meant to 'supervise' their king, but instead they humoured him – intent on restoring their private fortunes, which could be done most easily through royal favour. He was allowed to spend most of his time hunting, and even introduced a new 'friend' to the court – Ludovick Stewart, son of the murdered Earl of Moray.

The returning Presbyterian ministers might have expected protection, but they didn't get it. James held the Presbyterians in contempt. Those who agreed with his opinions about bishops and respect for the throne formed the Episcopal Church in Scotland.

Negotiations for a treaty with England were renewed, with Elizabeth expressing surprise at the lords' actions in seizing James – as if she hadn't supported them at the time. In 1586, an alliance in defence of true religion and for mutual assistance in case of invasion was agreed. In return, James sought a pension, and recognition of his right to succeed to the English throne. He got less money than he had wanted, and Elizabeth's 'firm promise in the word of a Queen that she would never directly or indirectly do or suffer to be done anything that she could withstand to the diminution or derogation of any right or title that might be due to him in any time present or future, unless by manifest ingratitude she should be justly moved and provoked to the contrary.'

It was enough – for now. Soon, James would be put to another test. England's Secret Service was already gathering evidence of Mary's complicity in the Babington Plot.

CHAPTER TWENTY-ONE

THE BABINGTON PLOT

Queen Elizabeth's most valued advisor William Cecil, eventually rewarded the title of Lord Burghley, knew that one day he must retire or be removed from the scene. Therefore, in 1573 he had supervised the appointment of two new secretaries of state to work under him.

Sir Thomas Smith was a scholar and civil servant noted for his hard work, honesty and intense patriotism. Sir Francis Walsingham was from a different mould. As an ambassador to Paris, he had displayed keen skills in diplomacy and espionage, and as a fanatical Protestant he would become Elizabeth's shield, taking charge of the Secret Service. He is remembered as one of England's great spymasters – perhaps the greatest of them all. In terms of gathering intelligence and acting on it or otherwise, Burghley was exceptional, but Walsingham was better.

Burghley and Walsingham were all too aware of the support for the imprisoned Mary Queen of Scots. They also knew that Mary was active in encouraging those who sought to return her to Scotland's throne, and more. They believed that Mary would be a threat so long as she lived.

After Lennox had failed to 'convert' the young King James, the Duke of Guise returned his attention to James's imprisoned mother. Perhaps the French duke was weary of James's vagueness over religion – always hinting, but never committing himself – in contrast to the devoutly Catholic and comparatively straightforward Mary. Whatever his reasoning, Guise held meetings in 1582, in order to foster support for the invasion of England, the overthrow of Elizabeth, and the return of both England and Scotland to Catholicism. His support was split over who should lead in the discussions. Guise favoured the Jesuits, but many lay Catholics resented them. Gilbert Gifford was one such man – a hothead who acted as an agent for the Catholics, though they suspected that he also reported to Walsingham.

Wearing his Catholic hat, Gifford was not alone in favouring the assassination of Elizabeth. Such plots were taken seriously by the English Secret Service – not least following the assassination of the Protestant William of Orange in 1584 in Delft. It was known that Gifford had been in secret correspondence with Mary though she, like the French, was very suspicious of his motives. So many plotters, but few knowing who they could trust – realising that Walsingham was a master of turning Catholic agents with threats or inducements.

In 1584, Bernardino de Mendoza, the Spanish ambassador in London, was expelled following the discovery of his complicity in a plot to overthrow Elizabeth and put Mary on the English throne. Francis Throckmorton provided the evidence, under torture. Utterly broken, Throckmorton went on to confirm that Guise was planning to lead an invasion of England, financed by the king of Spain and the papacy. Finally, and with no more information to give, Throckmorton was executed.

In 1585, Parliament passed a new bill, called 'The Bond of Association', drafted by Lord Burghley and his protégé Walsingham. Under its terms, signatories pledged themselves to prevent anyone who overthrew Queen Elizabeth from taking power, and to pursue all plotters to the death. People signed in their thousands. Some members of parliament were concerned that if Elizabeth's life was seriously threatened, Mary would be executed and James might be in danger from 'an angry mob' – even if he was innocent. However, the worriers were advised that these were desperate times, requiring desperate measures.

The same bill that provided for the Bond of Association introduced new measures to be taken against Catholic priests, seemingly on the assumption that all and any of them might be agents and plotters. Those who had joined the priesthood since 1559 had just 40 days to leave the country. If they returned, they would be charged with treason.

England's fears and suspicions were raised, in part, by the activities of homebred plotters encouraged by foreign powers, but it was the military threat made by these self-same foreign powers that caused the greatest concern. Burghley and Walsingham were reasonably confident in their ability to shield Elizabeth from an assassin's knife, but a full-scale invasion by the papacy, France and Spain was a different proposition.

At the start of 1585, England's relationship with Spain was stretched to breaking point. Dutch Protestants were fighting to throw off the yoke of Spanish imperialism, and had sought England's help. In return, in order to discourage England, Philip II of Spain had ordered the seizure of English ships.

Spain had recently annexed Portugal and the Azores, and was hell bent on further expansion. England was in a quandary. Like Spain, she was looking to extend her foreign influence and trade. Indeed, it was in 1585 that Sir Richard Grenville returned to England having established a colony of 100 men on Roanoke Island, Virginia, seeking to relax Spain's grip on the New World. Some of Elizabeth's ministers advised that the best form of defence might be attack, but Elizabeth refused to make any sort of a pre-emptive strike while negotiations with the Dutch were continuing.

In August 1585, the negotiations reached a conclusion. A treaty was signed at Nonsuch Palace between England and the Netherlands (United Provinces) in which England agreed to support the Protestant Dutch against the Catholic Spanish. It was in England's interests to do so, for a conquered Netherlands would provide the Spanish with an ideal base from which to invade England. The Earl of Leicester commanded the 7,000 troops provided to support the Protestant cause.

Elizabeth had unleashed Sir Francis Drake against the Spanish – funding him to the tune of £10,000. He had the audacity to start his expedition by seizing the Spanish port of Vigo, where he calmly refitted his ships before sailing off to cause havoc in the Cape Verde islands. He then raided Spanish possessions in the West Indies.

Drake's activities broke whatever remained of Spanish patience. Philip of Spain was now the leader of Europe's greatest Catholic nation. As such, he had a responsibility to destroy the 'illegitimate heretic' sitting on the English throne. The twin irritations of the Earl of Leicester in the Netherlands, and Drake on the high seas, settled the issue. Goaded into action, Philip appointed Don Juan de Zuniga to make the necessary arrangements, including the gathering together of a huge invasion fleet.

Part and parcel of the invasion plans were the assassination of Queen Elizabeth, and the rescue of Mary who the Spanish invaders, together with their Catholic allies, would place on the thrones of England and Scotland. Pope Gregory XIII had stated, in regard to the proposed assassination of the Protestant Elizabeth that, 'whosoever sends her out of the world with the pious intention of doing God's service, not only does not sin but gains merit'.

Mary was imprisoned at Chartley. Despite her suspicions about him,

Gilbert Gifford had established a secret means of corresponding with her. The brewer who supplied Chartley was recruited to take in letters contained in a waterproof container, hidden in a keg of beer. A few days later, he would collect the now empty keg, containing Mary's replies. At first, they were vague and non-committal, but confidence in Gifford's loyalty eventually blossomed and he was soon carrying far more important and potentially incriminating correspondence between Mary and various people, including foreign ambassadors. All these letters were written in a cipher.

As far as Mary and her contacts knew, they had established a successful means of contact. Their packages arrived without any suspicious delays, and with their seals intact. They were not to know, therefore, that their fears about Gifford were well founded. Walsingham had made the necessary arrangements. Gifford delivered the letters to Walsingham's decoding expert, Thomas Phellipes, who deciphered the messages with all speed. The packages were then handed to Arthur Gregory, employed by Walsingham for his exceptional skills in counterfeiting – including the replacement of the most intricate seals – then handed back to Gifford for delivery.

Walsingham knew the vital role that Mary would play in the planned Spanish invasion. She was the means by which Catholic control would be asserted. Inspecting her correspondence, he must have realised that Mary had said enough to demand her removal. He had a problem, however, in Elizabeth's reluctance to commit regicide, despite knowing that throughout nearly 20 years of imprisonment, Mary had constantly been plotting. If nothing else, Elizabeth did not wish to set a precedent, and she had probably developed a horror of the execution of queens during her childhood, in her father's reign. If Walsingham was to get Elizabeth's approval for Mary's removal – thus thwarting an important part of Spain's invasion plans – he would have to provide irrefutable evidence that Mary was at least supportive of a plot to assassinate Elizabeth.

In May 1586, Mary stated her position regarding her son, King James. She wrote to the ambassador Mendoza – who had been expelled from England in 1584 for his complicity in a plot against Elizabeth and was now orchestrating English Catholic agents from a base in France – stating that she would over-ride James's rights of succession, because of his prevarication amounting to refusal to convert to Catholicism, and naming Philip of Spain as her successor. Thus the woman who had 'given' Scotland and England to France was now offering them to Spain. Philip was suitably appreciative. He would later write to Mendoza that he valued Mary 'not so much because of what she says in my favour, but because she subordinates her love for her son, which might be expected to lead her astray, for the service of our Lord, the common good of Christendom, and that of England.'

Two months later, Elizabeth of England signed a 'mutual defence treaty' with James of Scotland who, presumably, had been informed of his mother's intentions. As a sweetener, the King of Scots received a pension of £4,000 a year. Though the ever-greedy James had wanted more, it was enough to ensure his loyalty. If Spain were intending to invade England through the back door, using Scotland as a 'friendly corridor', they would have to think again.

Mendoza was operating a group of agents out of France. Considering they were pitted against Walsingham, they were not a very impressive group. The majority were disgruntled young English Catholics, acting as much out of self-interest as from religious conviction. One such a man was Anthony Babington.

Babington was the eldest son of wealthy Catholic gentry. As a young man, and despite a recent marriage, he expressed a desire to travel abroad for male companionship and spent a year in France. It was there that he was introduced to several of Mary's exiled supporters and, perhaps, to Mendoza. He may also have visited Rome. When he returned to London, he rented a house in Barbican and studied at Lincoln's Inn. He did not seek his wife's company but was instead drawn into the company of young men involved in Catholic conspiracies against Elizabeth. He acted for a time as a courier, but it could be said that he was a reluctant plotter.

Evidently, he was considering a life abroad with a male friend when he received an unexpected packet of letters to be delivered to Mary. By now he had turned against such secretive and dangerous escapades, and returned them to the French ambassador, while applying for a licence to travel abroad with his friend, Thomas Salusbury. If he had travelled without this licence, he would have run the risk of forfeiting his estates. Walsingham saw to it that the licence was refused. The spymaster knew a loose cannon when he saw one.

So it was that Babington had no option but to stay in London, where he met with a Catholic adventurer describing himself as Captain Fortescue, whose real name was Ballard. He was a dangerous man, seeing a 'Catholic revolution' as his path to wealth and glory, and with a habit of convincing himself that whatever he wanted to believe was true. He was a great charmer into the bargain, and Babington fell for him.

Ballard was always short of money, and he may have borrowed money from Babington in order to pay for a trip to France where he met with Mendoza. After this meeting, Mendoza wrote to Philip of Spain, reporting that he had found a group of four men prepared to assassinate Queen Elizabeth, 'whether by poison or steel'.

Meanwhile, back in England, Babington continued to meet with his circle of Catholic friends. They included Chidiock Tichbourne, Thomas Habington, Henry Dunne, Robert Gage, Robert Barnewell, Thomas Salusbury and Edward Jones. Babington also met a new friend who he then introduced to his circle. Robert Poley described himself as a Catholic gentleman, and a fervent supporter of Mary and any efforts to place her on England's throne. He may indeed have been a Catholic, and he might even have been a gentleman. However, he was certainly an accomplished agent in Walsingham's Protestant Secret Service.

Ballard returned from France and told Babington his news. With Catholic Europe mustering for an invasion of England, Ballard had been entrusted to discover the views of Catholics in the north of England. Would they support the proposed invasion?

Ballard had other news. The assassination of Queen Elizabeth was to be entrusted to John Savage, a man described as 'an excellent soldier, a man skilful in languages and learned besides' who had been fighting for the Spanish in the Low Countries. For that reason alone, he stood out as a professional in the company of naïve amateurs.

It has to be asked why Mendoza was prepared to use the likes of Babington and Ballard. Perhaps he had no alternative. Walsingham and his agents played in a different league. Savage seemed to recognise this, and was reluctant to play his part. Meanwhile Babington and his friends, becoming increasingly nervous with the prospect of bold words becoming stern action, discussed whether it might be better to kidnap Elizabeth, and simply hold her till she agreed to grant toleration in religion. They were roughly split between assassination and kidnap.

Walsingham was expecting Mary to write to Babington. He was hoping that she would incriminate herself. The double-agent Gifford was sent to Chartley and, using the brewer's kegs as before, received a large packet that he forwarded to Walsingham's decoding expert.

At or about the same time these letters were being deciphered, events took an unexpected turn. Babington requested an interview with Walsingham. Perhaps he had finally lost his nerve. Once again, he was asking for a licence to travel abroad. Walsingham agreed to meet with him, but denied his appeal. Walsingham wanted the plot to proceed, while he watched and waited.

The contents of Mary's letters were not as damning as Walsingham had hoped. Therefore, he decided to use Gifford as an *agent provocateur* to encourage the hesitant Babington, and to find out more about the shadowy figure of John Savage. Pressurised by Gifford, Babington strengthened his resolve while describing the reluctance of some of his circle of conspirators to be involved in the assassination of the queen. It was finally agreed that the dark deed should be entrusted to a group of just six of the more determined, including Savage. Mindful of Walsingham's requirements, Gifford then encouraged Babington to write immediately to Mary, giving full details of the proposed assassination. She must be informed of the deed that was to be done in her name, in order that she might give her approval, and plan accordingly. Gifford may have suggested that Mary's approval of the plan was vital if the plan was to proceed. At the same time, Gifford assured the nervous Babington that invasion was imminent and he and his plotters would not be abandoned.

Babington wrote the letter to Mary. In it, he described how she would be rescued by 'ten gentlemen and a hundred our followers', and that, at the same time, Elizabeth would be executed by the gang of 'six noble gentlemen, all my private friends'. Shortly after its delivery, Gifford announced that he was needed in France. He knew that Walsingham's trap was about to be sprung, and there was nothing to be gained from 'blowing his cover'.

The conspirators were growing increasingly uneasy. Ballard's visit to the north of England had been a disappointment. There was little support among English Catholics for any sort of a coup that involved an invasion by Spanish and French troops, coupled with the murder of Elizabeth who had earned their grudging respect despite her persecution of Catholic priests.

Babington was called back for a second interview with Walsingham, ostensibly to discuss his application for a licence to travel abroad. In fact, it turned into a game of cat-and-mouse, and Babington suspected that Walsingham might know of their plans. Ironically, Babington turned to Robert Poley, who was in Walsingham's employ. Poley suggested that, in order to save himself, Babington should meet again with Walsingham and tell him all. In the meantime, Poley would hide him. Ballard was informed and agreed with Babington that they were discovered, and that their only course was to offer to act as witnesses against the rest of the group. Poley informed them that Walsingham was busy, but an interview would be arranged as soon as possible.

Elizabeth had been informed of events, and was sufficiently distressed to involve herself, suggesting ways that might be used to prompt more incriminating evidence from her rival, Mary, or to test her further. However, time was running out. Walsingham knew the plotters might flee at any moment, and so ordered their arrests. The guard on Mary was tightened to prevent any news getting to her, and her apartments were thoroughly searched.

Some of the conspirators were more than willing to confess their sins. Those who proved obstinate were broken on the rack. Ballard was one of those who tried to hold out, or perhaps he failed to convince his inquisitors that he had no more information to divulge. By the time of his trial, he was barely able to crawl, let alone walk.

The plotters were brought to trial on September 20 1586. Anthony Babington, John Ballard, John Savage, Chidiock Tichbourne, Charles Tilney and Edward Habington were dragged through the streets from Tower Hill to St Giles's Field where a high scaffold had been built – high enough to ensure the huge crowd that had gathered could see the hanging, drawing and quartering of the condemned. It is said that the executioners were particularly cruel, provoking some sympathy for the dying men. Elizabeth ordered that on the following day, when seven more conspirators were to be executed, they must be hanged till they were dead, and only then were they to be mutilated.

There was one more matter to be dealt with. It was announced that Mary Queen of Scots was to be tried for treason. Walsingham believed he had his evidence.

Those who view Mary Queen of Scots as a tragic-romantic figure are quick to point out the cold and calculating manner in which Walsingham trapped her. They might suggest that by intervening at an early stage, he could have halted her correspondence. This is true, of course, but only up to a point.

Following her abdication, Mary's status was anything but certain. Or rather, it was uncertain in English eyes. In Scotland, it might have been a different matter for, as she had sought to regain the throne after her abdication she might have been guilty of treason against her son. That is certainly the way that the Protestant Lords would have viewed matters. Rather than face that possibility – or further attempts to investigate her involvement in her husband's murder – she had decided to flee to England. She did not take the option of retiring to live out a relatively comfortable life in France.

Apologists for Mary state that she was 'illegally detained against her will' after her flight to England, but what did she expect from Queen Elizabeth, remembering that she had already claimed the throne of England as her own, and remembering that France, Spain and the Pope had declared their support for that claim? Did she think that she would be allowed to hold court? Perhaps, if she spurned the approaches of Catholic plotters, she might have been allowed a greater degree of freedom. As it was, she took every opportunity to encourage them.

In a list of *agent provocateurs*, Mary's name would be right at the top. Even then, Elizabeth had steadfastly refused to deal conclusively with the Marian problem. Walsingham knew the risks. It was his duty to protect Elizabeth – even from herself – while protecting England and, above all perhaps, the Protestant faith.

Philip of Spain may have written to his ambassador Mendoza that he valued Mary because she subordinated her love for her son, 'for the service of our Lord, the common good of Christendom, and that of England.' It could however, be suggested that here was the act of a spiteful woman seeking revenge on the son who had done little if anything to free her – as if he could.

Would England and Scotland's Protestant people be happy to know that, if Mary's will be done, they would be ruled in future by the Catholic king of Spain? The English people had emerged as a thoroughly xenophobic race. They were the veterans of centuries of foreign wars, the contemporaries and comrades of Raleigh, Drake, Sir Philip Sidney and the rest. Men who would die rather than surrender to a foreign flag. Perhaps this was part and parcel of their Protestantism – the rejection of outside interference in their nation's affairs. Who was this French-speaking, Scottish queen to deliver them into Spanish hands? This foreign queen who, just 20 years before, had openly sought the throne in France's name. She might be Tudor in blood, but in many English minds this simply compounded her treachery.

CHAPTER TWENTY-TWO

A QUEEN ON TRIAL

Just three weeks after the executions of the Babington plotters, Mary faced her accusers in the great hall of Fotheringay Castle in Northamptonshire. Dressed in black velvet, she attempted a regal start to the proceedings, pointing to a throne bearing the English coat of arms and announcing: 'I am queen by right of birth and my place should be there.'

Unimpressed by what they probably saw as an act of incriminating haughtiness, Mary's judges directed her to a simple chair. She sat quietly while the Lord Chancellor stated the charge of treason, and outlined the case against her. In return, Mary denied plotting with Anthony Babington, or anybody else, to kill Queen Elizabeth. 'Can I be responsible for the criminal projects of a few desperate men, which they planned without my knowledge or participation?'

In claiming that the assassination plans had been made without her knowledge, Mary set the tone for the proceedings. The intercepted correspondence was read out to the court. Mary's secretaries, Nau and Curle, had already made statements confirming that they were her letters. Evidently, she had written them in French, which they then translated into English before encrypting. The court also heard the confessions made by Babington and other conspirators.

Of all the correspondence, Mary's response to the letter written by Babington on Gifford's instructions was the most damning. Babington had informed Mary that there would be a Catholic invasion of England, led by Philip of Spain and in sufficient force to ensure success; that the invaders would be joined by loyal English Catholics; that Mary would be delivered from her imprisonment; and finally, Babington had described 'the dispatch of the usurping Competitor', that is, the assassination of Queen Elizabeth.

Mary had acknowledged receipt of Babington's letter on July 14, and then considered the matter for three days before making her full reply. She was concerned about the timing of things, seeking reassurance that there would be no delay between Elizabeth's murder and her rescue. She was afraid that she would be placed in mortal danger if her guards were to hear of Elizabeth's death while she was still in their custody, and she stated that the entire adventure depended on a successful invasion. Until that was ready, nothing must be done that would put her in peril.

Mary didn't expressly offer her support for the murder of Elizabeth, but she clearly accepted it as a means to her desired end – her release. Certainly, she wrote nothing to dissuade the conspirators from their chosen course. This must have shocked Elizabeth. For nigh on 20 years, Elizabeth had resisted suggestions to remove Mary from the scene, quietly or otherwise. However, Mary would not protect Elizabeth. She could have suggested that Elizabeth be held captive, but chose not to do so. In those terms, it might be said that it was Mary who was first to put her signature to a royal death warrant – by omission or otherwise.

Elizabeth was under no illusions about the conduct of her royal cousin, and wrote to her accordingly. 'You have planned in divers ways and manners to take my life and to ruin my kingdom by the shedding of blood ... I never proceeded so harshly against you; on the contrary, I have maintained you and preserved your life with the same care which I use for myself.'

Mary continued her defence. After 17 years of imprisonment, her seductive figure had filled out, she was crippled with rheumatism and her general health was clearly failing. She pointed this out to her accusers, saying 'I have only two or three years to live and I do not aspire to any public position.'

If the court had been prepared to take this statement at face value, they might have decided on exile rather than execution. However, the weight of evidence did not suggest that Mary sought an idle, foreign retirement. Indeed, this argument may have gone against Mary for, if true, it brought the prospect of Spanish rule into clearer focus.

The court heard of Mary's longer term plans. She would deny the succession to her son King James (unless he converted to Catholicism), handing it to Philip of Spain. Ironically and unintentionally, this threat would boost the English establishment's acceptance of James as the rightful heir to the English throne.

If Mary believed she had but a short time to live, then her priority was to hand England to Spain, rather than claim the throne for herself. From a

Spanish point of view, Mary was but a short term means to a valuable end. Philip's proposed invasion would secure England's throne for himself. After that, his domination of the Channel and North Sea would allow him to crush the rebellious Dutch. And after that? Surely, the conquest of England, Scotland and the Low Countries would have been the first steps in the Catholic reclamation of Northern Europe.

The apologists and romantics, and they are many, will point out that Mary was tried under the Act of Association, which they describe as an unfair law. It may have been so, but it was the law, good or bad, as passed through the English parliament. They might suggest that a Queen of Scots could not commit treason against a Queen of England. However, Mary had abdicated and it was her son (against whom she had plotted) who sat on Scotland's throne. They might also argue that under English law a person might only be tried by their peers – an argument used in the defence of Charles I and no doubt acceptable to those who believe in the divine right of kings to rule above and beyond the laws of the common herd. Does divine right extend to conspiracy to murder? One cannot help but question whether such protests are little more than the complaints of the fouler when fouled.

The court delivered a guilty verdict on Mary, but despite the overwhelming evidence, Elizabeth remained reluctant to sign Mary's death warrant. It has been said many times that Elizabeth hesitated because she feared it might set a precedent. Feared that by executing Mary, she would invite homebred or foreign retribution. Is this possible? The leading Catholic houses of Europe had been planning her assassination for years ... They were the powers behind the Babington plot, working hand-in-glove with a gang of desperadoes. Elizabeth was equally aware that the papacy had been involved in at least three plots to have her murdered, even before Babington came on the scene. In the pope's eyes, Elizabeth remained the 'illegitimate heretic' on who he had declared open season.

Elizabeth was her father's daughter. That is relevant, of course – none could ignore the impact of having Henry VIII as a patriarch. However, that immense, malevolent figure did not lurk alone in Elizabeth's background, as Bloody Mary had been her sister. Elizabeth had feared them both, and was determined not to be as they had been. Throughout her reign, Elizabeth was reluctant to put her signature on *any* death warrant. It is little wonder that she was reluctant to dictate the same fate for her royal cousin as had been visited on her own mother. Quite simply, Elizabeth had a deep-seated revulsion for the executioner's block.

Elizabeth's hesitancy to sign Mary's death warrant was equally prompted by a genuine concern for the stability of her country. She had to decide whether it would be better, on balance, to execute Mary or to send her into exile. Elizabeth was no fool, was well advised, and realised the risks involved. Up till now, the great majority of English Catholics, while no doubt resenting the persecution of some of their priests, sought little more than religious tolerance. They would have nothing to do with Babington and his kind, and while they were Catholics they were English, and deeply resented Mary's plans to put them under Spanish rule.

Elizabeth knew all this, but needed to be reassured that Mary's execution would not be interpreted as the martyrdom of a Catholic hero – as the papacy and European powers would undoubtedly portray it. Walsingham would have informed her of his agents' reports that the great Catholic lords of the north of England had given a lukewarm reception, at best, to Ballard's approaches when he sought their support for the proposed invasion. However, they might feel differently if Mary was executed and any rebellion, however small, could tie up Elizabeth's army, opening the door to the Spaniards – no army can be in two places at one time.

How would King James of Scots react to the execution of his mother? Might he ignore the mutual defence treaty he had signed with Elizabeth just months before? Whether Elizabeth sought reassurance or delay, she demanded to know these things before putting her signature to Mary's death warrant.

Much was known about King James's feelings for his mother. In 1583, Elizabeth had suggested to James the possibility of Mary's release, provided that he and the king of France would guarantee her good behaviour. If she had assumed that James held some affection for Mary and would welcome this approach, she must have been stunned by his reply. James had discovered that his mother was claiming precedence over him in Scottish affairs. He stated that her dealings with Catholic powers made her untrustworthy. He saw the prospect of Mary's release as a threat to his own position, and was therefore concerned to ensure her continuing imprisonment. It seems that as far as James was concerned, his mother could rot.

A year later, James was given more cause to fear Mary's release when Patrick, Master of Gray, a former agent representing Mary's interests, had swapped sides. He informed James of Mary's plans – which would exclude him unless he was prepared to take a back seat and dance to Catholic tunes. Recognising that his future would be best secured by allegiance to Elizabeth, James then sent Gray to London as his ambassador, with instructions to tell all he knew about Catholic plots and Mary's ambitions. In fact, Gray had little to tell that Walsingham had not already discovered, but this episode served to reassure Elizabeth of James's loyalty to her, though she was intelligent enough to perceive that his first loyalty, as ever, was to himself. In offering his allegiance to Elizabeth, the king of Scotland was seeking England's protection from Mary and her Catholic allies, while furthering his claim to the English throne.

While Elizabeth prevaricated over the death warrant, Walsingham was entrusted to sound out James's current opinions on Mary's fate. He discovered that while James was happy for his mother to be imprisoned, he would not support her execution. Not only would it be a blow to his pride and prestige, but also it might enflame wider resentment in Scotland – the sort of resentment that could provoke a revolution. That was too much to ask. James suggested that his mother be put in the Tower of London, her former servants hanged, and that keener jailors be appointed. He did not see exile as an option, fearing that Mary would be free to assert her claim to his throne.

Walsingham wanted to change King James's mind. James was represented in London by a lawyer, Archibald Douglas, and it was he who wrote to the Scottish king, pointing out the dangers in opposing Mary's execution. Mary had been tried under the terms of the Act of Association. Persons found guilty of plotting against Elizabeth forfeited any claim they might have to the throne, and if their descendants were in any way assenting or privy to they plots, they too would be barred from the succession. Therefore, if James's opposition to Mary's execution was interpreted as assenting to her plotting, or gave the impression that he had been a party to them, he must give up his hopes of the English throne.

King James was caught between a rock and a hard place. In Scotland, many believed that Mary's execution in England, by the English, would be tantamount to a declaration of war between the two countries. One Scottish noble told the king that if he allowed Elizabeth to execute his mother, he would deserve to be hanged the next day. Even those who had opposed Mary in the past, and been delighted to see the back of her, now came to her defence, as described by Gray in a letter he sent to Archibald Douglas on November 23, expressing his fear that James might feel forced to break the alliance.

'The King nor no man ever believed the matter would have gone so far ... If her [Mary's] life be touched or her blood meddled with, he can no longer remain on good terms with the Queen [Elizabeth] or estate of that realm. He will find it hard to keep the peace if her life were touched. I never saw all the people so willing to concur in anything as in this. They that hated most her prosperity regret her adversity.'

A few days later, Douglas received a second letter – this time from James himself. Clearly, he viewed Douglas as some sort of 'temporary London ambassador'. The king instructed the lawyer to ensure that Mary's life was spared, at least until the arrival of an honourable embassy. Unfortunately, he went on to describe, in quite strong terms, what he thought of Elizabeth for landing him in this mess, by allowing her subjects to pass judgement on a sovereign Prince – something far worse than her father had ever done, in his opinion, and which dishonoured him and injured her own reputation. 'Guess ye in what strait my honour will be in, this disaster being perfected, since before God I already dare scarce go abroad, for crying out of the whole people. And what is spoken by them of the Queen of England it grieves me to hear, yet I dare not find fault with it except I would dethrone myself, so is the whole of Scotland incensed with the matter.'

Douglas was an anything but honourable embassy for his king. In fact, he showed James's letter to Elizabeth, who flew into a high fury. This brought matters to a head. Elizabeth had but one question. Would James break the alliance if his mother was executed, yes or no? Douglas replied in the negative. He didn't think that James would accept the alternative, for to become an enemy of England would suggest alliance with her enemies, France and Spain, and it was now clear that the king of Spain wanted England (and Scotland) for himself. In these circumstances, while James might bluster, he had little alternative but to go along with his mother's execution. Or did he?

Some have suggested that a braver king than James might have realised that he was in the driving seat. True, he needed England, but England needed him just as much, if not more. He tried to play the game of bluff and counter-bluff, but he was too much the moral coward.

At the same time, he had another matter to consider. According to the rules of succession, it was Mary who was next in line to the English throne. His succession would have to be through her, but he knew that England's Protestant people would resist any claim she made. Therefore, if Mary was spared and outlived Elizabeth, his claim to the throne would be threatened. On the one hand, Mary had said that she would deny him the succession. On the other, the English would oppose her succession, and thus himself. Clearly, there was no advantage to James in keeping his mother alive. This was the trump card in Elizabeth's hand. She had no doubt that James would be upset by Mary's death. Equally, she was convinced that he would get over it.

James's 'honourable embassy' finally arrived in London, to plead for clemency. His ambassadors were Patrick Gray – who, as the English knew, had already betrayed Mary – and Sir Robert Melville. They brought a letter from James to Elizabeth, setting out his position and stating he would view his mother's execution as a sad return for the friendship he had shown Elizabeth. He argued that Mary should be sent abroad, under guarantee of good behaviour.

Sir Alexander Stewart, who accompanied the ambassadors, promptly threw a spanner in the works by announcing that he had instructions direct from James to inform Elizabeth that he would not oppose the execution. This was hardly a united negotiating team. The situation went from bad to worse when Gray, sticking to his plea for clemency, suggested that Mary might make over her succession claims to her son, in return for her life.

'By God's passion, that were to cut my own throat, and, for a duchy or an earldom to yourself, you or such as you would cause some of your desperate knaves to kill me', Elizabeth responded angrily. 'No, by God, he shall never be in that place. Tell your King what good I have done for him in holding the Crown on his head since he was born, and that I mind to keep the league that now stands between us, and if he break, it shall be a double fault.'

Gray and Melville realised they had overstepped the mark and begged for a delay, but Elizabeth had heard enough. 'Not for an hour', she replied. Mary was executed on February 9 1587.

Elizabeth put on an amazing display of grief after Mary's execution, claiming that she had been tricked into signing the death warrant. She put the blame on her secretary, William Davison, who had drawn up the document. The royal scapegoat was thrown into prison.

There are contrasting accounts of James's reaction. Some said he was so upset that he was quite unable to eat his supper. Others said that he was delighted at the news, declaring, 'I am now sole king.' Another account suggests that Maitland was so embarrassed by James's happy mood that he ordered courtiers from the grinning royal presence. It wasn't long before James started to consider how he might make a profit from his situation, however, and he quickly accepted the role of grieving son.

James let it be known that he was furious with Elizabeth. Seeking to appease those Scots who so deeply resented Mary's execution, he said that he would not be intimidated by an old woman, unloved by her subjects. He wept and wailed – then got to the point. He wrote to Elizabeth suggesting that she might heal his wounds by granting him lands in northern England, together with the title of duke. It is not known whether Elizabeth laughed, but she certainly refused.

Many Scots were thirsting for revenge. Among them was the fifth Earl of Bothwell who, like the fourth earl (Mary's third husband) was no stranger to violence. He scoffed at the mourning clothes worn by the king, saying that a better suit would be made of armour.

In July 1587, Maitland, now Chancellor and the king's principal adviser, made an impassioned speech to the Scottish parliament, demanding that Mary's death must be avenged. All those nobles present swore to support the king in this venture, if that is what he wished. James thanked them, but that was all. Meanwhile, the Border clans made profit from their outrage, sweeping through England's northern shires and leaving a trail of mayhem and murder wherever they reived and plundered.

Elizabeth was angered and perhaps a little fearful at this distraction, but her confidence must have been raised by Sir Francis Drake's action against the Spanish fleet, gathering for the proposed invasion of England. In April, just a couple of months after Mary's execution, Drake boldly sailed into Cadiz with four warships and 23 armed merchantmen. In a battle that lasted for two days, Drake's fleet sank 30 large Spanish ships and countless smaller ones, before burning thousands of tons of stores. He reported to Elizabeth that he had 'singed the king of Spain's beard.' England was safe from invasion, for the time being.

ROME, FRANCE
AND SPAIN

Following the execution of the Catholic mother he had never known, the Protestant King James of Scots was deeply hurt when Queen Elizabeth of England refused to compensate him with lands and titles, or to name him as absolute heir to her throne. In this dark mood, and egged on by those Scottish nobles who thirsted for revenge, he sought to pressurise Elizabeth by contacting her enemies.

James might have known that his correspondence with foreign powers would come to Walsingham and Elizabeth's attention. He was probably counting on it, as a vital part of a dangerous game of double bluff. In truth, he had little to gain and much to lose from any foreign alliance, other than with England, but he was keen to bully Elizabeth into granting him some recompense, while making a show of grief in order to pacify those Scots who threatened to invade England, to extract revenge. Infuriated Catholic nobles might have thrown James aside to make way for one of their own persuasion – foreign or otherwise – and so needed to be appeased.

James passed the blame for failing to persuade Elizabeth to leave Mary's head on her shoulders, and Patrick, Master of Gray, was ruined. When told what had been said by Sir Alexander Stewart – that James would accept Mary's execution – the king denied all, swearing that if Stewart came back to Scotland he would 'hang him before he put off his boots'. In fact, Stewart returned to Scotland with impunity.

As he was endeavouring to avoid criticism at home, James saw a need to reassure foreign powers that he had not supported his mother's execution. He coveted the throne of England, but recognised that country was seriously threatened. If it was invaded, then what future for him? He may have entertained the belief that a quick conversion to Catholicism would save him, but not if he was judged guilty as an accessory to what was becoming 'the martyrdom of Saint Mary'.

A trident of powers – the papacy, France and Spain – threatened England and ultimately Scotland. James considered which, if any, would listen to his pleas.

The Spanish position was clear. Their intention was to invade England as a colonial force. In truth, they had been reluctant to invade if it was simply in order to place Mary on the throne, and then retire. Indeed, they may have welcomed Mary's execution as removing an obstacle between Philip of Spain and the English throne. As long as Mary was alive, the Spaniards would have to recognise her as the legitimate Catholic heir, or risk Rome's disapproval. For Spain, there would be no advantage in waiting while Mary lived out her three score and ten. True, it had been reported that she suffered ill health, but that was no guarantee. England and Scotland under Mary might be offered as a base for the suppression of the Protestant Low Countries, and extending Spanish power throughout northern Europe, but they would be subject to Mary in their operations, albeit she would be little more than a puppet queen.

For the same reason, Spain did not want James to rule – either in Scotland or England. Philip made his feelings clear on this subject – telling the pope that the king of Scotland was a hopeless heretic who should be dethroned, not converted. Indeed, Spain viewed the prospect of James's conversion with some alarm, for it would remove their excuse to invade. Such a conversion might suit the papacy, but it would hinder Spain's plans to become the dominant power in the world. Philip then announced that he was the indisputable heir to the English throne, by descent from John of Gaunt.

The pope was not convinced, either way. James had been given ample opportunities to convert in the past and had refused, but this didn't rule out the possibility that he might yet come to his senses. In order to test which way the wind blew, a mission was sent to Scotland, headed by the exiled Catholic Bishop of Dunblane. James behaved in character – talking, but making no commitment either way – and using up the last shreds of papal patience.

The Scottish Catholic nobility were outraged by Mary's execution. Led by Huntly in the north, Crawford and Montrose, and by Maxwell and Lord Hamilton in the south, they were determined on action, but undecided as to what form it should take. One possibility was to invite a Spanish army to invade Scotland and force the king to convert to Catholicism. Unaware of Philip of Spain's belief that James was unfit to rule, converted or otherwise, they may have been surprised when they received a refusal to their invitation. That left them with little option but to rebel on their own account. They assembled their forces at Dunfermline and Linlithgow, but after much shuffling, and upon hearing that Edinburgh's defences had been strengthened, rebellion no longer seemed like such a good idea. They then considered another popular Scottish activity – kidnapping. James was invited by Huntly to a banquet in Dunfermline and, strangely for such a nervous soul, actually turned up. However, on the day following his arrival, in that coldest hour before the dawn, he leapt from his bed and fled as if the Hounds of Hell were on his trail.

James's attendance at Huntly's banquet might be explained if, once again, he was playing a double game. He did little to curb the Catholic nobles, because he hoped they would increase the pressure on England. He sought their support – hoping that they would intercede on his behalf if ever there were a successful foreign invasion. But he lost his nerve.

The only obvious course left open to James was to approach his French relations. He wrote to Henry III of France, Catherine de Medici and the Duke of Guise, asking for aid to avenge his mother. He must have known that they did not favour him. As far as they were concerned, he had done little if anything to help his mother during her lifetime, while remaining stubbornly Protestant, and they were not impressed when he sought to make a bargaining token out of his religion.

France was torn apart by civil war between Catholic and Protestant. Protestant Henry of Bourbon, King of Navarre threatened Catholic Henry III of Valois, King of France. Therefore, when James wrote to Henry of France, it was to reassure him that no king should have to tolerate rebellion, and stating he would ensure than no Protestant Scots would fight with Navarre's forces. However, because he couldn't resist trying to be on both sides of a fence at the same time, James also wrote to Henry of Navarre, offering his support and friendship.

The Duke of Guise paid little attention to James's pleas, for he was in league with Philip of Spain. Together, they were trying to rid France not only of the threat of Protestantism, but also of a weak Catholic king. The duke was one of the most powerful nobles in France, so it might be assumed that his first loyalty was to the French king. However, this simple conclusion fails to acknowledge that the duke was extremely ambitious and had his own agendas, both at home and abroad.

Under Salic law, Henry of Navarre was the legitimate heir to Henry of Valois, King of France; but the king of Navarre was a Protestant and therefore a heretic to the majority of Frenchmen. As an alternative, Henry, Duke of Guise, claimed descent from Charlemagne, suggesting he had a better claim to the French throne than Henry of Navarre – and none could doubt his allegiance to the Catholic Church. Henry of Valois, King of France, had given his tentative support to Henry, Duke of Guise, who publicly returned the compliment, but Guise was impatient and already planning to overthrow the French king at the earliest opportunity, with Spain's support and the backing of Catherine de Medici, the dowager queen. Thus Henry of Guise was determined to have the throne of France for himself, and both Henry of Valois and Henry of Navarre were painfully aware of Guise's desire to seize total power.

Philip II of Spain was the champion of Catholic orthodoxy. Within France, he was represented by his ambassador, Don Bernardino de Mendoza – a grand master of cross-Channel intrigue and closely involved in plots to assassinate Elizabeth and free Mary. The Spanish ambassador was the paymaster of the ultra-Catholic conspiracy known as the Holy League, under Philip's overall command. Guise and his brothers – who put loyalty to the League and themselves ahead of any expected loyalty to Henry of Valois, King of France – headed the League in France.

It was very much a case of mutual back scratching. The League and Catholic Church supported Guise, because he supported them. And he supported them as a means of toppling Henry of Valois and denying the succession to Henry of Navarre. In this arrangement, there was a great deal of self-interest, but little if any affection or admiration.

It was the Guise's current grudge that Elizabeth of England would not have executed their kinswoman, the Catholic Mary, without the reassurance of the French king, Henry of Valois, that any objections he might raise would be nothing more than empty words that could safely be ignored. In the opinion of the Guises, the king's lack of resolve in this matter simply confirmed his readiness to make deals with Protestants. Their efficient propaganda machine swung into action. Backed by the Church and the League, it was put about that the French king favoured alliances with heretics, such as Elizabeth and the Henry of Navarre, to loyalty, to the truth, faith, and its ultimate champion, Spain.

In the eyes of many of the French Catholic clergy, their king had sold his soul to the devil – and they preached this message from their pulpits. His power had long been crumbling as one after another of the great provinces slipped from his control – into the hands of Protestants or ultra conservative Catholics, or local lords intent on filling their own coffers. The French people had suffered long and hard as the rule of law was swept aside in a flood of anarchy and religious wars, characterised by atrocities such as the slaughter of 3,000 Protestants by the Parisian mob on St Bartholomew's Day, 1572. While the mob carried out the massacre, it was orchestrated by leading members of the Catholic establishment, headed by Catherine de Medici and the Guise family.

After years of fighting, in late October 1587 – the year of Mary's execution – the Protestant army of the Huguenot hero Henry of Bourbon, King of Navarre, was trapped in the village of Coutras in the junction of the Drone and Isle rivers. Their escape route was blocked by a vastly superior Catholic army, commanded by the Duke of Joyeuse whose wife was a cousin of the Guises.

Like Guise, Joyeuse was an ardent member of the Holy League, backed by Philip of Spain. Together, the Leaguers saw their chance to stamp out Protestantism in France for all time. They would emerge as the heroes, headed by Guise and creating a stark contrast with the king's failings. Henry of Navarre would be defeated, and Henry of Valois would be left without any credibility.

Catholic forces had slaughtered entire garrisons in the past, and hanged hundred of defenceless Protestant prisoners. This time would be no different. Recognised as a brilliant and merciless military commander, Joyeuse ordered that not one heretic, not even Navarre himself, should survive. With Navarre out of the way, it would clear Guise's road to the French throne. Any wounded Protestants were to be killed where they lay.

When the heavily-armoured Catholic cavalry charged at the psalm-singing Huguenots, they cannot have imagined that they would be broken on the stubborn Protestants ranks and they, the superior force, would soon be fighting for their lives. The Huguenots wouldn't have asked for quarter or received it, nor did they give it. Huguenot cavalry captured the Duke of Joyeuse who was trying to escape. The man who had ordered 'no quarter' begged for mercy, but one of his captors put a bullet through his brain.

All over the battlefield of Coutras, the Huguenots killed their prisoners, including dukes, marquises, counts, barons and common soldiers. It is said that 3,000 were shot or put to the sword before Navarre finally ordered an end to the killing.

In the aftermath of Coutras, the Huguenots found themselves in an incredible position. Only weeks before, they had been seeking to avoid a pitched battle, relying solely on hit-and-run tactics, but now they had defeated the full might of the Catholic army. What was more, they were about to be reinforced by a powerful mercenary force, paid for by the Protestant Elizabeth of England. Under the command of Baron von Dohna, it included 8,000 German cavalry, a similar number of German infantry, and 18,000 Swiss led by the Duke of Bouillon.

Paris and the French throne were there for the taking, but Henry of Navarre surprised them all. He disbanded his army and rode off to dally with his mistress. Navarre had been fighting for Protestant survival, rather than a Catholic defeat. As heir to the throne of France, he had little to gain and everything to lose by continuing the war. Such a course would undoubtedly infuriate the French people still further, allowing Guise to gather far wider support for his claims. Navarre's philosophy seemed to be that simply because his Protestant forces had won a battle, there was no point in pushing matters to the point where he might lose the war. He was not impatient.

Henry of Navarre was not alone in recognising the Duke of Guise as a threat. King Henry of France had grown wary of him, and no longer trusted the Leaguers' motives, nor their hollow protestations of allegiance to him. He suspected that Joyeuse had gone over to the League's cause – to gain control of France by placing Guise on the throne – and therefore didn't shed many tears over his death at Coutras. Guise and the rest of the Leaguers were becoming a far greater threat to Henry of France than the Protestants who sought little more than religious tolerance after decades of persecution.

The French king may have hoped the huge mercenary army, funded by England, would march into Guise's territory in the north. Without reinforcements – and it was within the king's power to withhold them – Guise would almost certainly be defeated and his power destroyed. Then, and only then, would the French king throw his forces into the fray.

Henry of France was confident that the vast army of 40,000 he had garrisoned between Etampes and La Charite could destroy the Protestant threat. In fact, the mercenary army made up of men from Germany and Switzerland was practically destroying itself. Internal bickering was the start of its downfall – that and the mercenary's desire for loot and easy living. It was said that French women and the owners of wine cellars had more to fear than the Catholic soldiery from the foreign Protestant mercenaries.

When it was clear that the mercenaries were not interested in his lands in the north, Guise saw an opportunity to enhance his popularity with the French people. With a force of just 6,000 men, he shadowed the Germans and Swiss, occasionally swooping down on any stragglers who were promptly marched to Paris to be displayed to the mob. Such easy victories earned him great kudos with the French Catholics.

Guise was an exponent of the art of self-publicity, and enjoyed the backing of many Catholic priests who gave their allegiance to Rome and the Holy League, rather than their king. Parisians were convinced that the Duke of Guise was the only man standing between them and the marauding Protestant mercenaries. As for the unpopular king, who knew where he might be skulking? Some priests suggested that he might already be negotiating with the Protestants, as he had done in the past.

Eventually, the mercenary army blundered into the neighbourhood of Montargis where, thinking they had nothing to fear, they set up in disorderly camps. Guise and his brother, the Duke of Mayenne, decided on a night attack. Many of their army were killed, but the attack served its purpose. They had taken prisoners, horses and wagons, various items of baggage including two camels, and the personal banner of the German commander, Baron von Dohna. Guise carried these off to Paris, which he entered like a victorious Caesar, assuring the people that he had enjoyed a massive victory over the Protestants.

Meanwhile, the French king was indeed in negotiations with the mercenary army. Elizabeth of England had not paid Dohna's troops. The Swiss were ready to head home, but the Germans were keen to see if they could extract some blackmail from Henry before they left. From his point of view, this would be a small price to pay to rid his country of a foreign horde whose drunken excesses and communal stomach was costing his country dear.

Guise learned of these developments and feared the king might regain something of his reputation if the negotiations proved successful, so he moved quickly to regain the initiative. Dohna was half-heartedly besieging the

French town of Aunea with a small force of his German troops when Guise's army attacked. Dohna was lucky to escape with his life and a handful of followers. The rest of his force was slaughtered.

The survivors from Dohna's forces joined the Swiss contingent who were already on their way home, having accepted the French king's terms. Henry was pleased with what he had achieved through peaceful negotiation, but the people of France, particularly the Parisians, were not impressed. In their eyes, it was the Duke of Guise who had ridded the country of the murdering foreigners, and the pulpits rang with his praises. Made bold with victory, the doctors and masters of the Sorbonne declared that it was as lawful to depose a prince who had failed, as it was a trustee suspected of malfeasance. King Henry, who had expected to be hailed as a hero, was openly jeered.

Bernardino de Mendoza summed up the public mood for his master, the king of Spain and power behind the Holy League. 'On the whole ... events here could hardly have gone more happily for Your Majesty's affairs. The people of Paris can be relied on at any time. They are more deeply than ever in obedience of the Duke of Guise.'

The inference was clear. He who obeyed the Duke of Guise ultimately obeyed the King of Spain. Here lay the threat to Protestant England and Scotland – the united Catholic powers of Rome, Spain and traditional France.

Historians of Old Scotia seem remarkably vague about the Spanish Armada, as if it was of no concern to Scotland. Equally, the historians of Merry England see it as their affair, and theirs alone. Both are right, and wrong. They are right in that the immediate threat was to England. They are wrong in assuming that a defeated England under Spanish rule would have ignored its neighbour. And on the larger front, if we can drag ourselves away from parochial attitudes for a few moments, we might look at a map of Europe and ask whether Protestantism could have survived if England had fallen.

Philip II of Spain's possessions make impressive reading. As well as Spain and Portugal, they included Sardinia, Sicily, Naples, Lombardy, Franche Comte and what was then the Spanish Netherlands. In France, while the Protestant claimant to the throne still lived, Spain could be confident that the Catholic majority would oppose his succession and put the Duke of Guise on the throne. Thus united, Spain and France would dominate Europe and might go on to conquer those northern states that had fallen into heretic hands. It was this promise of a mighty counter-reformation movement that earned the papacy's support.

Rome supported Spain, because Spain supported Rome. And Rome supported the Duke of Guise in France because they saw him as the best Catholic defence against the Protestant threat of Henry of Navarre. Thus it was that the Church was to undermine the position of the incumbent King Henry. It wasn't enough that he was Catholic. He was too tolerant for the Church's liking, so they chose Guise who had proved he would fight the good fight with all his might.

Christian compassion, as we might understand it, was not to be wasted on Protestants. So it was that Rome did not so much support the invasion of England as demand it – just as they had demanded the invasion of the Holy Land in former times. And if Spain was to profit from that invasion, then so be it.

Sir Francis Drake's destruction of some Spanish ships and stores in the port of Cadiz in 1587 was just as he described it. He had singed the king of Spain's beard – nothing more than an inconvenience. The preparations for an invasion were quickly resumed.

At the start of 1588 the gathering Spanish fleet was faced with another problem. This time it was a typhus epidemic, which claimed the lives of many, including the fleet's commander, the Marquis of Santa Cruz. His replacement was the Duke of Medina Sidonia. Apparently, he was reluctant to accept this position, arguing a lack of naval experience, but King Philip insisted.

Sir Francis Drake was back in England at this time. He persuaded the Lord Admiral, Lord Howard of Effingham, to base the English fleet at Plymouth. The Spaniards' plans were an open secret. They would sail up the English Channel to the Flemish ports where they would be loaded with troops commanded by the Duke of Parma. These were battle-hardened veterans of the war against the Protestant rebels in the Netherlands. As such, they were the finest troops that Spain could muster.

It was the English commander's intention that the Spanish fleet should be engaged long before it reached the Flemish ports. A running battle, up the full length of the Channel, would best suit the fast English ships whose main tactic was repeated broadsides from their cannons, rather than immediately closing to board in a pitched battle. Hit, hit, hit and run, then hit and hit again until the enemy lowered his colours, or was so weakened as to be easily boarded.

English gunners prided themselves in that they were the finest of any fleet in the world. The size of the Spanish fleet, 132 ships in all, would give them every opportunity to prove whether this was so. However, it was another form of firepower that would settle the Armada's fate.

According to plan, when the Spanish Armada was sighted off the Lizard in Cornwall, messengers raced to inform Lord Howard of Effingham, commanding the fleet in Plymouth. Howard set to sea immediately, having divided his ships into four squadrons commanded by himself, Sir Francis Drake, Sir John Hawkins and Martin Frobisher. Their initial 'hit and run' tactics met with little success, however, and the Spaniards sailed on to Gravelines with few casualties.

So far, so good for the Spanish, but then Medina Sidonia was frustrated. The Duke of Parma announced that he would not embark his men in unescorted transports while the English fleet were prowling in the Channel. The big Spanish ships could not reach Parma's men, who would not try to reach them, forcing the Armada to turn south-west and anchor in close ranks off Calais.

When the Spanish anchored, the English saw their opportunity and grabbed it with both hands, sending in fire ships packed with burning pitch and gunpowder. Suddenly all was chaos, with Spaniards attempting to flee in all directions. Medina Sidonia managed to rally most of them, while others burnt, but the English were ready to attack again, firing broadsides, and there was a running battle up the Flemish coast before a stiffening wind scattered the Spaniards into the North Sea, with the English sharks snapping at their heels.

CHAPTER TWENTY-FOUR

IN THE ARMADA'S WAKE

In the violent storm that followed the Armada, England feared that the Spanish ships might put in to Norwegian ports to refit before a second attempt at embarking Parma's troops, but nobody was sure about anything. Out of touch with her fleet, England was working in the dark. With no way of knowing what to expect, they prepared for the worst. A force of 20,000 men gathered at Tilbury in Essex, under the command of the Earl of Leicester. They were joined by Queen Elizabeth, who offered words of encouragement.

'I know I have the body of a weak and feeble woman, but I have the heart and stomach of a King, and of a King of England too, and think foul scorn that Parma or Spain; or any prince of Europe should dare invade the borders of my realm, to which, rather than any dishonour shall grow by me, I myself will take up arms ... By your valour in the field we shall shortly have a famous victory over these enemies of my God, my kingdom and of my people.'

Elizabeth was not to know it, but that famous victory had already been won. Her God had played his part, blowing her enemies to kingdom come – or far enough away to make them lose all interest in continuing. Whatever was left of the storm-tossed Spanish fleet was heading for home.

The survivors had to circumnavigate the British Isles, losing ships along the way in mighty storms that lasted for weeks. At least 17 ships were torn apart on Ireland's rocky coastline. Most of the survivors were hunted down and killed. The Lord Deputy, Sir William Fitzwilliam, had but 2,000 English troops to police the 'rebellious' Irish, and so decided he couldn't allow any Spaniards to survive, lest they cause trouble. Those who were saved by sympathetic Irish were slipped over to Scotland, to join their comrades whose ships had been lost on Scottish shores. With a keen eye for easy money, the Scots started confidential negotiations with Spain for their release.

More than 11,000 Spanish souls were lost before they reached their home waters. Some in battle, some in storm, some massacred and some who perished of thirst and starvation for the ships had not expected such a long voyage. Then there was scurvy and typhus. King Philip had gambled much and won nothing, but refused to accept that he had been defeated. He had lost the battle, he admitted, but the war had just begun. With that in mind, he welcomed back his vanquished heroes as they struggled ashore from their broken ships. This was in marked contrast to the treatment of the wounded and injured English sailors for whom no provision was made. In effect, they were left to rot. Perhaps Elizabeth and her courtiers were just too busy celebrating to concern themselves with the fate of their saviours.

In Scotland before the Armada, King James had declared his intention to stand by England, while quietly keeping his options open. The Elizabethan Secret Service had been well aware that Spanish agents were operating in Scotland, and that James might be prepared to negotiate through them with Philip. They were particularly concerned about a Colonel Semple – a Spanish agent from the Netherlands. So while Elizabeth and her advisors were fairly confident of Scotland's support, or at least its neutrality, they had seen the need to cement their neighbour's position.

Elizabeth called on God to witness that she was innocent of Mary's blood, and sent James a gift of £2,000 with a plea that he 'seal his ears with the wax of Ulysses' against siren offers from the continent. In return, James promised 'his forces, his person, and all that he commanded against yon strangers'.

Still, he left the Spanish agents free to wander over his country. Indeed, it was only when James had received definitive news of the Armada's defeat that he ordered the arrest of Colonel Semple, who languished for a short time in prison before making his escape.

Protestants at home and abroad were quick to declare that God had been on their side, some barely acknowledging the role of the English fleet. Armada medals state, 'God breathed and they were scattered'. From the Protestant perspective, God had intervened, sinking Spain's ships and drowning thousands of her sailors in order to preserve the Protestant faith. In the eyes of the Elizabethan court, here was proof positive that God was a Protestant – and an Englishman.

With renewed confidence and God's help, England planned to build on the defeat of the Armada. They were determined to take the offensive. Younger commanders would be favoured – men like Sir Francis Drake, whose ability to raise morale apparently excused his frequent reluctance to get close to the action. Despite his heroic status, Drake was more the scavenging hyena than the marauding lion. Nevertheless, he would be trusted to take the war to Spain's back yard.

Meanwhile, Philip of Spain displayed a great stoicism and dignity in learning of his fleet's defeat. Father Famiano Strada described how the king took the news. 'I give thanks to God by whose hand I have been so endowed that I can put to sea another fleet as great as this we have lost whenever I choose. It does not matter if a stream is sometimes choked, as long as the source flows freely.' Another version has Philip saying: 'I sent my ships to fight against men, and not against the winds and waves of God,' before returning to his papers. He would be kept busy planning another fleet, stronger than the last. Bigger ships, better equipped and with more guns, paid for with gold from Spanish territories in the New World.

The Spanish threat had not been destroyed, but simply delayed. The war would continue – that much was certain. Indeed, the Spanish were more determined than ever to destroy Protestantism. They acknowledged that God had destroyed their Armada, but accepted this as part of their faith – that He works in mysterious ways. Bernardino de Mendoza highlighted this in a letter to his king, pointing out that even the noblest crusaders had suffered defeats and it may be that God humbles those who fight in His cause so that through humility they may learn the way to victory. Philip agreed with this sentiment, which gave the Spaniards renewed confidence. It was not the English who had defeated them, but God who tested his most faithful. Indeed, they had not been defeated so much as delayed. Next time, they would be better prepared, and then God might smile on them, or otherwise.

'It is impiety, and almost blasphemy, to presume to know the will of God,' Philip once stated. 'Even kings must submit to being used by God's will without knowing what it is.'

Compared to the pragmatic Philip of Spain, King James VI of Scots might have been described as a wishful thinker. Despite his love of hunting, he had a deep-seated revulsion for violence between men, and convinced himself that it might be stopped by kind words. Scotland was constantly torn apart by civil war, raids, murder and feuds that were handed down from one generation to the next. In 1587, with the Armada looming on the horizon,

James had dreamt up what he saw as a solution. Not so much a war to end all wars as a party to end all enmities.

Most of the Scottish nobles had attended the banquet in Edinburgh, though they may not have known its purpose. After they had been fed and watered, they were taken on a procession through the streets of the capital, each one holding hands with his bitterest enemy – like battling schoolboys forced to shake hands by a well-meaning teacher. Yes indeed, James was a wishful thinker. Then again, as he abhorred violence, his options were strictly limited.

One of those options was to reform the law in order to make his nobles more accountable. Scottish nobles tended to regard themselves as minor kings within their own areas of influence, indeed, that was pretty much what they were, often combining the roles of chief of their clan, feudal landlord and magistrate – judge and jury, sitting on one often comfortable chair, dispensing 'justice' or making war on his neighbours. This was particularly true of the chiefs and heads of families in the Borders, Highlands and Western Isles. From their positions of eminence, the great but seldom good tended to regard the King of Scots as a partner in their noble business, rather than as any sort of supreme ruler. They acknowledged the law of the land, most of the time, but administered it as they saw fit, and were past masters at turning a blind eye to those parts of it that did not suit their purposes. The clan system was very much a family affair and many Scots, from the highest to the low, protected their kith and kin, both near and far – even against the courts of justice.

James recognised that it was not so much the law as difficulties in its enforcement that was at the heart of the trouble. It was one thing to pass laws, but a very different matter to ensure that they were followed throughout the kingdom. By regularly ignoring the laws of the land, while enforcing their own versions of justice, the Scottish nobles had elevated their position among their own folk. The man who contemptuously ignored the king's writ might slit his neighbour's throat if his chief ordered it.

As far as King James was concerned, this situation was intolerable and he became an ardent champion of modernisation and reform of the law, coupled with a vigorous administration of the same. In this, he had a great supporter – a companion and advisor who could match his intellect and, perhaps most importantly, make him laugh. That man was Sir James Maitland, who Spottiswoode described as, 'A man of rare parts, of a deep wit, learned, full of courage, and most faithful to his King and master. No man ever carried himself in his place more wisely nor sustained it more courageously against his enemies than he did.'

Maitland became the king's principal adviser – all the more remarkable because he had remained loyal to Queen Mary and deeply resented her execution – although he was a Protestant. He was a man with high ideals who could not accept the 'rough justice' that had been dealt by England to the former Scottish queen. However, he was no idle dreamer. Rather, he was a pragmatist and, despite his feelings regarding Mary, believed that alliance with England offered Scotland's best option. If nothing else, it would give King James the means and power to deal with his rebellious earls – means and power that had been siphoned off for far too long into attempts to cool internal strife. Maitland didn't have to like the English in order to do business with them, and was ever loyal to his king's interests, present and future.

 Maitland the reformer was a force to be reckoned with, a man described as wise and courageous, literate and courtly (despite his often sharp Scots tongue), who was extremely witty and loved a good joke. James had every confidence in this paragon of a statesman, promoting him to Secretary in 1584, Vice-Chancellor in 1586, and Chancellor just one year later. He was a man of great power and influence, and therefore viewed by many as an intolerable nuisance. Noble enemies surrounded him.

The reforming partnership of King James and Sir James Maitland was a direct threat to the long-held power of the Scottish aristocracy, and they reacted accordingly. The aggressively proud and hot-headed Protestant Earl of Bothwell, who had itched to invade England after Queen Mary's execution, was among the leaders of those opposing reforms, and was quick to sneer at Maitland's origins – from outside the nobility.

By favouring one, King James had offended others, and many nobles were deeply jealous of Maitland's advancement, so rallied to Bothwell. Together, Bothwell and his allies provided an effective opposition to the king's desire for change. Hampered on all sides, Maitland was unable to bring in the reforms he sought, and his attempts at enforcement were spurned.

Perhaps the greatest threat of all came from the Catholic earls of the north. They would have liked nothing better than to return Scotland to Catholicism, and were fervent in their hatred of the Elizabethan court and all who dealt with it – including Maitland, who they regarded as an upstart collaborator. They were led by the earls of Huntly, Errol, Angus and Crawford, who had been in close contact with the Spanish both before and since the Armada.

Huntly might be singled out as the most devious and treacherous of the plotters. In 1588, he had married a sister of the Duke of Lennox, placing him on the fringes of the royal family and ensuring that he would be in contact with the king. He fulfilled all the qualifications that James sought in one on whom he might lavish his affection, for Huntly was young, handsome and amusing. At this stage, the king did not view Huntly as any sort of a threat, thinking him to be altogether too delightfully frivolous to involve himself in matters of state. Indeed, the king set about converting Huntly to Protestantism, and the handsome young earl apparently went along with this, agreeing to attend the Kirk. In truth, however, Huntly was displaying his contempt and hypocrisy.

Huntly may have been a charming psychopath. Certainly, a wolf lurked behind the courtier's smile; his frivolity a thin veneer over a cruel core. He was in the habit of adorning the turrets of Strathbogie Castle with the severed limbs of his foes, and was capable of combining irony with his barbarism – when his men captured two cooks from an enemy clan, Huntly ordered that they should be roasted alive.

England's Secret Service and Scotland's Protestants were well aware of the treacherous dealings being conducted by Huntly and the other Catholic earls, and pressed King James to take action against them. Many would have done so, but not James, who almost seemed to encourage them, Huntly in particular, by seeking their friendship. He even appointed him Captain of the Guard. It might be wrong to assume that James was fooled by Huntly's double-dealings. He may have been attempting to bring the wolf to heel, against the day that he might be protection against a far more threatening adversary, the Earl of Bothwell.

The Earl of Bothwell was an opponent of Maitland's reforming zeal, and as opponents go, he was about as bad as it got. Francis Stewart Hepburn had inherited the earldom through his mother, Jane Hepburn, a sister of the former Earl of Bothwell who had married Mary Queen of Scots. Any badness that had been witnessed in the former earl (and there was surely badness aplenty) was seemingly magnified in his nephew. He had grand ideas about his own importance and status, for his father was one of James V's illegitimate sons – a brother of Lord James Stewart, later the Regent Earl of Moray. He believed this gave him rights in regard to the Scottish throne. Like Huntly, he was certainly a lad of parts, as described by William Fowler. 'There is more wickedness, more valour, and more good parts in him than in any three of the other noblemen.'

On one of his dalliances in England, Bothwell met with the Dean of Durham, who described him thus: 'This nobleman hath a wonderful wit and as wonderful a volubility of tongue as agility of body on horse and foot; competently learned in the Latin; well languaged in the French and Italian; much delighted in poetry; and of a very resolute disposition both to do and to suffer; nothing dainty to discover his humour or any good quality he hath.'

Bothwell had been another royal favourite. In the early 1580s, King James had been in the habit of hanging about his neck while slobbering sweet nothings in his ear, irrespective of the company. Affection faded into impatience, however, when Bothwell's wildness led him into one scrape after another, ranging from assaults and disturbances of the peace through to vicious feuds and rumours of plotting for rebellion.

In the end, Bothwell was virtually an outlaw. The only thing that saved him was his political status as an opponent of Maitland, which found favour with his fellow Protestant nobles, and the support of the Kirk, as an energetic enemy of the Catholic earls. However, survival was not enough for Bothwell. He decided to reverse his fortunes, and came to the conclusion that the best way would be to seize control of the king. This in itself was enough to anger James, but that anger turned to blind fury and terror when James discovered that Bothwell was in league with warlocks, witches and sorcerers, despite his reputation as the Kirk's enforcer.

England's Secret Service had long been aware of the Catholic earls' dealings with Spain and finally, in February 1589, they had their proof. They intercepted letters written to Philip of Spain by Huntly, Errol and Crawford, lamenting the failure of the Armada, and promising to invade England if Philip sent assistance.

Elizabeth was furious, and wrote to James, virtually ordering him to deal with the traitors. 'Good Lord! Methinks I do but dream!' she stormed. 'No King a week would bear this!'

James had to do something, but he was still besotted with Huntly and, as ever, his loyalty to handsome young men knew few bounds. He dismissed Huntly from his post as Captain of the Guard and had him imprisoned in

Edinburgh Castle. At the same time, he promised the English ambassador that Huntly would be dealt with severely. However, James dined with Huntly the very next day, and treated him with his usual affection. 'Yea, kissing him at times to the amazement of many; and the next day was with him again and hath given his wife, servants and friends free access to him.'

Just days later, Huntly was released and restored to the captaincy of the guard. Maitland objected in the strongest possible terms, knowing that Huntly's release would infuriate Elizabeth to the point where she might reconsider her position regarding James's eventual succession to the throne of England. James's determination to keep Huntly at his side was finally defeated by Maitland's stubborn threat to resign from the king's service unless Huntly was punished, and a weak compromise was finally agreed. Huntly was dismissed from his captaincy again, and ordered to return to his estates in the north.

A few weeks later, the king was hunting when he received news that Huntly had indeed returned north, but only to raise his clansmen and to be joined by Errol and Crawford. Together, the three earls were marching south at the head of a Catholic army. Just to make matters worse, Bothwell had thrown in his lot with them – perhaps for no better reason than that he couldn't resist a fight, whatever the cause – and was marching north from his stronghold in the Borders.

King James's response was exemplary, despite his reputation for cowardice. Short of money, as always, he summoned the Protestant lords and lieges of southern Scotland. A force was also raised in Edinburgh. With a minimum of delay, they decided the greatest threat was from Huntly, and marched north to meet him.

The opposing forces met at the Bridge of Dee, but it was too late in the day to wade into each other, so the two armies encamped. Nobody seemed sure what to do next, with both sides fearing a night attack. Realising their predicament, King James sought to cheer his troops, as described by one member of the expedition. 'That night we watched in arms, and his majesty would not so much as lie down on his bed, but went about like a good captain encouraging us.'

The stalemate might have continued longer, or fighting started, but news had reached the rebel earls' army that the king himself was in the field against them. This served to remind them, perhaps, of the seriousness of rebellion and they started to slip away in twos and threes, then hundreds and more, until Huntly accepted the majority decision and followed in their wake. Thus the king won his victory in the field, without a blow being struck.

While this came as a relief to many, it meant, in practical terms, that the king's expedition had failed. Huntly and the rest were still at large, and might return to rebellion at any time. Having marched his army to Aberdeen, James found that there was little enough food to sustain them, and they were soon expressing their impatience at being kept away from their homes. Therefore, a message was sent to Huntly, promising that if he and his allies surrendered immediately, they would be dealt with leniently, and it was so. Huntly, Crawford and Bothwell were tried for treason, which demanded a harsh punishment in Scotland, but they were simply imprisoned for a few months, with all comforts and privileges.

Queen Elizabeth was both furious and dismayed at this outcome, but the reforming King James was well enough satisfied at this display of his authority, and the enforcement of the law. Many monarchs would have had the rebels' heads, but James could see no advantage in that. He not only preached tolerance and forgiveness, but practised them also. Here was a man who wanted to be remembered as a Solomon – the king who put brains before brawn – and now he had put down a rebellion without shedding a drop of blood.

There was intelligence in King James's actions. To have executed the Catholic earls would have been to create more martyrs for their cause. The memory of James's mother, Mary Queen of Scots, was trouble enough, and while championing the Protestant cause, James had no desire to become a persecutor of Catholics. He believed in the philosophy of toleration, and avoidance of violence. In direct contrast to so many monarchs, James viewed war as an admission of failure – a last resort to be avoided at all costs. He had taken the heat out of the Catholic earls' anger, and done enough to ensure that Scotland would not be used as a base for a Spanish invasion of mainland Britain. It was enough, for now.

France was not immune from the effects of the defeat of the Armada. In order to appease Philip of Spain and the Parisian mob, King Henry of France had been favouring the Duke of Guise and when it was rumoured that the Spanish had successfully invaded England, the French king reluctantly made Guise his Lieutenant General. However, when it was discovered that the Armada had failed, the French king grew confident. Guise was out on a very weak limb.

King Henry's first move was to sack his entire government, believing that they had remained loyal to his mother, Catherine de Medici, and therefore to the League which favoured Guise. He kept Guise at his side, perhaps to keep his rival where he could see him. Meanwhile, Guise learned from anonymous sources that the king was planning to have him killed. He was not impressed, however, for he viewed his king with scorn.

Henry was under no illusions. 'It is my life or his,' he told one of his loyal nobles. Members of Henry's bodyguard assassinated Guise, practically in the royal presence. According to one account, Henry appeared and looked down at the body of the duke, riddled with stab wounds. 'How tall he is. I had not thought he was so tall. He is even taller dead than alive'.

Neither Spain nor Rome was particularly troubled at the news. They had long been aware that Guise was an egotist, acting out of self-interest. He was, in some ways, little better than any greedy and sometimes careless mercenary. He had been employed to serve the interests of Spain and Rome, but they would not mourn him.

Leading members of the League were immediately arrested, but King Henry never gained true control and, just seven months later, he too was struck down by an assassin's knife. Despite the Catholic Church and Leaguers' best efforts, Protestant Henry of Navarre succeeded to the throne of France in July 1589.

Following the destruction of the Armada, England had decided to go on the offensive, rather than wait for Spain to make its next move. In April 1589, Sir Francis Drake and Sir John Norris sailed from Plymouth with 150 ships and 15,000 men. Their orders were to attack and destroy those Spanish ships that had survived the storms and then, when that had been achieved, to support a coup in Portugal against Spanish rule.

This expedition turned into a fiasco. Within a couple of months, Drake was back, minus half his men. The rest had been killed or had died of disease. The hand of a fickle God had intervened, yet again; only this time it was English ships that were battered by storms. It would later emerge that Drake had been intent on plundering the Azores, rather than sinking Spanish ships. As ever, Drake was more interested in loot than military objectives or political orders. This was naturally what made him so popular with his men, who received a share of any captured treasure, ransoms and the like.

Queen Elizabeth was disappointed, but not dismayed at Drake's failure. Indeed, her spirits were raised by the news from France that Henry of Navarre had succeeded to the throne, though not without opposition. Once again, civil war was raging between Protestant and Catholic. Philip of Spain threw his weight behind the Leaguers who were particularly strong in Picardy, Normandy and Brittany. In turn, and in defence of the Protestant faith and to keep Philip occupied with France, rather than have him free to renew his invasion plans, Elizabeth threw English troops into the fray, sending over an army of 4,000 men under the command of Lord Willoughby.

CHAPTER TWENTY-FIVE

WEDDINGS AND WITCH HUNTS

Above all things, King James of Scots coveted the English throne. While he held strong opinions on what form it should take – Episcopalian with bishops rather than Presbyterian without – he was essentially a champion of 'Protestantism with toleration'. In this, he recognised theological and political arguments, for while both countries were Protestant, they had adopted very different forms of the faith. Scotland's Calvinist Presbyterians were, in fact, very disapproving of England's Church. Meanwhile, the English Church was being openly criticised by a new generation of puritans seeking more radical reforms. As far as the puritans were concerned, the break with Rome was not enough because, essentially, the Church had remained Catholic. Tempers had long been frayed and many of the most dogmatic were intensely irritated by the fence-sitting antics of King James.

James might have converted to Catholicism if his life or throne depended on it, for he was not of the stuff from which martyrs are made. Whenever he seemed to be drifting toward Rome, it was perhaps out of a sense of insecurity, or because he recognised some advantage in bending with the wind. He could simply have been considering the alternative as an intellectual exercise, for he was ever the academic theologian, prepared to look at both sides in an argument, recognising faults and favours. This was the approach that had been encouraged by one of his tutors, Peter Young, reflecting the Renaissance origins of the Reformation in which men were encouraged to think for themselves. Young believed in the logic of Calvinism and was keen to foster argumentative solutions to complicated theological questions. Thus encouraged, the young king had branched out into logical discourse on all manner of subjects, both spiritual and secular, and he maintained this philosophy throughout his life. If he seemed, at times, to lack moral fibre, individuals must decide for themselves whether that made him a coward or otherwise.

Some would argue that his revulsion to violence was not a fault. It was said that he swooned at the mere sight of a drawn sword or dagger, although his much faceted character is revealed in details of his hunting expeditions when he paddled merrily in the blood of slain stags. Remembering his strange upbringing, surrounded by plotters and murderers, and the violent deaths of so many of his contemporaries, it is possible that his fear was not so much of the naked blade as the intentions of the man wielding it.

Along with his intellectual endeavours and desire for reform – not forgetting his scheming and prevarication – James recognised the need to enhance his acceptability to Protestants in the widest sense. There were clear teachings on the family unit as the foundation on which the Protestant faith was built, and James was well aware that many were openly questioning his sexuality. The defeat of the Armada gave him renewed confidence in the future of Protestantism, and he wished to establish his position in it. There was no reason to delay his finding an acceptable, Protestant wife. His councillors had long been pressing him in this regard. Indeed, serious negotiations had been started several years previously. Many had been considered, but since 1587 there had been just two names on James's list. Significantly, they were the names of countries, France and Denmark, rather than suitable girls.

Protestant politicians favoured an alliance with Protestant elements in France. This arrangement was particularly attractive to those Scots whose sense of national identity caused them concern at ever-closer links with England. A continuation of the Auld Alliance, perhaps, but based on the reformed religion. Henry of Navarre's sister, the Princess Catherine de Bourbon, was their favourite, but when negotiations were under way, Navarre had still to defeat Guise and the Leaguers, and long years of war had drained his coffers. He was not minded to produce a large dowry for his sister.

Some felt a light French purse should not stand in the way of a strong cross-Channel alliance, but it was a major stumbling block for James who favoured the wealthier Denmark – a Protestant country that had maintained lucrative neutrality from the religious wars raging to the south. Denmark was an orderly country, focused on trade. Thus an alliance with Denmark was particularly attractive to Scotland's burgesses, merchants and craftsmen.

Equally, from the king's point of view, a Danish bride might bring a larger dowry – certainly larger than France could offer.

Elizabeth of England was not keen on a Danish bride for her heir, the Scottish king, and said as much. The problem, in her mind, was that Denmark followed the Lutheran form of Protestantism. She suggested that James should marry his first cousin, Arabella Stewart, but James was far from keen. From his deep interest in horses and hounds, he might have feared the consequences of such close line breeding, and Arabella was just ten years old. She wouldn't have brought a large dowry, and James was desperate for funds. Therefore, he was prepared to ignore England's objections.

Tentative negotiations with Denmark had started in 1585, but it wasn't until 1587 that James sent two ambassadors to formally request a match with Princess Elizabeth, the older daughter of Frederick II. The Danes were anything but enthusiastic. Elizabeth was already promised to the Duke of Brunswick. However, they said that Elizabeth had a younger sister, Princess Anne, and James could have her, if he wanted.

Anne was just 12 years old in 1587. Not as beautiful as Elizabeth, perhaps, but attractive and 'more fully developed' and taller than her sister had been at the same age. The ambassadors made their inspection, said they would speak with their king, and returned to Scotland.

The arguments went this way and that. James had still to rule out a match with France, so those who favoured a Danish alliance whispered that Anne was young and beautiful, while Catherine of Bourbon, Henry of Navarre's sister, was 'old and crooked and something worse if all were known'.

James wanted to know how much he could wring out of Denmark, and the 'rank and file' of the Protestants – merchants, burgesses and the like – were keen to know if an alliance with wealthy Denmark might improve their trading opportunities. They felt that this was the greatest attraction of a Danish match – the opening up of a lucrative trade with the Baltic, rather than a bankrupted France. In their opinions, Scotland's prosperity, and their personal fortunes, seemed to be hanging in the balance. Financial gain through increased trading opportunities was their primary interest and, at that time, the Scottish 'middle class' might have lynched anybody who publicly argued for Catherine of Bourbon, or a home-bred queen.

The Danes hadn't seemed particularly keen with their 'take her or leave her' approach, but this might have been a negotiating stance. The Earl Marischal, no less, was sent to Denmark in 1589 with orders to call their bluff, if bluff it was. He was instructed to ask for a dowry of £1,000,000 Scots, various trading concessions and a promise of mutual military support. Denmark was also to give up an ancient claim to the Orkneys.

The Danes didn't know whether to laugh or cry. Anne's father had recently died, leaving her a small amount of money. That would be her dowry, they stated, and not a penny more. Then something quite amazing happened – or so we are told. James received a portrait of Princess Anne, and fell hopelessly in love. He announced that he must have her, with or without a dowry, saying he would not be a merchant for his bride. It was a truly spectacular turnaround.

Scotland was in a sorry plight to receive a new queen. A contemporary, William Fowler, wrote that James 'had neither plate nor stuff to furnish one of his little half-houses, which are in great decay and ruin. His plate is not worth £100, he has only two or three rich jewels, his saddles are of plain cloth ... no bread but of oats.' The English ambassador, Sir William Asheby, confirmed James's financial straits: 'Surely Scotland was never in worse state to receive a Queen than at present, for there is not a house in repair.'

In truth, the Scottish Parliament had provided £10,000 to pay for the marriage celebrations, but this had already been spent. James was at his wits' end, and begged Queen Elizabeth to help. In recognition of her hesitant approval of this Protestant match, she sent £1,000 in cash, and advanced £2,000 to purchase plate in England. It was something, but still not enough.

Princess Anne set sail for Scotland at the end of August 1589, but her Danish ship was delayed. James's impatience turned to concern then fear as days slipped into weeks without any news. Storms raged out at sea, and James feared the worst. He was almost mad with grief when the news arrived, in mid-October, that after several attempts at the crossing the Danish ship had been forced to turn back. Anne was safely housed in Oslo. Ten days later, at the start of November, James set sail for Norway. He did not return until May of the following year.

The couple were married in Oslo on November 23. David Lindsay, minister at Leith, who was among the 300 or so Scots who had accompanied their king, conducted the service. Lindsay was clearly impressed with the bride, describing her as, 'a Princess, both godly and beautiful, as appeareth by all that know her. I trust she shall bring a blessing to the country, like as she giveth great contentment to his majesty'. His Nordic blonde, 'with lovely white skin and golden hair, slender, graceful and of a good height', infatuated James.

The marriage ceremony was followed by a month of festivities, laid on by the royal couple's Norwegian hosts. There was some talk of a return to Scotland, but then an invitation arrived from Denmark. The Scottish royal party travelled overland by sledge, passing through Sweden and finally arriving at Kronborg Castle in late January, where the Danish royal family welcomed them.

James was in his element. He couldn't remember when he had enjoyed himself so much, dividing his time between intimate moments with his young and beautiful wife and attending lectures on theology and medicine, not to mention numerous hunts and 'falling over' drinking parties with the Danish royal family and sundry nobles. The festivities simply moved up a gear with the arrival of the Duke of Brunswick, who married Anne's elder sister, Princess Elizabeth, on Easter Day.

The romantic will draw what impression they choose of James's whirlwind romance and honeymoon, though the cynic might suggest that he had prudently avoided the expense of having his wedding at home. All good things must come to an end, however, and James and Anne finally sailed for Scotland, arriving at Leith on May 1.

King James of Scots returned with more than a bride. While in Norway and Denmark, rubbing shoulders with some of Europe's great Protestant leaders and intellectuals, he had been treated to the sort of praise that he had received as a boy, when he was paraded before visiting dignitaries. To a man, they had praised his wit and wisdom. Given this encouragement, James let his imagination fly to new heights. Might he unite Europe into an alliance of tolerant, Protestant states? Would the great and the good sit at his feet while he made solemn pronouncements?

Anne was crowned Queen of Scots in the Abbey Kirk on May 17 1590. Danish guests took their leave soon after. Scottish hospitality was no match for that displayed across the North Sea, and James was still so infatuated with Anne that he may hardly have noticed their departure. Ever the rhymester, he wrote verses in which he pictured three goddesses bestowing their graces upon Anne at her birth.

That blessed houre when first was brought to light
Our earthlie Juno and our gratious Queene,
Three Goddesses how soone they had her seene
Contended who protect her shoulder by right.
But being as Goddess of equal might
And as of female sexe like stiffe in will
It was agreed by sacred Phoebus skill
To joyne there powers to blesse that blessed wight.
Then, happie Monarch sprung of Ferguse race,
That talks with wise Minerve when pleaseth thee
And when thou list some Princlie sports to see
Thy chaste Diana rides with thee in chase
Then when to bed thou gladlie does repaire
Clasps in thy arms thy Cytherea faire.

The 'happie Monarch sprung of Fergus race' was James, of course. He was clearly delighted with his new queen, but unfortunately it was not to last.

There can be little doubt that James had discovered he could be as attracted to his queen as he had been to handsome, young males. Then, after the first flush of passion, James realised that his Danish princess fitted in with the Protestant notion that women were, to use John Knox's words in his *The First Blast of the Trumpet against the Monstrous Regiment of Women*, to be considered as 'weak, frail, impatient, feeble and foolish'.

Anne was all these things and worse. Frivolous and empty-headed, childish rather than courtly, and increasingly expensive. When he tried to curb her spending the king discovered something of the shrew. She had a quick temper and childish tantrums. She could be violent, spiteful and indiscreet and began to cause all sorts of trouble. She was ready and willing to take sides, sometimes against the king's favourites or trusted servants, and she allowed herself to be drawn into the murky world of Scottish politics, where angels feared to tread. Knowing that Chancellor Maitland had not been overly keen on the king's Danish marriage, she encouraged those opposed to him in devious ways.

King James's actions did not help. Though he was patient with his young queen, and maintained his affection for her, his interest was returning to his bright male companions. Matters went from bad to worse. Queen Anne became openly critical of the Presbyterian Church. True, the king had found a Protestant mate, but she was of the Lutheran variety, as practised in Denmark. Although Elizabeth of England had warned against the wedding for that very reason, even she could not have predicted what happened next. Queen Anne converted to Roman Catholicism, possibly to annoy her husband. By that stage, the honeymoon was well and truly over.

The northern earls seemed to have settled down after their failed rebellion and a sojourn in prison, but Bothwell was another matter. Making his base in Liddesdale in the Scottish Borders – surrounded by notorious reivers, thieves and murderers who regularly raided into England, thus stoking the fires of animosity between the two countries – he looked for new opportunities to commit mayhem.

At the start of 1591, James learned that a brawl was brewing in Kelso, in which Bothwell would undoubtedly take part. Recognising another opportunity to prove his authority and enforce the law, the king galloped south and ordered Bothwell to appear before him. The earl got a right good dressing down. Was this the way Bothwell repaid the king's former kindness and affection? James emphasised that Bothwell had received his last warning, and vowed to God that the law would be enforced with all vigour if there was any more trouble.

The erring earl was sent on his way, and the king returned to Edinburgh where he had much to hold his attention, for his courts in the Lothians were trying a number of witches. Nowadays we may scoff, but in those days the threat of witches and warlocks and other devil worshippers was taken very seriously.

It has been said that there are two sides to every coin, and both Catholic and Protestant churches preached that just as there was a God, so there was a Devil. Add a letter here and subtract one there, and you have Good and Evil and, heaven knows, for every one who followed the path of goodness, others seemed intent on wreaking evil in the world. From there, it was a short jump to conclude that while good people worshipped God, others worshipped the Devil, also known as Satan, and sought his help in their ungodly ways. If not, then why was there so much evil in the world? Why did crops fail, cows abort, and so on and so forth. Even the most ardent atheist, while denying both God and the Devil, can accept that as there are millions who worship the one, there might at least be a few who worship the other.

The problem was, of course, that ignorance led to the belief that some simple souls, or those with mental health problems, were bewitched or possessed by devils. In some cases, it was even suggested that they were devil worshippers and, in a weakened condition, they might admit to being so, after prolonged questioning, abuse or torture.

Initially, James approached the question of witchcraft and its associated subjects with a healthy degree of scepticism. If nothing else, he had a fascination with the abnormal and unexplained. He made a study of it and published a treatise on the subject, which he titled *Daemonologie*. In his opinion, witches and sorcerers had been lured by Satan to repudiate God. In a parody of Christian rites, they met in congregations to worship the Devil, who appeared before them with his latest instructions, supplying them with enchanted stones, powders, poisons and waxen figures. Witches and sorcerers could raise storms; induce insanity and cause impotence, heightened sexual desire or even death. The list of their achievements went on. They could fly, but only for so long as they held their breath ... The most striking thing about *Daemonologie* is that its intellectually argumentative author never questions the reality of witches, as such. He was obviously convinced of their existence and powers.

All in all, the king's treatise provides an intriguing insight to the beliefs of the time. One can picture James sitting in the law court, or some room of inquisition, listening intently and scribbling notes. He was delighted when one poor soul capered and shrieked, and astonished when a reputed witch, named Agnes Simpson, asked to whisper in his ear. When he agreed, Agnes told him things that he had said to his wife on their wedding night. The king then 'swore by the living God that he believed all the devils in hell could not have discovered the same.' Others might have concluded that wedding night conversations tend to follow a fairly standard form.

James was equally fascinated to learn that the witches of Lothian regularly met at North Berwick. The Devil came to them in the form of a man and, in some sort of fertility rite, had sex with the younger and more attractive witches. Then came evidence that made the king's blood run cold. One witch let it slip that the Earl of Bothwell was acting in league with the Lothian coven, encouraging them to use their satanic powers against the king. Never the hero, James was terrified, and demanded to know more.

The coven had tied cats to severed human limbs and thrown them into the sea, hoping to raise storms while the king was crossing to Denmark. Poisons had been concocted, and they had passed a man's image among them while chanting, 'This is King James the Sixth, ordained to be consumed at the instance of a nobleman, Francis, Earl of Bothwell.' One witch added that James was to be destroyed, 'that another might rule in his place and the government might go to the Devil'.

Under closer questioning, one witch let it slip that Bothwell was in fact their leader. It was he who appeared before them as the Devil or his representative at North Berwick, ordering them to destroy the king, before taking his pick of the coven. A wizard from North Berwick, one Richie Graham, confirmed Bothwell's leadership in summoning the powers of darkness against the king.

The evidence contained those flashes of the mundane that made it all the more convincing. Evidently, Bothwell was getting rather impatient with the witches failure. 'Because a poor old silly ploughman named Grey Meill chanced to say that nothing ailed the King yet, God be thanked, the Devil gave him a great blow.'

All this was just too much for the nervous King James. When terror came in the door, logic and humanity flew out the window. With the notion of evil directed against his person firmly rooted in his mind, James recalled that on his return from Denmark, accompanied by his new queen, they had run into a storm off the Bass Rock, near North Berwick. Irrational with fear, perhaps, James described having seen witches in the raging seas, in the form of hares bobbing about on sieves.

Everything seemed to centre on North Berwick. According to some accounts, King James gathered a small band of trusted followers and went down to see what was happening for himself, hiding in the grounds of the church at St Andrews. They witnessed a gathering of six wizards and nearly a hundred bare-breasted witches who danced and cavorted when their leader appeared with a blackened face, wearing the skin of an animal. The witches then took it in turns to kiss his exposed backside – evidently a standard satanic practice. At that point, the king's men rushed from their positions. They were able to catch a few of the witches, but their leader escaped. King James was convinced that the bare-arsed figure was none other than Bothwell.

Alongside his abiding faith in God, the king had one other defence against the satanic arts. It was part of the lore of witchcraft that a witch or sorcerer would lose their powers if they confessed. Therefore, if they could all be forced to confess, the threat to the king would be removed. Nobody knew how many were involved, but James's appointed witch-hunters would leave no stone unturned in rooting them out.

Believing in his own powers of persuasion, James interviewed many of those who were arrested. Those who would not confess were handed on to torturers.

James couldn't deal with all the cases personally, so he gave a dire warning to those who might stand in his stead. Any magistrate who was lenient would be committing a heinous crime, and must expect to come under suspicion. Suddenly, all sorts of old debts were paid off. A whisper here or a word there and an unpopular neighbour would be hauled off to the magistrate's court, or worse. The beatings and torture would continue for years – women and girls, men and boys. Mostly they were women because according to the king the Devil had seduced Eve in the Garden of Eden, and ever since they had been frailer than men. The desire to dance was evidence of their wantonness, he added, confirming the teachings of the Presbytery.

In later times, when his fear and hatred had mellowed, King James would explain his actions, which some have misinterpreted as nothing more than a sadistic cruelty. 'For these witches, whatsoever hath been gotten from them hath been done by me myself, not because I was more wise than others, but because I believed that such a vice did reign and ought to be suppressed.' He had travelled a long way from his initial stance of intellectual curiosity, declaring witchcraft to be 'the highest point of idolatry, wherein no exception is admitted by the law of God.'

It was believed that witches and sorcerers had sold their souls to the Devil, and no punishment could be too severe. Some were burnt or drowned, others died under torture. Much the same thing was happening in England. In 1589 a number of women were hanged at Chelmsford for witchcraft. God's children couldn't be too vigilant in their war against the evil one and his followers.

A primitive form of stretching was commonly employed to extract confessions. The suspect was suspended by the wrists from a wall, with heavy weights tied to their feet. Flesh was lacerated and pierced. In some cases, the suspect was tied between two strong horses, and literally pulled apart – a variation on the rack. Sometimes, the children of the accused were forced to watch while their parents screamed for mercy – presumably as an example of what would happen to them if they followed in their parents' footsteps. Other times, it was the children who screamed. Barbarous, to be sure, even for those barbarous times.

The *First Book of Discipline* prepared by the new Presbyterian Church in Scotland had recommended death for adulterers. Here was the vicious theology of John Knox and his like, taken straight out of the pages of the Old Testament. This sentence was rarely, if ever, imposed, but bare-footed baillies and their women were forced to wear paper crowns describing their sin as they were marched to the whipping post in the Market Cross. Those who made comments critical of the Kirk were sentenced to, 'stand at the kirk-stile on the Sabbath, with branks upon their mouths.' A brank was a metal helmet with a hinged face-piece that enclosed the head, to which it was fixed tight with a padlock. That face-piece was fitted with a large, sharp-edged metal wedge, which was forced into the wearer's mouth. It was also used on nagging wives, though they might also have been banished, as could those with dirty hands. Fornicators were also to be banished, after suitable chastisement. If they returned, they would be burnt. The list of fines, indignities, privations and other punishments imposed by the early Kirk runs on and on.

John Prebble described it thus in his popular book, *The Lion in the North*. 'Obscene and degrading punishments were imposed in the righteous belief that they were necessary for the salvation of the sinner ... The scourge and the brank, the stocks and stool of penitence, sackcloth and the ducking pond, banishment and burning, were all revolutionary weapons of the dictatorship of the presbytery'.

And then there was the secular law.

PLOT AND COUNTERPLOT

Sir Francis Walsingham died on April 6 1590 at Barnes near Richmond Palace. During his 17 years as Secretary of State, he had taken over the Secret Service administered by William Cecil, later Lord Burghley, and honed it to near perfection for its time. It became a major weapon in England's armoury, and the Protestants' international struggle against a Catholic counter-Reformation, with more than 50 spies at home and abroad, not to mention countless informants and 'occasional' agents, recruited as and when the need arose. Walsingham's greatest skill was in turning Catholic agents. For that, he might be considered the father of double agents.

Few knew the extent of Walsingham's service to England for it was, by its very nature, kept secret. Much of the country was enjoying something of the fruit of his labours and improved security, though the poor still faced hard times and low wages. This was particularly true of the north of England: geography, the problems inherent in long distance travel and other economic factors undoubtedly played their part in drawing England's wealth and power into the southeast, but that wasn't the whole story. The north was being bled dry because of its nobles' adherence to Catholicism as an expression, in part, of the independence they had claimed since before the arrival of the Normans. And everywhere the countryside suffered while urban dwellers prospered. The face of England was changing.

London was in the grip of a new fashion for theatre going. Perhaps it provided a short abstention from the realities of life – the Spanish threat, punitive taxation to pay for a never-ending succession of wars, soaring prices and crime rates, and the terrible plight of the poor in a land increasingly divided between the haves and have-nots. The hanging judges had never been so busy. Meanwhile, the playwright Christopher (Kit) Marlowe was the toast of the town following the successes of *Tamburlaine the Great* and *The Jew of Malta*. At the theatre, the Curtain and the Rose, rowdy audiences revelled in performances presented by companies of players with wealthy patrons such as the earls of Pembroke and Worcester. Such patronage fostered popularity with 'the masses', if theatregoers can ever be thus described. Lord Howard of Effingham, the Lord Admiral, supported a company known appropriately as the Lord Admiral's Men, which included the up-and-coming actor Edward Alleyn. His lordship's mind was already on more lucrative ventures, however, as England was still intent on capitalising on the failure of Spain's Armada.

In the summer of 1591, Lord Howard was close to the Azores, cruising in close formation with Sir Richard Grenville on his ship the *Revenge*. They were hoping to intercept and plunder Spanish treasure ships returning from the New World. However, they understandably decided to make a tactical withdrawal when they learned of the proximity of a greatly superior fleet of Spanish men-of-war. The hunters had become the hunted.

In the course of their withdrawal, Howard and Grenville were separated. Howard got away, but Grenville was engaged by the Spaniards. The *Revenge*, with just 150 crew, was hopelessly outnumbered by the 15 Spanish ships and 5,000 men, but the battle raged on for nearly 15 hours. Finally, the *Revenge* was boarded and Grenville captured in desperate hand-to-hand fighting. He later died of his wounds on the Spanish flagship *San Pablo*, but is still remembered as one of England's naval heroes.

One year later, another famous old salt got into something of a pickle. Sir Walter Raleigh was imprisoned for seducing Bess Throckmorton who, ironically, was one of the queen's maids of honour. He was released in under a month when his country, or rather his queen, needed him – to quieten a gang of rowdy sailors. 'And we'll rant and we'll roar, like true English sailors. We'll rant and we'll roar, across the Spanish Main,' but when they returned to their home ports, England expected very different standards of behaviour., particularly when the queen's purse was involved.

Where Howard and Grenville failed, others had succeeded. English privateers (legitimised pirates), backed in part by Queen Elizabeth, had seized and looted the Spanish treasure ship *Madre de Dios*. Their haul was valued at £800,000 of which a proportion was due to the backers, including the queen. When they returned to Dartmouth, it was discovered that the crew had helped themselves to most of the treasure and were refusing to return it. When another of the backers, the Earl of Cumberland, tried to press the matter of payment, the sailors ran amok and Cumberland withdrew in some haste. It was after this fracas that Elizabeth had Raleigh brought before her. Clearly, she was not amused at being denied her just rewards and ordered Raleigh to intercede with the privateers. They gave him a rousing welcome, but declined his request, though they did produce some of the less valuable trinkets in order that Raleigh might mollify the queen.

King James of Scots had more weighty matters on his troubled mind. Principally, there was the unresolved problem of the Earl of Bothwell. James was convinced that Bothwell was planning to kill him by means fair or foul, earthly or diabolical, but punishing him would not be easy.

Bothwell had to be caught. When that was finally done, he was imprisoned in Edinburgh Castle. The king made it clear that he intended to punish Bothwell with the utmost severity, but he miraculously escaped and returned to the Borders. It was clear that somebody in the castle had been turning a blind eye, either out of sympathy with Bothwell, or because they had been paid to do so. Either way, the king's efforts to enforce the law had been frustrated – another slap in the face for the reformers.

Bothwell remained very popular both with the Kirk and the nobles. The king was sure that one or both had organised Bothwell's escape. He wasn't the first 'wild man' favoured by the Presbytery. Apparently, they saw a need for such storm troopers in the defence of their faith – hard men who might take the fight to the enemy. Such a status brought its own privileges. A commoner suspected of sorcery would be interrogated, abused and finally tortured into giving a confession. But the Kirk indulged in blatant hypocrisy where Bothwell was concerned, minimising his crimes as 'youthful exuberances'.

To his fellow nobles, Protestant and Catholic alike, Bothwell was something of a hero in the resistance movement against the king and Maitland's reforming zeal – reforms that would have curtailed the nobles' powers. It was put about that all the talk about witches and warlocks was nothing more than a crude attempt to blacken Bothwell's name and reputation. Universal popularity in aristocratic circles became most significant when this champion of the Protestant cause allied himself with Catholic earls in open rebellion against King James. It seems that most of his fellow Protestant nobles simply shrugged and smiled.

As for the common people, the same Protestants who would happily watch the burning of a witch came to Bothwell's defence. They contrasted the leniency displayed to the treacherous Catholic earls with the harshness promised for Bothwell. Gossips and propaganda merchants set to work, suggesting that the king was favouring Catholics over Protestants. From being the accuser, James had become the accused.

Meanwhile, Bothwell was living off the fat of the land, shielded by his many friends and allies. Never staying too long in one place in order to avoid recapture, he was seen here then there, moving closer and closer to the capital where the terrified king hid in his palace, unable to determine whether his foe was man or devil.

Emboldened by drink, Bothwell appeared one night in the Canongate, shouting challenges to Chancellor Maitland to come out and fight him. When nobody appeared, the earl staggered off with his cronies. He made a far more determined assault on the night of December 27 1591 when he forced his way into Holyroodhouse at the head of a body of men. Maitland fled to his chamber while the king scurried to a remote tower room. Strong doors guarded both, but Bothwell's men set about breaking them down with heavy hammers, and by setting fires. While this was going on, a messenger got word to the provost of Edinburgh. A mob rushed to Holyrood to save the king. Bothwell withdrew – or vanished into thin air – but it was a near thing.

James's rescue by the townspeople convinced him that they had come to their senses and seen Bothwell for what he was, but he was quickly disillusioned. When he attended a service at St Giles, announcing his wish to thank the people of Edinburgh, he was rebuked by the clergyman who went on to justify the raid, suggesting it was the king's inequitable treatment of Bothwell that lay behind the affair. Or rather, his harshness in this particular case, compared to his leniency in dealing with the Earl of Huntly and other 'traitorous' Catholics.

Bothwell had a young cousin, the Earl of Moray. Like Bothwell, the handsome heir and son-in-law of the late regent was hugely popular with the Kirk, as an opponent of the Catholic earls. Indeed, Moray enjoyed far greater popularity than Bothwell, for he had few of the latter's wild faults.

Moray and his family, the Stewarts, were involved in a long-standing feud with Huntly and his Gordons. Again, this served to enhance Moray's popularity with Presbyterians. Any enemy of Huntly was a friend of the Kirk. Recently, Huntly had been pushing the pace of this animosity, and it may be that Moray had come south to ask King James to intervene. Equally, it may be that he came south to support his cousin Bothwell.

Whatever the circumstances, in February 1592 it was known to the king and his chancellor that the suspect Moray was at his mother's castle, Donibristle, on the northern shore of the Firth of Forth, accompanied by just a few servants. They wanted to be reassured, at least, as to the purposes of his visit. As none of the Protestant nobles would act against their champion, the king had to use one of the Catholic earls and chose Huntly, ordering him to arrest Moray for aiding and abetting Bothwell.

James and Maitland knew of Huntly's deadly feud with Moray, so should have expected trouble. Certainly, that is what they got. Instead of arresting Moray, Huntly's Gordons surrounded Donibristle and set it on fire.

In one version of what happened next, Moray managed to fight his way out of the burning castle and tried to escape along the shore, but Huntly found him hiding in a cave and had him dragged out, and savagely butchered. In another version, Moray ran naked from the castle, his hair aflame, and was confronted by Huntly who slashed him across the face with a dagger. Moray had time to say, 'Ye hae spoilt a better face than your ain, my Lord,' before he was run through by the Gordons' swords.

The Scots have a liking for famous last words, and often include them in their tales. Whichever way it happened, the end was certain and a lament was penned to commemorate the evil deed.

Ye Highlands and ye Lawlands,
Oh! Where have you been?
They hae slain the Earl o' Murray,
And laid him on the green.

'Now wae be to you, Huntly!
And wherefore did ye sae?
I bade you bring him wi' you,
But forbade you him to slay.'

He was a braw callant,
And he rade at the ring;
And the bonnie Earl o' Murray,
Oh! He micht ha' been a king.

He was a braw callant,
And he rade at the glove;
And the bonnie Earl o' Murray,
Oh! He was the Queen's luve.

This ballad is worth studying, for it reflects the opinions of the time. The words of the second verse purport to be those of King James who is excused, up to a point, by the suggestion that while he ordered Huntly to bring Moray with him, he had said the earl must not be harmed.

Then there is the notion that Moray might have been a king. This was more than some vague reference to his ancestry, or wishful thinking. In the eyes of the Kirk, kings ruled only by the will of the people. The Presbyterian's position was that a king might be replaced if he offended public opinion, and James had been causing deep offence both with his stated allegiance to the Episcopalian version of Protestantism (viewed by Presbyterians as little better than popery), and his reluctance to deal with Huntly and his kind.

James was well aware that Moray had inherited his father-in-law's popularity, and would have been high on the Kirk's list of potential replacements for the throne. As such, he had offered a clear threat to James – all the more so if he formed an alliance with his cousin, Bothwell. Moray had been Bothwell's most influential protector.

Finally, there is that reference to Moray being the queen's love. Whether or not this is to be taken literally, it is known that Queen Anne was lavish in her praise of Moray, and showed him much affection at a time when the royal marriage was virtually on the rocks. This may have been a deep irritation to the king.

The deepest irritation to the king's people, however, was that after Moray's murder, James still refused to act against Huntly. It is known that James wrote to Huntly, saying, 'Always, I shall remain constant'.

A Catholic earl had brutally murdered a leading member of the Protestant nobility, but the king was doing nothing to bring him to justice. This proved two things to the Kirk and its people. Firstly, that the king favoured Catholics. Secondly, that he may have entered a pact with Huntly and that Moray had been murdered at least with his consent, and probably at his instigation – to remove a threat to his throne and marriage. Presbyterians remembered that James was the son a queen described by many of their number as a 'murdering whore'.

Scotland was in turmoil, teetering on the brink of rebellion. In the circumstances, King James and Chancellor Maitland decided they should lie low until Catholic arrogance and Presbyterian anger had cooled. Maitland fled to his house at Lethington, barricading the door behind him, while the king went on an aimless trip, wandering here and there with a body of loyal retainers on the pretext of hunting for Bothwell.

James knew his absence would be insufficient to satisfy the Kirk, but he needed time to make plans. He had to find some way to appease the Presbyterians, knowing they opposed him because of his loyalty to the Episcopalian Church. The solution must have been obvious to an intelligent man who could bend like a reed, according to the winds of change.

King James summoned a Parliament in May 1592, to announce a change in his policy. In a complete turnaround, he announced full support for the Kirk. He thanked God that he had been born into a Kirk like that of Scotland – the sincerest Kirk in the world. He also rejected the Episcopalian alternative: 'As for our neighbour Kirk in England, it is an evil mass said in English.'

When James finished his speech, there was a stunned silence then much praising of God and praying for the king. The Presbyterians viewed the king's pronouncement as some sort of deliverance; he was telling them what they wanted to hear. His allegiance to Episcopalianism, with its bishops, had threatened the Presbytery, and now that threat had been removed. The more cautious of the brethren may have decided to see if James was havering – or disseminating, as the English would have it.

That aside the king's 'conversion' couldn't have come at a better time for the Kirk. Recently, there had been a serious falling out between the churches of Scotland and England, fuelled by the rise of Puritanism in England. The English establishment saw the Presbyterians as the Puritans' allies – as they both denounced the role of bishops and anything else that suggested 'popery' – so in attacking one, they attacked both.

Matters came to a head when an English cleric, Richard Bancroft, delivered a sermon described as 'an abusive and violent attack upon Scottish Presbyterianism, declaring it to be subversive of all order and government.' Of course, this had been King James's view, prior to his recent shift, but now he went along with James Melville who replied on behalf of the Kirk, denouncing 'the belly-god bishops in England'.

At this time, the Church of England was trying to steer a middle course between Catholicism on one side, and the extremes of Puritans on the other.

In 1587, Puritans had sought to replace the English (Anglican) Church with a form of Presbyterianism when Anthony Cope introduced a reforming bill to parliament, but Queen Elizabeth immediately forbade its discussion. Cope was sent to the Tower of London. Peter Wentworth, who objected to the queen's intrusion, soon joined him.

One year later, in 1588, anonymous Puritans produced pamphlets pouring scorn on the English clergy, particularly the bishops. For example, one tract announced that John Bridges, the Dean of Salisbury, had been a dunce while he was at Cambridge. Hard hitting stuff indeed. However, these pamphlets were published during the threat of the Armada and its aftermath, so were described as subversive. Puritans were arrested and tortured in efforts to discover the pamphlets' authors. The pamphlets had also upset some Puritan leaders who felt they served no useful purpose and effectively weakened the case for reform by allowing the establishment to brand all Puritans as dangerous troublemakers – which it did.

Archbishop Whitgift was determined to impose uniformity on the Church of England by stamping out the Puritan threat. In 1591, ten Puritan clergymen were hauled before the Court of Star Chamber, and accused of treason. At the same time, some enthusiastic but misguided Puritans were hailing William Hackett as the new messiah. Hackett, who was little more than an illiterate simpleton, played out the role that had been given to him, and was executed for his ungainly efforts.

Scottish Presbyterians had been consistently alarmed at these and other persecutions of English Puritans. Encouraged by King James's change of mind, the Scots offered sanctuary as well as prayers for their English colleagues. Three particularly radical English Puritans accepted this asylum, much to Queen Elizabeth's annoyance. She wrote angrily to James.

'There is risen both in your realm and mine a sect of perilous consequence, such as would have no kings but a presbytery and take our place while they enjoy our privilege. Yea, look well unto them. I pray you stop the mouths or make shorter the tongues of such ministers as dare presume to make orisons in their pulpits for the persecuted in England for the Gospel.'

James acceded to Elizabeth's demand that one of the Puritans, John Penry, be expelled from Scotland. The king then adopted his habit of hunting with the hounds while running with the hare by acting slowly and interceding with Elizabeth on behalf of other English puritans. It wasn't until 1593 that the English forces of law and order finally caught up with the pamphleteer Penry, whose printing press had been kept on the move between secret locations. He was charged with 'writing with intent to cause rebellion', found guilty and hanged.

Meanwhile, Puritans in the English Parliament were causing trouble by complaining of repression whenever Queen Elizabeth forbade discussion of reform. In response, the queen dissolved parliament – the ultimate censorship. She had also moved her court to Windsor, in order to escape plague-ridden London. It was estimated that plague had killed 15,000 Londoners in 1592 alone.

In order to further appease the Kirk, King James allowed the passing of legislation remembered as the Golden Act, or Charter of the Presbytery. It established ecclesiastical government by presbyteries, synods and general assemblies, rescinding an Act of 1584 that had established the status of bishops and Episcopal jurisdictions. King James and Chancellor Maitland, by now elevated to Lord Thirlestane, were simultaneously determined to draw a line over which no man should step, asserting the royal authority and blocking any clerical influence in the temporal government of the realm.

In private, and despite his promises to the Kirk, King James was still determined to impose Episcopacy on Scotland at some time in the future, though he was prepared to be patient. In the meantime, with his new reputation as a supporter of the Presbytery, he may have thought that Moray would soon be forgotten and that things were going his way. If so he was quite literally in for a rude awakening.

At or around midnight on June 27 1592, Bothwell resumed his assault on the king. With about 300 supporters, he surrounded the palace at Falkland where the royal family and household were sleeping, and set about the gates with a battering ram. James fled to a tower, which Bothwell besieged until the following morning when he finally went away. A very nervous king finally emerged to demand an investigation into what had occurred.

James suspected that Bothwell had somebody working for him on the inside, perhaps recalling his earlier escape from Edinburgh Castle. In fact, the investigation revealed that Bothwell enjoyed widespread support, while the king was literally surrounded by treachery. One after another of his courtiers were implicated, in turn implicating others, until James realised that if he punished one, he must punish them all. Nevertheless, he was determined to make an example of somebody, and that body was no less than a Gentleman of the Bedchamber, the young laird of Logie, John Wemyss, who had been in league with Bothwell.

Wemyss was arrested at Holyrood, but his lover, one of Queen Anne's Danish serving women, helped him to escape. This prompted a furious row between James and Anne. Finally, and realising the extent of his unpopularity, James dissolved into tears. It was at or about this time that Chancellor Maitland, Lord Thirlestane, returned to his house at Lethington and bolted the door a second time, perhaps realising that as bad as things were, they were about to get worse.

George Ker was arrested as he was about to sail for Spain. He was a Catholic, and that, together with his destination, and perhaps a whisper in the right ear, had brought him to the authority's attention. Several sheets of paper were found in his possession, all blank except for the signatures of various Catholic nobles – Huntly, Errol, Angus and Sir Patrick Gordon of Auchindoun. These papers were to be known as the 'Spanish Blanks'.

Ker was interrogated, then tortured. With his foot being crushed to a pulp in a device known as 'the boot' he revealed a plot with a familiar ring to it. An exiled Scottish Jesuit, Father William Crichton, living in Spain, who insisted that King Philip of that country would invade Scotland and return it to Catholicism if he could be sure of Scottish Catholics' support, had instigated the plot which was virtually the same deal that Huntly and his allies had offered to Spain immediately after the Armada. It was said that the papers had been left blank in case they were intercepted, but that Ker and Crichton had been instructed as to what should be written on them at a later date – confirmation that the signatories would support Philip's invasion.

From a Presbyterian perspective, the Spanish Blanks were discovered at a very convenient time. Amazingly convenient, in fact. When James was loath to act against the Catholic earls, evidence was produced to link them with another plot to invade Scotland and thence England. In truth, however, there was little if any credible evidence, other than the 'confession' of a man subjected to brutal torture. That and some signatures on blank sheets of paper – at a time when the English Secret Service employed expert forgers. It is certainly possible that those who had given their allegiance to the Earl of Moray, and their support to Bothwell, would use all and any means to have revenge against Huntly.

The unfortunate George Ker provided evidence against King James into the bargain. Again, very convenient, but in this case unquestionable – notes in James's own hand, in which he had mused on the likely outcome in the unlikely event of his invading England. These notes were found in Ker's possession, but they had been written by James for himself alone, and put away in some private place. There they must have come to the attention of a light-fingered courtier who recognised their significance as weapons in the Presbyterian propaganda war against the Catholic earls and Scottish king. We know that James was surrounded by treachery in the wake of Bothwell's attack at Falkland.

King James's notes, however they were obtained, revealed his attitudes towards Scotland, England and Elizabeth. He quickly ruled out the possibility of his invading in 1592, acknowledging that Scotland was in such disorder that he must conquer it first, before thinking about foreign ventures. Perhaps at some time in the future, he mused, with a little help from abroad, but not now.

'In the meantime, I will deal with the Queen of England fair and pleasantly for my title to the Crown of England after her decease, which thing, if she grant to, we have attained our design without stroke or sword. If by the contrary, then delay makes me to settle my country in the meantime and, when I like hereafter, I may in a month or two (forewarning of the King of Spain) attain to our purpose, she not suspecting such a thing as she does now, which, if it were so done, would be a far greater honour to him and me both.'

There was nothing much in this to surprise or upset England. Indeed, it simply confirmed what they must have suspected, that if James was denied the throne of England, he might try to seize it, with a little help from his friends. But was that a serious threat? Hardly.

One wonders whether it was naïvety or a willingness to convert to Catholicism that made James consider that he might be offered Spanish aid. Perhaps, at this stage, he hadn't considered the full ramifications of the proposal. Incidentally, he did not consider the possibility of aid from the Protestant states of Northern Europe because they had already stated that they would remain neutral, while wishing him well. They would be reluctant, to say the least, to become embroiled in a war, satisfied that Elizabeth would be succeeded by a Protestant, whoever that might be, for the majority of England's people would settle for nothing less. And who wanted to take on England, still riding the wave of the Armada's defeat? Nobody – other than the king of Spain and a handful of adventurous Scottish Catholic nobles, perhaps hidden from reality behind the thick walls of their northern strongholds.

Some have suggested that James's notes are a clue to the thinking of the Catholic Earls. Their enemy was the Queen of England, not the King of Scots, who might well profit from their plotting, a point which James fully appreciated, they say.

This is an interesting proposition, giving the Catholic earls something of a patriotic status, but is it true? One might be tempted to suggest that it was the Presbyterian earls who were the true enemy of the Scottish Catholic earls, rather than Elizabeth. It was they who rattled her cage, not her theirs.

Neither James nor Elizabeth was friendly towards the Presbyterians and puritans who sought to hijack the governments of their countries. If James were to profit from the plotting of the Catholic earls, it would be as a balance for the plotting of their opposite numbers, who had supported Moray and continued to shield Bothwell. If their plotting bore fruit, it would be a very different matter – but that was a very big if. In the meantime, James would strive to play one against the other.

DAYS OF RECKONING

Following the discovery of the Spanish Blanks, and with George Ker's account of what was to have been written on them – offers of support for a Spanish invasion from various Catholic nobles – the Kirk demanded action. They suggested that King James's notes, musing on the possibility of invading England with Spanish support, meant that if he did not take that action, then he should be considered as guilty as Huntly or Errol. Elizabeth of England let it be known that she had reached the same conclusion.

Thus caught between a rock and a hard place, James agreed that the northern Catholic earls must be taught a lesson, although significantly he announced that he would take charge of the expedition. His meagre force arrived in Aberdeen in February 1593, but the conspirators had already fled into the wilds of Caithness where, in the king's opinion, pursuit would prove impossible. Therefore, declaring that he could take no other action, the king accepted bonds of good behaviour from various towns and gentry whose involvement had been minimal, at most. He also seized the rebels' estates, but placed their houses in the custody of their friends. Seemingly satisfied, the king then returned south.

The Kirk and English court were far from satisfied. Lord Burgh, the English ambassador, suggested that the confiscation of the earls' estates was nothing more than pretence, and he was not far from the truth. No official action was taken to forfeit the rebels' property. Indeed, a parliament that might have passed forfeiture upon Huntly and his allies was dissolved before it could take action. Queen Elizabeth, who viewed the Catholic earls as backstabbing traitors, was furious. If King James would not deal with them, she growled, then she would find somebody who was equal to the task.

It came to James's attention that Elizabeth had contacted Bothwell, and now it was the Scottish king's turn to lose his temper. He demanded an interview with Lord Burgh, and made his feelings clear. 'Touching that vile man, as his foul affronts to me are unpardonable and most to be abhorred by all sovereign princes, so we most earnestly pray the Queen to deliver him in case he have refuge within her dominions, praying you to inform her plainly that if he be reset or comforted in any part of her country, I can no longer keep amity with her, but will be forced to join in friendship with her greatest enemies for my own sake.'

Once again, King James was making threats, as if he had lost his place in the plot. After all, it was his refusal to deal with Huntly, accused of murder and treason, that was the cause of the trouble. Instead, he concentrated on Bothwell alone. He wrote to Elizabeth, saying that he 'would rather be a slave in the Turks' galleys' than show leniency to one who had dishonoured him in such barbarous fashion. Did she think, he demanded, that Bothwell had bewitched him from a king into a senseless ass?

Elizabeth sent a conciliatory reply, but James's angry protestations had not addressed England's concern – that Catholic earls who were plotting for an invasion by Spain had not been dealt with. Whatever she might say to James in a letter, Elizabeth was planning to apply stronger pressure in order to make him come to his senses.

She had been left with little alternative. It was as if James had failed to realise the full enormity of the Spanish threat. It wasn't simply a matter of religion. In former times, the undoubtedly pious Philip might have been prepared to let England go her own way on that account. It was only when religion became intertwined with politics and trade that Spain ruled that the time had come to speak of war. It is true that Philip was something of a crusader for the Catholic Church, but his attacks on England were attempts to see off a business competitor as well as a nation of heretics.

Foreign policies were dominated by the economic theory known as mercantilism, based on the belief that world trade was finite in nature. Hence it was argued that one nation's (English) trade could only expand if another nation's (Spanish) trade was reduced. Thomas Mun of the East India Company, founded in 1600, produced more philosophical discussions of mercantilism. *A Discourse of Trade, from England unto the East Indies* was published in 1621. He followed this with *England's Treasure by Forraign Trade, or, the balance of our foreign trade is the rule of our treasure*. Written in about 1630, it was not published until after his death in 1664.

How did the English see themselves and their country at that time? It seems appropriate to quote from Shakespeare, who knew how to pluck his nation's heartstrings and had John of Gaunt speaking magnificently of:

This royal throne of kings, this sceptr'd isle,
This earth of majesty, this seat of Mars,
This other Eden, demi-paradise,
This fortress built by Nature for herself
Against infection and the hand of war,
This happy breed of men, this little world,
This precious stone set in the silver sea,
Which serves it in the office of a wall,
Or a moat defensive to a house
Against the envy of less happier lands;
This blessed plot, this earth, this realm, this England...

The seafaring people of that sceptr'd isle had a raging thirst for adventure, money and commerce. Spain's closely-guarded monopolies in the New World were a huge temptation to a nation that believed it had the sailors and ships to run rings around the lumbering Spanish galleons. This happy breed of men ... Little England had big ambitions. Too big for mighty Spain to swallow. Elizabeth knew that the future of England was hanging in the balance. She wasn't about to let James tip it in Spain's favour, for the sake of some rebellious earls.

By now if not before, Elizabeth must have realised that James's loyalty to his handsome male friends could come between him and his reason – that and his highly dubious belief that Huntly and the other Catholic earls might win England for him, if the need arose and he so ordered. In this, James was once again displaying that unhappy knack of finding bizarre solutions to barely existent problems, and thus provoking very real troubles for himself and his country.

Elizabeth had all but promised him the throne of England – if he behaved. His response was to make threats as to what he might do if he was denied. In this and many other ways, James could be his own worst enemy. Elizabeth of England was not one to be threatened and James had to be taught a lesson concerning the long arm of her influence and power. Others would help in bringing him to his senses ...

On the morning of July 24 1593, King James was still dozing in his solitary bed when he heard voices in the adjoining room. Bleary-eyed and somewhat confused, he staggered out to discover the cause of the commotion. Feeling somewhat grumpy at this interruption of the royal slumber, he threw open his door to demand an explanation. But anger turned to abject terror when a sword-carrying Bothwell confronted him.

James was never brave in the presence of naked steel. Quite the opposite, in fact. He took off down the corridor to Queen Anne's rooms, screaming 'Treason!' at the top of his voice.

The door to the queen's chamber was locked, and nobody responded to his shouts. It was then that James looked back at Bothwell and realised that the latter was on his knees, with the sword lying on the floor in front of him. James demanded to know what was going on – or words to that effect, for he was still noted for 'the florescence of his obscenities'.

If Bothwell wasn't about to run him through, then he might be planning to use his black, satanic arts. Once again, terror defeated reason and the king screamed that while Bothwell might take his life, he should not have his immortal soul. Nor would he live in shame and captivity.

At this, Bothwell offered his sword to James, telling him to strike – the ultimate act of homage. And since that wasn't enough to calm the terrified king, the entrance of several of Bothwell's friends helped James to realise that the erring earl was intent on a parley, rather than a killing. Thus reassured, James took control of the situation. His shouts had indeed been heard, and a group of armed citizens had already rushed to his assistance. Seeing this, he leaned out of a window, laughing, and told them all was well and they should return to their homes.

James was confident that, when it came to talking, he had few equals and nothing to fear. Despite his hatred of Bothwell, he made a great point of saying how much he appreciated Bothwell's contrition – ignoring the circumstances in which it had been offered. He spoke to Bothwell as if he were among his most loyal subjects, gently rebuking him for having dealings with England. Then they got onto the nitty-gritty.

It was agreed that Bothwell would withdraw, and later attend trial charged with witchcraft. It being agreed, of course, that the trial would end in acquittal. James also agreed that Bothwell would be pardoned for all his other offences, but that he must withdraw from the royal court. Satisfied with these concessions, Bothwell took his leave. Apparently, he had forgotten Elizabeth's instructions to insist that James should deal with Huntly, once and for all. If his reputed powers had included an ability to predict the future, Bothwell might not have departed so gladly.

Bothwell's actions made wise men stop and think. Up till then, Bothwell had been little more than a thorn in James's side – a constant reminder to the king that the Kirk had teeth, that it might use, if the need arose. But now he had gone too far in acting on his own behalf while representing Elizabeth of England, who was no friend of the Scottish Presbyterians, and all this at a time when James had announced his support of the Kirk – wholehearted or otherwise – and allowed the passage of the Charter of the Presbytery.

Times and priorities were changing. In acting with Elizabeth of England, Bothwell had already placed himself outside the body of the Presbyterian Kirk, whose power brokers asked what might have happened if Bothwell had kept control of the king, perhaps in Elizabeth's name. She could have induced him to the English Church. Equally, Bothwell had allied himself to the Catholic earls in the past. He was too much of a loose cannon, increasingly unpredictable and too big a risk. The decision was made by the political wing of the Scottish Protestants to distance themselves from their former champion. In a dozen ways, his support was undermined. He would no longer be forgiven for his 'youthful exuberances'.

The political powers behind the Presbyterians decided that King James, for all his faults, could be forgiven. He had been caught between the extremes of the outlaw Bothwell and the rebellious Catholic earls, and left virtually without support. This had left him vulnerable, and it was a vulnerability that they might seek to exploit by rallying to his cause.

Side by side, King James and Presbyterian politicians could offer a united front, inducing an atmosphere of mutual support. One of the first to feel the warm glow of its benefits was Chancellor Maitland. After years of fearing for his life, the brave reformer suddenly found himself in the company of new and influential friends, some of whom had been his former adversaries in parliament. Lord John Hamilton, one of the greatest of Scotland's nobles, was among the first to offer a nod of approval in Maitland's direction, along with Glamis, the Treasurer. They were followed by many of the leading families of Stewarts and Douglases. Catholics were also joining the new alliance, including the Homes and Maxwells of the Borders – if for no better reason than they were at feud with Bothwell, and because they knew enough to recognise a winning team when it emerged from the pavilion.

With a newfound confidence, King James realised that he might settle with Bothwell. In a compromise that allowed the king's former promises to be acknowledged, Bothwell was informed that his agreement with James would not be honoured unless he went into exile.

Bothwell's supporters were turning their backs on him. He had already been outlawed and his estates forfeited, though nobody had dared take over his property lest their enjoyment of it be curtailed by a knife across the throat. Now that fear had faded, others found comfort where Bothwell had once ruled.

Yet still the earl did not recognise when he was beaten. In April 1594 he galloped a small force in ever decreasing circles centred on Leith and Arthur's Seat. The raid was a fiasco, highlighting the need to have him removed. It cost him the last of his support in Scotland, and Elizabeth of England finally realised that he was a lost cause.

Broken and beggared, Bothwell left Scotland in April 1595, never to return. In that year, however, he was not the only noble to leave Scotland with a heavy heart.

In 1593, King James had been stubbornly resisting demands for him to deal finally with the Catholic earls. Instead, he seemed to support them, as if he was in awe of them. He described Huntly, Errol and Angus as the most powerful nobles in his kingdom and informed Bowes, Elizabeth's representative, that 'if he should again pursue them and toot them with the horn he should little prevail.'

The king still held a lingering affection for Huntly. In November 1593, James cajoled a small convention of nobles to pass an Act of Oblivion, effectively forgiving the Catholic earls for past crimes, including charges arising out of the Spanish Blanks. This despite the fact that it renewed the wrath of Queen Elizabeth and the Kirk. The Synod of Fife proceeded to excommunicate the earls, without reference to the king.

This tricky situation might have continued, leading to the destruction of the new alliance within Scotland, but needs must when the devil drives and James's personal devil was Bothwell whose raid on Leith, while achieving little, had deeply upset the king. In its wake, James determined that he would sacrifice Huntly in order to be rid of Bothwell, once and for all. He made an unequivocal promise to the Kirk. 'If ye will assist me against Bothwell at this time, I promise to prosecute the excommunicated lords so that they shall not be suffered to remain in any part of Scotland.' This was part and parcel of the new deal.

Alongside his desire to settle with Bothwell, James had recently discovered that Huntly was once again scheming with the king of Spain. The Kirk had discovered that the increasingly desperate Bothwell had renewed his contact with the Catholic earls. Therefore, James's offer and the Kirk's acceptance provided an opportunity to kill at least two birds with one stone.

Once again, King James headed north at the head of a punitive force, but this time he meant business and the earls realised it. Despite an early success against advanced troops commanded by the Protestant Earl of Argyll, the Catholic nobles broke and fled, once again, into the wilds of Caithness. Their homes, which had formerly been placed in the care of their friends, were burnt to the ground.

It may have been their negotiations with Bothwell that finally turned the king against them. Whatever the cause, and despite his earlier excuse to Bowes, King James the hunter was now prepared to pursue his quarry 'and toot them with the horn' right vigorously. He offered them just one alternative. Huntly and Errol agreed to go into exile from Scotland, which they did in March 1595.

Queen Elizabeth of England was able to express satisfaction with King James of Scots, at last. By exiling the Scottish Catholic earls, James had effectively removed the possibility of a Spanish invasion of England through the back door. The possibility of a second front being opened on England's northern border, whether to assist France or Spain, had been a military and diplomatic headache for England over many centuries, repeatedly soured relations with Scotland, and cost many thousands of lives and untold financial expenditure. With that threat removed, at least for the time being, England could concentrate on its internal problems and the ongoing war with Spain, not only for the defence of the realm, but to expand trade and eventually to pursue colonisation.

In 1593, Queen Elizabeth's court had celebrated the 35th anniversary of her accession to the throne. In that same year, England's leading playwright, Kit Marlowe, aged just 29, was stabbed to death in a pub brawl. The exact circumstances of his death are not known, but he had been a government spy,

serving under Sir Francis Walsingham, and it has been suggested that his
assailants were connected to the Secret Services' enemies. Whatever, his
departure cleared the way for the up-and-coming Will Shakespeare, who was
already enjoying success with plays like *The Comedy of Errors*. Such diversions
helped the citizens of London to forget the woes of the world for a few hours
for, yet again, plague stalked the streets of England's capital city.

Just as Scotland's king had his problem earls, so Elizabeth of England had
to suffer the power games of ambitious nobles. Following the destruction of
the Armada, England had decided to go on the offensive, rather than wait for
Spain to make its next move. The Protestant Henry of Navarre had
succeeded to the throne of France, though not without opposition. Philip of
Spain had thrown his weight behind the Catholic Leaguers. In response, and
in defence of the Protestant faith and to keep Philip occupied with France,
Elizabeth had sent English troops into the fray, originally sending over an
army of 4,000 men under the command of Lord Willoughby.

Willoughby had returned from France in January 1590, to be replaced in
August 1591 by Robert Devereux, the young Earl of Essex, who proved more
ambitious than competent as a military leader. He was summoned back to
London in February 1592 with the survivors of his expedition, after
infuriating Queen Elizabeth by rewarding 24 of his officers with
knighthoods, despite their distinct lack of action. It was said that for every
one of Essex's men lost in battle, ten more died of disease. Despite this, Essex
joined the Privy Council at the start of 1593.

In that same year, Henry IV of France, the great Huguenot hero of
Protestantism, finally wearied of war. After so many years of slaughter,
anarchy and mayhem, he realised that religious differences among his people
would tear his country apart till nothing was left standing. As a Protestant, he
had sought nothing more than religious toleration. As a king of France, he
came to believe that it might never be achieved. And so, as a pragmatist, he
converted to Catholicism while reassuring England that he would not
become her enemy. He was still a believer in toleration. For that reason alone,
though there were many others, he could not become an ally of Philip of
Spain. Indeed, despite Henry's conversion, the war with Spain continued.

Meanwhile, the Earl of Essex had been striving to flex his political muscles
in England. He was still just 25 years old in March 1594, when matters came
to a head between him and Queen Elizabeth. Just as he had made knights of
his officers in France, he now sought to increase his kudos and power – what

he described as his 'domestical greatness'- by rewarding his followers with valuable appointments. Among them was Francis Bacon, who had offended the queen with a speech he had made in parliament, so she blocked his advancement to the post of Solicitor General.

Essex was not a man to be thwarted, and decided to 'make an example' of one of the queen's favourites. He accused the queen's physician, the Jewish Rodrigo Lopez, of being a Spanish agent, and plotting to poison the queen. When the queen dismissed these suggestions with unguarded scorn, Essex was even more determined to teach her a lesson. He rounded up various suspected Spanish agents and had them tortured. Naturally enough, they confirmed whatever their torturers suggested. In the face of this evidence, Elizabeth was powerless. Dr Lopez was castrated, disembowelled and finally hanged in front of a large crowd, jeering anti-Semitic slogans.

Elizabeth and Essex would continue their stormy relationship. It was to be the most curious of love-hate affairs between an ambitious young noble and an ageing queen.

Meanwhile in Scotland, the marriage of King James and Queen Anne had proved fruitful with the birth of a son on February 19 1594. Prince Henry Frederick Stuart was named in memory of his two grandfathers. His father, the king, had adopted his own mother's spelling of their surname – Stuart rather than Stewart – thus setting the royal family apart from others of that name.

Malicious gossips (a species inhabiting Scotland since the dawn of time), suggested that James might not be the true father of the prince. The Duke of Lennox was one name that was bandied about in these 'guess the paternity' games involving bawdy jibes about the king's sexuality. In later years, there would be no doubt as to the parentage of James's children. Unfortunately for James and his descendants, he had inherited porphyria through his mother from his grandfather, James V, and passed it on to succeeding generations of the Stuart royal family. Porphyria goes a long way to explaining the king's character and condition. He was ever subject to excessive swings in mood, from hysteria to morbidity, and while it might be suggested that he had reason enough to feel persecuted, this was insufficient to account for his occasional paranoia and frequent obsessions. Added to this were his physical problems, including a tongue that was too large for his mouth, causing him to drool, and a skin so tender that he never washed –

using a damp cloth to gently wipe his flaking hands. In many cases of porphyria, the sufferer's skin is easily damaged, and even the slightest knock can cause it to break. This is caused by skin photosensitivity, requiring exposure to sunlight to cause the skin to become fragile, and is therefore confined in most cases to the hands, neck and face, which develop blisters and open sores. Unfortunately for James, he was virtually addicted to hunting and hawking, and so was regularly exposed to the elements.

James had no reservations concerning the parentage of the baby prince, and was clearly delighted with his wee ane. He went so far as to bleed the royal coffers dry in scraping together sufficient funds to pay for a right royal baptism, to which he invited many of the great and good of foreign lands. Of course, he had a hidden agenda. He still had his dream of becoming Europe's Solomon, and would portray himself as such to his guests. A masque was arranged in which James appeared as a Christian Knight of Malta. He was clearly delighted with this role, which is more than can be said for those of his nobles, including the bold Buccleuch, who were instructed to wear women's clothes and play the part of Amazons. Not quite wolves in sheep's clothing, but something very similar.

After the celebrations were over, there remained the matter of the prince's upbringing. Rather like the man who hated his public school, but later insists on sending his son through the same ordeal, King James was determined that the prince should be raised in the same Spartan surroundings that he had suffered. Prince Henry was just one year old when he was sent to live in Stirling Castle. Significantly, perhaps, he was placed in the charge of the Earl of Mar – King James's childhood playfellow.

Like many a mother faced with such a loss, Queen Anne was furious, to put it mildly. As in the past, she reacted by flirting with various nobles, practically plotting against both James and Mar. The attractive young queen could wrap the sternest of men around her little finger. Unfortunately, this made James all the more determined to maintain control over their son.

King James knew that his popularity was tenuous, and there can be little doubt that he saw his son as being as much of a threat as a blessing. He feared that his wife might gather together a group of nobles who would seize control of the prince in her name, and overthrow him, the king – as had been done to his mother, Mary Queen of Scots. He feared that history might repeat itself, knowing that a significant number of his nobles would be more than willing to become Regent during the prince's minority, possibly with the promise of admission to the beautiful Queen Anne's bed into the bargain.

In truth, James was probably letting his imagination run riot. Once again, in seeing trouble where it hardly existed, he created it for himself. The queen's priority was to have her son returned to her side, to be raised by her at Holyrood. True, she flirted outrageously with various nobles, both in her husband's presence and absence, but is this so hard to understand when that same husband was gawping at favoured young men? Some might say that Anne was simply seeking attention.

By now, James had moved his household, apart from his queen, to Falkland Palace. Anne begged him to return to Holyrood in order that they could settle matters. Finally, the king returned nervously, fearing that he might be abducted at any moment. The meeting of the royal couple started with a quarrel, which brewed into an outright screaming match, with hatfuls of reproaches on both sides. Finally, the queen dissolved into tears. After this, various witnesses removed themselves to allow the royal couple some time alone. There was reconciliation, 'and they returned to Falkland very lovingly together'. And they say such things only happen in storybooks.

DIVINE KINGS
AND IRISH REBELS

Chancellor Maitland died in October 1595, shortly after the reconciliation of King James with Queen Anne. Remembering the support that Maitland had provided for James in his endeavours to reform the Scottish legal system, it was perhaps to be expected that James would mourn the loss of his old ally. However, the complicated king was ever ready to surprise the unsuspecting. Rather than praising Maitland, he seemed to blame him for all that was wrong in Scotland, as if Maitland had been holding the king back from achieving his goals.

It seems that while James had accepted the need for a political ally, he did so grudgingly. Whenever possible, he preferred to act alone, with a huge confidence in his own abilities. The boy begets the man, and the boy had received constant praise for his intellectual powers. James grew up believing that he had few if any equals in the brains department, and this attitude was further encouraged by his attitude towards kingship.

In public, he might have paid lip service to Presbyterian ideals of democracy – even to the point of a king's right to rule being open to question but in private he rejected this philosophy and was still determined to establish Episcopalianism in Scotland. This despite his concessions to the Kirk, because he had been forced into granting them, which rankled with him. He did not like being bullied, and was not one to forgive easily.

King James believed that people should know their place in life, and that his was that of a supreme ruler who answered only to God. In effect, he believed that kings ruled by a divine right that no man could or should question. In 1595, he knew to keep such thoughts to himself, but he would finally reveal his true beliefs – for example, when addressing the English House of Commons.

'The state of monarchy is the supremest thing on earth. For kings are not only God's lieutenants upon earth and sit upon God's throne, but even by God Himself they are called gods ... they make and unmake their subjects. They have power of raising and casting down, of life and of death, judges over all, and yet accountable to none but God only. They have the power to exalt low things and abase high things and make of their subjects like men at the chess, a pawn to take a bishop or a knight, for to emperors or kings their subjects' bodies and goods are due for their defence and maintenance.'

This explains King James's attitude towards Chancellor Maitland who, in James's opinion, had approached his job as too much the partner in the royal business. His lack of deference, and his ability to match James's wit and wisdom, had not always been appreciated. In his later years, Queen Anne had befriended Maitland, and James had believed the Chancellor was too ready to take her side in various arguments. James was glad to see the back of Maitland for Maitland, despite his unfailing loyalty to James, had treated him as a man, failing to acknowledge that kings 'even by God Himself they are called gods'.

With Maitland out of the way, James sought to shape Scotland to his exclusive designs. He would lose his all-supreme position if he appointed a replacement Chancellor, so was determined to leave the post vacant. When questioned on this, the king asserted that if he appointed a noble, that man would soon 'be better attended upon than the king himself'. In fact, James seemed to resent most of his nobles, believing they sought to fly too high – close to heaven where only kings had any right to be. Throughout his adult life, James sought to pluck his nobles' flight feathers. On the other hand, if he appointed a commoner to the Chancellorship, then that man would undoubtedly seek to extend his powers, indulging in all manner of intrigue, fraudulent practices and the favouring of cronies. Ironically, the clamour arising out of his refusal to appoint a Chancellor, for which there was no shortage of candidates, convinced the king that he had made the right decision, for if he had favoured one, he would have offended many. Thus, James felt that he had acted again as the Solomon of his age and it became a habit with him to leave offices unfulfilled whenever there were a number of candidates. This simply offended all and satisfied none, other than himself.

Having determined to delegate as few of 'his' powers as possible, King James threw himself wholeheartedly into governing his realm. He was a great believer in the furtherance of education and culture, and still believed in the need to reform the law and ensure its enforcement – partly as a visible means of imposing his authority on his subjects, to prove he had 'power of raising and casting down, of life and of death,' and to 'make of his subjects like men at the chess'. But how would his subjects respond?

The Highlands and Islands had made their own reputation in standing above and beyond the king's law. In turn, James dreamed of the day when he would bring the great chiefs to heel – men who aped the godly powers that were the king's alone. He announced his opinion of them and theirs. 'I shortly comprehend them all in two sorts of people: the one that dwelleth in our mainland, that are barbarous for the most part and yet mixed with some show of civility; the other that dwelleth in the Isles and are utterly barbarous without any show of civility.'

James started his campaign to 'civilise' those he described as wolves and wild boars by summoning the western chiefs to Edinburgh, to show titles to their estates. Few could produce such titles in a land where the sword had ever been mightier than the pen, and even fewer came to the king's call. James used this as an excuse to impose a colonial system. Responsible Lowlanders, mainly drawn from Fife, were given title to various wild lands, which they were expected to settle.

An Act of 1597 allowed for the creation of three burghs – in Kintyre, Lochaber and on the Isle of Lewis. However, the gentlemen-adventurers who sought to establish their rights were met with open hostility rather than red carpets and cheering crowds. They soon returned to the Lowlands.

One of the great problems in the north and west was the difficulty of access and transport, other than by sea. No such problem existed in the Borders, however, which were well within reach of the king's law. Within reach, perhaps, but a tough nettle to grasp.

For hundreds of years, the Scottish Border clans and families had lived by their own laws and rules – based largely on the concepts of get your retaliation in first, an eye for an eye, and devil take the hindmost. Armstrongs, Elliots, Grahams, Kerrs, Littles, Scotts and a dozen more names had proved that only the fittest survive in centuries of warfare and raiding. And for every Scottish reiver, there might be one or more operating from the English side. Indeed, cross-frontier marriages became common and, by regularly taking the law into their own hands, Borderers had developed a habit of standing apart from both Scotland and England, with a willingness to swap sides at the drop of a hat or, more likely, a purse. Many Borderers acted as if the old kingdom of Northumbria still existed and represented the core of society, while everybody else, in both Scotland and England, Edinburgh and London, were beyond their frontiers, as well as their understanding. Nor were they an altogether unruly mob. It depended on who was issuing the orders. The majority of them rode a horse and carried a lance, and were described as possibly the finest light cavalry in Europe. Many had remained Catholic – probably more from habit than conviction.

These reivers operated against a backdrop of 'gentlemen's agreements', some of which had been committed to parchment, and all of which they considered as binding. One such an agreement was 'the truce day', when men from both sides could meet, mingle and bring cases before the Wardens of the Marches, without fear or favour. In brief, such truce days had the potential to stop bad blood or hurt feelings getting any worse.

One such truce day in the spring of 1596 was attended by a notorious reiver, Kinmont Willie Armstrong. His open presence in Carlisle was evidently too much for some of the English to stomach, and he was seized and thrown into a cell in the castle. Naturally, the Scottish Borderers were outraged and demanded his return. When this was refused, a 'fighting patrol' of Scottish reivers under the command of Scott of Buccleuch assembled at Morton Rig, and then crossed the border under cover of darkness. It may be that one or more of Willie's guards was a true man of the border, or felt sufficiently threatened to turn a blind eye, but whatever the truth behind the tale, Willie was freed and carried back triumphantly to Scotland.

King James was seeking to impose some order on the reiving clans, but they answered to nobody but their leaders – and then only when it suited their purpose – and those chiefs had been offended by the English breach of a truce day. All hell broke loose. In a land where the raid and counter, feud, blackmail, murder and looting were common events for hundreds of years, 1596 saw a stunning escalation in violence.

James was furious and denounced the 'barbarity' of the Scottish raids, swearing he would 'not approve them against his most deadly foes, much less against the subjects of Elizabeth.' He made sallies into the wild frontier, hanging various miscreants, but it would be a number of years before he could take his final revenge on those who had openly flouted his will. In the meantime, he sought to appease the queen of England by naming his new baby daughter Elizabeth. The princess was born at Dunfermline in August.

For all his confidence in his abilities, King James was wise enough to recognise his limitations in the management of his finances. He was a bit of a fool where money was concerned, owing his servants as well as more established lenders, and finally teetering on the brink of ruin. Meanwhile, Queen Anne, whose money was managed separately, was doing rather well.

James demanded an investigation into his Exchequer, and came to suspect that some of its officers had been dipping their fingers. In reality, they were probably trying to claw back something of that which they were owed, though James chose to ignore this. He then spoke with the queen's councillors, who offered to administer his revenues and provide him with a healthy income. It is said that James was encouraged to throw out the old and bring in the new when Anne shook a purse in his face, containing a thousand pounds in gold which she had just received. As there were eight of these councillors, they were known as the Octavians. They formed a new and formidable power base within the Scottish government, and one not based on religious loyalties.

Meanwhile, English Anglicans and Scottish Presbyterians, despite their differences, were still concerned with Catholic threats, at home and from abroad. Despite the activities of the likes of Drake and Raleigh, or rather because of them, Philip of Spain was showing an astonishingly dogged determination to follow through on what he had started with the Armada of 1588. After nearly ten years of warfare on land and the high seas, Philip was sticking to his task of restoring Europe to the Catholic faith. Following his failure to establish an invasion route to England through Scotland, he had concentrated on Ireland.

The history of Ireland and its unhappy relationship with interfering neighbours is a vast subject – far too vast a subject to be covered here. Suffice to say that in the middle and later years of the 16th century, the Catholic Irish people were striving to throw off the yoke of English colonialism, which was now a domineering force for Protestantism.

At the end of 1591, Hugh Roe O'Donnell, son of the Lord of Tyrconnell, escaped from Dublin Castle where the English had held him prisoner since 1587. Thus encouraged by the return of his son, Tyrconnell expelled the English sheriff of Fermanagh before stepping aside for young Hugh to become chief of the O'Donnell's and Lord of Tyrconnell in May 1592. Later in that same year the new Tyrconnell submitted to the English Lord Deputy of Ireland, Sir William Fitzwilliam – a situation made more complicated by rumours that Fitzwilliam had earlier accepted a bribe to allow O'Donnell to escape from Dublin.

Before the year was out and despite his submission, O'Donnell arranged a synod of Catholic bishops in Tyrconnell. Such a gathering allowed for political as well as religious discussion. In the spring of 1593, just months after the discovery of the Spanish Blanks in Scotland, O'Donnell sent the Catholic Archbishop, James O'Hely of Tuam, to meet with Philip of Spain. The Spanish king saw that Ireland offered an alternative to Scotland as a route to England, and agreed to assist the 'Ulster Lords' in their struggle with the English government of Ireland, based in Dublin.

Hugh Maguire, the Lord of Fermanagh and a son-in-law of Hugh O'Neill, Earl of Tyrone, was already fighting the English who were trying to have him removed. He seized Enniskillen, and held it against an English counter-attack in October but they were back in February, and this time victorious. The tables were quickly turned with the besieged becoming the besiegers. Tyrconnell joined Fermanagh, and together they surrounded Enniskillen before destroying an English column that attempted to relieve their comrades in August 1594. With their supplies exhausted, the English held out until May 1595 when the town was recaptured by Fermanagh and Tyrconnell's jubilant forces.

In May 1594, Sir William Russell replaced Sir William Fitzwilliam as Lord Deputy. In the following year, he converted the cathedral of the city of Armagh into a garrison. Clearly, he was expecting more serious trouble.

The following month, as a sign of their readiness to accept foreign aid, Tyrconnell joined with Tyrone in offering the crown of Ireland to the Governor of the Spanish Netherlands, Habsburg Archduke Albert. A Spanish fleet set out immediately for Ireland, but it was lost like the Armada before, and Tyrone and Tyrconnell saw little alternative but to seek a peace with the government in Dublin.

Hugh O'Neill, Earl of Tyrone, had been declared a traitor in 1595. Now he was granted a royal pardon, having agreed to break off negotiations with Spain and to take no further part in what had become a widespread 'rebellion' against the imposition of English. It seems that Tyrone was simply playing for time as in July 1596, he announced the resumption of hostilities against the English. Another Spanish fleet was heading for Ireland. Unfortunately for Tyrone, not to mention the Spanish sailors and troops, it was wrecked in a storm off Finisterre at the end of October. Perhaps deciding not to place any more of his faith in Spanish ships, and with negotiations no longer an option, Tyrone immediately attacked the English garrison in Armagh.

It was a sign of Spain's wealth and power that she had been able to put a fleet to sea at all, for just months earlier a combined English and Dutch fleet had scored a great victory over the Spanish in their home port of Cadiz. This served to restore English morale just months after the deaths of Sir John Hawkins off the coast of Puerto Rico, and his nephew, Sir Francis Drake – struck down by dysentery off Panama – while these two English heroes were making a joint expedition against Spain's territories and treasure ships.

Hawkins and Drake epitomised the English sailor in Elizabethan times. On the whole, they loved their queen and country, but that love was nothing compared to their hatred of foreigners. It was said that they hated the pope, the Turk and the Devil, but mostly the pope for it was he who had allotted the East Indies to Portugal and the West Indies to Spain. As for the high seas, they regarded them as a no-man's-land where they might murder and pillage to their hearts' content. If they had been told they were fighting the good fight for Protestantism, they might have laughed. They fought for Elizabeth and England, and their financial backers, but above all they fought for themselves. Drake's compatriots described him as 'The Master Thief of the Unknown World'.

Robert Devereux, the Earl of Essex, had commanded the surprise attack on Cadiz. Rather than lose their ships to the enemy, the Spaniards had scuttled their Indies fleet, carrying 12 million ducats. Denied this prize, the English and Dutch sailors vented their anger on the city. The killings, rape, looting and burning had continued through the streets of Spain's wealthiest port for a fortnight, leaving little more than a smoking ruin.

Back in Ireland, Lord Burgh replaced Sir William Russell as Lord Deputy in March 1597. Having organised his troops, he then marched against the Earl of Tyrone in July. He did not survive long, dying of typhus in October. Thomas Dubh Butler, Earl of Ormond, was then appointed Lieutenant-General of Queen Elizabeth's army in Ireland, with orders to destroy the rebellious Tyrone. By now Tyrone had completely despaired of Spanish aid arriving in one piece, and therefore submitted to Ormond.

It would be nearly a year before Tyrone went back on his word – again. He joined forces with his old allies Hugh Roe O'Donnell, Lord of Tyrconnell, and Hugh Maguire, Lord of Fermanagh, to defeat English forces in Ulster, commanded by Sir Henry Bagenal, at the Battle of the Yellow Ford. Bagenal was among the many English dead.

News of this victory spread like wildfire, thus encouraging rebellion and threatening Protestant settlers who had recently been 'planted' in areas such as Munster, in much the same way that King James of Scots had sought to plant loyal Lowlanders in parts of the Highlands and Islands. This plantation policy caused deep resentment, in Ireland as in Scotland, but this did not deter the English authorities.

Social unrest was hardly confined to Scotland and Ireland. In England, there was a 'revolt' in Oxfordshire in 1596. Its leaders had threatened to break down enclosures and murder the local gentry. In truth, it received little support, but served as a warning of the unrest caused by rural poverty, and highlighted the accelerating depopulation of the countryside.

Much of the tilled land – worked for the production of crops – had been converted to permanent pasture on which to graze sheep. This suited England's lucrative wool trade, but required fewer workers living on the land. In February 1598, in recognition of this burgeoning problem, Parliament decreed that any land that had been tilled for 12 years or more and had subsequently been converted to pasture must be returned to tillage. Workers' dwellings that had been destroyed – increasing the already huge numbers of homeless beggars – were ordered to be rebuilt. However, it was recognised that these measures might amount to too little, too late, as rural England was already experiencing a crime wave. Therefore, the role and responsibilities of justices of the peace was increased.

Most English counties now required about 50 justices to settle all manner of civil and criminal cases. With over 300 statutes to enforce, theirs was a somewhat onerous task, which was not always appreciated by those who were brought before the bench. Many of the poor felt they received a very rough form of justice, because those sitting in judgement were drawn exclusively from wealthy, local families. From 1597, those justices had a new form of punishment to deal with both serious and petty criminals – transportation to 'the colonies'. This helped them protect everything from a gentleman's purse and silk kerchief to his rabbits.

A German visitor to England in 1599, Thomas Platter, left an interesting if not necessarily accurate account of the woman's role in English society. 'The women-folk of England have mostly blue-grey eyes, are fair and pretty, and have more liberty than in other lands ... Women as well as the men – in fact more often than they – will frequent the taverns or ale houses for enjoyment ... they gaily toast each other ... often stroll out in gorgeous clothes, laying great store by ruffs and starch them blue, and the men must put up with such ways and may not punish them for it – indeed the good wives often beat their men.'

After his victory against the Spanish fleet at Cadiz in 1595, but having been denied prize money and treasure when the Spaniards scuttled their Indies ships, Essex had returned to England a happy commander, but a frustrated man. His lifestyle invoked heavy expenses that were not matched by his income, mainly derived from customs duties on sweet wines, which had been granted to him by Queen Elizabeth in 1590. In these circumstances, he could not resist the temptation of raising another fleet in an attempt to intercept Spanish treasure ships – thus serving the needs of his country and empty money chest.

The taking of Spanish galleons lined English purses, while denying Philip of Spain some of the wealth that he would otherwise use to fund his ongoing war to destroy Protestantism throughout Europe, and expand his territories both at home and in the New World. However, Essex's expedition was a disaster and he returned to Plymouth in late October 1597 – certainly no wealthier and perhaps little wiser. He retired from court, but in December Queen Elizabeth made him Earl Marshal. He was still short of funds, and rowed bitterly with Elizabeth. Another example of their strangest of love-hate relationships. There was a great falling out.

Coming to his senses finally in October 1598, Essex apologised to Elizabeth for his behaviour. Perhaps he had seen a renewed opportunity for advancement with financial rewards because Lord Burghley, formerly William Cecil, had died in August after 40 years' service to the queen as her closest advisor. As a reward for his apology Essex was appointed Lord Lieutenant of Ireland, and set off for Ulster at the head of 16,000 troops with orders to deal with the rebellious Earl of Tyrone.

After his earlier victory at the Battle of the Yellow Ford, Tyrone had been joined by Edmund Butler, Viscount Mountgarret, and Thomas Butler, Lord Cahir. With their tails up, they had confidently raided right up to the defences of Dublin.

If these 'rebels' were concerned at the arrival of Essex in Ireland, they soon found that they had nothing to fear. The new Lord Lieutenant appeared to have lost his nerve. Rather than attacking Tyrone, as ordered, Essex negotiated a truce with him. Then, as if realising the enormity of his mistake, he fled back to England in order to be first to break the news to Elizabeth. Outraged, she had him thrown into prison to await trial while the whole sorry affair was investigated.

Essex pleaded with the queen in a series of increasingly desperate letters, but to no avail. Elizabeth had turned her back on him. She removed his income derived from custom duties, his 160 servants were dismissed and his household dispersed on the orders of the Star Chamber.

In February 1601, Essex was released from house arrest. Amazingly, he attempted to stage a coup. It was a gross miscalculation, for he had little if any support and Elizabeth was at the height of her popularity.

Elizabeth's new Chief Minister, Sir Robert Cecil (son of the late Lord Burghley) harangued Essex at his trial. 'The difference between you and me is great. For wit I give you pre-eminence. For nobility I also give you place. I am no swordsman – there also you have the odds. But I have innocence, conscience, truth and honesty to defend me, and in this court I stand as an upright man, and your lordship as a delinquent.'

Financially ruined and now publicly disgraced, Essex had nothing to look forward to, other than a quick end. This was provided in February 1601, when he was beheaded at the Tower of London. Still his queen did not desert him entirely, allowing Essex the dignity of a private execution, rather than being paraded in front of a howling mob.

King James of Scots had been in dubious contact with Essex, seeking a pact to their mutual benefit regarding James's claim to the English crown – a claim that Elizabeth still refused to officially acknowledge – but he would not mourn the earl's passing. Rather the opposite, because James had long been fearful of an overly powerful nobility. If he were to inherit England, he would prefer it to be a land without the likes of Essex who might seek to oppose him, even to the point of rebellion or assassination. This was ever the problem with plotters – if they would plot with you, then they might plot against you.

At the same time, James was taking a very close interest in the Irish debate, realising that it was a problem that he would inherit along with the crown of England. Therefore, he had every reason to be pleased at the appointment of a new Lord Deputy. In May 1600, Charles Blount, Lord Mountjoy, took up the cudgel so quickly dropped by the disgraced Essex.

Mountjoy was a very different kettle of fish to Essex, announcing sternly that he meant to settle this Irish matter once and for all. Here was no dandified aristocrat, but an experienced soldier and skilled administrator. He had been given three connected tasks: the destruction of the Earl of Tyrone, the recovery of Ulster, and finally the English conquest of all Ireland.

From the start, Mountjoy made his intentions clear. He meant to get the job done as speedily as possible, seeking to destroy Tyrone's resources and support – operating a scorched earth policy that caused untold suffering, while knowing that the Irish earl was receiving the bulk of his money and arms from Spain. He set up permanent garrisons in Ulster, and could call upon English warships to support his land operations. He would further the process of 'Anglicisation' by all and any means, fair or foul. Of course, his ultimate goal was to ensure that Ireland would never be used as a Spanish base for an invasion of England and, by now, that was of as much or more concern to King James as it was to the ageing Queen Elizabeth.

GOWRIES AND GODS

King James of Scots lived in constant fear of assassins and, if he was to be believed, miraculously survived an attempt on his life in August 1600. 'If to be believed' because the circumstances of the event remain far from clear and, in his account of it, James was more inclined to disseminate than enlighten.

The event is remembered by some as the Gowrie Plot, and by others as the Gowrie Conspiracy though just who plotted or conspired to do what is far from certain. Indeed, it might be better described as a tragedy.

The principal characters, along with King James, were the 22-year-old Earl of Gowrie and his brother Alexander, the 19-year-old Master of Ruthven. Two younger brothers, William and Patrick, were not involved in the event, but would suffer some of its consequences.

The boys' grandfather, Lord Ruthven, had been the one holding a knife or pistol to pregnant Mary Queen of Scot's belly and therefore the embryonic King James, during the murder of David Riccio. Their father had later been executed for treason, as a leader of the Ruthven Raid and their sister was a lady-in-waiting and confidant to Queen Anne. These and other things stood between James and Gowrie, though the king seemed kindly disposed towards Alexander – a handsome, young man.

As well as the family history, James saw other reasons to be nervous about Gowrie. Principally, he believed that Gowrie had dealings with Moray and Bothwell, and he certainly enjoyed a happy relationship with the Kirk. To put these matters into context, the 22-year-old earl had but recently returned from six years of study abroad, though this in itself might have raised suspicions in James's mind. Also, there seemed to be a certain jealousy. Gowrie had been well received in London, which he visited while travelling home to Scotland, and James was certainly angry when he heard that some Edinburgh citizens had turned out to welcome the young earl. Sneering at

Gowrie's popularity, James commented that more folk had turned up to watch Gowrie's father's execution.

To make matters worse, Gowrie angered the king by opposing him in Parliament in June 1600. After that, life at court was made intolerable for the earl and he retired to his estates, apparently to lead a quieter life.

Despite the ill feeling, James borrowed heavily from the comparatively wealthy Gowrie. The sum of £80,000 has been mentioned. While the king may have been superficially grateful, this could have increased his resentment, and it created another problem. At some time in the future, the money would have to be returned. Or would it?

Less than two months after their row in the Scottish parliament, King James was hunting near Falkland. Gowrie's younger brother Alexander, the Master of Ruthven, was in the company. After the hunt, they rode to Gowrie House at Perth where they dined. And after that, according to reports, King James and Alexander withdrew from the rest of the guests. Some time later, the king was heard shouting for help. His attendants rushed to his aid and, without hesitation, killed Alexander and then his brother, Gowrie.

In an attempt to stop speculation, the king issued a statement. The hunt was about to begin when he was drawn aside by the Master of Ruthven who told him that he had discovered a stranger carrying a pot of gold through the streets of Perth. Alexander then asked him to come to Perth and investigate. At first, the king had refused, but he finally changed his mind and rode to Perth with 16 attendants.

In the king's account, the Earl of Gowrie, who had been warned of the king's approach by his brother, met him outside the city. The king noted an uneasiness and lack of cordiality in the earl's manner, but accepted his invitation to dine at Gowrie House.

After dinner, the king asserted, he went alone with Alexander to investigate the stranger and the pot of gold. Alexander then led him through a series of chambers – carefully locking each door behind them. Finally, they entered a small room. There was no pot of gold, but a man dressed in a suit of armour and holding a dagger. Ruthven seized the dagger, accusing the king of murdering his father, and saying that he must die.

The anonymous man in the suit of armour stood still, amazed and trembling. However, employing his negotiating powers, the king convinced

Ruthven to think again. At this, the lad said he must consult with his brother, and left the room ...

According to the king, a servant had already announced to his attendants that he had departed – presumably to get them to leave. Gowrie had risen from the dinner table with his guests, who went out to their horses. Meanwhile, the king had turned his eloquence on the trembling suit of armour, persuading it to open a window so that he could escape. One must assume that there was something about the window latch that was beyond the king's understanding ...

James was just about to climb through the window when Ruthven returned to the room, and said again that the king must die. There was a struggle in which, according to James, he got the better of the young and active Ruthven before shouting for help through the open window. The king's attendants, about to mount their horses, then rushed back into the house.

One of the king's pages, John Ramsey, was in the lead. He rushed into the room where the king was masterfully holding Ruthven on his knees and gripping his head under his arm. Presumably, despite his earlier care, the lad had failed to lock all those doors in the series of chambers on his return. Ruthven, thus pinned, was still able to hold his hand to the king's mouth, in an effort to stop him crying out a second time. Ramsey immediately struck with his sword from behind, killing Ruthven.

Meanwhile, Gowrie had apparently grabbed a sword and was rushing to aid his brother. He was still racing up the stairs when he was met by Ramsey, who ran him through. The rest of the king's attendants finished the job.

What really happened that night at Gowrie House? Arguments involving premeditation on either side may be misdirected. None of the parties to the incidents were fools, leaving the probability that the killings arose out of a spontaneous quarrel – though we only have the king's account of things.

Sir William Bowes, the English diplomat, expressed his belief along such lines, describing Ruthven as 'a learned, sweet and artless young gentleman'. Bowes suggested that perhaps the king, when they were alone, had said something about Ruthven's late father having been executed as a traitor, 'whereat the youth showed a grieved and expostulatory countenance, the King, seeing himself alone and without weapon, cried Treason! The Master, abashed to see the King to apprehend it so ... put his hand to stay the King's showing his countenance in that mood, immediately falling upon his knees to

317

entreat the King ... Ramsey ran the poor gentleman through.'

Some might suggest that 'a grieved and expostulatory countenance' when one's dead father's memory is dragged through the dirt is hardly grounds for accusing 'the poor gentleman' of treason, or justification for having him killed. In James's account, the page had struck Ruthven without hesitation. However, in another account, James had ordered Ramsey to 'Strike him high, because he has a chain doublet upon him.'

Bowes was effectively saying that King James was a liar. The king's account might have been a total fabrication from start to finish. Indeed, we cannot even know whether the lad Alexander died before or after his brother.

In a fanciful flight of the imagination, one might imagine a scene where Gowrie, growing concerned at Alexander's absence with the king, who had notorious leanings toward handsome young men, had found them together 'in a delicate condition', leading to an almighty row, threats and then the king's scream of treason. Might it have been Alexander who sought to protect his brother, rather than the other way about? Who can say? The problem with obvious lies is that they leave the road open to all sorts of speculation. The king might even have been outside, sitting on his horse, guarded by some of his attendants, while the earl and his brother were slaughtered.

Were there any other witnesses to the events at Gowrie House? Would they have dared to talk? King James was determined that nobody should question his account of events. He immediately sent word, commanding the five ministers of Edinburgh to gather together their congregations, give thanks for his deliverance, and read out his statement. They refused to do so, insisting that they would not relate a story of which they were not certain – not when it involved a champion of the Kirk, lying dead alongside his brother and both accused of treason.

In his frustration, James revealed a new side to his character, somewhat reminiscent of his great-uncle, Henry VIII. Who were these ministers to question his word? He demanded that they be dragged before his Council, asking each in turn whether they believed his account, and angrily addressing one thus, 'I see that ye would make me a murderer. It is known very well that I was never bloodthirsty. If I would have taken their lives, I had causes enough, I needed not to hazard myself so.'

Still the ministers expressed their doubts. They might have been remembering the murder of the Earl of Moray, in which James was implicated. By his own admission, he had 'causes enough' to have taken the lives of Gowrie and Ruthven (though what the lad had done wrong, he did not make clear). Or perhaps they were thinking that the man who 'was never bloodthirsty' had not shown any reluctance in ordering the torture and death of suspected witches, and had recently commanded two military expeditions. All that the ministers knew, for sure, was that James had virtually invited himself to Gowrie House and that when he left, the earl and his younger brother were dead. King James was incandescent with rage. Did these stubborn ministers not know that he was recognised as a god, even by God himself, and therefore responsible to God alone?

The last thing James needed at that time was a scandal. Elizabeth might be sprightly enough, and still liked to be portrayed as beautiful and strong, but the years had taken their toll. At 66, she might cover her face with layers of potions, creams and powders, but it was only a matter of time. Her first minister, Robert Cecil, was already in secretive correspondence with King James. Anybody with half a grain of sense in England could see the inevitability of James's succession, and were already vying for his favour.

James's reaction to the Edinburgh ministers was short and sharp. They were banished from the city and their livings. Their shocked reactions may have planted the seeds of a cunning scheme in King James's mind. He announced that acceptance of his version of what had occurred at Gowrie House would be a test of clerical loyalty. Any who questioned it would be punished in the same manner as the Edinburgh ministers.

James had got the measure of the Presbyterians. They might rant from their pulpits, but threaten their pockets ... Indeed, some were already applying for the newly vacant posts in Edinburgh. As for the rest, when James demanded a thanksgiving for his deliverance to be said from every pulpit in the land, it was universally obeyed and James obtained approval for what had been done from a convention of the clergy.

As for the five Edinburgh ministers, four changed their minds and accepted James's version. They were ordered to travel throughout the length and breadth of the land, repeating their submissions at public places. That left just one, a Robert Bruce, who refused to back down. This leader of the Kirk and a former confidant of the king was banished from Scotland, on pain of death.

Whatever he might force on his own people in Scotland, James was not believed abroad. In France, King James's account of events was met with such howls of derision that the Scottish ambassador considered it wise to have the story suppressed.

James did all in his power to signal Ruthven and Gowrie's guilt, although in the king's own account, Gowrie seemed guilty of nothing other than rushing to his younger brother's aid. As a final seal of his disapproval, James ordered that the bodies of the 'traitors' be hacked into pieces – gibbeted, quartered and displayed throughout the country. Their estates were forfeited and the very name of Ruthven abolished.

Gowrie's sister, Beatrix, was banished. Queen Anne was furious at the loss of her lady-in-waiting and sulked in her room, but by now the increasingly wily James had the measure of her, as well as the Kirk. When the king presented her with a tightrope dancer, the queen forgot poor Beatrix.

Gowrie and Ruthven's younger brothers were smuggled into England, to escape James's wrath. From there, William slipped away to the Continent, but Patrick lingered too long, finally being imprisoned in the Tower of London, on James's orders, for 19 years without trial.

As everybody seemed to accept James's succession to the throne of England, the Kirk might have felt bound to accept pragmatism over dogma in the aftermath of the Gowrie affair. Assuming that he survived to unite the crowns of England and Scotland, James would truly be a force to be reckoned with, and it seems that the powers behind the Presbytery decided that it wasn't worth falling out with him over the circumstances of Gowrie's killing – lawful or otherwise. By now, they must have realised that in dealing with King James, they were seeking to guess the intentions of a wily hill fox crossed with the most slippery of eels. When taken together with the Earl of Moray's murder, the Gowrie killings certainly suggested a ruthless side to the king's character.

While they had previously enjoyed James's shift in position – favouring Presbyterian over Episcopalian – the leaders of the Kirk recognised that the king might change back without notice. Therefore, they must have feared for their futures once James was installed as leader of the English, Episcopalian Church. Any hopes that he would cast out England's bishops and convert the land to Presbyterianism, were dashed by the publication of *The Trew Law of Free Monarchies: Or The Reciprock and Mutuall Dutie Betwixt a Free King and his Naturall Subjects* in September 1598, followed by the *Basilikon Doron*.

Basilikon Doron is a fascinating read, arising from James's dream that he hadn't much longer to live. In these circumstances, he decided to set down some advice for his son, Prince Henry. Among many other things, he gave a warning about Puritans. It would have made interesting reading to the more obstinate members of the Kirk in Scotland.

'Take heed, therefore, my son, to such Puritans, very pests in the church and commonweal, whom no deserts can oblige, neither oaths nor promises bind; breathing nothing but sedition and calumnies, aspiring without measure, railing without reason, and making their own imaginations the square of their conscience. I protest before the great God that ye shall never find with any Highland or Border thieves greater ingratitude and more lies and vile perjuries than with these fanatic spirits. And suffer not the principals of them to brook your land if ye like to sit at rest, except ye would keep them for trying your patience, as Socrates did an evil wife.'

Returning to the *Trew Law*, as well as setting out the role of a king, his position and duties – as passed on to the English Parliament virtually word for word, as described in the previous chapter – King James laid down the law regarding the people's duty to their king.

James started with a consideration of the scriptures, quoting Samuel as an indicator that the people must ever be obedient to their king. God made a king, reluctantly at first and only because the people insisted, and only He could unmake him. God's ordinance was that as the people had asked for kings, then they must obey their king in all things, fearing him as their judge, loving him as their father, praying for him as their protector.

From ancient times, Scottish and English kings had obtained rights in their kingdoms, by conquest, uninterrupted use and possession, James continued. These rights amounted to absolute ownership, and thus absolute power over the whole land. 'So he is master over every person that inhabiteth the same, having power over the life and death of every one of them.'

The Kirk had stated and many others proposed that kings must obey the laws of the land. James countered that as there were kings before any parliaments were held, or laws made, it followed that kings were the authors and makers of the laws, rather than the laws being the makers and authors of the kings. In other words, it was for a king to make laws, not to be subject to them. An interesting point of view, to be sure.

Dealing with the Presbyterian notion that kings ruled only with the will of the people and might be removed should they prove tyrannical, James pointed out that evil kings as well as good ones came from God. Therefore the people had no right to resist, save by tears and sobs to God.

It might appear that James was on some crazy power drive, deluding himself that he could do whatever he wanted, when he wanted, answering only to God. However, whether crazy, deluded or otherwise, James was convinced that it was only by asserting 'the divine right of kings' that the royal family could hope to survive. If he was 'just another man', why should his people obey him? If they would not obey him, how could he hope to rule? Acceptance of the divine right of kings as supreme rulers, answerable only to God, was not so much a philosophy as a necessity and this is what he taught his children.

This was the essence of the *Basilikon Doron*, originally written for Prince Henry, and it was never to leave his side. It starts with a sonnet, quoted here as it appeared in the edition of 1603 – chosen for brevity because the 1599 edition contains an extra sonnet. Incidentally, the original was written in Scots, but the following is a translation into the English of the time. By 1603, James wanted both Scots and English to understand and heed his words.

God giues not Kings the stile of Gods in vaine,
For on his throne his Scepter doe they sway:
And as their subiects ought them to obey,
So Kings should feare and serue their God againe.
If then ye would enjoy a happie raigne
Obserue the statutes of your heauenlie King,
And from his Lawe, make all your Lawes to spring,
Since his Lieutenant heere ye should remaine.
Reward the iust, be stedfast, true, and plaine
Represse the proude, maintaining aye the right,
Walke alwaies so, as euer in his sight,
Who guardes the godlie, plaguing the prophane
And so ye shall in Princelie vertues shine
Resembling right you mightie King Diuine.

Some have described the *Basilikon Doron* as an outstanding work. Others have praised its 'fresh, natural and spontaneous style'. Perhaps, in order to appreciate it fully, one should remember its target audience – the young prince.

After the sonnet, the work is divided into three books. The first concerns the duty of a king towards God, the second deals with the duty of a king in his office, and the third is concerned with more mundane matters ranging from how a king should dress and eat – in a 'manly, round and honest fashion' to sport and pastimes, suggesting for example that chess is 'over fond and philosophic a folly'.

In many passages, the hypocrisy is nothing less than stunning. The historian D H Willson, summed it up thus: 'James's combination of shrewdness and naivety, his pious satisfaction at abstinence from vices which did not attract him, his capacity for combining lofty ideals with sordid practice, his astonishing vanity – all are revealed in the *Basilikon Doron*.'

The volume of instruction might be amusing, but for one thing. Prince Henry died before he could inherit. Therefore, it was his brother who closely studied its pages, accepting his father's notions of the divine right of kings, virtually word for word. That boy grew into a man, and was crowned and later executed as Charles I.

CHAPTER THIRTY

RITES OF PASSAGE

At the start of 1601, the *Basilikon Doron* was still a well-kept secret, with a tiny print run circulated only to James's most trusted confidants. The English people must have been more than interested in the identity of King James VI of Scots, soon to be James I of England. Undoubtedly, some would have been fearful for their futures, and keen to discover which way the wind blew, and already various Englishmen of influence were in correspondence with James, offering to help him in any way that they could, clearly hoping to maintain their high positions at court.

Elizabeth was keeping a brave face on things – quite literally, because she had outlawed any unofficial portraits. Thus she was seen as she wanted to be seen – an iconic, proud and beautiful queen. The truth was that she had been ageing dramatically, and did not enjoy the best of health.

Leaving aside the fact that his grandmother had been English, James was born in Scotland, his father was a Scot, and his mother, though born a Scot, had been practically French. Mary had called her son Jacques, was a Catholic raised in France and married to the French king, and had plotted with France and then Spain before the English finally executed her. Most Englishmen believed that the only race worse than the Scots was the French, so why would they accept James as their king?

James asked himself that question many times and it drove him to distraction. He was forever searching for reassurances that the Promised Land wouldn't slam its gates in his face.

In truth, England faced the prospect of accepting James, probably sooner rather than later, simply because there was no better alternative. They believed him to be a champion of Protestantism – probably in its Episcopalian form, though they were not altogether sure on that point. He seemed to favour religious toleration, allowing the majority of English Catholics to believe that if they didn't bother him, he might not bother them. What they all approved of was the fact that he was a man, and had already proved himself capable of producing sons, thus settling the succession.

Despite Elizabeth's massive popularity with her people – a popularity amounting to a 'Gloriana cult' – England's history was that of stern kings and strong leaders. This was the land of Edward Longshanks, Richard the Lionheart and Good King Hal of Agincourt, 'blessed be his memory'. Wives and courtiers might have feared the likes of Henry VIII, but the people had been reassured that they were in strong hands. Perhaps they would be again.

Elizabeth's great popularity was far from universal among the poor. A labourer in Essex was heard saying that he prayed for a king. When questioned, his reply was that, 'the Queene is nothing but a woman and ruled by noblemen so that poor men get nothing … We shall never have a merry world while the Queene liveth.'

He was not alone in expressing such sentiments. There was a strengthening undercurrent of discontent with the ageing queen. Some of her critics were hauled in front of magistrates and subsequently mutilated or pilloried for the effrontery of wanting the work, ale and bread that Elizabeth's England was failing to supply. Was it fair to blame Elizabeth? She did have a habit of taking the credit when things went well – up to and including the defeat of the Armada – so she might not have complained quite so much about having to shoulder some of the blame when things went wrong – up to and including the country's struggling economy.

In these circumstances, Englishmen who moved in powerful circles were keen to glean any snippet of information concerning King James. Sir Henry Wotton, the diplomat and poet, returned from Scotland in 1601. His impressions of James were recorded in *Life and Letters of Sir Henry Wotton* by L Pearsall-Smith.

'This King, though born in 1566, does not appear to be more than twenty-eight years old. He is of medium stature and of robust constitution; his shoulders are broad but the rest of his person from his shoulders downwards is rather slender. In his eyes and in his outward appearance there is a natural kindliness bordering on modesty. He is fond of literary discourse, especially of theology, and is a great lover of witty conceits. His speech is learned and even eloquent. In imitation of his grandfather, James V, he wears his hair cut short. About food and clothing he is quite indifferent. He is patient in the work of government, makes no decision without obtaining good counsel, and is said to be one of the most secret princes of the world. On occasion he has shown bitter hatred, especially against the Earl of Gowrie, and he reduced to obedience the ferocious spirit of Bothwell whom he banished. Yet by his lavish creation of marquises, earls and barons, he does not appear jealous of the great lords. Such creations, far more numerous than in England, he uses to bind his followers to him since he lacks the means to reward them in other ways. An admirable quality is his chastity, which he has preserved without blemish, unlike his predecessors who disturbed the kingdom by leaving many bastards.

'His court is governed more in the French than in the English fashion. Anyone may enter the King's presence while he is at dinner, and as he eats he converses with those about him. The domestics who wait upon him wear caps on their heads. Dinner finished, he remains at table for a time before he retires, listening to banter and to merry jests in which he takes great delight. With his domestics and with the gentlemen of his chamber he is extremely familiar, but with the great lords he is grave. He has no guard, either because he cannot afford one or because he relies upon the love of his people, which he calls the true guardian of princes. Though his kingdom is small, his court is composed of a large number of gentlemen, who, either from curiosity or from zeal to protect their Prince, accost newcomers at once and ask them what they want.'

Clearly, Sir Henry had seen King James in a complimentary light. A foreigner might not appreciate just how much such a description would appeal to the average Englishman. Kindly and modest, a lover of witty conceits, quite indifferent about food and clothing, patient, chaste, doesn't appear jealous, doesn't stand on ceremony … These are the qualities that the English have always admired and looked for in their leaders.

Whether or not James was fully worthy of such praise, Sir Henry produced a basically honest account, as might be judged from mention of James's financial straits, and his dealings with Gowrie and Bothwell. In this Wotton hints at the contrast between James at ease and when crossed.

King James had, by his mid-30s, matured into a man who might be a good friend or an unforgiving enemy. Again, this was something that the English could admire. Part of this was in his character. Those who inhabited his world had moulded the remainder – those who blocked his every attempt to move his country forward.

King James preferred the ways of peace to war. Many had seen this as a sign of weakness and sought to exploit it, but he was quick to learn. He preferred intellectual discussion to rabid argument, and was bullied for it by those who, in the fullness of time, would discover that he was slow to forgive. He sought to preach religious tolerance, and in this he was opposed, not least by zealous Presbyterians. The sort of men who took John Knox as their role model – a man whose attitude might be summed up as: 'the only good Catholic is a dead Catholic'. James had sought to protect the Catholics, risking much to do so. In return, they plotted with Spain. James sought to reform and modernise the Scottish legal system, and in this the mighty nobles opposed him. Little wonder that he made so many marquises, earls and barons from the ranks of those who supported him, in an attempt to redress the balance. He tried to bring law and order to the Highlands, Islands and Borders and his approaches were turned back with disdain. In a world full of feud and faction, he sought to act as an arbiter. His efforts were largely ignored, making him a vigorous proponent of law enforcement.

Perhaps he went too far in his proclamations on the divinity of kings, but what had his people made of the democracy they had been given or taken? Government by the people – or rather, by a cadre of nobles – seemed to drift toward self-interest and fraudulent greed. Once James had got the measure of the Kirk, he treated it with scorn, refusing to accept that such men should be left to decide the religion of his kingdom and preach against him, whenever they chose. But those who did not cross him found that he could be a true and loyal friend – just as long as they didn't overstep the mark. Then they would discover that he had all but run out of patience.

We do not know what happened, really, to the Earl of Gowrie, but we might suspect that King James was not prepared to wait for him to become another Moray or Bothwell – a stick for the political wing of the Kirk to beat him with. James was already planning his move to England, and perhaps he had concluded that Gowrie was becoming too powerful, and popular, to leave behind. In James's mind, Gowrie was all too closely linked to Bothwell, even to the point of his taking an interest in the black arts and other magic. Queen Elizabeth hinted at this in her response to news of his death. Congratulating James on his deliverance, she commented, somewhat tongue-in-cheek, that since Gowrie had so many familiar spirits she supposed there were none now left in hell. It may be that the young earl died not for what he had done, so much as what he might do or become. King James seemed to offer the simplest of messages: I am a supreme ruler, answerable only to God, and this is the law of my land. Obey it and prosper, or break it and be damned. To modern ears, that might sound totally unacceptable. However, James was a man of his times and cannot be judged on democratic notions involving one man, one vote.

James had long since grown petulant at Elizabeth's longevity. Did she mean to thwart him, by lasting as long as the sun and the moon? Obsessed with the English succession, in his nervous state he had spent many a long hour pondering the various obstacles that might stand in his way.

James believed that the surest way to ensure an easy passage to the throne of England was to have Elizabeth's public blessing. If only she would acknowledge him as her heir, then all would be well. But time and again she had refused. 'She would have no rising sun to eclipse her glory,' particularly not when that rising sun had shown such ingratitude and waywardness as in the past – as in favouring Lennox over Morton, prompting Elizabeth to exclaim, 'That false Scottish urchin! What can be expected from the double dealing of such an urchin as this?'

Elizabeth might have forgiven, perhaps, but she had not forgotten. Nor was she prepared to issue James with a blank cheque or right of passage. All she would say was that she would not injure any right or title that was due to him – if he behaved. In 1586 when pressed, she had replied with a veiled threat suggesting that his ingratitude might prompt her to reconsider her position.

Faced with Elizabeth's refusal, one of James's concerns was that if he had to make a case to inherit England's throne after Elizabeth's death, the common law of England disallowed any alien from inheriting land, though it might be gifted. On many occasions, he had asked Elizabeth to grant him the English estates of his grandparents, the Earl and Countess of Lennox. After all, he wasn't asking for the English crown – not this time– but again she had refused.

In James's mind, that refusal led to all sorts of further fears. Principally, he feared the claim of his first cousin, Arabella Stewart, born and bred in England's green and pleasant land. Like James, she was descended from Margaret Tudor, but through Margaret's second marriage. Elizabeth knew of this fear and may have refused him the Lennox's estates as a means of scolding him for ignoring her advice that he should marry Arabella. James's angst may have been a source of amusement to Elizabeth and her circle and James, when faced with another of Queen Anne's sulks, could have wished he had not let his heart rule his head when he was young. With Arabella at his side, his claim would have been complete.

Then there was the matter of Henry VIII's last will. The obese and syphilitic tyrant had developed a hatred of all things Scottish – a hatred arising from the failure of his 'rough wooing' – and so vested the succession, should his own children (Edward, Mary and Elizabeth) die without issue, in the line of his younger sister Mary, who had seen off the aged King of France before marrying Charles Brandon, created Duke of Suffolk. At the time of James VI, the succession in this line fell to Edward Seymour, Lord Beauchamp. Again, this was a worry to James who was not altogether convinced that Englishmen would deny Henry's will and Beauchamp's claim, despite questions over the legality of his parents' marriage and the plain fact that Beauchamp was not considered fit to rule himself, let alone England.

On top of all this, James remained deeply troubled by the bill passed through the English Parliament in 1585, designed specifically to protect Elizabeth from James's mother, Mary Queen of Scots, as a focus for those who plotted for a Catholic restoration by any means. The bill was linked to the Bond of Association. It sought to bar James from the succession if he supported any such plot and, under the terms of the bond, avowed that he would be hunted down and killed if he did. In effect, anybody who failed to oppose plots against Elizabeth, let alone supported them, would forfeit any claim they might have to the throne of England. Any hint of involvement, however small, might block James's path and he took this very much to heart, as shown in the case of Valentine Thomas.

Thomas was a Catholic Englishman, and a bit of a villain according to all accounts. Taking advantage of the easy access to King James, as described by the diplomat Sir Henry Wotton, he had obtained an informal audience with the king in Scotland. He then returned to England, and some time later was arrested on an unrelated matter.

During the course of his interrogation, Thomas hinted that James had suggested that he should assassinate Queen Elizabeth. It may be that Thomas thought that by protesting he would never undertake such a thing that he would be rewarded as a patriot, rather than punished as the ruffian he undoubtedly was. Nevertheless, his interrogators knew their duty, and the matter was reported to Elizabeth.

Elizabeth's reaction was exemplary – up to a point. She wrote to James, telling him what Thomas had said, and adding that she didn't believe a word of it. However, she did see this as an opportunity to tighten the reins on her heir. She sent orders that Thomas was to be 'encouraged' into signing a 'confession' regarding the plot that never was, and kept in prison without trial, at her pleasure.

James was furious. Elizabeth knew exactly what she was doing. Thomas could be brought to trial at a moment's notice, and if he repeated his accusations, James would be barred from the succession. James wrote back in fear and outrage, demanding that Elizabeth should erase his name from anything to do with Valentine Thomas. More than that, she must issue a declaration of James's innocence.

Elizabeth refused, yet again, to which James's anger knew no bounds. He ranted and raved that Thomas had been tortured on Elizabeth's orders into making a false confession. He recalled that it was by linking his mother's name to just such an assassination plot that England had justified her execution. This was intolerable! He would vindicate his innocence. He would print Elizabeth's letter in which she had said she didn't believe one word of Thomas's confession, and circulate it to every royal household in Europe. More than that, he would issue a public challenge involving 'trial by combat' with any accuser. Presumably, he was planning to appoint a champion although he was angered beyond reason.

Elizabeth was unmoved. She may have taken some delight in taunting the man who would one day sit on her throne. Thomas languished in prison, remaining a threat until after Elizabeth's death, when he was promptly executed on James's orders.

King James was ever keen to distance himself from his mother, Mary, both in life and death, from fear that he would be linked with her plotting. He would not, however, tolerate any criticism of her – certainly not from outsiders. In 1596, ten years after her execution, he had pushed the Scottish Parliament into passing a bill that made it treasonable to slander either of his parents. It was no idle threat, as at least two people discovered when they danced at the end of a hangman's rope. Of course, this bill was aimed at muzzling the more vociferous members of the Presbyterian clergy.

As was to be expected, Roman Catholicism was not about to deny its interest in the English throne. Their claim had been set out in 1594 by an

English Jesuit, Robert Parsons, based on the notion that succession in monarchies was derived from something more than hereditary rights.

Parsons wrote *A Conference about the Next Succession to the Crown of England* under the name R Doleman. Predictably, he found objections to all the known contenders, until he came to Philip of Spain and his daughter, the Infanta Isabella Clara Eugenia, as descendants of John of Gaunt. To them, Parsons extended all honour, cleverly concocting a seemingly impeccable claim on their behalf. Impeccable enough to outrage James, even if it failed to impress many others – at least, not in England.

In part, James wrote the *Trew Law* in response to Parsons' efforts. Both it and the *Basilikon Doron* stressed the hereditary nature of kingship, asserting that it was God's method of selecting kings, and as such was inalienable and indefeasible. In short, to oppose hereditary rights, as Parsons had done, was to go against God's will.

Some of those who witnessed James's angst saw a means to ingratiate themselves with him. There was a veritable flood of scribblings in James's defence and praise, some of which was published while the rest was suppressed as being just too provocative. The renegade parson, John Colville, wrote one of the more curious pieces. Taking the role of the prodigal, he claimed that he had opposed James in the past, but had come to his senses. He deserved to be hanged for his past mistakes, wailed the prodigal, before commending James to the English people. James laughingly commented that Colville must have gone mad and refused to return him to favour, but nevertheless published his words.

Denied Elizabeth's public approval, and kept on a tight rein by her over the years – a situation involving more stick than carrot – James's greatest fear was that his succession to the English throne might yet be opposed, either internally or from abroad. Therefore, he had a habit of trying to ingratiate himself with anybody and everybody – be they Catholic or Protestant – Lutheran, Calvinist, Episcopalian or even Presbyterian and Puritan.

This 'need to ingratiate' explains his having chosen a Danish wife, rather than the homebred Arabella Stewart suggested by Queen Elizabeth. Believe the tale of him falling in love with Anne's portrait if you will, but recognise that Denmark was one of the wealthiest, and therefore potentially the most powerful, Protestant states in Europe. James wisely decided that they would make better friends than enemies or disinterested neighbours, and saw that such an alliance would foster the trade for which Scotland thirsted. Trade that would encourage a distribution of wealth and power away from a handful of noble families. Even to the impoverished King of Scots, that prospect made up for the lack of a dowry.

In seeking alliances with other Protestant states, James was not simply self-serving – at least, not entirely. He had long believed in a league of Protestant nations – he had spoken of it openly, as early as 1585 – if only as a pact for mutual support and defence against Philip of Spain and his Catholic allies. It is true that he had enough confidence in his own abilities to picture himself as taking some major role in it – as some sort of latter day Solomon, applying his intellect to tricky problems and basking in the light of others praise and thanks for his solutions, but was that so terribly wrong? Is the swift runner to be criticised for knowing he is faster than his fellows?

As an academic and man of letters, James's confidence in himself was not misplaced. In his time, he was zealous in his efforts to modernise and reform the law. He encouraged the arts and was recognised as one of the prime movers in an educational and cultural renaissance within Scotland. Of course, he had to be in the right place, at the right time and in the right company in order to be involved in, say, the founding of a university in Edinburgh, but that shouldn't detract from his many achievements.

James was particularly keen to promote Scottish poets, believing that some might stand alongside the likes of England's John Donne and Andrew Marvell. Consider these lines by Captain Alexander Montgomerie, Master of the King's Poetry in 1583, on a typically metaphysical theme.

So swete a kiss yistrene fra thee I reft,
In bowing down thy body on the bed,
That evin my lyfe within thy lippis I left;
Sensyne from thee my spirits wald never shed;
To folow thee it from my body fled,
And left my corps als cold as ony kie.
Bot when the danger of my death I dred,
To seik my spreit I sent my harte to thee ...

James had used his extended honeymoon in Norway and Denmark, passing through Sweden, to discuss his ideas for an alliance of Protestant states, and his ideas were well received. Later, he took the opportunity provided by Prince Henry's christening to further his discussions with the various foreign envoys attending – draining the royal coffers in his attempts to put on a good show. Unfortunately, his anxieties over the English succession, which he wanted above and beyond all things, came to the fore and marred his case.

James had developed a habit of complaining about Queen Elizabeth and her refusal to publicly declare him as undisputable heir to her throne. Never wealthy, in 1598 he managed to find the money to pay for ambassadors to Denmark and the north German Princes. It was this sort of spending that led him into debt, forcing him into borrowing from the likes of the Earl of Gowrie. The ambassadors' purpose was to further James's arguments for a Protestant alliance. They also discussed James's title to the English crown, suggesting that foreign powers might bring pressure on Elizabeth to acknowledge his claim, even going so far as to ask what help might be offered to James if he had to fight for his prize. Evidently, they also spent some effort in highlighting Elizabeth's advancing years and suggesting that she was not, well, the queen she once was ...

In the fullness of time, all this was brought to Elizabeth's attention. To say that she was upset would be an understatement. She wasted no time in telling James exactly what she thought of him and his, and ordered him to desist. She had words with those Protestant states that James had approached. In the end, they did little other than 'commending him to the protection of the Almighty by whose will kingdoms were disposed'. Of course, they were enjoying a bit of a joke by quoting from his recently published *Trew Law*.

Despite incurring Elizabeth's wrath, James had not felt it necessary to be secretive about his dealings with Protestant states. Approaches to Catholic states had to be far more circumspect.

It would have been far kinder to King James's already taut nerves if he had distanced himself entirely from those who were, on the face of it, England's enemies. He certainly couldn't afford to be linked with the merest whisper of some foreign plot to have Elizabeth removed. But James had seen an opportunity that he couldn't resist. It would be a mistake to assume that all the Catholic states of Europe worked in harmony, with a common aim of overthrowing the Protestant states and returning them to Catholicism. It was Philip of Spain who sought the overthrow of Protestantism as a priority – partly as recognition of his faith, but largely as a means of expanding his already huge empire. That empire not only threatened Protestant states, but also neighbouring Catholics into the bargain. Thus it was that Spain continued its war with France after the formerly Huguenot Henry of Navarre, now King of France, had converted to Catholicism. Many European Catholic states were jealous of Spain's power, and felt that its king was just too big for his boots. They made their feelings known to the Vatican in Rome. There was no love lost between the Italian city states and their trading rivals in Madrid – Jesuits outside of Spain tended to be anti-Spanish. There was little support for Spain's claim among English Catholics in exile, who seemed far more interested in James's promise of religious toleration.

James knew of the widening Catholic split and sought to exploit it, recognising that Philip of Spain, acting virtually alone, was the most serious threat to his succession to the crown of England. Philip, who had already staked his own claim and who, in his dealings with Scotland and Ireland's Catholic earls, not to mention the Armada and continuing war, had shown that he was ready, willing and potentially able to force that claim on the English people. Perhaps this was James's greatest fear. In talking of having to fight for England, there was just one other serious contender.

Steering the most cautious of courses, and ever mindful of the eyes and ears of Elizabeth's Secret Service, James had the wit to send the most unlikely agents to make first contact with Catholic states. Men who nobody would suspect. Indeed, they might not even have known what they were about. Some travelling salesman, perhaps, complete with samples of Scottish cloth, honoured if somewhat confused to have been asked to present his king's compliments, and report back on how he had been received. Nothing more...

If the man were rebuffed, that would be an end to it. However, if things went well, he might receive further instructions for a return visit. Something fairly vague. Something that could be denied. Nothing in writing. Later, a second emissary might be sent. Somebody more responsible, though still not likely to attract attention. Again, he would present James's compliments and in conversation might sound out opinions on James's claim to the English throne. Again, all this would be reported back.

Eventually, if his agents' reports had been favourable, James would follow up with a more direct approach, spelling out his position. In return for certain favours, he offered to grant toleration to English Catholics and even hinted that he might convert to Catholicism – at the right price.

James's greatest hope was to get Henry IV of France on his side. Henry's conversion to Catholicism had earned him the undying support of Rome, which thought little of Philip's continuing aggression. James sought to employ Henry as a go-between, lavishing gifts upon him, even suggesting that they should renew the Auld Alliance, hoping that Henry would put in a good word for him.

Truth be told, Henry was far from impressed, describing James as a charlatan who practised with everybody but was true to none. Indeed Henry went much further than that in his sneering: well might the great king who wrote little books be called Solomon, he said, for was he not the son of David? The David to whom Henry referred was Riccio ... It was Henry of France who first described James as the wisest fool in Christendom, a description that has been remembered down through the centuries.. Despite all this, in 1601 Henry wrote to Rome, stating his opinion that King James of Scots was the rightful heir to England. Even the wisest fool was infinitely preferable to the Spanish bull.

In the summer of 1601, the Spaniards attacked Ostend, but were beaten off by its Anglo-Dutch defenders. Catholic Spain was clearly determined to continue the war against Protestantism, and as summer faded into autumn, England received the news it had been dreading. After so many failures, Spain had finally succeeded in landing a force in Ireland. They came ashore at Kinsale in Co Cork in September – 4,500 troops intent on supporting Hugh O'Neill, Earl of Tyrone, and Hugh O'Donnell, Earl of Tyrconnell, in their fight against the English forces of occupation.

Juan del Aguila, the Spanish commander, had intended to land in Donegal, allowing easy access to Ulster, but was advised that the Cork coastline would provide a better option – which it did, but that wasn't the point, for it positioned his troops at the opposite end of the country from Tyrone and Tyrconnell. The earls were marching their forces to join him, but Mountjoy, the Lord Deputy, was already on the move, at the head of 10,000 hardened troops – roughly the same number as the Irish irregulars.

Mountjoy arrived in Co Cork at the end of October, ahead of the Ulster earls. Faced with a force twice their size, and still waiting for local support, the Spaniards retreated into Kinsale and manned its defences. Sir George Carew, President of Munster, joined the besieging Mountjoy in November.

Despite the trouble in Ireland, it was business as usual at Westminster. Many in parliament were expressing concerns about royal grants bestowing sole trading or manufacturing rights. They complained that these monopolies of various commodities had led to inflated prices. For example, salt had recently doubled in price.

Queen Elizabeth knew the value of these monopolies to her exchequer, and was determined to protect them. At the same time, she may have wanted to make a public display that she could still maintain a tight grip on the reins of power. Therefore, she called for a delegation of 160 parliamentarians to appear before her. Gently but firmly, she proceeded to scold them, assuring them, to their embarrassment, that she was 'no greedy scraping grasper' and reminding them that 'to be a king and wear a crown is a thing more glorious to them that see it than it is pleasant to them that bear it,' to which King James might have said 'Amen', if he had been present.

Elizabeth sensed she had convinced the delegation of the need for royal monopolies, or embarrassed them to the point of losing interest in the subject, so cleverly thanked them for bringing the matter to her attention. Finally, she made a statement that might later serve as her epitaph. 'Though you have had and may have mightier and wiser princes yet ye have never had, nor never shall, have any that will love you better.'

Meanwhile, the besiegers of Kinsale had been fighting a war on two fronts since the arrival of Tyrone and Tyrconnell. Mountjoy was kept juggling between keeping the Spaniards in, and the Irish out.

After months of bitter fighting and the wasting of the surrounding country, Mountjoy's disciplined army finally drew Tyrone's brave but wild irregulars into a pitched battle on December 24. It was brought to a conclusion in less than three hours. With most of their force either dead or fleeing, the Irish commanders finally admitted defeat. A week later, the Spanish commander saw that he had no option but to surrender. Tyrconnell sought sanctuary in Spain, while Tyrone withdrew to Ulster.

Tyrone might have expected the traditional punishment handed out by England to those they deemed rebellious traitors – hanging, drawing and quartering in front of a jeering crowd – but first they would have to catch him. After two years of trying, Mountjoy finally sought Elizabeth's authority to grant a royal pardon to Tyrone, if he agreed to surrender. She gave him the royal nod of approval, but Mountjoy was still waiting for Tyrone's response when news came from London that the queen had died on March 24 .

Rather than leave matters waving in the breeze, with the possibility that the offer of a pardon might be withdrawn, Tyrone rushed to sign the treaty, which he did on March 30. It offered a better deal than he could have hoped for, allowing him to retain all his lands and feudal rights. Mountjoy may have felt that this was a small price to pay to see an end to the thing. It was just a shame that Elizabeth had not been allowed to die content, knowing that the English conquest of Ireland was all but complete. Of course, the Irish might have felt rather differently ...

CHAPTER THIRTY-ONE

CROWNS UNITED

Queen Elizabeth I of England died on March 24 1603. Seventy years old, she had reigned for almost 45 years during which time Protestant England had seen off a string of threats encouraged in no small part by Catholic Mary Queen of Scots, who had consistently presented herself as Elizabeth's competitor since being declared by the French, during her marriage to their king, as Queen of France, Scotland and England. The same Mary who, in later years – when her son disappointed her – offered Scotland and England to Catholic Philip of Spain, as if they were hers for the giving.

Things might have been different for England without the support of Scotland's Presbyterians, just as things would certainly have been very different for Protestant Scotland without the support of England. Stability in England aided Scotland, and vice versa. As a result, the last half of the 16th century saw a new spirit of cooperation between the two countries at governmental levels, after centuries of warfare with all that implied in both human and financial terms.

John Knox's name is remembered, but it was the Lords of the Congregation and their supporters whose steadying hands were on the Scottish tiller. Those supporters included an emergent class of minor lairds and burgesses. King James recognised both need and advantage in encouraging craftsmen, merchants and traders, and by doing so shifted some of the power to urban settlements, and away from the countryside and a sometimes uncontrollable aristocracy. The Reformation had led to a new era of land grabbing as the Catholic Church was stripped of its assets, and this in itself created a redistribution of power.

Together, the two Protestant kingdoms were creating the conditions that would eventually lead to the incorporation of a British trading Empire that sprawled across the face of the globe. The realisation of that profit-inspired dream, and the acceleration of colonisation beyond something more than trading posts, still lay far into the future on the fateful day that the Tudor dynasty finally faded and died.

During the last days of Elizabeth's illness, Scotland was eager for news. Rumours were rife and every traveller from the south was closely questioned. Some ambitious Scots were already packing their bags, for many looked to England as the Promised Land in which they might seek to further their fortunes. It was a land denied to them in the past, but things would be different, they believed, with King James on the English throne. This created a new tradition of Scotsmen seeking acceptance in England, together with the English retort, taken up by Samuel Johnson, about Scotsmen on the make. Certainly, for many an ambitious Scot in the spring of 1603, there were few finer prospects in Scotland than the high road leading to England.

Prince Henry was still at Stirling Castle, being educated under the guardianship of the Earl of Mar, but King James and the rest of his expanding family were waiting for news at Holyroodhouse. Queen Anne was not enjoying the best of health. The younger royal children, Elizabeth and Charles, were with their parents. In his book *James I*, Charles Williams described the scene: 'Holyrood was in a state of expectation. James refused to go anywhere, waiting, always and only, for the final news ... He was on fire to be gone; thirty years of vigil burned in him towards the dawn, and what now if the dawn still delayed?'

Meanwhile in England, an ambitious gentleman was keeping one eye on his finely tuned horse. Sir Robert Carey, son of Lord Hunsdon, was determined that he should be the first bearer of news to King James in the event of Elizabeth's death. She had hardly breathed her last on Thursday before he leapt into the saddle. A relay of fast horses was waiting at various points to gallop him north. His only fear could have been of a fast ship with a following wind. He finally clattered into Edinburgh on Saturday, splattered in mud and blood, for he had taken a bad tumble in which his horse had kicked him in the head. Having presented himself at the gates of Holyroodhouse, he was quickly ushered into the royal presence.

More than 400 miles in less than 60 hours was a fantastic achievement. Weak from hunger, hurt and exhaustion, Carey gratefully fell to his knees before saluting his king. The man once known to his mother as Jacques was now King of England, Wales, Scotland and Ireland, with claims to France. Union Jacques stretched out his hand and Carey touched it with his lips.

Carey was given food and had his wounds attended to, while being subjected to a battery of questions. He was an influential Elizabethan courtier and the English Warden of the Middle March, entrusted to bring some notion of law and order to that troublesome part of the border with Scotland. His father was the son of Anne Boleyn's sister Mary, and therefore Elizabeth's first cousin and closest relation. His elder brother Henry was Governor of Berwick and Warden General of the Scottish Marches.

As a member of what amounted to the queen's family, Robert Carey had visited London and been able to talk with Elizabeth in her final days. It had helped that his sister Philadelphia, wife of Lord Scrope, was one of Elizabeth's ladies-in-waiting at that time. The queen had been suffering a cold, they said, which was aggravated by her insistence on going out in foul winter weather. She then fell into some sort of depression at the loss of her lifelong companion, the Countess of Nottingham (Carey's elder sister), refusing food and medical attention. When Carey was brought into her presence, she was running a high fever. Carey reported that, 'she tooke me by the hand, and wrung it hard, and said: "No, Robin, I am not well," and then discoursed with me of her indisposition, and that her heart had been sad and heavy for ten or twelve days ... she fetched not so few as forty of fifty great sighs.'

Having tried unsuccessfully to raise the queen's mood, Carey had the temerity to suggest she must go to her bed. At that, Elizabeth showed a spark of her old self. 'Little man, the word must is not to be used to princes,' she exploded.

In later times, Carey admitted that his main concern was for his own future. Elizabeth was dying, but he could do nothing to help her and so must look to himself – as many others were doing. Recognising the advantages that might accrue from serving King James, Carey had written to him, explaining the situation and promising to ride north without delay to tell him whenever the queen died.

Having made the necessary arrangements regarding a chain of horses, Carey returned to Elizabeth's side during her final hours. By now, she was indeed confined to her bed – too weak to argue. Between their prayers, those around her asked if she would name James as her successor. By now her voice had gone, but she made some signal that Carey interpreted as confirmation.

The king continued his questioning of Carey, as if doubting his report. Finally, as proof that Elizabeth was truly dead, Carey presented James with the queen's coronation ring, cut from her finger in the last few moments of her life. 'It is enough, said James. 'I know by this you are a true messenger,' but he still harboured doubts.

James's concern was whether his powerful English allies had been successful in ensuring that nothing should obstruct his path to the vacated throne. He sat down to write a letter to the man who had, until but a few days previously, been Elizabeth's closest advisor. Even she had not been aware that her most trusted servant had been in James's 'employ' for a number of years.

Ever desperate for reassurances regarding the English succession in the last years of Elizabeth's reign, James had singled out one Englishman above all others who would best serve his purpose. That man was the ambitious Robert Cecil, son of Elizabeth's former right-hand man, William Cecil, Lord Burghley, with all the privileges that implied. Robert had inherited the old spymaster's influence at court. In 1591, he was knighted and joined the Privy Council. In 1595, he was appointed Principal Royal Secretary, and in 1599, Master of the Court of Wards. In a comparatively short period of time, he had risen to become one of the most powerful men in Elizabethan England.

At the start of Robert Cecil's relationship with Scotland, when he inherited his father's diplomatic and Secret Service contacts, he and King James had circled each other warily, uncertain whether they should become friends or enemies. Finally, James laid his cards on the table, instructing his ambassador to London to inform Cecil that if he would not assist him now, while Elizabeth still lived, he must expect no favours in the future.

Cecil asked for time to think this over, though he must have been expecting such an approach and would have already decided how to respond – men like Cecil were seldom taken by surprise. Nevertheless, he insisted on a suitably decent interval before requesting a secret meeting with the Scottish ambassadors.

At that meeting, he offered to promote King James's interests in England, but with two conditions: absolute secrecy, and James's undertaking that he would not ask him to act against Elizabeth, or do anything to cause her the slightest harm. It was that insistence, above all things, that convinced James of Cecil's worth, for James coveted such loyalty. Cecil believed that he could be loyal to both Elizabeth and James, at one and the same time. There is a hint in this that he saw England rather than its monarchs as his master.

Cecil had made his position clear and James applauded him for it, commending the fact that he had been 'so honourably plain'. Right from the start of their secret correspondence, there was plainness in their dealings which points to the blossoming trust and respect they had for each other. For King James, to have a trustworthy confidant was something of a new experience. Cecil was able to say what James wanted to hear – reassuring him that the road to Elizabeth's throne was clear, and he should look forward confidently to uniting the crowns of England and Scotland.

Maintaining his 'plain honesty', Cecil then requested that he should be remembered in the future government of the kingdoms. This request helped to endear the Englishman even closer to the Scottish king. Clearly, James saw nothing wrong with such a straightforward declaration of self-interest.

'My dearest and trusty Cecil,' James replied. 'My pen is not able to express how happy I think myself for having chanced upon so worthy, so wise, and so provident a friend ... your happy and honest concurrence for my weal doth force me, out of the abundance of a thankful mind, to write in a loving, plain and familiar style.'

Cecil was happy enough to reply in a similarly fraternal style, though he was just too cautious to be so enthusiastic. Indeed, behind the expressions of affection, Cecil's involvement was largely cynical for, like his father before him, he knew how to please the ears and minds of the great in order to feather his own nest. And by securing James's friendship – simply by undertaking various offices that would have fallen to him anyway, in the inevitable flow of events – Cecil was able to secure his own position. In the meantime, he would instruct James to sit still and stop rocking the boat.

As part of his course of instruction, Cecil had provided precise details on how best to correspond with Elizabeth. This produced a startling change in the nature of the relationship between the two monarchs. In her last years, Elizabeth must have been shocked then delighted at James's transformation from a whining sponger into a loving and affectionate godson. 'Your letters fill my heart with more contentment than pen or tongue can express ... They make me more happy than if I had won the Golden Fleece ... I protest to God that you shall ever be my oracle.' And so on – seemingly heartfelt devotion offered alongside prayers for her long life with the protection of the Almighty.

At first, Elizabeth may have raised a quizzical brow at such unexpected expressions of affection from 'the ungrateful Scottish urchin', but Cecil knew his queen and recognised that (like many an elderly person in the autumn of their years) she could be bought with sweet smiles and empty promises. It might be said that Cecil provided the bait for James's trap, and Elizabeth took it. The old queen finally smiled on the young king. If her acceptance of him was not stated, then it was adequately implied. This created a general climate of acceptance of James as her successor, both at home and abroad. In the end, even the Papacy and Philip of Spain had apparently accepted the seemingly inevitable.

King James's correspondence with Cecil touched on many matters, including his beliefs concerning religious tolerance, together with his misgivings about the extremes of papists and puritans. He did not wish his intentions to be mistaken by Cecil. Of course, such correspondence was highly secret and employed the English Secret Service system of referring to individuals by numbers alone, in order to preserve their anonymity.

My dear 10,

The fear I have to be mistaken by you ... enforceth me to pen an answer and clear resolution of my intention. I did ever hate alike both extremities in any case, only allowing the middes for virtue, as my book now lately published doth plainly appear ... I will never allow in my conscience that the blood of any man be shed for diversity of opinions in religion, but I would be sorry that Catholics should so multiply as they might be able to practise their old principles upon us...

Your most loving friend,

30.

During the final days of Elizabeth's last illness in March 1603, Cecil spoke privately with fellow members of the Privy Council, warning them that only those who assisted James's smooth passage into the Promised Land should expect favours in the future. To a man, the members of the Council bowed to the inevitable, hoping to be rewarded for their acquiescence.

While Carey was preparing his horse, Cecil and other members of the Privy Council had been overseeing more weighty matters. Warnings were sent to major cities and towns, stating that any unrest must be dealt with immediately and firmly. Troops based at strategic points throughout the land were ordered to come to a high state of readiness. Malcontents were rounded up and imprisoned. Nothing was left to chance.

Cecil had already drawn up a proclamation announcing James's succession, and sent him a copy, asking if he required any changes. James described it as perfect, needing no corrections. According to James's servant, George Nicholson, it was, 'Music that sounded so sweetly in his ears that he could alter no note in so agreeable a harmony.'

Nicholson also recorded that King James's mood seemed jovial enough on the Sunday, despite his having talked into the small hours with Carey and others, but this was not reflected in the letter James wrote that day to Cecil.

His words reveal his continuing unease, as if he couldn't bring himself to accept that England finally lay in his grasp. James was ever the wishful thinker, but his sometimes blind enthusiasm was now tempered by his characteristically nervous caution.

James's letter started with a description of his receiving the news that Elizabeth was dead and that he, James, had been proclaimed her successor – which was true, though Carey had simply assumed it so, for the official pronouncement wasn't made until after his departure. James then went on to say how much he valued Cecil's help. 'How happy I think myself by the conquest of so faithful and so wise a counsellor I reserve it to be expressed out of my own mouth unto you'.

Yet there is a hint of something else. A feeling that here was a man who had just won a prize that he had coveted for most of his life, and couldn't believe his luck. So it was that James sent the Abbot of Holyrood to Berwick, just across the border into England. Later, when the abbot reported back that he had received a joyful welcome as befitted a representative of England's new king, James might finally have realised that he was indeed bound for the Promised Land.

Five days after Elizabeth's death, James received the letter he had been waiting for. In it, the English Council confirmed what James was almost too fearful to believe. England's grief for Elizabeth's death was mitigated, in the Council's words, by hope of James's heroic virtue. Joy filled all English hearts, they said, and they promised James their obedience and urged him to come to them with all speed.

With this document to hand, James announced that an official proclamation should be read out at Edinburgh Cross. Heralded by a fanfare of trumpets, it would stop the wild rumours that had been racing through the city's streets. England's acceptance of James was described in the first, long sentence, part of which is reproduced here.

'Forasmekle as it hes pleisit the maist heich God to call to his maircie out of this transitorie lyff his Majesties dearest suster Elisabeth, leat Quene of England, France and Ireland, of worthie memorie, for the quhilk as we have just caus of sorrow sua aucht we to rejoyse in that it not only pleissit hir befoir her depairtar, according to the princilie dispositioun of hir hart towardis his Majestie in all the course of hir lyfe, to declair his Majestie only air maill and lawfull successour in the imperiall crounes of England, France and Irland, bot lykwayis, conforme to hir said will and his Majesteis undoubtit richt, the Lordis spirituall and temporall of England, being assemblet at Londone the xxiii day of March instant, assistit with his Majesteis lait dearest susteris Previe Counsall, and with great nowmeris of utheir principall gentlemen of qualitie of that kingdome, the maior, aldermen and citicenis of his Majesteis citie of Londone, and a multitude of utheris guid subectis and commonis of that realme, be oppin proclamatioun proclaimit his Majestie thair only richteous leige Lord and undoubtit Soverane...'

It was enough. As many were leaving the listening crowd as were joining it – rushing here and there in their haste to tell family, friends and colleagues what they had heard. It was a done deal.

On Sunday, April 3, King James attended divine service in St Giles. It must have been a strange affair. The king, puffed up with all sorts of heady notions, triumphantly marching into the same building where he had met such hostility in the past. Some of the congregation hoping, no doubt, that past words and actions had been forgotten. Hearts and minds filled with a heady mix of fear and wonder at the man who now held higher office than any before in either England or Scotland – the supreme and seemingly undisputed ruler of both kingdoms. Indeed, King of England and Wales, Scotland and Ireland, and not forgetting that lingering claim to France ... Edward Longshanks and Henry VIII must have been birling in their graves.

Amidst the pomp and ceremony, however, the future seemed bleak for many Scots. Some had been hoping that James would see fit to rule his kingdoms from Edinburgh. From the parochial point of view, there was much to be said for ruling a kingdom from its geographical centre. But it was not to be. King James was clear in stating his intention to move to London, and without delay. When he saw the grief this caused among his people, he took it as a token of their affection for him. However, they were grieving for the loss of what he represented, rather than the man himself. Before he left, James promised that he would return to Scotland one year in every three. In truth, Scotland's children would have grown into adulthood before they set eyes on their king again.

Despite their differences, most of the Lowlands acknowledged the prosperity they had enjoyed under James. During his reign, there had been a cultural renaissance and, most significantly, a marked improvement in trade. The blubbering burgesses of Edinburgh who waved a fond farewell to James's travelling circus mourned more for their purses than the loss of their king. They knew the likely ramifications of his move. They suspected that Scotland would become a financial backwater, and that the modernisation of the country's laws, and an adequate enforcement of the same, would be neglected.

As if to confirm the citizens' worst fears, it was learned that the reiving clans and families, taking advantage of the uncertain situation, had 'shaked loose the Border' in a violent spree of raids and looting. At that early stage, they couldn't know that James, even in distant London, would remember the scores he had to settle. In less than a decade, he would impose peace on the Border, with many of the reivers sent as fodder for the Protestant plantations, or left hanging from the branches of handy trees – the macabre fruits of a new era of law enforcement.

Others would also learn that while James was squeamish in some matters, there were few things he liked better than to see miscreants swinging at the end of stout ropes – symbols of the divine power that kings held over their subjects. 'They have power of raising and casting down, of life and of death, judges over all, and yet accountable to none but God only.'

As part of his final preparations before leaving Scotland, James had found time to write a few lines to his eldest son, Prince Henry, who was to continue his cloistered education in Stirling Castle. Some say his letter reveals a genuine paternal affection, but whatever the intention, the prince must have felt that he was being abandoned. So much pomp, ceremony and merriment in which he would take little if any part. One thinks of a boy at the harshest of boarding schools, hearing that he won't be going home for Christmas. Nor Easter, nor summer, not this year nor next ...

My son,

That I see you not before my parting, impute it to this great occasion, wherein time was so precious ... Let not this news make you proud, or insolent, for a king's son and heir was ye before, and no more are ye yet. The augmentation that is hereby like to fall unto you is but in cares and heavy burthens. Be therefore merry but not insolent: keep a greatness, but *sine fastu*: be resolute but not wilful ... Look upon all Englishmen that shall come to visit you as your loving subjects, not with that ceremony as with strangers ... Be diligent and earnest in your studies ... Be obedient to your master, for in reverencing him ye obey me and honour yourself. Farewell.

Your loving father,

James R.

Cecil and Carey were not alone in seeking to win the new king's favour. Before he had left Scotland, and heaven knows he did not tarry long, the rich and powerful, or simply ambitious, were seeking audiences with him – eager to express their undying devotion. Stunned by it all, James would knight no less than 300 suitors on his journey through England. Every town vied to offer a greater welcome than the last. Cannons roared while the people shouted 'God save King James,' till their throats were raw.

Among the first to pay their compliments to England's new king was the Dean of Canterbury, sent in haste by Archbishop Whitgift, eager to discover James's intentions towards the Church of England. James's answers were encouraging. Indeed, he was seemingly encouraging to all and any, other than a motley collection of criminals that were dragged into his presence at various points along his route. He hanged most of them, including two 'gentleman cutpurses'.

The celebrations were such that James slowed his journey in order to make the most of them. Indeed, he hadn't crossed the River Tyne before he was taking time out to hunt, and presiding at a succession of banquets. Nor did it help when the king fell from his horse and broke his collarbone while hunting a pack of hounds provided by members of England's desperate-to-please nobility. When news of all this reached London, the Privy Council realised that if the king would not hurry to them, then they must go to him.

Robert Cecil packed his bags and headed north. No doubt he was welcomed with open arms by the deliriously happy James, who had little on his mind but savouring every delicious moment of his triumphant journey through a land apparently flowing with wine and honey. Cecil maintained his reputation for honesty and plain speaking. Things were not as they seemed in the Promised Land ...

England's loyalty to its new king wasn't the issue. Rather, it was the state of the royal exchequer. That and the overall economy of the country. Standards of living had rapidly declined during the Elizabethan era for the great masses of the English people. Along with the immensely expensive involvement in foreign wars, England's income had not grown with its population – about 2.25 million in 1500 had almost doubled to 4 million in 1603.

As a result of increasing demand for a fairly fixed supply, food prices had soared. This put money in farmers' pockets, and had created vast fortunes for a few great landowners, but at the expense of the rest of the population. Throughout the land, the gap was widening between the haves and have-nots.

While the king was being so lavishly entertained, many were literally starving. Real wages had fallen by about 60 per cent. Beggars and paupers clogged the streets of all the major towns and cities. The Puritans were gathering support, and there were increasing mutterings of social unrest while radicals travelled from town to town, intent on causing trouble.

James didn't want to hear about this. Not while he was enjoying himself so much. The festivities continued.

Finally, James was close to London. Queen Anne had not been well enough to travel with him, but news came that she was already hot on his heels, eager not to miss any of the fun and games. She and her children caught up with her husband at Westminster, where he was holding court. 'There was such an infinite number of lords and ladies and so great a court as I think I shall never see the like again,' gushed Lady Anne Clifford, daughter of the Earl of Cumberland. She and her mother had killed three horses in their wild ride to be there.

The royal family were clearly delighted to be reunited. James swept up his seven-year-old daughter in his arms, showering the Princess Elizabeth with kisses. He even seemed pleased to see his wife.

King James's buoyant mood appeared to continue through his coronation on July 25, and even into the following year. At the opening of the English Parliament in 1604 (the crowns were united, but the parliaments were to maintain their independence, for the time being) James was 'as royally attended as if the gods had summoned a parliament and were all in their steps of triumph to Jove's high court,' and seemed to appreciate it well enough. In truth, however, his patience was already beginning to thin.

James felt that lavish entertainments and queues of self-serving sycophants, that had once been so pleasing, were coming between him and his divine right to rule. He had long since formulated on how best to administer his kingdoms, transforming them into a cohesive unit that might become a real force in Europe and a leader of Protestant states and interests.

King James declared that his wish above all things 'was at his death to leave one worship to God: one kingdom, intirely governed: one uniformity of laws.' This was Union Jacques's grand vision – his noble ambition. His wish was to be king of the British Isles, rather than of the separated Scotland, England and Ireland. He would speak of a *Great* Britain whenever he addressed parliament – and of himself as its king. King of Great Britain,

France and Ireland was how he styled himself, though he concentrated on Scotland and England.

'What God hath conjoyned then, let no man separate. I am the Husband, and all the whole Isle is my lawfull Wife; I am the Head, and it is my Body; I am the Shepherd, and it is my flocke: I hope therefore no man will be so unreasonable as to thinke that I that am a Christian King under the Gospel should be a Polygamist and husband to two wives; that I being the Head should have a divided and monstrous Body, or that being the Shepherd to so fair a Flocke (whose fold hath no wall to hedge it but the four Seas) should have my Flocke parted in two.'

One land, one religion, one government, one law and one people, 'the union of kingdom'. But for now, its people were getting in his way. It was as if they weren't listening. For some time, the king had scowled at the smiling faces in the press of humanity seeking audiences with him. Finally, the scowls became curses as James wearied of the demands being placed upon him.

'What do these people want of me?' he wailed. Sugar-tongued courtiers told that they came of love to see him. 'God's wounds!' roared James, reverting to broad Scots and florescent obscenities. 'Then I will pull down my breeches and they shall also see my arse.'

The honeymoon was ended with a curse. English and Scots would discover the realities of married life. An arranged marriage, no doubt, but a marriage nevertheless. For better or worse, richer or poorer. Would this new arrangement prove to be as difficult as the bitter centuries of courtship? Scottish brides and English grooms producing contented British children? And what of those unhappy bridesmaids – the Irish and Welsh? Time alone would tell.

✍ INDEX ☙

Center header: INDEX